Embodying Language in Action

"This splendid book intrigues, astonishes and enlightens. Grounded in Piazzoli's candid personal stories, it seamlessly interweaves pedagogy and artistry—embodiment, feeling, cognition, research, performance, culture and linguistics—into a rich tapestry of insights. It is a model of praxis, blending encyclopaedic grasp of theory and literature with assured practice."
—John O'Toole, *University of Melbourne, Australia*

"This timely publication is an excellent introduction to the artistry of process drama in second language education and a significant contribution to the scholarly debate on performativity in education. Erika Piazzoli offers rich theoretical perspectives on Embodying Language in Action, complemented by ten very inspiring examples of teaching practice, and engages the reader by drawing on autobiographical vignettes and personal memories. The book promises to become an important reference point for all those who believe that creative doing should be at the centre of education, who are eager to understand better in what sense and to what extent language teaching is an art, the teacher is an artist and the students are co-artists."
—Manfred Schewe, *University College Cork, Ireland*

Erika Piazzoli

Embodying Language in Action

The Artistry of Process Drama in Second Language Education

Erika Piazzoli
School of Education
Trinity College Dublin
Dublin, Ireland

ISBN 978-3-319-77961-4   ISBN 978-3-319-77962-1 (eBook)
https://doi.org/10.1007/978-3-319-77962-1

Library of Congress Control Number: 2018936588

© The Editor(s) (if applicable) and The Author(s) 2018
This work is subject to copyright. All rights are solely and exclusively licensed by the Publisher, whether the whole or part of the material is concerned, specifically the rights of translation, reprinting, reuse of illustrations, recitation, broadcasting, reproduction on microfilms or in any other physical way, and transmission or information storage and retrieval, electronic adaptation, computer software, or by similar or dissimilar methodology now known or hereafter developed.
The use of general descriptive names, registered names, trademarks, service marks, etc. in this publication does not imply, even in the absence of a specific statement, that such names are exempt from the relevant protective laws and regulations and therefore free for general use.
The publisher, the authors and the editors are safe to assume that the advice and information in this book are believed to be true and accurate at the date of publication. Neither the publisher nor the authors or the editors give a warranty, express or implied, with respect to the material contained herein or for any errors or omissions that may have been made. The publisher remains neutral with regard to jurisdictional claims in published maps and institutional affiliations.

Cover image: © Cultura RM/Alamy Stock Photo
Cover design by Jenny Vong

Printed on acid-free paper

This Palgrave Macmillan imprint is published by the registered company Springer International Publishing AG part of Springer Nature
The registered company address is: Gewerbestrasse 11, 6330 Cham, Switzerland

Acknowledgements

I would like to acknowledge the School of Education, Trinity College Dublin, particularly Andrew Loxley and Carmel O'Sullivan and the Arts in Education Research Group (AERG), who supported the publication of this book. I am grateful to all the students I have worked with at the Drama in Education Summer Schools, at the TCPID, Embodying Language module and Arts in Education module. I would also like to thank Julie Dunn and Claire Kennedy from Griffith University, Brisbane, for their guidance during my PhD; Fiona Dalziel (University of Padova) and the wonderful Padova Summer School 2017 team; all students and staff at the Dante Alighieri Society in Brisbane, my lifelong community of practice. Thanks also to Tomás Motos Teruel (Universitat de València) for his wisdom and generosity in granting the copyright of his cube diagram; John O'Toole and Brad Haseman for their mentorship and feedback, and for granting copyright of the Dramawise diagram; artist Patricia Ariel for the copyright of Hecate painting; and artist Nihad Nino Pušija for his photograph. A sincere thank you to Maureen Todhunter for making me appreciate, again, the artistry of punctuation. I also need to acknowledge that copyright for Leonardo da Vinci's *La Scapigliata* (Galleria Nazionale di

Parma) was granted by the Ministry of Cultural Heritage and Tourism (Ministero dei Beni e delle Attività Culturali e del Turismo), Complesso Monumentale della Pilotta, Parma (Italy).

On a personal note, *grazie di cuore* to Luca Marrucci, who has been present every single day throughout the two-year process of writing this book—encouraging me to keep going, inspiring me to dig deeper, listening, and making me laugh. If writing is manual somnambulism, as Coleridge put it, Luca was my beam of wakefulness.

Finally, I wish to pay homage to Koichi Tamano, Butoh Master from the Hijikata lineage. As it happens, I wrote the first page of this book after a Butoh workshop with Koichi in San Francisco. Two years later, I wrote the last page of this book after a workshop with Koichi in Cork. She has taught me 'the rare chance to accept'—allowing the body, images and movement tell a story.

"The body is a metaphor for words and words are a metaphor for the body." Tatsumi Hijikata[1]

References

Nanako, K. (2000). Hijikata Tatsumi: The Words of Butoh. *TRD/The Drama Review, 44*(1), 12.

Coleridge, H. N. (Ed.). (1836). *The literary remains of Samuel Taylor Coleridge* (Vol III). London: William Pickering.

---

[1] Hijikata Tatsumi, The Words of Butoh (Nanako, 2000, p. 12)

Contents

1 Introduction: What Is 'Artistry' and Why Do We Need It in Second Language Education?   1

Part I: Key Definitions in the Aesthetic Dimension

2 Drama as Process in L2 Education   21

3 Aesthetic and Intercultural Engagement   53

4 The Elements of Drama: An Intercultural Perspective   79

5 Knowing-in-Action   109

Part II: Navigating the Aesthetic Dimension

6	Play, Emotions and Distancing	133
7	Language Engagement and Teacher in Role	163
8	Navigating Performative Language Pedagogy	183

Part III: Researching the Aesthetic Dimension

9	Performative Research: Methodology and Methods	225
10	Learner Engagement	259
11	Teacher Artistry	295
12	Conclusion: Embodying Language in Action	321
References		335
Index		361

Abbreviations

ASD	Autistic Spectrum Disorder
ASIAP	Arts, Science and Inclusive Applied Practice
CEFR	Common European Framework of Reference for Languages
CLIL	Content and Language Integrated Learning
DA	Dynamic Assessment
DiE	Drama in Education
DOL	Drama and Oral Language
EAL	English as an Additional Language
ELP	European Language Portfolio
ESL	English as a Second Language
FL	Foreign Language
IRF	Initiation Response Feedback
L1	First Language
L2	Second Language
L3	Third Language
L2/Process Drama	Process Drama in a Second Language
LD	Learning Disabilities
QR	Quadripartite Response
QT	Quadripartite Thinking
RAI	Radiotelevisione Italiana

SCT	Sociocultural Theory
SLA	Second Language Acquisition
TCPID	Trinity College for People with Intellectual Disabilities
TiE	Theatre in Education
TiR	Teacher in Role
TPR	Total Physical Response
TT	Teacher Talk
VSR	Video-Stimulated Recall
ZPD	Zone of Proximal Development

List of Figures

Chapter 1
Fig. 1 *La Scapigliata* [The Head of a Woman] Leonardo da Vinci   6

Chapter 3
Fig. 1 Vicolo Savini, Roma   71

Chapter 4
Fig. 1 The elements of drama (Haseman & O'Toole, 2017)   81

Chapter 6
Fig. 1 An illustration from the Gruffalo's child   148
Fig. 2 Work on leaves   150
Fig. 3 Teacher in Role holding the message, next to the leaves prepared by the children   152
Fig. 4 A pupil finds the poisoned leaf   153

Chapter 8
Fig. 1 CEFR Levels Global Scale. Adapted from https://www.eaquals.org/our-expertise/cefr/   189
Fig. 2 3D Map of Dramatic forms. Motos (2016)   196
Fig. 3 Hyper Cube: Four Dimensions in Performative Language Teaching and Learning   198

Chapter 9

Fig. 1	Hecate, Patricia Ariel (2008)	227
Fig. 2	Breaking down the construct of learner engagement	233
Fig. 3	Aesthetic engagement indicators	236
Fig. 4	Engagement questionnaire template	237
Fig. 5	Research methods, research question one	240
Fig. 6	Pre-text (case study one)	252

Chapter 10

Fig. 1	Hecate, Patricia Ariel (2008). Detail, first voice	262
Fig. 2	Hecate, Patricia Ariel (2008). Second voice, detail	268
Fig. 3	Hecate, Patricia Ariel (2008). Third voice, detail	275
Fig. 4	Hecate, Patricia Ariel (2008). A polyphony of voices, my interpretation	286

Chapter 11

Fig. 1	Underhill's (1992) teacher development model	297
Fig. 2	Unconscious incompetence in micro reflection-in-action (inter-episode level)	301
Fig. 3	Conscious incompetence in micro reflection-in-action (inter-episode level)	304
Fig. 4	Conscious competence in micro reflection-in-action (inter-episode level)	308
Fig. 5	Progression of reflection-in-action from unconscious incompetence to unconscious competence	311

List of Tables

Chapter 5
Table 1   Reflective practitioners' contract (Schön, 1983, p. 300)   112
Table 2   O'Mara (1999) reflection-in-a action (p. 318)   115
Table 3   A comparison of the models of O'Neill, O'Mara and Bowell and Heap   117

Chapter 8
Table 1   Overall spoken interaction (CEFR, 2018, p. 85)   191

List of Drama Workshops

Workshop 1	Names and identity	45
Workshop 2	At the gypsy camp	72
Workshop 3	The Jugglers	104
Workshop 4	High Tide in Venezia	126
Workshop 5	The poisoned leaf	157
Workshop 6	Pygmalion	178
Workshop 7	David and Goliath	215
Workshop 8	The Journalists	253
Workshop 9	Mirrors	290
Workshop 10	The secret strategy	316

Prologue

In April 2016 I was in Madrid to attend an international conference on *gloctodidáctica teatral*, drama and theatre in education for second language learning. After a day of research presentations, conference delegates were invited to attend a series of performances of language students' plays. Several groups of Spanish students performed plays in English, Italian, and German. I recall sitting in a small theatre during a play by Spanish undergraduates in German. The piece alternated a series of fast-paced abstract images, followed by naturalistic scenes. I could not understand the German dialogues, but the mood of the piece was strong and I thought I'd need no translation. Surely I would be able to follow—having done one semester of German twenty years ago! However, as the play progressed, frustration set in; I could not follow at all. The language content was too difficult. I disengaged.

More precisely, I engaged elsewhere. I was physically 100% present in that theatre. But where was I really? My mind went back to my German learning experience, twenty years earlier. Why did I not continue learning German after that semester of study? Why didn't I pay more attention in class? The language sounded alien to me in that theatre. Impermeable. I recalled that semester of German, in Italy, my native country; we would study German grammar systematically, and the teacher had us watch German crime series on television at the end of each class. Obviously, it didn't work for me.

As the play progressed, my thoughts kept flying: What about Spanish? The official conference language was Spanish, a language in which I felt comfortable, having majored in Spanish studies in my college years. Yet, it had been almost fifteen years since I spoke any Spanish, and re-discovering my Spanish self, after living in an English-speaking country for half my life, was intriguing. It was like finding an old treasure box in the attic. What about French then? Why was it that while French was my first choice of language to study at school, having been exposed to French from childhood and having acquired a native-like accent, I barely scratched pass level in five years of schooling? It's not that I disliked French; I just made no emotional investment in it.

Which brought me to the elephant in the room: what was that *desire* of mine, as a teenager, to identify so strongly as an English speaker? What was behind that 'otherness' that I was constantly chasing, which brought me to score top marks in English at school; to enrol in an English-speaking university; to migrate; to live in English-speaking countries for half my life? And in an ironic twist of fate, what was it, again, that brought me to become so committed to teaching Italian as a foreign language, and to focus so intently on drama to facilitate language teaching and learning? This passion had, no doubt, made it possible for me to be at that very conference, to sit in that very theatre.

All of that was going through my head, alas, as I sat in front of those beginner language students acting in German—a German they and I had studied; a German *they* had learnt; a German *I* couldn't connect with. At that point it occurred to me that although a language may be 'taught' rationally, our emotions process it beyond our rational selves. Kramsch's (2009) words echoed in my head:

> We are fooling ourselves if we believe that students learn only what they are taught. While teachers are busy teaching them to communicate accurately, fluently, and appropriately, students are inventing for themselves other ways of being in their bodies and their imaginations. Success in language learning is an artefact of schooling. (p. 4)

I started to think about second language acquisition, drama and embodiment. Lulled by the foreignness of an unfamiliar language, in the familiarity of a theatre space, I was inspired. Scribbling key words in the dark of that theatre, I drafted the structure of this book. The discussion that follows is an expansion from that moment.

1

Introduction: What Is 'Artistry' and Why Do We Need It in Second Language Education?

> Consciously we teach what we know; unconsciously we teach who we are. (Hamachek, 1999)

When I was eight years old, I started learning English at my primary school in Milan, Italy. I remember the first day clearly, when the English teacher came into the classroom. She told us: "Children, we're going to study English; as a first step, you're going to change your names. I'll give you your English names now." I didn't understand the concept of learning English. What *was* English? She had a big dictionary with her, a name dictionary. She went through the roll and one by one she re-baptised, so to speak, each one of us with our new English names. So our classmate Angelo became *Angel*; Davide became *David*; Daniele became *Daniel*. When it came to my name, tragedy struck: there was no name translation for Erika. No English name for me. Anxiety crept in as the teacher re-baptised me *Heather*. "From now on, in the English classes your name is Heather!" she proclaimed. I still remember the feeling of displacement as she addressed me by my new name. I was alarmed by this new identity. Little did I know that the plant 'heather' is translated as *erica* in Italian. Instead, the obvious connection for me and my classmates was with Heather Parisi, a voluptuous Italian showgirl popular in the 1980s.

This was definitely too much of an identity stretch for an eight-year-old introverted child. All through primary and middle school, I disliked English. I remember a vague sense of confusion mixed with shame, not understanding what I had to say, what the right answer was. Classes were a blur. My name didn't make sense. I didn't make sense.

As van Lier (2004) argues, our sense of identity is essentially tied to our motivation to learn a foreign language, as "we can only speak the second language when thoughts, identities and self are aligned". He continues:

> I cannot speak in that foreign language from the depth of my self, and with integrity in my thoughts, the learner might say. Or, more practically, I cannot make my mouth say these sounds and things. The identity that has been allotted to me in this new culture, country or language, creates a barrier between my thoughts and my self, and I feel tongue-tied. (Van Lier, 2004, p. 128)

If our new identity does not align with our sense of self, the motivation to learn a foreign language may vacillate. In my childhood example, my teacher's best intentions turned sour as my allotted identity did not match my eight-year-old self. In hindsight, if I could have stepped into that teacher's shoes, I might have asked the children to choose their own names, gifting them the agency to reinvent themselves.

The role that emotions play in second language acquisition (SLA) has been largely documented; it is widely accepted that affective factors, like attitude, motivation and disposition, are paramount (Ellis, 2008). In a sociocultural perspective on second language learning (Lantolf & Poehner, 2014; Lantolf & Thorne, 2006), affect and cognition are inextricably linked. Since Damasio's (1999, 2010) foundational work on the brain, the self, emotions and consciousness, we are well aware that cognition and emotions are interconnected in learning. In this sense, the experience of learning is not just cognitive, but also connected to the emotions and the body. As Kramsch (2009) eloquently argues in *The Multilingual Subject*, language learners "rely not only on cool reason, but on the embodied aspects of a cognitive and socialized self: emotions, feelings, memories" (p. 53). More recently, affective and educational neuroscience research confirms that the role of emotions is essential to acquiring new knowledge. Neuroscientist Immordino-Yang (2016) notes:

Understanding the role of emotions in learning goes far beyond recognizing the emotion a student is having about a situation in order to design learning environments that strategically manipulate students' reactions. [...] Instead, understanding emotions is also (and perhaps even more critically) about the *meaning* that students are making – that is, the ways in which students and teachers are *experiencing* or *feeling* their emotional regions and how their feelings steer thoughts and behaviour, consciously or not. Emotions are not add-ons that are distinct from cognitive skills. Instead emotions, such as interest, anxiety, frustration, excitement, or a sense of awe in beholding beauty, become a dimension of the skill itself. (p. 21, original emphasis)

In this light, emotions are defined as the dimension of a skill, rather than a response generated by the skill; "the rudder that steers thinking" (p. 28). Thus, Immordino-Yang and Damasio effectively replace Descartes' formula *cogito ergo sum* (I think therefore I am) that set off the cognition/affect divide in the seventeenth century, with "we feel, therefore we learn" (p. 27), the cornerstone of embodied pedagogy. Interestingly, in the quotation above, Immordino-Yang points to "a sense of awe in beholding beauty". Seeking beauty in education, Winston (2010) reminds us, is a vital yet underestimated endeavour, which connects language learning to an aesthetic experience.

1 Teaching as an Art Form

Consider the dynamic relationship between a lesson plan and the actual unfolding of a class. Berghetto and Kaufman (2011) see this relationship as a gap between the "curriculum-as-planned and the curriculum-as-lived" (pp. 94–95). These, as any experienced teacher knows, are never identical; there comes a moment when the 'curriculum-as-lived' departs from the 'curriculum-as-planned', taking on a life of its own. That very same moment may be gratifying for one teacher and may provoke anxiety in another, according to levels of expertise, personality, circumstances, and many other context-specific issues. Reflecting on the gap between the curriculum-as-planned and the curriculum-as-lived, they continue: "Rather than trying to forcefully close or attempt to bridge this gap, it is much more fruitful to find ways to work in the 'in-between' space of the gap" (2011, pp. 94–95).

How can we, as teachers, confidently work in such 'in-between' space? How do we find inspiration in the threshold between what we plan and what is happening? When things depart from the plan, a degree of improvisation is obviously needed. Yet, improvisation is not to be confused with chaos; the above authors refer to a 'disciplined' kind of improvisation, as they suggest in the title of their essay, 'Teaching for Creativity with Disciplined Improvisation'. Although disciplined improvisation may initially appear to be an oxymoron, it holds an important truth: improvisation is not random. In the classroom, a teacher may improvise how to facilitate learning with a particular group of students. While 'delivering' a lesson plan, s/he may realise it is not pitched at the right level and change the plan, on the spur of the moment. The very use of the verb 'delivering' needs to be entirely questioned here, as it constructs teaching and learning based on an outdated transmission model, in which knowledge is constructed by delivering content from A (teacher) to B (student). Clearly, teachers who operate between the 'curriculum-as-planned' and 'curriculum-as-lived' are doing much more than just 'delivering' teaching. As Morgan believes, teaching is not about covering the curriculum, but *uncovering* it (in Saxton, 2015, p. 259).

In *The Educational Imagination*, Eisner (1985) argues that teaching is an art form guided by the educational values, personal needs and beliefs held by the teacher. With Stolnitz (1960), I define art form as the sensory elements that have been chosen from a particular medium, and exist only in their relation, as "a web organising the materials of which it is made" (p. 27). The assumption underpinning this book is that teaching can be seen as an art form, following Eisner's rationale of teaching as an art. In this context, Eisner identifies four parameters (pp. 153–155), which he calls 'senses', to justify teaching as an art:

- *The aesthetic dimension of teaching.* Teaching is an art in the sense that teaching can be performed with such skill and grace that, for the student as well as the teacher, the experience can justifiably be characterised as aesthetic.

- *The spontaneous dimension of teaching.* Teaching is an art in the sense that teachers, like painters, composers, actresses and dancers, make judgements based largely on qualities that unfold during the course of an action.
- *The complex nature of teaching.* Teaching is an art in the sense that the teacher's activity is not dominated by prescriptions or routines but is influenced by qualities and contingencies which are unpredicted. [...] It is precisely the tension between automaticity and inventiveness that makes teaching, like any other art, so complex an undertaking.
- *The process-based dimension of teaching.* Teaching is an art in the sense that the ends it achieves are often created in process. (1985, pp. 153–155)

To elaborate his point, Eisner defines 'art' as "the process in which skills are employed to discover ends through actions", while 'craft' is defined as "the process through which skills are employed to arrive at preconceived ends" (p. 154). This definition is arguable; does Eisner mean that art is related to improvised work only? Such a notion would be narrow, as some of the greatest works of art have been created with a preconceived end in mind. When Leonardo da Vinci painted *La Scapigliata* (Head of a Woman) in 1508, for example, he certainly had countless technical and anatomical drawings where he studied the human face, and a series of preliminary sketches that enabled him to capture a specific moment in time. He used these to paint an astonishing expression of calmness and intense beauty with such delicacy and precision in the face of the woman he depicts in his masterpiece of the Italian High Renaissance (Fig. 1). No one would dispute that Leonardo was a master craftsman and a timeless artist, and that *La Scapigliata* is a work of art.

In *The Craftsman*, Sennett (2008) discusses craft in a different light, viewing craftsmanship as the act of being engaged in concrete practices, with high attention to detail, grounded in the body. He argues: "First, that all skills, even the most abstract, begin as bodily practices; second that technical understanding develops through the power of imagination" (p. 10). He also tackles the differences between art and craft:

The most common question people ask about craft is how it differs from art. [...] In terms of practice, there is no art without craft; the idea for a

Fig. 1 *La Scapigliata* [The Head of a Woman] Leonardo da Vinci[1]

> painting is not a painting. The line between craft and art may seem to separate technique and expression, but as the poet James Merrill once told me, 'If this line does exist, the poet himself shouldn't draw it; he should focus only on making the poem happen. (p. 65)

Surely, an 'idea' for a painting is not a painting. However, why confine art just to the *idea* stage? In doing so, Sennett fails to acknowledge that art-making, just like craft, can go beyond the idea stage, into practical doing. Another distinction made by Sennett to elucidate differences between art and craft relates to agency and originality. Artists exercise agency and autonomy to create *original* work, for self-expression:

---

[1]Granted by The Ministry of Cultural Heritage and Tourism (Ministero dei Beni e delle Attività Culturali e del Turismo), Complesso Monumentale della Pilotta, Parma (Italy). Any unauthorized use or reproduction is forbidden.

"Autonomy as a drive from within that impels us to work in an expressive way, by ourselves" (p. 65). A third parameter that Sennett takes to distinguish the artist and the craftsman is collaboration; he talks about the artist acting alone (the lone artist), as opposed to craftsmen acting collectively (a body of craftsmen). This distinction may apply to some circumstances, but it does not apply to all art; certainly it does not apply to drama which, as we will see, is a collective, participatory art form. Rather than getting lost in arguments on what art is, or is not, and how it differs from craft, let us take Sennett's point above that it is not productive to separate technique from expression, and that 'if this line does exist, the poet shouldn't draw it', focussing instead on 'making the poem happen'. In our case, then, this book focuses on the *processes* involved in second language learning through drama, on making engagement with learning happen.

Going back to Eisner's teaching as an art, in a later writing (Eisner, 2002) he talks about teachers *crafting* an experience: "Teachers craft experience by shaping the environment that both students and teachers share" (pp. 382–383). Blindly sticking to the lesson plan as a pre-conceived end is a mechanical form of 'delivering' the curriculum, which does not align with craftsmanship, or with artistry. It is in this sense that Eisner related to teaching as an art form—a complex undertaking where teachers make judgements based on qualities that unfold during an action and where "the ends it achieves are often created in process" (1985, p. 154). What I find fascinating is that the artist can have a blueprint, but things do not always go according to plan. Events often turn out different from what was anticipated, because of unpredicted circumstances and/or unexpected external factors. At this point, we may freeze, ignore the accident, or work to rectify the mistake. Alternatively, we may pause, take the time to reassess, and take the mistake as a springboard to create new solutions. Such moments of the 'unexpected' are what Schön (1983) considers to be at the heart of the reflective practice—one of the methodological pillars of teacher artistry.

As we will see in Chapter 5, Schön is interested in an epistemology of practice implicit in the intuitive processes that practitioners bring to situations of uncertainty, instability and uniqueness. Eisner (2002) also makes this connection between teaching, artistry and improvisation:

> Good teaching depends upon artistry and aesthetic considerations. It is increasingly recognized that teaching in many ways is more like playing

in a jazz quartet than following the score of a marching band. Knowing when to come in and take the lead, knowing when to bow out, knowing that when to improvise are all aspects of teaching that follow no rule, they need to be felt. (p. 382)

Eisner talks about the "in-flight actions of the teachers" (p. 383) as matters of artistry. We will be examining those contexts, especially in light of reflective practitioners navigating between more than one language and culture in educational settings.

If we consider teaching as an art form in the language classroom, then where or what is the work of art? Is it in the effectiveness of the lesson plan? The teacher's delivery skills? The teacher's feedback to learners? The selection of curriculum's content? The students' output? From a socio-cultural, ecological perspective (Van Lier, 2004), the work of art lies in the *exchanges* within the classroom microcosm between the teacher and the learners; between the learners themselves; between each learner and the educational resources. This classroom ecology, thriving on a pattern of exchanges, creates various forms of learner engagement. Seen from this perspective, the classroom can be framed as an ecosystem in which the teacher/artist engages students as co-artists in a process involving not only cognition, but also affect, imagery, sensation, different forms of memory, emotion and embodiment. This dynamic relation between teacher and students' artistry and engagement *is* the work of art.

2 The Teacher/Artist

The expression 'teaching artist' was first coined in the 1970s by educator June Dunbar at the Lincoln Center Institute in New York. In the first issue of the *Teaching Artist* journal, Booth (2003) interviewed a number of key practitioners to formulate a working definition of the teaching artist. The main features emerging from the responses included: using practices of an art form but going beyond the art form to connect to other areas of life; embodying the teaching; a capacity to activate participation; and a focus on process (pp. 6–7). After more than a decade of inquiry, Booth (2015) reflects:

> A TA [teaching artist] does not 'perform' set workshops but generatively brings her creative thinking, learning interests, and ways of thinking to bear on every opportunity with participants. We don't *teach* something, we co-learn, co-create in skilfully shaped inquiries. (p. 152, original emphasis)

This definition aligns well with the philosophy of process drama: a collective, improvised form where, to borrow Booth's words, teachers co-learn, and co-create. Process drama as a collective art form and pedagogy will be defined in greater depth in Chapter 2. For now, however, it will suffice to say that it is an embodied approach to engage learners in a felt-experience. O'Neill (1995) suggests that the process drama teacher functions as an artist, working alongside the participants in a process of dramatic exploration. She argues that, in drama, the teacher is likely to function most effectively from "*within* the experience" (p. 64), inside the creative process, as a co/artist with his/her participants, rather than remaining on the outside of the work.

> Improvised drama is a group activity. In drama in education, this group will include the teacher. It is becoming clear that the teacher is likely to function most effectively in educational drama from within the creative process, as co-artist with the pupils. (O'Neill, in Taylor & Warner, 2006, p. 51)

Schewe (2017) concurs and points out that teaching through drama is not about using techniques alone; rather, the drama teacher needs to have an artistic inclination. Here is where, perhaps, the distinction between art and craft becomes clearer. Schewe (2013) advocates for teacher/artists embracing a performative approach to teaching. 'Performative', he holds, is to be interpreted from its roots *form* and *formative*, honouring the performative nature of language and education. Schewe suggests that performative language teaching should "be used as an umbrella term to describe (the various culturally-specific) forms of foreign language teaching that derive from the performative arts" (p. 18). He proposes a teacher/artistry continuum for teachers as artists and artists as teachers, with experience fluctuating as we further our training, and deepen our knowledge and 'creative doing'—using sound, voice, image, movement, space and embodied action (Schewe, 2017).

While in arts-based circles the statement above would be well-received, in L2 settings it may not be as obvious. L2 teachers may not see themselves as 'artists' and may not necessarily conceive of a lesson unfolding as a work of art.

For those educators interested in understanding and apprehending embodied approaches, the construct of identity, particularly teacher identity, needs to be considered. Identity formation in teaching is a complex topic that has received a lot of attention in the last decades (Akkerman & Meijer, 2011; Alsup, 2006; Beijaard, Meijer, & Verloop, 2004). How do teachers see themselves, and how does this impact on their work? To attempt tackling this question, it is important to realise that identity is not a fixed, stable construct, but a fluctuating, and at times contradictory construct involving not one but multiple sub-identities (Akkerman & Meijer, 2011). Each sub-identity may have its own stance, or position, and these I-positions may, at times, disagree with or contradict each other in the dialogical landscape of the human mind (p. 311). For example, when I was in college I had a friend who was completing her education degree (primary). She was also a singer in a local punk band. When she graduated, she secured a full-time job as a primary school teacher. It was 'a good job', some would say. For a year, she was both a teacher working with six-year-old children wearing uniforms in a Catholic school, and a punk rocker. She quit one year later and continued to write songs and perform in her own band. Ten years on, she is a punk rock musician. Akkerman and Meijer suggest that 'identity' can be considered as a 'narrative' about ourselves: 'I' as the author of a play about 'me', with 'myself' as a character in it, mediated by the context. If the self is constructing identities that are not aligned with our intended play, an internal conflict may occur. My singer friend, for instance, had various sub-identities casting different narratives. Teaching was 'a good job', but it wasn't the job for her.

A further distinction involves thinking of 'self' as 'the storyteller' and 'identities' as the stories being told (Akkerman & Meijer, 2011, p. 311). In the case of an L2 teacher learning drama-based pedagogy, if a teacher's sub-identity does not align with that of the teacher as artist, for instance, there may be a block, or resistance, to undertaking the work independently. This may account for the reluctance on the part of some teachers to use drama approaches, even after being involved in ongoing professional development and acknowledging its benefits for language learning (Araki Metcalfe, 2008; Stinson, 2009). Perhaps, for some, the notion of the artist is too intimidating, or connected with the all-pervasive myth of the artist as a rebel, and a talented genius. Far from it. The genius in teaching lies in the act of listening: listening to our students; listening to our pedagogical hunches; listening to the context; listening to the responses they generate.

A reference point in the performative language teaching literature who advocates for the teacher/artist identity is Peter Lutzker. In *The Art of Foreign Language Teaching: Improvisation and Drama in Teacher Development and Language Learning* (2007), Lutzker reports his own study on the effect of clowning workshops on fifty-five language teachers' professional development. The research tools encompass seven interviews with clowning masterclass leader, Vivian Gladwell, as well as fifty-five written responses from the teachers who took part in the workshops. A common thread in almost all the teacher/artists' responses was developing an awareness of "renouncing of all preconceived plans, becoming completely open to what will develop" (p. 134). Recurring themes that appear in the participants' responses are, among others, a heightened receptivity to the moment, an acceptance of oneself, a deep feeling of openness and liberation, and a new dimension of contact with others (p. 137). Lutzker concludes that the common element between language teaching and the clowning workshops is the development of a certain kind of 'fluidity' or awareness. In order to heighten awareness, both teaching and improvisation require "continually listening, waiting, being acutely receptive to everything that is occurring both outside and within, in order to respond fluidly and creatively" (p. 183). Lutzker provides a historical overview of key educators who have influenced the teacher/artist paradigm, advocating teachers as 'educational artists' (Weber, 1907); 'conscious artists' (Stenhouse, 1983); the 'artistry in teaching' (Rubin, 1985); 'teaching as a performing art' (Sarason, 1999); and the teacher as a 'creative improviser' (Sawyer, 2004). From his study on teacher development, improvisation and clowning, Lutzker concludes that "the incorporation of artistic processes into language teaching is seen as being inextricably tied to a teacher's own artistic training and growth" (2007, p. 455).

More recently, Crutchfield (2015) also advocates for performative language teaching as an art. He observes that this artistry involves engagement with the emotions, both pleasant and painful emotions. When intense emotions arise, teachers should not avoid them, but manage them competently. Teachers, he holds, need to be deeply familiar with the artistic processes in which they wish to engage their students: "This is especially true of artistic processes involving performance, where the 'work' is the body itself, or rather, *embodied action before witnesses*, and the performer is exposed in a profound, frightening and unpredictable way" (p. 103, original emphasis). This is an essential aspect of teacher artistry and drama practice, related to emotions and learning, which will be explored more in-depth in the second part of the book (see "Protecting into Emotion" in Chapter 6).

Lutzker (2016) makes a useful contribution here, as he distinguishes between training and practice. While in the former what is important is achieving a specific goal, in the latter the focus is on the time and effort invested to achieve a goal. Practice takes time, and this time changes us. Discussing a master carpenter and a master violinist's practice, Lutzker notes that they don't train, they *practise*, and "their practice sits deeply in their bodies and in their movements" (p. 234). It is interesting to note that, in this distinction, Lutzker refers to a craftsman (master carpenter) and an artist (master violinist), grounding their doing in a practice, anchored in the body, echoing Sennett's point above. Embodiment, in this sense, is highly relevant to practice, in both craftsmanship and artistry. Lutzker also discusses practice as affecting the carpenter and violinist in terms of their emotional lives, and the way they think (p. 234). He connects practice to Csikszentmihalyi's (2013) famous notion of flow in creativity, for which action and awareness merged into one, and the concept of time is distorted.

Lutzker suggests that L2 education should aim for such notion of practice, as opposed to training:

> One of the most disturbing aspects of so much foreign language teaching and learning is that pupils are constantly being asked to train for something – whether vocabulary, grammar, a test, or an exam – and are very seldom given the opportunity to practice in a foreign language and thus have no chance to experience flow in the context of their language learning. (p. 235)

In closing, I return to Hamachek's statement in the opening of this chapter: "Consciously we teach what we know; unconsciously we teach who we are". If we agree with Hamachek, if we concur that teaching is more than mechanically delivering a lesson plan, but involves "the aesthetic dimension of teaching" (Eisner, 1985, p. 153), then it is worth investigating what the aesthetic dimension of teaching may entail. A question emerges: *How can teacher/artists navigate the aesthetic dimension to facilitate performative language learning?* This book is my attempt to address this multifaceted issue, setting out to explore the artistry of process drama in second language education, and the kind of engagement generated, when language is embodied in action.

3   Organisation of the Book

The attentive reader will have already noticed from this introduction that the book is written in a particular style, drawing on autobiographical vignettes and personal memories. This style exposes what Kramsch (2009) would call my "narratorial self" as a multilingual subject. In her words: "The narratorial self brings into focus the indispensable role of private memory and imagination in language learning: *remembering how* (past experiences and emotions) and *imagining what if* (p. 74, original emphasis). In this book I share personal memories and emotions from my narratorial self as a learner of English, as a language teacher and as a teacher/artist. These memories are interwoven with theory and practice.

At the end of each chapter, a practical drama workshop is included, for a total of ten process drama workshops. The drama structures have been included as examples to support the theory. They are workshops I have designed and facilitated in a variety of contexts. Rather than conceiving them as rigid templates, the drama workshops are intended as real examples of practice. In a spirit of respect for the "ephemerality and immediacy of the form" (O'Neill, 1995, p. xiii), I acknowledge that the process dramas outlined have occurred in specific moments in time and will take different directions when used with other participants, in different contexts. I also wish to clarify, in alignment with Bowell and Heap (2017), that this book is not intended as "a recipe book of model lessons" (p. 7), but a praxial exploration of knowledge.

This style of writing—drawing on theory, practice and reflexivity—aligns with the praxis-oriented philosophy underpinning the theoretical framework of the book. On the one hand, praxis is a cornerstone of drama practice and research (Neelands, 2006). On the other hand, sociocultural theory (SCT) for second language learning also emphasises praxis-based research, "intervening and creating conditions for development" (Lantolf, Thorpe, & Poehner, 2015, p. 207). As will become clear, SCT with its emphasis on development and praxis-based research is the connecting tissue between process drama, aesthetic learning and embodiment.

The book is divided into three parts. Part I aims to introduce key concepts related to the aesthetic dimension of performative language teaching and learning. This introduction discussed the notions of teaching as an art, identity and the teacher/artist. Chapter 2 defines embodiment, drama-based learning, and process drama in second language education, positioning it as a performative approach to language teaching. Chapter 3 explores the realm of aesthetic and intercultural engagement in L2/process drama. Chapter 4 introduces the elements of drama, that is, the coordinates to navigate the aesthetic dimension, again with particular attention to the intercultural domain. Chapter 5 discusses knowing-in-action, the intuitive decision-making needed to interpret those coordinates.

Part II turns to *how* can teacher/artists navigate the aesthetic dimension *to facilitate learning*. From an SCT perspective, learning is viewed as symbolic mediation. Part II thus considers process drama as symbolic mediation for second language learning. Chapter 6 examines Vygotskian theories of play and dual affect, and how play mediates learning. It also introduces the concepts of protecting 'into' emotion and distancing in L2/process drama. The theoretical discussion is supported by a reflective practitioner account of a Content and Language Integrated Learning (CLIL) project in a primary school, where CLIL was combined with drama-based pedagogy. Chapter 7 focusses on engagement with language, Teacher in Role, and the art of questioning in L2/process drama. Chapter 8 advances a 4D model to orientate the teacher/artist in the rich depth of performative language pedagogy, considering language development over time and knowing-in-action.

It also covers the Common European Framework of Reference for Languages (CEFR) levels, alignment with various dramatic forms, and assessment. The chapter draws on a case study on teaching Italian working with adult Irish students with intellectual disabilities, through an embodied, visual arts and drama-based approach.

Part III switches to a research-based focus. Chapter 9 illustrates the methodological foundations of my doctoral research project, a reflective practitioner study on the constructs of 'learner engagement' and 'teacher artistry' informed by a performative paradigm. Chapter 10 provides an overview of the findings related to 'learner engagement'—within the domains of SLA, Intercultural Education and Aesthetic Learning. Chapter 11 reports findings related to 'teacher artistry', mapping my own progression as I learn to reflect in action and reflect on action, letting go of a covert tendency to control improvisation.

I have argued above that this book aims to address the question: *How can teacher/artists navigate the aesthetic dimension to facilitate performative language learning?* Part I addresses the first part of the question; Part II addresses the second part of the question; Part III consolidates the discussion and grounds it in reflective practitioner research. The Conclusion revisits the main focus of the book, embodiment in second language education. It touches on some long-lasting myths related to the nature of creativity that may still pervade L2/drama settings, and on the phenomenology of practice. The book ends with some considerations on future directions for practice-based research.

References

Alsup, J. (2006). *Teacher identity discourses: Negotiating personal and professional spaces*. Mahwah, N.J: Routledge.

Akkerman, S. F., & Meijer, P. C. (2011). A dialogical approach to conceptualizing teacher identity. *Teaching and Teacher Education, 27*(2), 308–319.

Araki-Metcalfe, N. (2008). Introducing creative language learning in Japan through educational drama. *NJ: Drama Australia Journal, 31*(2), 45–57.

Beijaard, D., Meijer, P. C., & Verloop, N. (2004). Reconsidering research on teachers' professional identity. *Teaching and Teacher Education, 20*(2), 107–128.

Berghetto, R. A., & Kaufman, J. C. (2011). Teaching for creativity with disciplined improvisation. In R. K. Sawyer (Ed.), *Structure and improvisation in creative teaching* (pp. 94–109). Cambridge: Cambrige University Press.

Booth, D. (2003). Seeking definition: What is a teaching artist? *Teaching Artist Journal, 1*(1), 5–12.

Booth, D. (2015). Something's happening: Teaching artistry is having a growth spurt. *Teaching Artist Journal, 13*(3), 151–159.

Bowell, P., & Heap, B. (2017). *Putting process drama into action: The dynamics of practice.* London: Routledge.

Crutchfield, J. (2015). Fear and trembling. *Scenario: Journal for Performative Teaching, Learning and Research, 9*(2), 101–114.

Csikszentmihalyi, M. (2013). *Creativity: The psychology of discovery and invention.* New York: Harper Perennial.

Damasio, A. R. (1999). *The feeling of what happens: Body and emotion in the making of consciousness.* New York: Harcourt Brace.

Damasio, A. R. (2010). *Self comes to mind: Constructing the conscious brain.* New York: Pantheon.

Eisner, E. (1985). *The educational imagination: On the design and evaluation of school programs.* New York: Macmillan.

Eisner, E. W. (2002). From episteme to phronesis to artistry in the study and improvement of teaching. *Teaching and Teacher Education, 18*(4), 375–385.

Ellis, R. (2008). *The study of second language acquisition.* Oxford: Oxford University Press.

Hamachek, D. (1999). Effective teachers: What they do, how they do it, and the importance of self-knowledge. In R. P. Lipka & T. M. Brinthaupt (Eds.), *The role of self in teacher development* (pp. 189–224). Albany: State University of New York Press.

Immordino-Yang, M. H. (2016). *Emotions, learning, and the brain: Exploring the educational implications of affective neuroscience.* New York: Norton.

Kramsch, C. (2009). *The multilingual subject.* Oxford: Oxford University Press.

Lantolf, J. P., & Poehner, M. E. (2014). *Sociocultural theory and the pedagogical imperative in L2 education: Vygotskian praxis and the research/practice divide.* Oxfordshire, England and New York, NY: Routledge.

Lantolf, J. P., & Thorne, S. L. (2006). *Sociocultural theory and the genesis of second language development.* New York: Oxford University Press.

Lantolf, J. P., Thorne, S. L., & Poehner, M. E. (2015). Sociocultural theory and second language development. Theories in second language acquisition: An introduction. In B. VanPatten & J. Williams, (Eds.), *Theories in*

Second Language Acquisition: An introduction (pp. 207–226). New York and London: Routledge.

Lutzker, P. (2007). *The art of foreign language teaching: Improvisation and drama in teacher development and language learning*. Tübingen: Francke Verlag.

Lutzker, P. (2016). The Recovery of Experience in Foreign Language Learning and Teaching. In S. Even & M. Schewe (Eds.), *Performative Teaching, Learning, Research — Performatives Lehren, Lernen, Forschen* (pp. 222–239). Berlin: Schibri Verlag.

Neelands, J. (2006). Re-imagining the reflective practitioner: Towards a philosophy of critical praxis. In J. Ackroyd (Ed.), *Research methodologies for drama education* (pp. 15–40). Sterling, VA: Trentham.

O'Neill, C. (1995). *Drama worlds: A framework for process drama*. Portsmouth: Heinemann.

Rubin, L. J. (1985). *Artistry in teaching*. New York: Random House.

Sarason, S. B. (1999). *Teaching as performing art*. New York: Teachers College Press.

Sawyer, R. K. (2004). Creative teaching: Collaborative discussion as disciplined improvisation. *Educational Researcher, 33*(2), 12–20.

Saxton, J. (2015). Failing better. In P. Duffy (Ed.), *A reflective practitioner's guide to (mis)adventures in drama education—or—What was I thinking?* (pp. 253–266). Bristol: Intellect.

Schewe, M. (2013). Taking stock and looking ahead: Drama pedagogy as a gateway to a performative teaching and learning culture. *Scenario: Journal for Performative Teaching, Learning and Research, 8*(1), 5–23.

Schewe, M. (2017, September). *The state of the art*. Key note address at the University of Padova Summer School: The role of drama in higher and adult language education — from theory to practice. Padova, Italy.

Schön, D. (1983). *The reflective practitioner: How professionals think in action*. London: Temple Smith.

Sennett, R. (2008). *The craftsman*. New Haven: Yale University Press.

Stenhouse, L. (1983). Case study in educational research and evaluation. In L. Barlett, S. Kemmis, & G. Gilliard (Eds.), *Case study: An overview*. Geelong: Deakin University Press.

Stinson, M. (2009). Drama is like reversing everything: Intervention research as teacher professional development. *Research in Drama Education: The Journal of Applied Theatre and Performance, 14*(2), 225–243.

Stolniz, J. (1960). *Aesthetics and philosophy of art criticism*. New York: Houghtoh Mifflin Co.

Taylor, P., & Warner, C. D. (2006). *Structure and spontaneity: The process drama of Cecily O'Neill*. Sterling, VA: Trentham.
Van Lier, L. (2004). *The ecology and semiotics of language learning: A sociocultural perspective*. Norwell, MA: Kluwer Academic.
Weber, E. (1907). *Ästhetik als pädagogische Grundwissenschaft*. Leipzig: Wunderlich.
Winston, J. (2010). *Beauty and education*. London: Routledge.

Part I: Key Definitions in the Aesthetic Dimension

2

Drama as Process in L2 Education

Let's start with silence. Arguably, silence carries several meanings and can be coloured by a wide spectrum of emotions. In first and second language acquisition (SLA), the silent phase that precedes speech is pregnant with expectation. But once one has become fluent, silence still characterises speech. King and Smith (2017) study silence and foreign language anxiety in Japanese English classrooms, denouncing "epidemic levels of learner disengagement" with "student silence as a trend that holds true". In their large-scale, multisite investigation into silence in L2 settings, they identify social anxiety as a main factor related to avoidance to speak. Social and language anxiety can also trigger another kind of silence in L2 speaking, one that is more difficult to pinpoint—not a verbal, but an affective silence. This was the case for Eva Hoffman, who wrote her memoires about learning to speak English as a Polish immigrant in Canada. Even when Hoffman became a proficient English language speaker, she felt there was something missing from her English-speaking persona. Granger (2004) analyses how Hoffman was able to communicate fluently in English, but it was deprived of the 'affective connotation' of the language. Here silence is said to represent:

> Something more elemental, more visceral: she knows the word, can think it, say it and write it, but cannot 'feel' its meaning. Hoffman is not literally silent; outwardly she functions very well in her second language. But in terms of her self-expression—that is, the expression of her self—this period of her life is effectively voiceless. (p. 69)

Silence, then, can also be interpreted as a lack of expressiveness in the feeling dimension. This lack of expressiveness was what motivated me in the first place to venture out of my comfort zone as a language teacher, and look elsewhere for inspiration.

My professional experience as a language teacher started in Australia in 2001, teaching Italian to adult students, in a language school nested within a university setting. During my initial teacher training, I was introduced to some techniques meant to lower what Krashen (1985) had famously described as students' affective filter. Part of the suggested routine to prepare our students for a 'relaxed' listening activity involved dimming the lights, playing some classical music and showing photographs of nature, printed in colour on glossy communicative textbooks. I used to draw a candle on the board and write: RELAX as I couldn't dim the lights. I remember feeling that my students did not particularly indulge in those alleged moments of relaxation. This was our pre-listening routine before the stereo spattered out a conversation between two natives.

The so-called 'relaxed' listening activity was followed by a series of 'analytical' listening tasks, aimed at reconstructing the exchange between two people reciting a fabricated script. I recall my students' disengagement with the pre-listening activities; their frustration at not comprehending the Italian dialogue; their polite obligation—so embedded in Australian culture—to engage in a series of sterile communicative exchanges, to indulge in their teacher's faith that this would somehow help them become better language speakers. More than anything, I recall the uncomfortable giggles every time I and my teacher colleagues would call out: *Non in inglese! Parliamo in Italiano*! (Not in English! Let's speak Italian!). This seemed to be the leitmotif of our lessons. In a classroom environment where speaking in the mother tongue was strongly discouraged, but without providing any real urgency to engage in L2 conversation, I was actively looking to fill that gap; I was trying to incorporate many creative activities in my teaching, although I felt they were not working.

By all means, I was not alone in my frustration; numerous teachers who I have met since then have reinforced, and continue to reinforce, this disenchantment. Surely, times have changed now, and it is a truism to state that some communicative language activities can flatten students' motivation. As Scarino and Liddicoat (2009) argue, by focussing solely on natural interaction, the communicative approach (Nunan, 1987), which gained popularity in the 1980s, overlooks that communication should also be purposeful. Discussing communicative teaching, Scarino and Liddicoat note:

> What is missing from such a view of interaction is an appreciation of the fact that interaction is purposeful. People do not talk in order to do language: they use language in order to talk. Therefore people need to have something to talk about and someone they wish to talk about these things with. By removing communicative purpose as a relevant consideration in classroom action, language teaching has tended to construct interaction as a sterile and pointless activity. (2009, p. 38)

Acknowledging the interactions in my L2 classrooms as 'sterile and pointless' is what made me encounter the work of actress, director, educator Viola Spolin (1906–1994), who designed a system of theatre improvisation games for the classroom. Shortly after I started my teaching career, I became an avid reader of Spolin's (1986) work, improvisation by *The Second City* in Chicago and Johnstone's (1999) *Impro for Storytellers*. I was so captivated by the benefits that improvisation could bring to L2 teaching, that in 2002 I enrolled in an improvisation course. Two levels were available, an introductory and an advanced level. Foolishly I believed that, having *read about* improvisation, I would be fit for the advanced level. Reality came crashing down on the first day, when the director asked us to share with the group the most embarrassing memory we had while acting on stage. While my classmates had extensive acting portfolios, I had never acted on a professional stage. Besides, all of them, except for me, were native speakers of English. I started to doubt myself.

During the course we practised a variety of formats from the *Theatresports* tradition, some of which included fast-paced entrance/exit improvisation skits, with members of the group calling out 'dead!' if the improviser wasn't funny enough. On one occasion, when I was made to 'drop dead' in the middle of my act, instead of quickly getting up and re-inventing my character, I stayed dead. I froze. I lay on the floor, in silence, in my 'dead' position, for the duration of the scene. Afterwards the director remarked that I should have quickly got up and invented a new character, and dismissed the incident as my lack of experience. In truth, I was attempting to improvise in a non-native language, surrounded by advanced improvisers, who were competing in charming the audience with ironic puns, rich in Australian cultural references, mastering a sense of humour beyond my command as a foreign language speaker. Overall, that course left me feeling inadequate. How could I think I was ready for the advanced level, in a foreign language? That experience made obvious how *foreign* English was to me.

Shortly after, eager to make up for that shameful introduction to improvisation, I decided to enrol in a second course—this time making sure it was at beginner level. It was in the same studio, but offered by a different company. This couldn't have been more different from the previous one; the facilitator was a physical theatre practitioner who introduced us to improvisation through movement, storytelling and mime. That course was also called *Improv*; it was also held in a theatre, and was also aiming for a public improvised performance. Yet, throughout it I was reinvigorated. It was grounded in movement, in the wisdom of the body. Words followed the body; silence was OK; comic relief was not necessary. I recall standing in awe, during a solo performance on stage, making eye contact with an intimate audience, thriving on the feeling of being *present*. As I improvised my story, my English words felt real and alive. That feeling of presence has accompanied me ever since when I dance, and when I improvise in role. That feeling of presence, I later discovered, is connected to what Barba (1995) calls scenic presence, the 'pre-expressive' and "body-in-life" (p. 7).

What made those two experiences so different from each other? Both improvisation courses were held in English, my second language; both were not designed for language learners. Surely, one was advanced, the other introductory. But one left me feeling inadequate—not funny enough; the other elevated me to an aesthetic plateau that fuelled a life-long commitment to practice. Most interesting for this discussion, understanding the principles of improvisation on a conceptual level did not translate to an applied understanding. After reading about improvisation, I thought I was ready for the advanced course. I had mixed up two very different kinds of knowing: knowing *that*, and knowing *how*. While the former involves a cognitive understanding, the latter involves a kind of embodied knowing—the subject of this book.

1 Embodiment

In order to define embodiment let me introduce the theory of 'simplexity': embracing 'complexity' and 'simplicity' in a research perspective—taking a complex concept and breaking it down to make it accessible, without losing its complexity. Simplexity is a paradigm that has become popular in educational theory, characterised by an active effort in decoding complexity, without reducing its depth (Berthoz, 2012). With Sibilio (2002), I take a 'simplex' perspective to perception, body and knowledge.

From a simplex perspective, embodiment in education relates to a kind of learning experience grounded in the mind, senses, body, imagination, reflection and social sphere: "Embodied pedagogy joins body and mind in a physical and mental act of knowledge construction" and therefore entails a thoughtful awareness of body, space, and social context (Nguyen & Larson, 2015, p. 332). Below I define embodied pedagogy in the interconnected fields of education, performative language teaching and sociocultural theory (SCT). While these theoretical definitions of embodiment are worthwhile and compelling, my fear is that they may become lost in the meanders of rational whirlwinds, leaving the reader bamboozled as to what embodiment actually means, in the classroom. As Perry and Medina (2011) recognise, writing about embodiment is challenging, as "the body is impenetrable by the means we have at our disposal—words, ink, page, computer" (p. 64). In a provocative chapter published in Perry and Medina's (2016) edited collection, St. Pierre (2016) highlights this danger: "I confess, I've never quite understood *embodiment*. I hoped that after reading and rereading the smart set of essays collected here […] I might finally get it. But I didn't" (p. 138, original emphasis). To overcome this trap, in the spirit of simplicity, at the end of the chapter I have included a drama workshop sequence—to illustrate, in practice, what embodying language in action may look like in an intermediate L2 classroom.

In *Nature, Life and Body-Mind*, John Dewey (1859–1952) develops the notion of body and mind as interconnected (Dewey, 1925/1981). He also elaborates on this notion in *Democracy and Education* (1916/2004) where he argues that "senses are avenues of knowledge not because external facts are somehow conveyed through the brain, but because they are used in doing something with a purpose" (p. 136). Pointing to the senses as avenues of knowledge was revolutionary, as effectively it shifted the perspective from knowledge belonging solely to the cognitive realm (the Cartesian paradigm) to knowledge as embodied. This argument, made by Dewey over a century ago, is now being echoed by educational neuroscientists; an example is Immordino-Yang and Damasio's statement, mentioned in the Introduction, "We feel therefore we learn" (Immordino-Yang, 2016, p. 27). Another influential player in embodiment studies is biologist, philosopher and neuroscientist Francisco Varela. Together with Thompson and Rosch, in 1991 he wrote *The Embodied Mind*, a seminal text that paved the way to embodied cognition research, recently revised into a new edition (Varela, Thompson, & Rosch, 1991). Looking at learning from an embodied perspective, the authors note, implies looking not only at the cognitive plane, but also at the perceptual, sensory and emotional awareness planes, with reflection as key to experience:

> By *embodied*, we mean reflection in which body and mind have been brought together. What this formulation intends to convey is that reflection is not just *on* experience, but reflection *is* a form of experience itself – and that reflective form of experience can be performed with mindfulness/awareness. (2016, p. 27, original emphasis)

This definition of embodiment lends itself well to performative pedagogy. As Duffy (2014) puts it: "A basic maxim in theatre is that drama is doing. The study of how that *doing* impacts and even accentuates learning is embodiment" (pp. 9–10, original emphasis). An important aspect of embodiment is the possibility it affords to express the 'what if' through the faculty of imagination. Lev Semyonovich Vygotsky (1896–1934) describes this 'what if' of drama as what makes the art form *embody* elements of reality through imagination. In *Imagination and Creativity in Childhood* (1930/2004) he writes about drama enabling a drive for action, a drive for embodiment:

> The dramatic form expresses with greatest clarity the full cycle of imagination … Here the image that the imagination has created from real elements of reality is *embodied* and realized again in reality, albeit only the contingent reality of the stage; the *drive for action*, for *embodiment*, for realization that is present in the very process of imagination here finds complete fulfilment. (p. 70, my emphasis)

Going back to my experience discussed above, I can identify this difference between the two improvisation courses. While in the first experience when I 'dropped dead' on stage I struggled to find a 'drive for action', to draw from reality and incorporate its elements into an imagined new character, in the second experience a different texture was created, a felt-experience, where the body was leading the imaginative action. This enabled me to incorporate real elements into the imaginative sphere, feeling an impulse for action and, consequently, for language.

Vygostky (1933/1994) identifies this kind of felt-experience as an important unit of analysis for development. To describe this unit of analysis as experience, he uses the term *perezhivanie*, a Russian noun that cannot be directly translated into English. Interestingly, the term *perezhivanie* is also contained in Stanislavski's (1936/1980) original version of *An Actor Prepares*, translated as "the creative process of experiencing". This term, however, was later dropped in the English translation (Carnicke, 1998, p. 109). Throughout Stanislavski's text, the term *perezhivanie* is translated in many different ways: "the art of living a part"; "sensation"; "living and experiencing"; "the capacity to feel"; "emotional experience" and "creation" (p. 109). Vygotsky's notion of *perezhivanie* draws on Stanislavski, and resonates with embodiment in second language learning.

Perezhivanie relates to an embodied felt-experience—in a way, it is the antonym of the "lack of feeling expressiveness" described above in

Granger's (2004) affective silence. The French have a wonderful way of referring to 'foreign' languages: *langues vivents*, literally, 'living' languages. By experiencing a 'living' language, as we speak it we feel it triggers an emotion, stimulated by imagination and turned into action. In my early years of teaching, my embodied felt-experience of the English language through improvisation inspired me to introduce some drama strategies into my teaching practice. I was following a hunch that by engaging in performative approaches, my students could find, like I had found, ways to make the language less foreign and more alive. We could also make a language *vivent* (alive), connected to felt-experience.

An embodied approach to language learning is at the heart of what Schewe (2013) refers to as performative teaching in language education. Performative language teaching is "an approach to language teaching and learning that emphasises *embodied action* and that makes use of techniques, forms and aesthetic processes adapted from the performing arts" (Crutchfield & Schewe, 2017, p. xiv, original emphasis). Schewe further reflects on the integration of performative elements in L2 teaching, pointing to body, voice, space and physical presence. He sees the body as an "instrument of perception" advocating for "the conscious incorporation of the body into the learning process" (in Even & Schewe, 2016, p.181). As Coleman (2017) argues:

> Rather than reject the interference of the body, drama recognises its centrality to learning and channels that physical energy. Through the body, a language learner may communicate, well before mastering the words to speak a sentence, feeling or idea aloud. (p. 32)

In other words, language learners use the body to mediate meaning.

From a sociocultural perspective of second language learning, the term 'embodiment' is associated with development, self-regulation and gesture. SCT is a Vygotskian orientation to second language development that views learning as a mediated phenomenon. As Haught and McCafferty (2008) state: "Language in use is necessarily an embodied phenomenon" (p. 139). Embodiment research, or gesture studies, is a branch of sociocultural research that focuses on how the body mediates expression and development in SLA. From this perspective, the underlying assumption of embodiment is that gesture and speech are two facets of the same process, part of a single integrated system. In a collection of essays on gesture study research, McCafferty and Stam (2008) state:

> For our purposes we want to embrace the general principle that as human beings we live our lives through embodied experience within specific cultural historical contexts, and that this has an impact on how we communicate as well as how we think. (p. 3)

The authors go on to say that the basic tenet of gesture studies is the close connection between language and gesture in relation to meaning-making. McNeill (1992), the psycholinguist associated with gesture studies research, draws on Vygotsky's work to posit that gestures are a window on the mind, and speech and gesture develop *inter*dependently in speech. Analysing the various kinds of gestures that L2 speakers make, as they interact, can offer an insight into the learners' acquisition process, according to the type of gesturing they engage in.

Drawing on McNeill, Lapaire (2014, 2016, 2017) construes speech as an embodied social practice. Informed by a background in linguistics and dance, Lapaire considers language as action in motion; he teaches English as a second language (ESL) through a choreography of speech, gesture and dance. Even (2011) explored similar territory, developing a performative approach to teaching German grammar through drama pedagogy. She describes 'drama grammar' as a performative approach, where "the fictionality of the dramatic context serves as a secure environment for learners to try out combinations of words, gestures and movements in collaborative efforts to drive the action forward" (2011, p. 307).

Embodiment is also tightly interconnected with intercultural education. A focus on the body in L2 and intercultural education gained momentum in the early 2000s, through edited works like *Body and Language: Intercultural Learning through Drama* (Bräuer, 2002) where a conscious attempt was made to conceive embodiment as an active medium to foster intercultural awareness. In this context,

Fleming (2003) argues for drama as a form of intercultural education. More recently, Rothwell (2017) has made a case for process drama and intercultural language learning.

In a praxis-based approach to knowledge (Lantolf & Poehner, 2014), educational discourse moves from theory to practice and back—informing theory with practice, and reflecting back on it. In this spirit, I now shift the focus to the first four strategies of the drama workshop below, to anchor theory in educational practice.

2 Embodiment in Practice: A Classroom Example

Names and Identity (Workshop 1) is an introductory drama workshop that I have conducted in a variety of language contexts, with undergraduate students learning Italian (L2) in Italy, mature age students of Italian (FL) in Australia, pre-service foreign language teachers in Ireland, and, most recently, asylum seekers learning Italian (L2) in Italy. The workshop was developed for L2 students new to drama-based work, at an intermediate level of proficiency. I created this workshop spontaneously, and later put it in writing for documentation purposes. Each time I have facilitated this workshop, it has moved in different directions given the flexible nature of drama, and it will take a different course every time it is put into action. As O'Neill (1995) puts it, "the experience is impossible to replicate exactly" (p. xiii). My purpose in sharing the structure I discuss below is to use a real classroom example to illuminate the theoretical discussion on embodiment.

Looking at the first warm-up activity of Workshop 1 with fresh eyes, a number of observations spring to mind. In Step 1.a, the warm-up activity incorporates breathing awareness exercises. While this may be routine for voice and drama-based classes, it is rather unusual for an L2 class, making the first, solid point of departure between embodied and more traditional approaches to L2 teaching: awareness of breath. As Varela et al. (2016) note, "breathing is one of the most simple, basic, ever-present bodily activities" (p. 25). Yet, in an educational context where learning is equated with the mind only, breathing can become completely overlooked. Second, an emphasis on the prosodic dimension of language can be easily identified in activities. Specifically, the voice exercises in Step 1 are inspired by the voice studies tradition, with practitioners such as Berry (2011), Rodenburg (2015), and Linklater (2006) at the forefront. Linklater in particular advocates restoring the balance between intellect and emotion—a balance which, she argues, has been conditioned out of us by the mind–body split promoted by Western educational strategies (Linklater, in Berry, Rodenburg, & Linklater, 1997, p. 51).

The *Emotional Palette* routine (Step 1.b) lends well as an example of embodying language in action. Participants are encouraged to call out, in the target language, a number of emotions, ideally a dozen. Those emotions are written down as a spider diagram on a chart or on the white board. Next, the participants suggest a key word, or key sentence, in the target language. Comparing the range of emotions written on the board to the watercolours in a painter's palette, we proceed to explore how the key word/s can be 'coloured' with different emotions. Thus, saying *benvenuto* (welcome) in a suspicious manner may reveal a particular quality of expression, or sub-text, different from whispering it in a jealous, euphoric or horrified manner.

A gradual build-up follows: after using our voices to 'colour' the key word/s with various emotions, we use our eyes, our hands, our whole posture to express the emotions. Participants may initially be taken aback when I ask them to express those emotions with eyes only, or hands only, or through a movement in space, but they soon grasp, and enjoy, the freedom and lightness this exercise evokes. Here, gaze and gesture come to the foreground of the L2 speakers' awareness. Body, in this sense, is intended as body in space, as I would encourage them to use chairs, desks, indeed any object around our kinesphere—the sphere around our body whose periphery can be reached by our hands and legs (Laban, 1966). Ultimately, participants discover the expressiveness of their bodies in motion, experimenting with basic locomotion like walking, jumping, sliding—first in isolation, then acknowledging each other.

My personal passion for Butoh, an improvised Japanese dance form that I have practised in the last ten years, informs this phase. In this exercise, participants are encouraged to play with micro movements, levels and rhythm, action and stillness, interpreting key words, coloured by key emotions (in the target language) as they connect to their body awareness. This is a simple, yet effective exercise that can be repeated at the beginning of every class with increased levels of difficulty—key word/s, sentences, idiomatic expressions, building towards still images, individually or in groups (also called freeze frames or tableaux). As a basic form of embodiment, it is surprising how this sequence of exercises can be liberating for those L2 students experiencing foreign language anxiety (MacIntyre, 2017). At the end of the *Emotional Palette* routine, participants are encouraged to reflect (Step 1.c), in pairs and as a group. This phase of reflection is where all the insights and observations are externalised, letting the group engage in a reflection on language learning and body language. Undeniably, embodied pedagogy involves the body, but it does not leave out the mind; reflection is essential after having experimented with voice and body.

The next step is a practical voice exercise, focused on name and identity. Here we focus on the resonance and vibrational textures of our names, pronounced in a variety of ways (Steps 2–3). This connects to a discussion that prompts reflection on what our name symbolises, for us, in our culture and personal lives. Recently I conducted this workshop with a group of asylum seekers, who initially seemed quite taciturn. I was taken aback by how talkative the group became when we began to discuss their names, and what their names represented for them.

The activities so far have focused on prosodic elements of language. Although prosody has been gaining some momentum in L2 teaching (Haycraft, 2010), with some advocating for a 'prosodic turn' in the field (Boureux & Batinti, 2003), the L2 classroom reality is that the set of texts associated with prosody-specific activities are often flat and uninspiring (Piola Caselli, 2017). The difference between standard texts used for prosody-specific activities, and the exercise discussed here, is that these activities function as a warm-up to stimulate awareness of our name, of our voices and bodies, after which participants can focus on a meaningful exploration through drama. On the other hand, traditional prosodic exercises seem to exist for their own sake, stripping the speaker of purpose and context. The rest of the workshop, discussed below

(Steps 4–12), shifts focus from prosodic elements of language to storytelling. It functions as an introduction to an embodied L2 approach—using body and voice to playfully practise speaking in another language, introducing some basic features of process drama.

3 Process Drama

Process drama is an improvised form associated with Drama in Education (DiE), a drama-based approach to teaching and learning that emerged in the 1970s in England through the practice of Dorothy Heathcote, as documented by Wagner (1976), Johnson and O'Neill (1991), and O'Neill (2015). One of the core features of DiE is that the teacher takes on a role within the story (Teacher in Role) to engage participants in an embodied make-believe that is interconnected to an aspect of the curriculum. Heathcote's approach was originally described as 'drama for understanding' and 'drama as a mode of learning'. It was initially conceptualised by Bolton (1979) who drew on Vygotsky's (1930/1978) theories to ground DiE in symbolic play, emotion and development. The term 'process drama' is tightly connected to DiE; it was first used by O'Toole (1990) and Haseman (1991) and later elucidated by O'Neill (1995). In his seminal paper on process drama, Haseman (1991) describes it as "an improvised form which is designed to evoke an artistic response to participants" (p. 19). More recently, Haseman and O'Toole (2017) offer the following definition of process drama:

> Process drama is an improvised form of drama in which you construct a coherent dramatic story with yourselves as the character in that story. It is a powerful way to explore, through experience, all of the elements of drama. This approach brings mind, body, emotions, imagination and memories into the classroom to shape and deepen your learning. (2017, p. viii)

This explanation of process drama puts an emphasis on emotions, embodiment and learning. It makes clear reference to the elements of drama (see Chapter 4) that, the authors suggest, can be explored through imagination and experience. This is precisely in keeping with O'Toole's (1990) very first address on process drama, where he defines it as the negotiation of the elements of the art form. O'Toole later expanded this definition in *The Process of Drama* (1992), where he lays the foundation of the form. Haseman (1991) also defines process drama in terms of the elements of drama, adding that "it is shaped by an educational context which places an emphasis on the quality of learning from educational art encounters" (p. 19). These early definitions capture the dual nature of process drama as art form as well as pedagogy.

O'Neill (1995) describes process drama as a "complex dramatic encounter", which "evokes an immediate dramatic world bounded in space and time" (p. xiii), and shares with theatre its emphasis on aesthetic form and meaning. She identifies some characteristics of process drama:

1. An episodic structure
2. The absence of a script
3. An integral audience

To clarify these concepts, it is worth exploring each point separately. (1) The structure of a process drama implies a series of 'episodes' connected by temporal and spatial relationships, which together form a "web of meaning" (O'Neill, 1995, p. xiv). In order for this 'web of meaning' to effectively connect the episodes, the teacher/artist needs to make choices on several levels. The first choice relates to the pre-text, that is, a source or input that defines the nature of the dramatic world. Choosing a pre-text wisely is critical, and will be discussed in greater depth when exploring the elements of drama (see "Pre-text and Dramatic Tension" in Chapter 4). From the pre-text, the participants are invited to actively create and explore these episodes, which together form a collective narrative. Following the pre-text, the structure overarching the episodes can be divided into three phases, which, adopting O'Toole and Dunn's (2015) terminology, I call the initiation, the experiential and the reflective phases. The workshop I discuss below (Workshop 1) and the others in this book are structured around these phases (initiation, experiential, reflective).

I would define Workshop 1 as an introduction to process drama and embodied learning, rather than as a full-length process drama. While in this case the pre-text is a theme (the connection between name and identity), the actual story is chosen by the participants in each group (Step 7). Ideally, the pre-text connects or 'hooks' (O'Toole & Dunn, 2015) to the participants' interests or motivations. Workshop 1 is designed as an introductory workshop where the teacher does not know her/his students. Having the students choose the story to work with here is an invitation for them to choose something that they as participants can connect with. Often, in this situation the students will choose the funniest story, or the story that breaks the most taboos. This may not always lead to the most insightful discussion, but then again, it is up to the teacher/artist to then steer the reflection around the story; in a way, breaking taboos is the raw essence of play and performance (Schechner, 2006). The focus is precisely on the group becoming familiar with the playfulness of drama, and with working as a group, using their bodies to tell stories in space (Step 8). This is not at all for granted when working with L2 adult groups who are doing drama for the first time. This workshop also aims to introduce participants to the episodic nature of process drama: in Step 9, participants are invited to identify a key moment in their story, and imagine what happened *five minutes before* and *five minutes after*. This helps to familiarise with the form of process drama, where episodes are connected by temporal or spatial relationships.

Second, process drama is characterised by (2) the absence of a script. This brings us to one of the common misunderstandings related to the form. In process drama, the script emerges in action, through the improvisation of the group rather than being pre-defined. This can be recorded or documented for assessment, if needed, but it is created ad hoc and will therefore change from group to group. With O'Neill (2017): "There should always be an openness to the contributions of the participants to the process and the possibility of the work developing in unexpected ways" (p. 27). It follows then that process drama does not involve fixed structures, memorising lines of a pre-determined script, blocking movements, rehearsing or staging a theatre play. The very concept of being on a 'stage' does not apply to process drama, as most activities are performed collectively. Even when students volunteer to perform on their own, the focus is not on their acting skills. Stage fright, or being a 'bad actor' are common objections that L2 learners and L2 teachers may have, based on this misconception of the form.

Moreover, although it is based on improvisation, process drama fundamentally differs from improvised skits like, for example, the *Theatresports* tradition, where the exercises are isolated and one-off. In process drama, the episodic nature of the form connects the various episodes, and reflection follows and/or precedes each episode. This reflection, in L2/process drama, is directed towards language and intercultural meaning-making. For example, in Workshop 1, should the participants choose a 'funny' story that breaks taboos, provoking laughter, the discussion can veer on the perception of such taboo/s across cultures (the target culture; the culture/s of participants). The emphasis is on engaging rather than "playing for laughs" (Bolton, 2007). No one will call out 'dead!' if we are not being funny enough, for it is not on entertainment, but on meaning-making that this kind of improvisational work revolves.

Third, a crucial aspect to understand process drama is (3) the notion of 'integral audience'. In O'Neill's (1995) words: "The imagined world is created by and for the participants themselves" (p. 118). Rather than having *no* audience, as it is sometimes erroneously indicated, in process drama everyone *is* audience—an active audience doing, witnessing, reflecting and making meaning. What is meant by 'integral audience' is that there isn't a predefined group off stage, *gazing* at the actors while another group on the stage is *being gazed* at. This is bypassed in process drama by having the whole group engaged together—gazing inwards and outwards simultaneously. Indeed, drama workshops often begin in a circle formation. The circle convention, a common routine for drama practitioners, serves to question, re-configure and equalise personal boundaries through space (at least metaphorically), reducing the status differential that an elevated stage may create.

The concept of re-balancing hierarchies does not stop at the distribution of space in a room. Rather, it permeates to the philosophy of process drama, with the status and hierarchy of the teacher and students also being re-balanced. This operates on two levels: a paradigm level and an operational level. The former relates to the drama teacher endorsing a reflective practitioner stance (Schön, 1983) and therefore viewing reflection as integral to teaching. The latter relates to the kind of roles adopted by the teacher and by the students in the drama. Workshop 1, discussed below, serves an important function: introducing language students to the idea of re-negotiating agency in the student/teacher hierarchy. This takes time and is fundamental for the co-artist relationship to take place. Letting the students choose the story (Step 7) is one important step to indicate this negotiation of agency. Listening to students' opinions in the reflections that precede/follow the episodes is another indicator of this shift. Reversing the status hierarchy is not a straightforward matter; it is an invitation that participants can accept, but also resist. It can take time if students are not used to it, especially with new groups where trust is still forming. Ultimately, it can empower the participants, giving them the confidence to try out new possibilities through the 'as if' mode of drama.

The renewed confidence endowed by the 'as if' mode of drama is precisely what inspired SLA researchers to take an interest in process drama as a learning medium. One of the most prominent pedagogical features of the DiE and process drama tradition is Heathcote's Teacher in Role (TiR). Equally, TiR is also one of the cornerstones in L2/process drama practice: its unequivocal pedagogical value is that it affords the L2 teacher the possibility to expose students to rich sociolinguistic registers, breaking free of standardised classroom exchanges. TiR will be discussed more in-depth in the second part of the book (see "Teacher in Role and SLA" in Chapter 7).

Shin Mei Kao (1994) was the first researcher to conduct an empirical study in this field, using discourse analysis to investigate process drama in the L2 classroom. The study was ground-breaking at the time, as illustrated in *Words into Worlds*, a seminal text through which Kao and O'Neill (1998) have inspired two decades of research (Stinson & Winston, 2014; Winston, 2012). Aspects of L2/process drama that have been considered so far include motivation and cultural sensitivity (Bournot-Trites, Belliveau, Spiliotopoulos, & Séror, 2007); oral communication (Stinson, 2008); teacher development (To, Chan, Lam, & Tsang, 2011); multi-modality (Yaman Ntelioglu, 2011); questioning and turn-taking (Kao, Carkin, & Hsu, 2011); foreign language anxiety (Piazzoli, 2011); Teacher in Role and digital technology (Dunn, Bundy, & Woodrow, 2012); role and L2 learners' sense of self

(Tschurtschenthaler, 2013); epiphany (Pheasant, 2015); intercultural/intracultural understanding (Rothwell, 2015); creativity and innovation (Hulse & Owens, 2017); and vocabulary acquisition (Kalogirou, Beauchamp, & Whyte, 2017).

While it would be beyond the scope of this chapter to review all these studies in depth, I briefly mention one major research development. The largest L2/process drama research project published to date is Madonna Stinson's (2008, 2009) research in Singapore, consisting of two multi-site projects. The instruments used included standardised tests looking at language progress over time, as well as comparison of control groups and experimental groups. The *Drama and Oral Language* (DOL) study involved 140 students who engaged in four process dramas for ten sessions of one-hour classes, and were tested orally using a standard test instrument (Stinson & Freebody, 2006). The *Speaking Out* study was longitudinal design research, involving eight teachers and twelve classes, for up to 480 students engaged in L2/process drama for one year. In both studies, proficiency in English was measured through pre-intervention and post-intervention testing, analysed statistically. Findings showed that L2/process drama was beneficial for students' oral development, writing, confidence and active participation. Four key findings Stinson (2008) identified are: "contextualising language" (p. 199); "confidence and motivation" (p. 200); "the safe space of drama" (p. 200); and "shifting the power from teachers to students" (p. 201). The DOL and the *Speaking Out* studies support the use of process drama for second language learning, and they unearth interesting dynamics related to resistance in teacher education (Stinson, 2009). For a more comprehensive overview of L2/process drama research, see Belliveau and Kim (2013) and, more recently, McGovern's (2017) discussion on conceptualising drama in second language learning.

4 Performative Language Teaching

The term 'performative language teaching' was first introduced by Schewe (2013) in the context of second language education, with the aim to create a shared terminology through which to consolidate an international community of practice. The term encompasses DiE and theatre in education (TiE) in FL/L2/AL contexts; *theaterpädagogik* and *dramapädagogik* in Germany, *glottodidattica teatrale* in Italy, *gloctodidáctica teatral* in Spain, and several other context-specific ways of describing theatre and drama pedagogy in language education. From a performative language teaching approach, Schewe holds, "emphasis is placed on forms of aesthetic expression" (p. 16). His use of 'performative' relates back to its roots 'form' (per*form*ance) and 'formative' (per*formative*) with the Latin suffix *per* meaning 'through', 'by means of'. '*Per*formative' in this sense implies being formative (educating) through form, a simplex notion that captures well the richness of the field. Schewe clarifies that by 'form' he means art and language, as well as the body: "'Form' also implies the ways in which the body speaks and how sound, word, sentence and movement all interact with each other" (p. 16). Clearly, then, a 'performative' approach to language is an embodied approach, with particular attention to the aesthetic domain.

The use of the term 'performative' also evokes the performance studies field. Schechner (2006) defines performance studies as an open, evolving area, encompassing theatre and anthropology, folklore and sociology, history, performance theory, linguistics and performativity, where "questions of embodiment, action, behaviour, and agency are dealt with interculturally" (p. 2). He frames performance as 'restored behaviour', that is "me, behaving as if I were someone else"; or behaving "as I am told to do"; or again, behaving "as I have learnt" (p. 34). In this sense, performance is seen as a spectrum of ritualised behaviours that can be more or less self-conscious, from staged performance to everyday life: "Performing on stage, performing in special situations (public ceremonies, for example), and performing in everyday life are a continuum" (p. 170).

Interestingly, Schechner differentiates between performance as 'make-believe' and performance as 'make belief'. In make-*believe*, "performances maintain a clearly marked boundary between the world of the performance and everyday reality"; in make *belief*, "performances intentionally blur, or sabotage that boundary" (p. 43). In the former, the boundary between what is real and what is imagined is clear; in the latter, the boundary is blurred, with professional roles, status, gender and race influencing situations to "create the very social realities they enact"

(p. 42). This is a useful distinction, which we will come back to in the second part of the book (see "Make-Believe and Make Belief" in Chapter 7).

Performative, as used by Schechner, is connected to Austin's (1962) concept of 'performatives', later developed by Searle's (1969) theory of communication units as speech acts. For Austin performatives are those utterances that are not just describing, but actually doing, performing an action: "The uttering of the words is, indeed, usually a, or even the, leading incident in the performance of the act" (p. 8). However, Austin differentiated between 'authentic' and 'parasitic' performatives, the latter being performatives in fictional context, like an actor speaking on stage. With Schechner (2013), I reject Austin's view of 'the theatre as parasite', agreeing that Austin "did not understand, or refused to appreciate, the unique power of the theatrical as imagination made flesh" (2013, p. 124).

A sociolinguistic view to speech as performance also informs the definition of language learning in the Common European Framework of Reference for Languages (CEFR): "Language use, embracing language learning, comprises the actions *performed* by persons who as individuals and as social agents develop a range of competences, both general and in particular communicative language competences (2001, p. 9, my emphasis). In the latest CEFR Companion Volume (2018), the quotation above is reiterated, and followed by: "Thus, in *performing* tasks, competences and strategies are mobilised in the *performance* and in turn further developed through that experience" (CEFR, 2018, p. 29, my emphasis). The document does not refer to performative language teaching, but goes on to embrace an "action-oriented approach" (p. 29). In Even and Schewe's (2016) appropriation of the term 'performative language teaching', they define language pedagogy as 'performative' in the sense of "action-orientation" and in the sense of "verbal action" (pp. 176–177). At a meta-level, by appropriating this term to describe a kind of embodied approach to language teaching, Even and Schewe's contribution to scholarship is itself a 'performative' move, in Austin's sense.

As a community of practice, performative language teaching and research was reinforced by the birth in 2007 of the online journal *Scenario*, the only academic journal (to date) devoted to research and practice on teaching foreign languages through performative approaches. Within this realm, Schewe (2013) distinguishes between *small*-scale forms and *large*-scale forms. He points to process drama as a small-scale form, as it can be integrated within the curriculum, where a process drama unit can unfold for one, or several classes. Other small-scale forms include forum theatre, readers' theatre, improvisation and playback theatre, widely documented elsewhere (Blatner, 2007; Jackson & Vine, 2013; Menegale, 2016; Prendergast & Saxton, 2010; Prentki, 2013). Large-scale forms, on the other hand, are defined by Schewe (2013) as longer, product-oriented projects, aimed at the rehearsal and staging of plays, which span over months and often imply extra-curricular commitment.

What emerges from the discussion is that process drama belongs to the performative language teaching family, keeping an emphasis on performance as process. Rothwell (2017) sums this up eloquently in defining process drama as "a performative pedagogy approach, rather than a means to a theatrical end performance" (p. 149). This conceptualisation of performative language teaching, encompassing small-scale and large-scale forms, contributes to putting to rest the redundant drama/theatre binary opposition that characterised the turn of last century, in favour of drama and theatre being viewed as a continuum.

5   Theatre and Drama

Drawing on Schewe (2013), Fleming (2016) proposes that the term 'performative language teaching' can be a useful alternative to polarities like drama and theatre, product and process, spectator and participant. Fleming views 'performative language teaching' as a "concept that can re-focus theory and that embodies a culture of learning that promotes engagement, joy, ownership and active participation" (p. 203). In discussing a re-focus of theory, and polarities like drama and theatre, Fleming is referring to a fierce debate in the field known as the 'theatre/drama divide', which characterised the discourse at the end of the last century (Bolton, 1992; Hornbrook, 1985).

This debate originated in England and extended to other English-speaking countries. As Fleming recounts, advocates of theatre in the 1970s and 1980s accused drama of being too unstructured, leaving out the aesthetic component. Advocates of drama recognised the legacy of symbolic play, and accused theatre trainers and scholars of promoting a mood of "exhibitionism, staginess or artificiality" (2016,

p. 192). The argument is multifaceted. On one side, early drama educators were inspired by Slade's (1955) approach to play, as well as Way's (1967) work on play and their influence in England at the time. Bolton (2007) offers a lucid summary of those historical developments. Fleming (2016) makes an interesting point here, noting that after Slade and Way's initial contribution to the field, followed by Bolton and Heathcote, "for many drama education practitioners terms like 'acting', 'rehearsals' and, of particular interest, 'performance' were outlawed and instead words like 'living through', 'engagement' and 'experiential' were used" (p. 192). 'Living through' and 'experiential learning' are useful phrases. Yet, learning through drama is not just about living through; is it also about *reflecting* on having lived through.

In languages other than English, the difference between 'drama' and 'theatre' may not be as clear cut, making the theatre/drama debate come across as a rather Anglocentric affair. Fleming (2011) does acknowledge this, recognising that for those outside the United Kingdom, a debate between 'theatre' and 'drama' may appear confusing, especially in languages where the distinction is not as obvious. In Italian and Spanish, for example, the noun *teatro* can translate as both 'drama' and 'theatre'; to make things more complicated, the Italian noun *dramma* exists, and is specific to theatre plays. 'Drama in education' translates as *teatro didattico*,[1] making a distinction between 'drama' and 'theatre' initially perplexing for Italian speakers, who often need to employ the English terms to convey the message. While all this may leave us lost at sea, these terms do have different roots. Going back to Greek, 'drama' comes from *dran*, to do, act; while 'theatre' comes from *theatron*, as well as *theasthai*, to behold, from *théa*, to gaze, and *théama* 'spectacle', and *theatès*, 'spectator'. Moreover 'theatre', from Latin *teatrum,* also signifies the site where plays take place.

The so-called theatre/drama debate faded out in the mid-1990s. Around the same time, and responding to a yearning to overcome that

---

[1] While in English 'didactic' has acquired a connotation of a teacher-centred teaching style, in Italian the adjective *didattico* (from the noun *didattica*) is a general term that refers to teaching methods and approaches in education (similarly to the Spanish *didáctico* or the French *didactique*).

division, the term 'process drama' emerged. A process-based approach to drama shares common elements with theatre, as O'Neill (1995) illustrates in her *Drama Worlds*, a timeless masterpiece on the aesthetics of process drama. Indeed, the 'doing' mode of drama (*dran*) *and* the 'beholding' quality of theatre (*theasthai*) lie at the core of process drama. As O'Neill puts it: "Both theatre and process drama depend on the temporary acceptance of an illusion—a closed, conventional, and imaginary world that exists in the voluntary conspiracy between audience and actors" (p. 45).

As Fleming (2011) points out, some commentators view the theatre/drama debate as "a period of misdirection and confusion, an unfortunate aberration that thankfully now has been left behind and is best forgotten". Yet others see it as "a period of extraordinary growth in theory and practice which, despite some excesses and mistakes, gave rise to powerful new ways of thinking" (p. 10). I find the latter view more productive to the conversation, especially when the debate is positioned within second/foreign language education. In this sense, the adoption of the term 'performative language teaching', as Fleming (2016) argues, further departs from the theatre/drama distinction. It embraces drama *and* theatre as aesthetic form, within the context of second language education. Fleming advocates for:

> A more nuanced account of performance that does not always have to mean literally performing on stage, but refers rather to the phenomenology of experience, the element of self-consciousness and in-built reflection that marks it out from everyday experience. (p. 195)

As we began this chapter with silence, let us end with a comment on silence. Lutzker (2016) reflects on another role of silence, not seen as a deficit but as richness. He advances the concept of *attunement*—that is, coming into tune with our surroundings, in terms of presence, breath, silence. Lutzker sees attunement as an important notion in second language education, one that is ignored by an obsessive preoccupation to continue *talking* in the classroom. He adds: "Attunement cannot be separated from silence. Whereas to see invariably requires light, listening in the deeper sense of attunement generally requires its opposite, the very absence of sound – silence" (p. 229). Similarly, Kramsch (2009) notes how "as teachers of language we have been trained to hate silence" and advocates for a different view of silence, as "words have no meaning without the silences that surround them and silences have different meanings across cultures" (p. 209). The drama workshop below, *Names and Identity*, aims to consolidate how these concepts may be integrated in practice, transforming silence as social anxiety and avoidance of speaking (King & Smith, 2017), into silence as reflection, breath, presence.

Workshop 1: Names and Identity

Description: This workshop investigates the productive tension between the sound of our name in our mother tongue and in additional language/s, and perception of the connection these sounds may have with identity.

Students' Context—Inspiration for the Workshop: The *Cultura e Accoglienza* 2017 project provided 30 adult asylum seekers and migrants in Padua (Italy) with access to the University of Padova's library, the possibility to audit some modules, a tutor and access to Italian (L2) classes. As part of this project, in collaboration with Fiona Dalziel, in 2017 we conducted a series of performative language workshops. This particular workshop (Names and Identity) was the first workshop. Participants were male and female adults from Nigeria and Cameroon, they did not know each other, and had no drama experience. They had studied some Italian (L2) at various language centres.

Educational Aims: Creating group cohesion and intercultural awareness; introducing participants to performative pedagogy.

Pre-text: The connection between name and identity.

Level: A2 to B2 (CEFR).

Duration: Three hours.

Workshop 1 Names and identity

	Drama strategy
Initiation phase	**Step 1. Warm-up** a. Breathing awareness b. *Emotional Palette*: voice; eyes; hands; full body; space; locomotion c. Still images **Step 2. *Voicing* our name**: Call out (sound) your name, one by one, as: a. A foreigner pronounced it; b. Someone you love pronounced it; c. *You* pronounce it **Step 3. *Hearing* our name**: Again call out (sound) your name, but this time have the whole group echo it back, and listen to its sounds as: a. A foreigner pronounced it; b. Someone you love pronounced it; c. *You* pronounce it **Step 4. Discussion**: Engage the group in a discussion: Do you think that by changing name you can change identity? What *is* a name?
Experiential phase	**Step 5. Our name story**: What is the story of your name? And, if you have a nickname: How did you choose your 'adopted' nickname? What influenced you? According to language proficiency, write on the board the connectors required to construct a story, and/or some key sentences (My story begins...; while I was...; suddenly; but then, etcetera) **Step 6. Sharing stories**: Break the class into groups of 3 or 4, encouraging them to re-position chairs to form small circles, or triangles and share their story **Step 7. Choosing one story**: The teacher encourages each group to choose one story to work with. Once they have chosen, each group tells the story they have chosen to the rest of the class **Step 8. Tableaux**: Back in their groups, participants are invited to identify a key moment in the story. Once they have agreed, they embody it in a still image **Create**: Students work in their groups, to physically try out different solutions to embody their key moment in the story—using levels, body language and props **Present**: Groups show their interpretation to the others—frozen images with no dialogue **Respond**: After each group presents, the others are invited to describe the body language and the levels. Also reflect on meaning and storytelling. What is happening? What does it evoke? **Step 9. Tableaux (before and after)**: In the same groups, imagine what might have happened *five minutes before* the key moment, and what may have happened *five minutes after*. Follow the steps above to create, present and respond to the sequences. The teacher (or the participants) can incorporate key words, a countdown, sound effects, a short narrative, signs, or other, to link the sequences through cause and effect

(continued)

Workshop 1 (continued)

	Drama strategy
Reflective phase	**Step 10. Debrief**: Ask students how they felt, how was it to use their body, voice, imagination in the target language
	Step 11. Language revision: Ask students to recall all language learned during the session. Questions related to language structures, verbal patterns and idioms will emerge here. Concrete examples from the drama will be insightful to connect back to the grammar
	Step 12. Final reflection: Here the focus on language shifts back to the drama and to the meaning-making, including intercultural elements

This chapter situated embodiment—in education, in sociocultural theory for second language learning, and in process drama. Using a praxial approach, these concepts were explored not only through theory, but also through examples of classroom practice and reflection. It illustrated the key features of process drama, touched on research on drama and SLA, and contextualised the theatre/drama debate—revisited in a performative language key. A central aspect of embodiment relates to how the senses, feeling, imagination and reflection work together, when operating across one or more languages and cultures, and the heightened awareness that is aroused by these modes of knowing. This brings us to the aesthetic and intercultural engagement, a subject we turn to in the next chapter.

References

Austin, J. L. (1962). *How to do things with words*. Oxford: Clarendon Press.
Barba, E. (1995). *The paper canoe: A guide to theatre anthropology* (R. Fowler Trans.). Routledge: London and New York.
Belliveau, G., & Kim, W. (2013). Drama in L2 learning: A research synthesis. *Scenario: Journal for Performative Teaching, Learning and Research, 7*(2), 7–27.
Berry, C. (2011). *Voice and the actor*. New York: Random House.
Berry, C., Rodenburg, P., & Linklater, K. (1997). Shakespeare, feminism, and voice: Responses to Sarah Werner. *New Theatre Quarterly, 13*(49), 48–52.
Berthoz, A. (2012). *Simplexity: Simplifying principles for a complex world* (G. Weiss, Trans.). Yale: Yale University Press.

Blatner, A. (Ed.), (2007). *Interactive and improvisational drama: Varieties of applied theatre and performance.* Lincoln, NE: iUniverse.

Bolton, G. (1979). *Towards a theory of drama in education.* Harlow: Longman.

Bolton, G. (1992). Have a heart! *Drama, 1*(1), 7–8.

Bolton, G. (2007). A history of drama education: A search for substance. In L. Bresler (Ed.), *International handbook of research in arts education* (pp. 45–66). Amsterdam: Springer.

Boureux, M., & Batinti, A. (2003). *La prosodia: Aspetti teorici e metodologici nell'apprendimento-insegnamento di una lingua straniera.* Paper presented at the Atti delle XIV giornate del GFS.

Bournot-Trites, M., Belliveau, G., Spiliotopoulos, V., & Séror, J. (2007). The role of drama on cultural sensitivity, motivation and literacy in a second language context. *Journal for Learning Through the Arts: A Research Journal on Arts Integration in Schools and Communities, 3*(1), 1–33.

Bräuer, G. (Ed.). (2002). *Body and language: Intercultural learning through drama* (Vol. 17). London: Ablex Publishing.

Carnicke, S. M. (1998). *Stanislavsky in focus.* Amsterdam: Harwood Academic Publishers.

Coleman, C. (2017). Precarious repurposing: Learning languages through the Seal Wife. *NJ: Drama Australia Journal, 41*(1), 30–43.

Council of Europe. (2001). *Common European framework of reference for languages: Learning, teaching, assessment.* Strasburg: Cambridge University Press. Retrieved from https://rm.coe.int/1680459f97.

Council of Europe. (2018). *Common European framework of reference for languages: Learning, teaching, assessment: Companion volume with new descriptors.* Strasburg. Retrieved from https://rm.coe.int/cefr-companion-volume-with-new-descriptors-2018/1680787989.

Crutchfield, J., & Schewe, M. (2017). Introduction: Going performative in intercultural education: International contexts, theoretical perspectives, models of practice. In J. Crutchfield & M. Schewe (Eds.), *Going performative in intercultural education: International contexts, theoretical perspectives, models of practice* (pp. xi–xxv). Bristol: Multilingual Matters.

Dewey, J. (1916/2004). *Democracy and education.* New York: Dover Publications.

Dewey, J. (1925/1981). Nature, life and body-mind. In J. A. Boydston (Ed.), *John Dewey: The Later Works, 1925–1953. Volume I, 1925: Experience and Nature.* Illinois: Southern Illinois University Press.

Duffy, P. B. (2014). *Facilitating embodied instruction: Classroom teachers' experiences with drama-based pedagogy.* (Doctoral Dissertation). Retrieved from http://scholarcommons.sc.edu/etd/2810.

Dunn, J., Bundy, P., & Woodrow, N. (2012). Combining drama pedagogy with digital technologies to support the language learning needs of newly arrived refugee children: A classroom case study. *Research in Drama Education: The Journal of Applied Theatre and Performance, 17*(4), 477–499.

Even, S. (2011). Drama grammar: Towards a performative postmethod pedagogy. *The Language Learning Journal, 39*(3), 299–312.

Even, S., & Schewe, M. (Eds.). (2016). *Performative teaching, learning, research—Performatives Lehren, Lernen, Forschen*. Berlin: Schibri Velag.

Fleming, M. (2003). Intercultural experience and drama. In G. Alred, M. Byram, & M. Fleming (Eds.), *Intercultural experience and education* (pp. 87–100). Clevedon: Multilingual Matters.

Fleming, M. (2011). *Starting drama teaching*. London: Fulton Books.

Fleming, M. (2016). Exploring the concept of performative teaching and learning. In S. Even & M. Schewe (Eds.), *Performative teaching, learning, research—Performatives Lehren, Lernen, Forschen* (pp. 189–205). Berlin: Schibri Verlag.

Granger, C. A. (2004). *Silence in second language learning: A psychoanalytic reading: Second language acquisition*. Clevedon: Multilingual Matters.

Haseman, B. (1991). Improvisation, process drama and dramatic art. *The Drama Magazine, 19–21.*

Haseman, B., & O'Toole, J. (2017). *Dramawise reimagined*. Sydney: Currency Press.

Haught, J. R., & McCafferty, S. G. (2008). Embodied language performance: Drama and the ZPD in the second language classroom. In J. P. Lantolf & M. E. Poehner (Eds.), *Sociocultural theory and the teaching of second languages*. Oakville, CT.

Haycraft, B. (2010). Pillars of pronouciation: Approaching spoken English. *IH Journal of Education and Development, 29.* http://ihjournal.com/pillars-of-pronunciation-approaching-spoken-english-by-brita-haycraft.

Hornbrook, D. (1985). Drama, education, and the politics of change: Part one. *New Theatre Quarterly, 1*(4), 346–358.

Hulse, B., & Owens, A. (2017). Process drama as a tool for teaching modern languages: Supporting the development of creativity and innovation in early professional practice. *Innovation in Language Learning and Teaching,* 1–14.

Immordino-Yang, M. H. (2016). *Emotions, learning, and the brain: Exploring the educational implications of affective neuroscience*. New York: Norton & Company.

Jackson, A., & Vine, C. (2013). *Learning through theatre: The changing face of theatre in education*. London: Routledge.

Johnson, L., & O'Neill, C. (Eds.). (1991). *Collected writings on education and drama: Dorothy Heathcote*. London: Hutchinson Publications.

Johnstone, K. (1999). *Impro for storytellers*. New York: Routeledge Theatre Arts Books.

Kalogirou, K., Beauchamp, G., & Whyte, S. (2017). Vocabulary acquisition via drama: Welsh as a second language in the primary school setting. *The Language Learning Journal*, 1–12. https://doi.org/10.1080/09571736.2017.1283351.

Kao, S.-M. (1994). *Classroom interaction in a drama-oriented English conversation class of first-year college students in Taiwan: A teacher-researcher study*. (Doctoral Dissertation). Retrieved from https://etd.ohiolink.edu/.

Kao, S.-M., & O'Neill, C. (1998). *Words into worlds: Learning a second language through process drama*. London: Ablex Publishing Corporation.

Kao, S.-M., Carkin, G., & Hsu, L. F. (2011). Questioning techniques for promoting language learning with students of limited L2 oral proficiency in a drama-oriented language classroom. *Research in Drama Education: The Journal of Applied Theatre and Performance, 16*(4), 489–515.

King, J., & Smith, L. (2017). Social anxiety and silence in Japan's foreign tertiary classrooms. In C. Gkonou, M. Daubney, & J.-M. Dewaele (Eds.), *New insights into social anxiety: Theory, research and educational implications* (pp. 91–109). Bristol: Multilingual Matters.

Kramsch, C. (2009). *The multilingual subject*. Oxford: Oxford University Press.

Krashen, S. (1985). *The input hypothesis: Issues and implications*. New York: Longman.

Laban, R. (1966). *Choreutics*. London: Macdonald and Evans.

Lantolf, J. P., & Poehner, M. E. (2014). *Sociocultural theory and the pedagogical imperative in L2 education: Vygotskian praxis and the research/practice divide*. Oxfordshire and New York: Routledge.

Lapaire, J.-R. (2014). À corps perdu ou le mystère de la désincarnation des langues. *E-CRINI - La revue électronique du Centre de Recherche sur les Identités Nationales et l'Interculturalité*, Editions du CRINI, (6), 1–16.

Lapaire, J.-R. (2016). The Choreography of time: Metaphor, gesture and construal. In R. Gabriel & A. C. Pelosi (Eds.), *Linguagem e cognição: Emergência e produção de sentidos* (pp. 217–234). Florianopolis: Insular.

Lapaire, J.-R. (2017, September). *Talkers as social movers*. Paper presented at the University of Padova Summer School: The role of drama in higher and adult language education–from theory to practice. Padova, Italy.

Linklater, K. (2006). *Freeing the natural voice: Imagery and art in the practice of voice and language*. Hollywood, CA: Drama Publishers.

Lutzker, P. (2016). The recovery of experience in foreign language learning and teaching. In S. Even & M. Schewe (Eds.), *Performative teaching, learning, research–Performatives Lehren, Lernen, Forschen* (pp. 222–239). Berlin: Schibri Verlag.

MacIntyre, P. D. (2017). An overview of language anxiety research and trends in its development. In C. Gkonou, M. Daubney, & J.-M. Dewaele (Eds.), *New insights into language anxiety: Theory, research and educational implications* (pp. 11–30). Bristol: Multilingual Matters.

McCafferty, S. G., & Stam, G. (2008). *Gesture: Second language acquisition and classroom research*. New York: Routledge.

McGovern, K. R. (2017). Conceptualizing drama in the second language classroom. *Scenario: Journal for Performative Teaching, Learning and Research, 11*(1), 4–16.

McNeill, D. (1992). *Hand and mind: What gestures reveal about thought*. Chicago: University of Chicago Press.

Menegale, M. (Ed.). (2016). *Drama and CLIL: A new challenge to the teaching approaches in bilingual education* (p. 170) (S. Nicolás Román, & J. J. Torres Núñez, Eds.). Bern: Peter Lang.

Nguyen, D. J., & Larson, J. B. (2015). Don't forget about the body: Exploring the curricular possibilities of embodied pedagogy. *Innovative Higher Education, 40*, 331–344. https://doi.org/10.1007/s10755-015-9319-6.

Nunan, D. (1987). Communicative language teaching: Making it work. *ELT Journal, 41*(2), 136–145.

O'Neill, C. (1995). *Drama worlds: A framework for process drama*. Portsmouth: Heinemann.

O'Neill, C. (2015). *Dorothy Heathcote on education and drama: Essential writings*. Abington: Routledge.

O'Neill, C. (2017). Seal Wife—Random observations. *NJ: Drama Australia Journal, 41*(1), 27–29.

O'Toole, J. (1990). *Process, art form and meaning*. Paper presented at the 14th National Association for Drama in Education (NADIE) Conference, Sydney.

O'Toole, J. (1992). *The process of drama: Negotiating art and meaning*. London: Reutledge.

O'Toole, J., & Dunn, J. (2015). *Pretending to learn: Teaching drama in the primary and middle years*. Brisbane: Drama Web Publishing. https://pretendingtolearn.wordpress.com/.

Perry, M., & Medina, C. (2011). Embodiment and performance in pedagogy research: Investigating the possibility of the body in curriculum experience. *Journal of Curriculum Theorising, 27*(3), 62–75.

Perry, M., & Medina, C. L. (Eds.). (2016). *Methodologies of embodiment: Inscribing bodies in qualitative research*. Oxon: Routledge.

Pheasant, P. (2015). The epiphany in process drama and language learning. *p-e-r-f-o-r-m-a-n-c-e, 2*(1–2). http://p-e-r-f-o-r-m-a-n-c-e.org/?p=919.

Piazzoli, E. (2011). Process drama: The use of affective space to reduce language anxiety in the additional language learning classroom. *Research in Drama Education: The Journal of Applied Theatre and Performance, 16*(4), 557–573.

Piola Caselli, C. (2017, September). *Letteratura ad alta voce.* Paper presented at the University of Padova Summer School: The role of drama in higher and adult language education – from theory to practice. Padova, Italy.

Prendergast, M., & Saxton, J. (Eds.). (2010). *Applied theatre: International case studies and challenges for practice.* Bristol: Intellect.

Prentki, T. (2013). *The applied theatre reader.* London: Routledge.

Rodenburg, P. (2015). *The right to speak: Working with the voice* (2nd ed.). London: Bloomsbury.

Rothwell, J. (2015). Laying down pale memories: Learners reflecting on language, self, and other in the middle-school drama-languages classroom. *Canadian Modern Language Review, 71*(4), 331–361.

Rothwell, J. (2017). Using process drama to engage beginner learners in intercultural language learning. In J. Crutchfield & M. Schewe (Eds.), *Going performative in intercultural education: International contexts, theoretical perspectives and models of practice* (pp. 147–171). Bristol: Multilingual Matters.

Scarino, A., & Liddicoat, A. (2009). *Teaching and learning languages: A guide.* Melbourne: Department of Education, Employment and Workplace Relations.

Schechner, R. (2006). *Performance studies: An introduction* (2nd ed.). New York: Routledge.

Schechner, R. (2013). *Performance studies: An introduction* (3rd ed.). London: Routledge.

Schewe, M. (2013). Taking stock and looking ahead: Drama pedagogy as a gateway to a performative teaching and learning culture. *Scenario: Journal for Performative Teaching, Learning and Research, 8*(1), 5–23.

Schön, D. (1983). *The reflective practitioner: How professionals think in action.* London: Temple Smith.

Searle, J. R. (1969). *Speech acts: An essay in the philosophy of language* (Vol. 626). Cambridge: Cambridge University Press.

Sibilio, M. (2002). *Il corpo intelligente.* Naples: Simone.

Slade, P. (1955). *Child drama.* London: University of London Press.

Spolin, V. (1986). *Theater games for the classroom: A teacher's handbook.* Evanston: Northwestern University Press.

St. Pierre, E. A. (2016). Afterword: Troubles with embodiment. In M. Perry & C. L. Medina (Eds.), *Methodologies of embodiment: Inscribing bodies in qualitative research* (pp. 138–148). Oxon: Routledge.

Stanislavski, K. (1936/1980). *An actor prepares.* London: Eyre Methuen.

Stinson, M. (2009). Drama is like reversing everything: Intervention research as teacher professional development. *Research in Drama Education: The Journal of Applied Theatre and Performance, 14*(2), 225–243.

Stinson, M., & Winston, J. (2014). *Drama education and second language learning.* London: Routledge.

Stinson, M. (2008). Process drama and teaching English to speakers of other languages. In M. Jacqueline, H. John, & M. Anderson (Eds.), *Drama and English teaching: Imagination, action and engagement.* Oxford: Oxford University Press.

Stinson, M., & Freebody, K. (2006). The DOL project: An investigation into the contribution of process drama to improved results in English oral communication. *Youth Theatre Journal, 20,* 27–41.

To, L.-W. D., Chan, Y.-L. P., Lam, Y. K., & Tsang, S.-K. Y. (2011). Reflections on a primary school teacher professional development programme on learning English through process drama. *Research in Drama Education: The Journal of Applied Theatre and Performance, 16*(4), 517–539. https://doi.org/10.1080/13569783.2011.617099.

Tschurtschenthaler, H. (2013). *Drama-based foreign language learning: Encounters between self and others.* Munster: Waxmann.

Varela, F. J., Thompson, E., & Rosch, E. (1991). *The embodied mind: Cognitive science and human experience.* Cambridge: The MIT Press, Project MUSE.

Vygostky, L. (1934/1994). The problem of the environment. In R. Van Der Veer & J. Valsiner (Eds.), *The Vygotsky reader* (pp. 338–354). Oxford, UK: Blackwell.

Vygotsky, L. S. (1930/1978). *Mind in society: The development of higher psychological processes.* Cambridge, MA: Harvard University Press.

Vygotsky, L. S. (1930/2004). Imagination and creativity in childhood. *Journal of Russian and East European Psychology, 42*(1), 7–97.

Wagner, B. J. (1976). *Dorothy heathcote: Drama as a learning medium.* Washington, DC: National Education Association.

Way, B. (1967). *Development through drama.* London: Longmans.

Winston, J. (Ed.). (2012). *Second language learning through drama: Practical techniques and applications.* Padstow, Cornwall: Routledge.

Yaman Ntelioglu, B. (2011). 'But why do I have to take this class?' The mandatory drama-ESL class and multiliteracies pedagogy. *Research in Drama Education: The Journal of Applied Theatre and Performance, 16*(4), 595–616.

3

Aesthetic and Intercultural Engagement

In this chapter we explore some key areas in the aesthetic and intercultural dimension of learning, related to performative language teaching and process drama in particular. In the introduction I put forth a question as the focus of this book: *How can teacher/artists navigate the aesthetic dimension to facilitate performative language learning?* This is no easy question; attempting to address it requires careful elaboration.

Here we may find useful the notion of simplexity, introduced in the previous chapter as a paradigm characterised by active effort in decoding complexity, without reducing its depth (Berthoz, 2012). As Berthoz suggests: "The basis of meaning is in the act itself: meaning cannot be superimposed on life; it *is* life. To my mind, the concept of simplexity includes the idea of meaning" (p. 22, original emphasis). Through simplexity theory we are invited to process complex situations without making reality any less complex. Simplexity theory has been used to analyse action, perception and perceptual systems, including attention, gesture and body in movement. A simplex approach seems therefore apt to discuss aesthetic learning and process drama.

Maxine Greene (2001) describes aesthetic education as "an initiation into new ways of seeing, hearing, feeling, moving [...] a special kind of reflectiveness and expressiveness, a reaching out for meanings, a learning to learn" (p. 7). Greene talks about aesthetic learning as a mode through which we can bring students to an active perception, to "wide-awakeness" (p. 11). The issue is complex, and to proceed it is necessary to make it simpler or rather, *simplex*—that is, accept its complexity and carve our way through its undergrowth. In truth, 'aesthetic' is such a misunderstood word. Used as both a noun and an adjective, in contemporary language it has come to assume several meanings, from 'aesthetic surgery' to 'beauty parlour' and 'surface beauty'. In the spirit of simplexity, let us consider for a moment what 'aesthetic' is not and work backwards, like Greene suggests. What happens when, for a surgical operation, we are put under general '*an*aesthetic'? We cannot see, hear, touch, smell, taste, create, feel, think, imagine or remember anything. We are numb. Holding on to this image, it is worth dipping our toes in the enchanting waters of philosophy.

1 Aesthetics in Education

Aesthetics is a branch of philosophy concerned with art, beauty, perception and sensory experience. A highly debated, lively field of philosophical inquiry, it is enriched by multiple interpretations, so much so that an inclusive review of aesthetic theory is well beyond the scope of this volume. Instead, I will limit myself to introducing the etymology of the term, the foundations, and some key thinkers who have influenced education.

Aesthetic discourse can be traced to the ancient Greeks, notably Plato (250 BC) and Aristotle (330 BC). In the Western tradition, Immanuel Kant was the first philosopher to draw systematic attention to aesthetics. Drawing on Baumgarten (1750/1970), who coined the term 'aesthetics' in a two-volume treatise, Kant exposes this theory in *Transcendental Aesthetics* (1781/1990). Kant defines aesthetics in terms of 'sensation', from the Greek term *aistetika* ('of the senses'). As he states: "The capacity for receiving representations (receptivity) through the mode in which we are affected by objects is called sensibility", while "the effect of an object upon the faculty of representation, so far as we are affected by it, is sensation" (p. 43). Later, in *Critique of Judgement*

(1790/1928), Kant explains aesthetic judgement as the free interplay between 'imagination' and 'understanding' in a person's response to beauty. For Kant, aesthetic judgement necessitates a 'disinterested' stance, which allows one to appreciate a work of art for its own sake rather than for an underlying desire. Thus, to judge something as beautiful is to judge it on the basis of perceptual form, without a connection to its content (p. 48). Although ground-breaking at the time, and essential to establishing the foundations of aesthetics in Western philosophical tradition, Kantian aesthetics alone cannot underpin an embodied approach to learning, as it severs affect and cognition in the aesthetic experience. Moreover, Kantian aesthetics cannot be reconciled with the epistemology of embodied pedagogy as it divorces aesthetic form from content.

In contrast, Hegel's aesthetics emphasises the content of a work of art, framing it in its historical context. "The forms of art", he states, "are nothing but the different relations of meaning and shape" (1835/1975, p. 75). Hegel holds that the purpose of art is to unveil the 'truth' in the form of sensuous artistic configuration (p. 55). The kind of 'truth' Hegel is concerned with is spiritual truth. Hegel's philosophy is relevant to this discussion as his emphasis on historical situatedness inspired sociocultural theory. However, Hegel's aesthetics as spiritual truth does not fully align with the embodied paradigm of process drama. Rather, Schiller's (1795/1965) vision of aesthetics, which influenced Hegel's early writing, is better suited. Schiller frames the aesthetic in terms of playfulness, or the 'play instinct' (*Spieltrieb*), which he sees as a drive essential for humanity. He holds that only through play can a person be complete (letter XV). Schiller conceives of individuals as aesthetic beings: "There is no other way to make a reasonable being out of a sensuous man than by making him first aesthetic" (XXIII). He sees the prerequisite of the aesthetic being as an active determination, exercising freedom and choice. This emphasis on aesthetics as playfulness and agency resonates with sociocultural theory, performative language teaching, and process drama.

In the twentieth century, formalist aesthetics placed an emphasis on the perception of pure form, with content as a mere function of form. At the other end of the spectrum, Marxist aesthetics values content and its political function in shaping ideology over form (Eagleton, 1976). Vygotsky (1926/1971) absorbed the Marxist tradition, developing his own theory of aesthetics. Vygotsky argues that perception of art requires "a creative act of *overcoming* the feeling", resulting in a change of purpose (p. 248, original emphasis). He claims that art relates to the 'social' within us. In *Psychology of Art*, he rejects purist formalist views endorsing a view of aesthetics that involves both cognition and affect. Lima's (1995) analysis of Vygotsky's aesthetic theory notes that the Russian psychologist frames aesthetic experience as "the *collision* of the *contradictory* emotions" generated by *form* on *content*:

> Aesthetic experience is the product of the influence of form on content, more specifically, of their collision in the work of art, the collision of the contradictory emotions generated. (p. 418)

As Vygotsky holds, such collision transforms the nature of the affect, resulting in a *catharsis*, that is, "the transformation of these feelings into opposite ones and their subsequent resolution" (1971, p. 244). In this discussion, however, I do not adopt the idea of 'catharsis', as I suspect, with Nussbaum (1992), that the Aristotelian concept might have been misinterpreted from its original meaning (pp. 280–281). Instead, I frame Vygotskian aesthetic theory above within the theory of metaxis (O'Toole, 1992) a notion described more in-depth in the next chapter (see "Intercultural Dramatic Tension" in Chapter 4).

Within the Marxist tradition, Marcuse (1978) also holds that aesthetic content is extracted from the constant process of reality, and assumes a significance of its own, 'accusing' reality through form. Like Vygotsky, Marcuse maintains that "aesthetic form is not opposed to content, with form becoming content, and vice versa" (p. 41). My understanding of aesthetics is particularly influenced and interpreted through the key thinkers I have discussed here.

2   Aesthetic Engagement

Rader (1974), late president of the Association for American Aesthetics, states that "aesthetic experience is the *apprehension* of a certain kind of value" (p. 131, my emphasis). It is interesting to note the use of 'apprehension' here. The etymological meaning of 'apprehend' as used by Rader is different from 'comprehend'. These terms mean, respectively, a sensorial/affective and a cognitive mode of understanding. Rader identifies two phases of aesthetic interest: an attentional phase and an elaborative phase. Both phases, he holds, are important and complementary in the aesthetic experience. The attentional phase relates to what the "aesthetic observer is or is not attending to"; the elaborative phase relates to a situation whereby "the beholder greatly enlivens and enriches the object of imagination" (p. 132)—that is, creates his/her own meaning. Through the elaborative phase, "in the aesthetic *apprehension* of a great work of art, the full evocative power of understanding, feeling, and imagination may be brought into play" (p. 132, my emphasis). Maxine Greene's (2001) commentary on Rader's phases is illuminating, as she relates these phases to teachers in the classroom, at the same time highlighting the potency of the aesthetic experience and the vulnerability of the teacher:

> We presume there are phases of imaginative awareness (Rader, 1974, p. 136), and we also presume that each phase can be encouraged as we teach. The first phase involves the paying attention we have stressed: the focussing, the careful noticing; the phase that permits the dance or the musical piece to emerge in its uniqueness and integrity [...] But there is more. There is the savouring in inner time, the elaboration of what has been seen or heard, the seeping down. What has been encountered becomes an event within personal consciousness; it may begin shining toward the lived world. Clearly, we cannot *make* that happen; nor can we intrude when people are becoming aware in this way. We cannot grade them on whether or not such a phenomenon does occur. All we can do is try to invent situations that make it more likely – allowing for time, for privacy, for silences. (pp. 31–32, original emphasis)

Dewey, an influential figure on the aesthetic experience in education, would describe such moments for inner time, privacy, and silences as the students undergoing 'an experience'. He conceives art as being the experience itself, rather than being an object: "The actual work of art is what the product does *with* and *in* experience" (1934/1980, p. 3). He describes 'experience' as a 'heightened vitality', and art form as the organisation of time and space in the development of life experience. For Dewey, the aesthetic experience is based on 'perception', an *active receptivity* or "receptive perception" (p. 48) involving affect and cognition. This active quality of perception is echoed in Maxine Greene's (2001) description of aesthetic education, where she explains 'perceiving' as an act of "mental imaginative participation" (p. 13).

Vygotskian aesthetic theory shares similar points. As I've mentioned above, Vygotsky (1926/1971) frames the aesthetic as not just perception, or feeling, but as a creative perception, a creative act of elaboration of such feeling and perception, in a social context. In a later work, Vygotsky (1930/2004) analyses the relationship between imagination, creativity and reality, concluding that through the creative process, embodied imagination becomes reality: "Once it has been externally embodied, that is, has been given material form, this crystallised imagination that has become an object begins to actually exist in the real word, to affect other things" (p. 20). This is similar to Dewey's (1934/1980) notion of an active 'receptive perception', followed by reflection and assigning new meanings—making the idea or emotion "clothed with meaning" (p. 60)—and Greene's 'careful noticing', followed by imaginative participation and 'reaching out'.

Abbs (1989) highlights how this process of perception, elaboration and emergence of new meanings is enabled by the use of symbol and metaphor, channelled by the art form. The aesthetic experience aims at awakening a mode of perceptual intelligence—again, not working through concepts but through *percepts*, the structural elements of sensory experience. In essence, the aesthetic experience relates to an active perception, acknowledging a feeling, processing it through time and reflection, and re-expressing it through symbols, through the elements of an art form, to give it new meaning. As Abbs explains in his manifesto of arts education: "I have tried to show that the aesthetic refers to a basic modality of human intelligence and that it is enhanced and developed through the symbolic forms of the arts" (1989, p. 11). Abbs dismantles the cliché of 'aesthetic' as "refined, exquisite, arty", defining it rather as "a kind of bodily knowledge, an apprehension of patterns through the power of sensibility" (p. 172). In this light, we turn our attention to intercultural aesthetics.

3   Intercultural Engagement

Harbon and Moloney (2015) define the intercultural as an "actively critical process of cultural reflection", with the learner being in-between cultures, investigating 'self' and 'other' (p. 19). This definition is useful as it sheds light on the idea of 'other'—a key notion to hold on to in these simplex waters. The concept of 'other' originates from self-reflexive anthropology, evoking 'the elsewhere', and functioning as a vehicle that allows for an inverse image of home, place, self and power (Said, 1978). In a basic sense, looking at the 'other' helps us to understand who we are, and who we are not. However, if embedded in the rhetoric of discrimination, it can serve to reinforce racial stereotypes. Indeed, political propaganda is often constructed upon an image of 'us' and 'them', where 'otherness' is conveniently demonised to construct an opponent. An important element to recognise and deconstruct such narratives, so common now within media and political discourse, is an awareness of 'self' and 'other' in the intercultural encounter.

Heyward (2002) defines intercultural literacy as the understandings, competencies, attitudes, language proficiencies, participation and identities necessary for successful cross-cultural engagement (p. 10). It follows that an interculturally literate individual has the understandings, competences and identities to "effectively 'read' a second culture, to interpret its *symbols* and negotiate its *meanings* in a practical day to day context" (2004, p. 51, my emphasis). Heyward's (2002) model charts the development of intercultural literacy. It looks at, precisely, understandings, competencies, attitudes, participation, language proficiency and identities, mapping these from 'limited awareness' to an 'intercultural' level. His insightful analysis of the various stages, from monocultural to intercultural (pp. 16–17), suggests that travelling, or having an intercultural encounter, does not necessarily result in intercultural competence; it can expand one's vision and awareness, or, in some instances, reinforce stereotypes about 'otherness'.

The same applies to second language teaching. In L2 education, the notion of 'self' and 'other' is embedded in the nature of the syllabus, and, like travelling, can reinforce stereotypes or expand vision. The language teacher invites students to savour the otherness of another culture. After all, what is language teaching if not an open invitation to otherness? This invitation will be handled differently according to the power differentials emerging from the idiosyncrasies at stake: teachers' cultural and linguistic background/s; teachers' beliefs about intercultural education; students' cultural and linguistic background/s; students' beliefs (overt or covert) about intercultural education; group dynamics—a multicultural or mono-cultural group; relationship/s to host culture, and so forth. Each ad hoc context will impact on how this open invitation to experience otherness is received. Whatever the context, once being immersed in the practice of learning to communicate in another language, students are necessarily coming into contact with another culture—in other words, the cultural encounter is entrenched in the language learning experience. It is widely agreed that developing intercultural competence is one of the purposes of second language education (Byram, 2008, 2009, 2012; Byram & Zarate, 1997; Crichton, 2008; Deardorff, 2009; Harbon & Moloney, 2015). However, second language education will not always result in learners becoming interculturally literate or developing intercultural competence.

Many frameworks to evaluate intercultural competence have been created in the last two decades, with Taylor (2014) tallying up to eighty-seven different kinds of frameworks to assess intercultural sensitivity. In Taylor's meta-analysis of those frameworks, he identifies four main typologies: multidimensional constructs, developmental constructs, trait-based models, behaviour models (p. 26). A review of these intercultural competence models is beyond the scope of this discussion, although worth noting here is that none of these models seems to acknowledge the *aesthetic* dimension of intercultural engagement, which is a notable omission.

Going back to Byram's (1997) seminal intercultural competence model, he puts forth five dimensions, or *savoirs*: attitudes, knowledge, skills of interpreting and relating, skills of discovery and interaction, and critical/cultural awareness. Of particular interest to our discussion is the first dimension, the attitudes of an intercultural speaker.

For Byram, such attitudes are *curiosity* and *openness* toward cultural differences (what he called *savoir être*). The 2001 Common European Framework of Reference for Languages (CERF) lists the same attitudes (as well as motivations, values, beliefs, cognitive styles, personality factors) under *savoir être*. The CERF defines the attitudes needed by the second language learner as:

- "Openness towards, and interest in, new experiences, other persons, ideas, peoples, societies and cultures;
- Willingness to relativise one's own cultural viewpoint and cultural value-system;
- Willingness and ability to distance oneself from conventional attitudes to cultural difference." (CEFR, 2001, p. 105)

These attitudes, Byram explained in his original formulation, require a dual operation: (1) readiness to suspend *dis*belief; and (2) willingness to suspend *belief*. While the former involves suspending *disbelief* about the other's cultural meanings, the latter involves suspending *beliefs* about one's own cultural meanings. This evokes, on the on hand, Coleridge's (1817/1965) famous willing suspension of disbelief, his definition of dramatic engagement as poetic faith—and on the other hand, a reflexive stance in 'suspending belief' about our own cultural meanings.

I remember the very first time I felt a poignant sense of otherness. I was ten years old, on holidays in France with my grandmother. This was the first time I visited a country outside Italy. I was playing with my doll, in our hotel room. In the pretend play, I was explaining to my doll, who was feeling quite confused, that the reason why people looked at Nonna differently when she tried to communicate with the hotel staff in the lobby was because we were in a strange, 'non-home land', where others spoke 'non-Italian language'. It was called the French language, I told my doll. I had seen Nonna having to work hard to make herself understood by the hotel staff in her make-shift French. I had perceived others gazing strangely at Nonna, conferring her otherness in return. This was so at odds with the familiarity I felt with her. Nonna had been 'other' in those people's eyes; how could that be? It was an unresolved tension—one I still recall vibrantly—as I made my doll hop from one piece of furniture to the next in our hotel room, to explain to her how we had relocated from Italy to France for holidays, and the people here in France spoke non-Italian, but we would soon be back in Italy. Through play, of course, I was resolving in my own way the captivating paradox of travelling: shifting identity from the familiarity of one's home country, to the unfamiliarity of the elsewhere; being the same, but perceived to be 'other' by virtue of the new context.

Taliaferro (1998) frames this duality as a 'double-consciousness' and analyses this notion as used in the work of Maxine Greene. Double-consciousness, a term originally appearing in Dubois's (1973) *The Souls of Black Folk*, refers to being able to look at oneself with the eyes of the other. This discourse influenced African-American literature, critical pedagogy and black ontological thought. In Greene's (1988) work, Taliaferro argues, the dialogue between self/other occurs through *imagination*, and is revisited as a dialectic relationship rather than as a dichotomy. In Taliaferro's words: "The dialogic nature of the human mind is manifested in the relationship between the Self and the Other, and it is through the imagination that they dialogue" (p. 94). This boundary between self and other is constructed and interpreted differently, for Taliaferro, according to the positionality of the subject as oppressed or privileged by the system. In analysing Maxine Greene, she notes that "the task of those who possess a double-consciousness is to imagine beyond those images fixed upon us by the inner-eye of the Other" (p. 94).

Imagination, then, can be recognised as a pathway between self and other. This relationship is constantly evolving, troubled, unfinished, in a *productive tension*. In my childhood memory mentioned above, Nonna, completely entrenched within my own sense of 'self', was in dissonance with the 'otherness' that I perceived the French hotel staff bestowed upon her. This collision was resolved through play, as I spoke to the doll and made it physically hop from one piece of furniture to the other—a vivid action in that memory: here is self (home); there is other (elsewhere). As a ten-year old, my imagination kept the self/other differentiation very concrete. However, as we grow into adults, we have the possibility of embracing, through imagination, the liminality of the self/other in the double-consciousness spectrum.

In drama, this double-consciousness can be evoked, felt and analysed through playing a dramatic role (willingly suspending our disbelief), and reflecting on it (suspending belief). As Neelands (2010) put it:

> At the heart of all drama and theatre is the opportunity for role-taking – to imagine oneself as the other. To try and *find oneself in the other* and in so doing *to recognise the other in oneself*. This is the crucial and irreducible bridge between all forms of drama and theatre work. (p. 122, my emphasis)

In talking about 'imagining oneself as the other', Neelands is in line with Greene. This process requires a particular sensitivity to experience, reflection, and awareness. Alred, Byram, and Fleming (2003) note the qualitative nature of this process:

> Being intercultural implies a more qualitative judgement about the nature of such encounter. Experience of otherness in a range of ways creates a potential for questioning the taken-for-granted in one's own self and environment. Being intercultural is, however, more than this. It is the capacity to reflect on the relationships among groups and the experience of those relationships. It is both awareness of experiencing otherness and the ability to analyse the experience and act upon the insights into self and other which the analysis brings. Experience alone is therefore not enough. (p. 4)

Thus, experience of otherness can be followed by an active process of awareness, reflection, analysis and action upon it—recognised in these authors' understanding as '*being* intercultural'. Interestingly, parallels emerge with the aesthetic experience of active perception (Dewey, 1934/1980), wide-awakeness (Greene, 2001) and creative reception (Vygotsky, 1926/1971). In this sense, *being* intercultural is not just about having an intercultural encounter. As Byram (2008) argues, we act as intercultural speakers when we are mediating between ourselves and others. This involves "being able to take an 'external' perspective on oneself as one interacts with others and to analyse and, where desirable, adapt one's behaviour and underlying values and beliefs" (p. 68). It involves an active process of questioning of one's cultural norms, putting them into perspective:

> People born and socialised into specific groups tend to assume that the conventions and values by which they live within their groups are inevitable and 'natural'. It is when they have some kind of experience which leads them to *question* these given conventions and values – but not necessarily to reject them – that they begin to become 'intercultural' in our sense. (Alred et al., 2003, p. 3, my emphasis)

Questioning, but not necessarily rejecting; this evokes Greene's (1988) discourse above, in holding a productive tension between self and other as a dialogue, "to break through, wherever possible, the persisting either/ors" (p. 4).

This idea of questioning resonates with Byram's suspending disbelief and suspending belief, and also evokes what Rancière (2016) refers to as 'unlearning' in educational aesthetics. In *The Pedagogics of Unlearning*, Dunne and Seery (2016) describe unlearning as going outside one's comfort zone, turning certainties 'outside-in', rather than 'inside-out'. This is the process of becoming willing to question reality, to unlearn what was given for granted and releasing ourselves from the burden of having to cognitively understand—opening up the space for an aesthetic experience. As Dunne puts it: "The event(s) of learning and unlearning, not to *being-as-such*, but to *being as maybeing*, to the possibility that something might come from the other side of silence" (2016, p. 3).

If so, what comes from the other side of silence? Nicholson (1999) discusses the fascinating relationship between 'self-awareness' and 'other-awareness', connecting intercultural engagement, aesthetics and dramatic form. Drawing on Geertz (1973), who holds that the arts symbolise deeply felt cultural values and beliefs, she points out that through drama processes, participants are enabled to embody different ways of seeing the world. Drama processes can shift "other understanding" towards "self-understanding":

> If, as Geertz has argued, subjectivity is inscribed through cultural and aesthetic discourse, the process of engaging with other voices and experiences may challenge self-identity, values and beliefs. Other-understanding can change self-understanding. (1973, p. 87)

Nicholson argues that such an act of self-interpretation *is* part of the aesthetic experience in drama. With this claim, she prompts us to dive deeper into the simplex waters of aesthetic learning.

4 Aesthetic Engagement in Process Drama

By analysing the various definitions of process drama in the literature (Bowell & Heap, 2017; Dunn & Stinson, 2011; Haseman, 1991; Haseman & O'Toole, 2017; Kao & O'Neill, 1998; O'Mara, 2016; O'Neill, 1995; O'Toole, 1992; O'Toole, Stinson, & Moore, 2009; Pheasant, 2015; Weltsek-Medina, 2007) it becomes apparent that, as different as they may be, these definitions share a number of essential features. They recognise:

- Process drama is an art form, as well as pedagogy;
- Process drama employs a number of elements—the elements of drama;
- Process drama can generate aesthetic engagement.

For O'Neill (1995) the purpose of engaging in process drama is:

> The same as that of encountering any of the other arts. Because it is active and collaborative, participants in process drama are required to think in and through the materials of the medium in which they are working and to manipulate and transform these materials. (p. 1)

As we observed above, aesthetic engagement is referred to as a process of active perception, triggering the senses and engaging emotions, imagination and meaning, expressed as symbol and metaphor through a given art form—in a social context. The end tail of this sentence (in a social context) deserves special attention; process drama is a participatory form, where participants function as audience and as artists at the same time. As O'Neill (1995) pinpoints, in process drama: "Participants are in a continual state of tension between representing an experience and being *in* an experience" (p. 118, original emphasis).

In this vein, Gallagher (2005) describes the embodied, collective nature of the form: "One person's aesthetic engagement is, more often than not, intimately tied to another's in the collective enterprise that is improvised drama" (p. 85). She terms this dynamic the sociology of aesthetics. Her point is that, in drama practice, participants are both perceiving and creating as a collective: "Drama participants engage aesthetically through critically examining and physically embodying their own, and others' sensuous perceptions and interpretations of a shared world" (p. 93). Drawing on Syssoyeva and Proudfit's (2016) aesthetics in collective creation of devised performance, Scully (2017) refers to this concept as the 'groupness of the group' in a drama process, bonding the participants as a social collective.

However, crucially, the group as a social collective is formed by individuals, each bringing their own unique experience. Bundy (2003) suggests that aesthetic engagement in process drama can be observed, in an individual, in terms of three qualities: *animation* and *connection*, which together may give rise to a *heightened awareness*. By animation Bundy implies a feeling of alertness, as percipients respond to the drama. By connection she refers to participants engaging with an idea evoked by a response to the drama. Heightened awareness denotes participants becoming more alert to thoughts or feelings that have not been previously considered (p. 180). These are inter-related: when percipients experience a sense of invigoration (animation), they may connect to an idea at a metaphoric level (connection), and may become open to new understandings (heightened awareness).

It is interesting to transpose Bundy's (2003) theory of aesthetic engagement to second language education, particularly performative language learning. Tschurtschenthaler (2013) investigates the aesthetic dimension of drama-based learning in connection to L2 learners' sense of self and other. Her research, conducted in a multilingual South Tyrolean context, focuses on the construct of identity, role-taking and role construction. She positions L2/drama learners fluctuating between real and imagined worlds, between self and other, involving the learner in a subjective, social and aesthetic learning process across different languages and cultures. Here, she pinpoints a crucial feature of performative language learning: playing a character in a second language requires some degree of integration of the foreign language with one's role, in what she describes as wearing a mask-upon-a-mask, or "double masking":

By stepping into someone else's shoes the learner experiences the other not only in terms of the other role and character, but also in terms of the other context, culture and language. The experience of the other language from within the other's point of view leads up to a *double masking* for the language learner. The foreign language, together with the role, results in a mask-upon-a-mask. (p. 230, my emphasis)

Tschurtschenthaler thus frames performative language learning as "an aesthetic process which integrates the constitution of the language learner's self" (p. 245). This resonates with O'Neill's (1995) view of process drama, which sees role negotiation as "exploiting the tensions between appearance and reality, mask and face, and role and identity that lie at the heart of the theatrical experience" (p. 85). It is precisely this double masking effect, I argue, that characterises the texture of intercultural aesthetic engagement in the experience of a second language learner, with animation, connection and heightened awareness (Bundy, 2003) occurring across intercultural planes through different modes of knowing, tapping into insights on identity, self and other.

5 Intercultural Aesthetic Engagement in Process Drama

In an attempt to provide an example, in practice, of intercultural aesthetic engagement, I discuss some students' comments, generated by a drama workshop I created as part of a research study on process drama, spontaneity and intercultural awareness (Piazzoli, 2010). Findings in this study align with Fleming's (2003) argument that process drama can generate various degrees of intercultural engagement, and can be considered "by its very nature as a form of intercultural education" (2003, p. 97). Through the strategies outlined in Workshop 2 (*At the Gypsy Camp*), illustrated in greater depth in the next chapter (see "Intercultural Dramatic Focus" in Chapter 4), a group of undergraduate students from Australia and New Zealand who enrolled in a third-year Italian language module, experienced something very removed from their everyday Australian life: being in role as children living in a gypsy camp, in Italy.

The workshop started with a vocal warm-up and an opening discussion on the theme of integration (Step 1). The pre-text was then introduced, that is, a photograph of a gypsy camp, taken by artist Nihad Nino Pušija. I chose this photo (Fig. 1) as I felt a connection with it, as it evoked a vivid background and implied dramatic roles. From it, we engaged in a series of tasks (Steps 2–3) to analyse the photo. The experiential phase saw the participants meet Radi (Teacher in Role), the five-year old child in the photo (Step 4). Next, a short breathing relaxation proceeded a listening activity, an account of the 'here and now' living conditions of a child living in a gypsy camp, through the narrative biography of Adžović (2005). Participants then embodied their own representation of every day scene in the camp, through freeze frames (Step 6). The vocal interpretation of a poem followed (Step 7). Participants engaged in a series of episodes, through which they became, alternatively, the children in the camp, parents of the children's classmates at the local pre-school, and the pre-school director's internal dilemma dealing with a theft incident (Steps 8–12). A discussion on human rights was the catalyst for the final episode (Steps 11–12). The workshop culminated in a reflection on otherness (Step 14), related to the roles played in the drama, and their own understanding of the issue.

This workshop, the research findings revealed, generated various degrees of intercultural awareness, which enabled participants to understand issues of integration from a different viewpoint. Data from the video recordings, my reflective journal, interviews and concept map diagrams also confirmed this shift in other participants, with particular reference to the workshop discussed below (*At the Gypsy Camp*). In sharing the structure of the workshop, rather than suggesting a series of fixed episodes to reproduce ad hoc, my purpose is to illustrate the strategies that led to these comments.

Tina (not her real name),[1] a mature-age student, suggests in the interview that, from her involvement in the drama, her perception of Italy shifted from 'beautiful architecture' to an awareness of social issues:

> This subject has continued giving me that broad understanding, so that I'm not just looking at [Italy] in terms of… beautiful churches, beautiful paintings and beautiful piazzas… but it's helping me to have that broader

---

[1] Pseudonyms have been used throughout the book to protect the real identities of the interviewees.

understanding of Italy as a culture, as a nation, as a… group of people. (Tina, 7:27–30)

Sarah, on the other hand, realises how she had previously 'glamorised' Italy:

I think because I have had this… you know, desire to learn Italian and to be… at least, I know the word is *Italo-australiana*, but I wanna be… *Austral-italiano*! [Laughs] So I realise, and I understand that I'm always going to have that 'Australianness' or whatever, that I would never be… native-like or whatever… but, I think, because, as I said it's… I've had that feeling for so long, I think I've glamorised… Italian culture and when I went to Italy I was 16 […], I've kind of gone 'Oh, Italy is just amazing!'… for me [this course] it has taken a little bit of the glamour out of Italy, for me but… I feel like I'm better equipped, and that, you know, at the end of the day, even in my life I kind of think: 'Well if I can just like glean the truth out of anything…' (Sarah, 5:37–39)

Sarah's experience seems to delve into her identity formation, tapping into a *desire* to be a speaker of Italian, something she had previously glamorised.

I believe that 'desire' is an important component of intercultural aesthetic engagement in second language education. Drawing on Kristeva (1980), Kramsch (2009) describes *desire* in second language learning as: "The basic drive towards self-fulfilment. It touches the core of who we are. Anyone who has spent some time learning a foreign language while studying or working abroad knows the thrills and frustrations of desire" (p. 14). I myself have experienced this desire as an adolescent, when I fell in love with the English language, intensely desiring to become an English speaker. As Kramsch puts it, for adolescents, desire represents an escape, "a new mode of expression that enables them to escape from the confines of their language and culture" (p. 14). I cannot tell whether this was the case for Sarah, the participant discussed above; certainly it was for me, as an adolescent learning English, going back to the questions about language learning and desire that I pose in the Prologue of this book.

Sarah's argument points at a heightened awareness of her perception of Italian society:

Because the other funny thing is that [amazed] only since doing process drama… that I've heard about the [social] problems from the Italians at work… It's never come up before and I don't know if that's just a coincidence? [...] Do you know what I mean? Or maybe before I just wasn't noticing it because... *I didn't want to?* (Sarah, 5:46–6:4)

This level of meta-reflection points to the intercultural dimension of the aesthetic experience as being significant to trigger a shift in understanding. Sarah was an advanced language learner, whose proficiency allowed her to *comprehend* the Italian language and some features of the culture. This workshop, I argue, also allowed her to *apprehend* the language and culture. As mentioned in the opening of this chapter (see "Aesthetic Engagement" in this chapter), while comprehending refers to a cognitive mode of understanding, apprehending refers to a sensorial/affective mode. Through the drama experience she not only comprehended, but also *apprehended* some of the dynamics related to the workshop theme.

This workshop led participants, including myself, to a critical questioning of our own roles, power, status, values and beliefs in society, opening up an aesthetic dimension to intercultural engagement. It confronted the students with an issue that, from their white Australian perspective, was initially seen as other—through playing a dramatic role and reflecting on it. This resonates with what Tschurtschenthaler (2013) describes as mask-upon-a-mask, or double masking: "The experience of the other language from within the other's point of view leads up to a double masking for the language learner" (p. 230). It also resonates with Taliaferro's (1998) discourse on double-consciousness in her reading of Maxine Greene (1988), intended as the productive tension held while looking at self, from the eyes of the other. In other words, the experience of temporarily wearing a double mask, to then un-mask it, evokes a double-consciousness, provoking new and unexpected ways of seeing. In discussing 'unlearning' in education, Dunne (2016) points to the possibility that "something might come from *the other side of silence*" (p. 3, my emphasis). What if, we may ask, on the other side of silence we found that we look just as *other* as others appear to us?

Workshop 2: At the Gypsy Camp

Description: This workshop focuses on issues of integration of the Roma people in Italy, also referred to as travellers, or gypsy people.

Students' Context—Inspiration for the Workshop: The workshop was part of an undergraduate module in Italian Studies, co-designed with Claire Kennedy in 2008, on exploring the Italian language, culture and society through cinema and the theatre, at Griffith University (Brisbane). It was a final year undergraduate module, open to students enrolled in Italian Studies, Education and Linguistics degree. Participants were twelve male and female students from Australia and New Zealand, from 20 to 65 years old. This particular workshop (At the Gypsy Camp) was also part of my Honours research project in Applied Theatre (2008/2009), supervised by Julie Dunn at Griffith University (Brisbane).

Pre-text: A photograph of a gypsy camp, taken by artist Nihad Nino Pušija (Fig. 1).

Educational Aims: Reflecting on intercultural issues involving the co-existence of Roma people and Italian people, considering facts and stereotypes on minority ethnic communities.

Level: C1 to C2 (CEFR).

Duration: Three hours.

Fig. 1 Vicolo Savini, Roma

Workshop 2 At the gypsy camp

	Drama strategy
Initiation phase	**Step 1. Warm-up**: a. Breathing awareness b. Voice awareness c. Group discussion: The city of Rome. Has anyone been to Rome? What is it like? How can we describe the architecture of the city of Rome? Does anyone know *Vicolo Savini* (Savini road) in Rome? What could we find in an alleyway, in the city of Rome?Describe the pavement of the roads, style of the buildings, and urban look of streets in Rome **Step 2. Pre-text**: Show the photograph *Vicolo Savini, Roma* (Fig. 1) taken by Nihad Nino Pušija and published in *ROM: Il Popolo Invisibile* [*ROM: The Invisible People*] by Adžovic (2005) **Step 3. Pre-text analysis—in pairs and as a group**: a. Describe the photograph: what do you see? b. Interpret the photograph: what is the image suggesting to you? c. Interrogate the photo: think of three open-questions related to it
Experiential phase	**Step 4. Teacher in Role**: Come into the space taking the role as Radi, the child in the photo (foreground), five years old. Sit on the floor, looking up at participants. Initially shy, gradually open up to tell about everyday life in the gypsy camp. Show your sister Sara, in the photo (child in the background). Answer questions, revealing anecdotes that may suggest why you look sad: your best friend Nino can't play with you today. The uncles will *take him to the river*. Linger on the gravity of this image—being taken to the river. Then move on to wonderful games you usually play with Nino. Leave the space with some questions unanswered **Step 5. Reading**: After a short relaxation, sitting or lying down with eyes closed, read out a passage written by Adžovic depicting the everyday life of a child in a gypsy camp (2005, pp. 79–80) **Step 6. Tableaux**: Each group creates one freeze frame, of: a. Radi, his friend Nino, and other children playing in the camp b. Radi on his everyday bus going to pre-school c. Radi's mother looking after her children in the caravan Create, present, respond to the images (see *Workshop 1*, Steps 8.a–8.c) **Step 7. Soundscape**: In three groups, students work on performing three different stanzas of a poem from author Usin Kerin's *Birth in the camp*, ('Nascita nell'Accampamento') http://www.assopaceaurunca.altervista.org/4.html The groups vocally interpret this poem using volume (whispering, shouting key words), rhythm (pauses, repetition, echo, overlaps), colouring selected key words with different emotions. Twenty minutes preparation, then, with lights dimmed, each group performs their section of the poem. Hand out the text and discuss **Step 8. Role play**: In the pre-school's hall. Radi asks for €50 from the parent of another child. Improvise in pairs (one parent, one child)

(continued)

3 Aesthetic and Intercultural Engagement 73

Workshop 2 (continued)

	Drama strategy
	Step 9. Class improvisation with Teacher in Role: On the same day, Radi is caught by a teacher while he takes some change from another child's backpack. The teacher, alarmed, reports to the director. Teacher in Role as the director, who calls a special meeting with the parents. One participant in role as the teacher; all other participants in role as the parents. Some are Italian, while others come from different cultural backgrounds, including three from a gypsy background. Position the chairs to re-create a meeting. Parents discuss how to deal with potentially similar situations
	Step 10. Class improvisation *without* Teacher in Role: One week after that meeting, it's the day the photograph (pre-text) was taken, precisely half an hour before the photo was shot. All participants take on a role as gypsy children waiting for the bus to take them to pre-school, like every morning. Teacher narration: "It was a morning like every other morning. It was cold. [pause] The children were waiting for the bus to take them to school. [pause] The bus should be here any time. [longer pause] The bus should really be here. [pause] The bus was late. [pause] When is the bus coming? It'd be warmer on the bus. [pause] The bus is very late now. [pause] What if it doesn't come? [pause] The bus did not come." Participants, in role as children, improvise
Reflective phase	**Step 11. Discussion**: Discuss the regional law from December 2007 (*Regione Lombardia*, Italy), which stated that Roma (gypsy) children without an Italian residency permit were not allowed to access the pre-school education system in the Lombardy area—a law later removed as it was strongly criticised by UNESCO. This deeply affected the gypsy ethnic communities throughout Italy, as they are rarely granted residency permits (Rodari, 2008). Hand out photocopies of the law; as well as a photocopy of the *Charter of the Fundamental Rights of the European Union*, http://fra.europa.eu/en/charterpedia/article/21-non-discrimination Article 21 (Non Discrimination). Discuss
	Step 12. Conscience Alley: The participants form two parallel rows, creating an alleyway. The teacher, in role as the Principal, walks slowly through the alley way. The participants voice the inner thoughts/sensations of the director, after the school meeting with the parents, while she is reflecting on the situation
	Step 13. Debrief: Breathe, shake, stretch, laugh, have some water, discuss what your favourite moment of the drama was like. Share any comments, observations, questions
	Step 14. Language revision: Steer the direction of the conversation towards the language learning. Focus on new vocabulary that emerged during the improvisation
	Step 15. Final reflection: How did it feel to be 'other'? A child, a parent, a man, a woman, wealthy, poor, living in a caravan, having to rely on spare change, having change to spare? Put up the photograph (Fig. 1) again, and discuss. What else can you see in the photograph, now?

This chapter considered aesthetic and intercultural engagement in second language education, with attention to the construct of aesthetic engagement in process drama. It advanced a framework for intercultural aesthetic engagement, a pivotal concept underpinning the book. The discussion drew from a wide spectrum of key theorists, as well as research on intercultural awareness and spontaneity, to illustrate the main theoretical points. At this point, to fully embrace the construct of intercultural dramatic engagement, we need to explore intercultural dramatic tension, and particularly metaxis. So far, we have been drawn towards the door of metaxis, without daring to go in. Chapter 4 will take us peeking through that door, and beyond, discussing the elements of drama in an intercultural perspective.

References

Abbs, P. (1989). *A is for aesthetic: Essays on creative and aesthetic education*. New York: Falmer Press.
Adžović, N. (2005). Rom. Il popolo invisibile. Roma: Editore Palombi.
Alred, G., Byram, M., & Fleming, M. (Eds.). (2003). *Intercultural experience and education*. Clevedon: Multilingual Matters.
Baumgarten, A. (1750/1970). *Aesthetica*. New York: George Olms.
Barrett, C. (Ed.). (1966). *Wittgenstein: Lectures and conversations on aesthetics, psychology, and religious belief*. Berkeley and Los Angeles: University of California Press.
Berthoz, A. (2012). *Simplexity: Simplifying principles for a complex world* (G. Weiss, Trans.). New Haven: Yale University Press.
Bowell, P., & Heap, B. (2017). *Putting process drama into action: The dynamics of practice*. London: Routledge.
Bundy, P. (2003). Aesthetic engagement in the drama process. *Research in Drama Education: The Journal of Applied Theatre and Performance, 8*(2), 171–181.
Byram, M. (1997). *Teaching and assessing intercultural communicative competence*. Clevedon: Multilingual Matters.
Byram, M. (2008). *From foreign language education to education for intercultural citizenship: Essays and reflections* (Vol. 17). Bristol: Multilingual Matters.

Byram, M. (2009). Intercultural competence in foreign languages. In D. K. Deardorff (Ed.), *The Sage handbook of intercultural competence* (pp. 321–331). Thousand Oaks: Sage.

Byram, M. (2012). Language awareness and (critical) cultural awareness - relationships, comparisons and contrasts. *Language Awareness, 21*(1–2), 5–13.

Byram, M., & Zarate, G. (Eds.). (1997). *The sociocultural and intercultural dimension of language learning and teaching*. Strasbourg: Council of Europe.

Coleridge, S. T. (1817/1965). *Biographia literaria: Or, biographical sketches of my literary life and opinions* (Vol. 11). New York: Dent.

Council of Europe. (2001). *Common European Framework of Reference For Languages: Learning, Teaching, Assessment*. Strasburg: Cambridge University Press. Retrieved from https://rm.coe.int/1680459f97.

Council of Europe. (2018). *Common European Framework of Reference For Languages: Learning, Teaching, Assessment: Companion Volume with New Descriptors*. Strasburg. Retrieved from https://rm.coe.int/cefr-companion-volume-with-new-descriptors-2018/1680787989.

Crichton, J. (2008). Why an investigative stance matters in intercultural language teaching and learning. *Babel, 43*(1), 31–34.

Deardorff, D. K. (Ed.) (2009). *The Sage handbook of intercultural competence*. Thousand Oaks: Sage.

Dewey, J. (1934/1980). *Art as experience*. New York: Perigee.

Dubois, W. E. B. (1973). *The souls of black folk*. Millwood, New York: Kraus-Thompson Oranization Limited.

Dunn, J., & Stinson, M. (2011). Not without the art!! The importance of teacher artistry when applying drama as pedagogy for additional language learning. *Research in Drama Education: The Journal of Applied Theatre and Performance, 16*(4), 617–633.

Dunne, É. (2016). Teaching and the event. *Journalism, Media and Cultural Studies (JOMEC) Journal, 10*. http://dx.doi.org/10.18573/j.2016.10081.

Dunne, É., & Seary, A. (Eds.). (2016). *The pedagogics of unlearning*. New York: Punctum Books.

Eagleton, T. (1976). *Marxism and literary criticism*. London: Methuen & Co.

Fleming, M. (2003). Intercultural experience and drama. In G. Alred, M. Byram, & M. Fleming (Eds.), *Intercultural experience and education* (pp. 87–100). Clevedon: Multilingual Matters.

Gallagher, K. (2005). The aesthetics of representation: Dramatic texts and dramatic engagement. *Journal of Aesthetic Education, 39*(4), 82–94.

Geertz, C. (1973). *The interpretations of cultures*. New York: Basic Books.

Greene, M. (1988). *The dialectic of freedom*. New York: Teachers College Press.

Greene, M. (2001). *Variations on a blue guitar: The Lincoln Center Institute lectures on aesthetic education*. New York: Teachers College Press.

Harbon, L., & Moloney, R. (2015). Intercultural and multicultural awkward companions: The case of in schools in New South Wales, Australia. In H. Layne, V. Trémion, & F. Dervin (Eds.), *Making the most of intercultural education* (1st ed., pp. 15–34). Newcastle upon Tyne: Cambridge Scholars Publishing.

Haseman, B. (1991). Improvisation, process drama and dramatic art. *The Drama Magazine*, 19–21.

Haseman, B., & O'Toole, J. (2017). *Dramawise reimagined*. Sydney: Currency Press.

Hegel, G. W. F. (1835/1975). *Aesthetics: Lectures on fine art* (Vol. 1, T. M. Knox, Trans.). Oxford: Oxford University Press.

Heyward, M. (2002). From international to intercultural: Redefining the international school for a globalized world. *Journal of Research in International Education*, *1*(1), 9–32. https://doi.org/10.1177/147524090211002.

Heyward, M. (2004). *Intercultural literacy and the international school*. (Doctoral Dissertation). Retrieved from https://eprints.utas.edu.au/423/.

Kant, I. (1790/1928). *Critique of judgement* (J. H. Bernard, Trans.). Oxford: Oxford University Press.

Kant, I. (1781/1990). Transcendental aesthetics (J. M. D. Meiklejohn, Trans.). *The critique of pure reason*. Raleigh, NC: Alex Catalogue.

Kao, S.-M., & O'Neill, C. (1998). *Words into worlds: Learning a second language through process drama*. London: Ablex Publishing.

Kramsch, C. (2009). *The multilingual subject*. Oxford: Oxford University Press.

Kristeva, J. (1980). *Desire in language: A semiotic approach to literature and art*. New York: Columbia University Press.

Lima, M. G. (1995). From aesthetics to psychology: Notes on Vygotsky's "Psychology of art". *Anthropology & Education Quarterly*, *26*(4), 410–424.

Marcuse, H. (1978). *The aesthetic dimension: Toward a critique of Marxist aesthetics*. Boston: Beacon Press.

Neelands, J. (2010). Learning through imagined experience. In P. O'Connor (Ed.), *Crating democratic citizenship through drama education: The writings of Jonothan Neelands* (pp. 35–48). Sterling: Trentham Books.

Nicholson, H. (1999). Aesthetic values, drama education and the politics of difference. *NJ: Drama Australia Journal*, *23*(2), 82–90.

Nussbaum, M. C. (1992). Tragedy and self-sufficiency. In A. O. Rorty (Ed.), *Essays on Aristotle's poetics* (pp. 261–290). Princeton: Princeton University Press.

O'Mara, J. (2016). Thinking on your feet: A model for teaching teachers to use process drama. In C. Sharma (Ed.), *Drama and theatre with children: International perspectives* (pp. 98–112). Abingdon: Routledge.

O'Neill, C. (1995). *Drama worlds: A framework for process drama*. Portsmouth: Heinemann.

O'Toole, J. (1992). *The process of drama: Negotiating art and meaning*. London: Reutledge.

O'Toole, J., Stinson, M., & Moore, T. (2009). *Drama and curriculum: A giant at the door*. New York: Springer.

Pheasant, P. (2015). The epiphany in process drama and language learning. *p-e-r-f-o-r-m-a-n-c-e, 2*, 1–2. http://p-e-r-f-o-r-m-a-n-c-e.org/?p=919.

Piazzoli, E. (2010). Process drama and intercultural language learning: An experience of contemporary Italy. *Research in Drama Education: The Journal of Applied Theatre and Performance, 15*(3), 385–402.

Rader, M. (1974). The imaginative mode of awareness. *The Journal of Aesthetics and Art Criticism, 33*(2), 131–137.

Rancière, J. (2016). Unwhat? In É. Dunne & A. Seary (Eds.), *The pedagogics of unlearning*. New York: Punctum Books.

Rodari, E. (2008). *Rom, un popolo: Diritto a esistere e deriva securitaria*. Milano: Punto Rosso.

Said, E. (1978). *Orientalism*. New York: Vintage Books.

Schiller, F. (1795/1965). *On the aesthetic education of man: In a series of letters* (R. Snell, Trans.). New York: F. Ungar Pub. Co.

Scully, G. (2017, May). *From performance to the periphery and beyond: Group devised theatre for additional language acquisition*. Paper presented at the Scenario Forum Conference: Performative spaces in literature, language and culture education, University College Cork, Ireland.

Syssoyeva, K. M., & Proudfit, S. (Eds.) (2016). *Women, collective creation, and devised performance: The rise of women theatre artists in the twentieth and twenty-first centuries*. New York: Springer Nature.

Taliaferro, D. M. (1998). Signifying self: Re-presentations of the double-consciousness in the work of Maxine Greene. In W. Pinar (Ed.), *The passionate mind of Maxine Greene: "I am—not yet"* (pp. 89–121). London: Falmer Press.

Taylor, S. (2014). Globally-minded students: Defining, measuring and developing intercultural sensitivity: Part 2. *The International Schools Journal, 33*(2), 26.

Tschurtschenthaler, H. (2013). *Drama-based foreign language learning: Encounters between self and others*. Munster: Waxmann.

Vygotsky, L. S. (1926/1971). *The psychology of art*. Cambridge, MA: The MIT Press.

Vygotsky, L. S. (1930/2004). Imagination and creativity in childhood. *Journal of Russian and East European Psychology, 42*(1), 7–97.
Weltsek-Medina, G. J. (2007). Process drama in education. In A. Blatner (Ed.) *Interactive and improvisational drama: Varieties of applied theatre and performance* (pp. 90–98). New York: iUniverse.

4

The Elements of Drama: An Intercultural Perspective

Storytelling defines us as humans. Aristotle conceptualises drama and poetry as "elevated fine arts" (330 BC, 6), able to capture the universal values of human beings. He identifies six basic elements of drama: plot, theme, character, language, rhythm and spectacle. Throughout the centuries, the elements of drama have been explored, expanded and contested by key theorists—in a universal effort to shed meaning on what is drama, and how can we understand its elements to create engaging stories. The Aristotelian elements thus created a universal framework, to either be followed or rejected according to epoch and trends. For example, in the twentieth century its rejection became a platform for Epic theatre, Brecht's (1964) non-Aristotelian drama, as well as Ibsen's Theatre of Realism. Boal (1985) also criticised the *Poetics*, as he believed that Aristotle's notion of catharsis reinforces the oppression of marginalised groups. Across traditions, drama theorists have agreed upon the existence of identifiable dramatic elements used by playwrights and directors to create theatre or, in the case of performative language teaching, to create learning through drama.

Heathcote makes an explicit reference to the elements of drama, defining her practice as a "conscious employment of the elements of drama to educate" (in Wagner, 1976, p. 13). She describes these elements as 'the three spectra of theatre': darkness/light, silence/sound, and stillness/movement. Bolton (1979) identifies the dramatic elements as *tension, contrast, symbolisation*, as well as *a sense of time* and *focus*. Similarly, Morgan and Saxton (1987) pinpoint the elements of drama as *focus, tension, contrast* and *symbolisation*. Bowell and Heap (2001) identify key elements as: *focus, metaphor, tension, symbol, contrast, role, time* and *space* (p. ix). For Haseman and O'Toole (2017), the elements of drama are intrinsic to the definition of process drama:

> Process drama is an improvised form of drama in which you construct a coherent dramatic story with yourselves as the character in that story. It is a powerful way to explore, through experience, all of the *elements of drama*. This approach brings mind, body, emotions, imagination and memories into the classroom to shape and deepen your learning. (Haseman & O'Toole, 2017, p. viii, my emphasis)

Pheasant's (2015) definition of process drama also incorporates the elements: "Process drama as an art form in the context of this research refers to techniques that employ *elements of drama* to engage and make meaning for students through the art form to heighten aesthetic engagement" (para. 8, my emphasis). He is fascinated by what he describes as the "Eureka Moment in aesthetic engagement—a heightened state of being likened to an epiphany" (2015, para. 2). He connects peaks of heightened engagement in L2/process drama to key moments when narrative, dramatic role and dramatic tension are skilfully managed by facilitator and participants. As the definitions above suggest, an awareness of the elements of drama is quintessential to the comprehension, and the apprehension, of process drama artistry.

1   The Dramawise Model

In 1987, Haseman and O'Toole conceptualised the elements of drama in the *Dramawise* model, which has been influential at policy level in the Australian and UK curricula. Three decades on, in *Dramawise Reimagined*, Haseman and O'Toole (2017) refine the elements model (Fig. 1) illustrating the elements of drama as:

4 The Elements of Drama: An Intercultural Perspective

THE ELEMENTS OF DRAMA

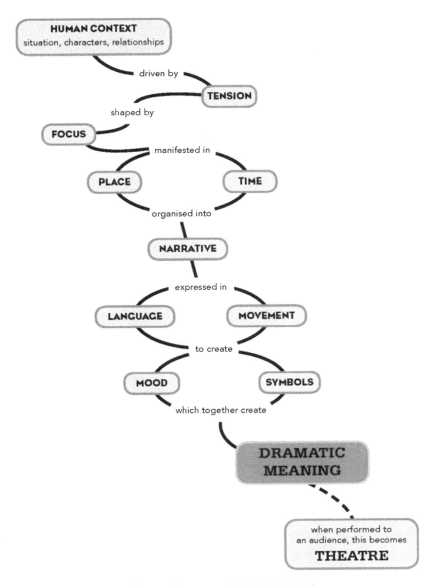

Fig. 1 The elements of drama (Haseman & O'Toole, 2017)

Situation, *character* and *relationships*, driven by *dramatic tension*, shaped by *focus*, manifested in *place* and *time*, organised into *narrative*, expressed in *language* and *movement*, to create *mood* and *symbols*, which together create *dramatic meaning*. When performed for an audience, this becomes *theatre*. (p. i, my emphasis)

In L2/process drama, the teacher/artist is concerned with the management of these elements, the essence to dramatic form, to create a felt-experience. This aims to generate what Kramsch (2009) calls "teaching language as a living form, experienced and remembered bodily, with a relation to an Other that is mediated by symbolic forms" (p. 191). In order to make the discussion as clear as possible, below I offer a real-life classroom example of how symbolic forms (the elements of drama) mediated an embodied experience for a group of second language learners reflecting back on their first day in a new country.

2 Sam's Story

The strategies of the drama described in this section also appear at the end of this chapter (Workshop 3, *The Jugglers*). This drama was inspired by working with a group of adult migrants and international students at the University of Padua, learning Italian as a Second Language (L2) through drama, in collaboration with Fiona Dalziel. Participants were asked to share a story related to their first day in Italy (Step 2). I was struck when Sam (not his real name), a twenty-year-old Nigerian participant, volunteered to share his story:

> On my first day in Italy I was in Bologna's train station, I had to get a train ticket to Padua. In front of the train station was a group of buskers, juggling and doing tricks on clown bikes. I was mesmerised by the jugglers, I stared at them for a long time. I just sat there, looking at them. They were brilliant. Then I realised I had been staring for… five hours. Five hours! I bought my ticket and left. I never saw them again.

What captivated me in Sam's story is hard to pin down on paper: it relates to a non-verbal nuance, to his emotional stance as he narrated the story, and how it was received by the group. The story generated laughter and appeared to trigger a pleasant memory in the storyteller. The content of the story was also intriguing: Sam had temporarily lost perception of time in a new country where he had just arrived. The mood of the story, as I perceived it from his portrayal, seemed to be a sense of wonder, of feeling temporarily lost in time, in-between countries, eager to start a new life. As all participants (including myself and Fiona) had experienced migration, the potential for a shared understanding was present. This is the first, important step, in choosing an aesthetically charged pretext: tapping into the feeling-dimension, connecting to an idea or theme beyond the story. I felt that a sense of connection (Bundy, 2003) was elicited by his storytelling and in the group's response.

Let's consider the elements of drama in this story. Sam's tale implies *characters* (himself, the buskers, passers-by) within a specific *situation* (a group of buskers performing juggling tricks) and a potential development of the situation (Sam joining the buskers). It also implies *relationships*, which could be amongst members of the busker group—perhaps there could be a set of twins—or between the group members and others: perhaps the ex-lover of one of the jugglers was amongst the audience? It is shaped by dramatic *focus*, manifested in *time* and *place* (on Sam's first day in Italy, before he caught the train, in front of the train station). The story is organised into a *narrative*, which allows it to be told in a chronological manner with a beginning, a middle and an end. It contains no dialogue, but certainly has scope for *language* (the buskers speaking amongst each other, Sam interacting with the buskers, passers-by interacting with the buskers). It hints at a degree of *movement* (the buskers juggling balls, performing tricks on the clown bike). The element of *mood* is open to interpretation; from Sam's recollection of the story, it seemed to be of anticipation and curiosity. The element of *symbol* is not explicit in the story, but could be woven into it: what if a set of juggling balls were given to Sam by one of the buskers, and what if he decided to keep those juggling balls until he had grandchildren of his own, as a symbol of starting a new life? What would he say to his grandchildren then, and what would the juggling balls signify?

A number of dramatic elements are present, or implied, in the story. Yet so far, *dramatic tension*, the queen of dramatic elements, is missing from the picture. As Dawson (1970) argues: "All works of art are fully grasped through the perception of the interrelatedness of their parts, and in drama the relation between parts is characteristically one of tension." (p. 30). Dramatic tension is a fascinating construct, the motor that powers good storytelling. In O'Toole's words (1992, p. 132): "The source of tension is the gap between people and the fulfilment of their internal purposes". This gap is created deliberately by imposing constraints in the story, to create an 'emotional disturbance', what O'Toole calls "impedance" (p. 135). O'Toole draws on Ryle (1949) who discussed inclinations and agitations using the metaphor of a rock in a current, or eddy in a stream: "An important feature of agitations [is] namely that they presuppose the existence of inclinations which are not themselves agitations, much as eddies presuppose the existence of currents" (p. 91). Ryle continues: "An agitation requires that there exists two inclinations, or an inclination and a factual impediment" (p. 91). Dramatic tension, then, can be seen as an *impediment* to what the characters are inclined, or urged, to achieve. O'Toole adds that the function of the playwright (or teacher) is to provide "a retardation of this urge towards swift gratification" to slow down the accomplishment of a task (1992, p. 134). Dramatic tension, inter-related to the other elements, creates an impediment within an emotional current. It is up to the teacher/artist, and participants as co-artists, to perceive and handle the inclination of that current, connected to the fulfilment of the characters' goals.

Haseman and O'Toole (2017) identify different types of dramatic tensions: tension of the task, tension of dilemma, tension of relationships, tension of surprise, tension of the mystery and the tension of metaxis. To illustrate each typology, I continue with the example of Sam above.

The *tension of the task* could be injected into Sam's story if the buskers were trying to raise a sum of money, perhaps by a certain day, perhaps by today, to enter a competition to perform at a national juggling arts event. The 'task' to complete could be to reach €1000 to enter a competition that closed at 8 p.m. The time constraint here would work hand in hand with the tension of the task, and it would be necessary to build some background about the event itself (building belief).

The *tension of dilemma* was also missing from the story—as it was told. It could be added as, for example, one of the jugglers received a phone call and was offered a chance to leave the group and join a more advanced, opponent juggling group, even if his best mates were there. His personal dilemma could be explored, looking at friendship and loyalty towards his friends who taught him the tricks of juggling, and his motivation to win the competition.

If he agreed to switch groups, *tension of relationships* would set in. It might become explicit in a dialogue where his mates confronted him about it. Yet, it would become even stronger if his mates asked him to play a main part in the act, just moments before he could break the news of him leaving the group; this would impose a further constraint.

Tension of surprise would emerge if, just before the 8 p.m. deadline, the head of the group received an unexpected message from the competition administrator, stating that they had been issued with a payment from an undisclosed donor for the group's fee to enter the annual Arts Council competition, and for a complementary one-week training retreat to prepare for it.

Tension of the mystery would creep in if, after the initial celebration at the donor's gesture, they realised more fully that the source of the funding was an unknown secret benefactor. If the unknown donor asked them to sign a confidentiality agreement, to attend an intensive one-week practice at his remote, undisclosed venue, the tension would rise. If, then, the secret donor asked them to reach the venue without any mobile devices, the tension would escalate.

Finally, there is a further type of dramatic tension, perhaps the most important one in relation to aesthetic engagement: the tension of *metaxis*. A Greek term, metaxis has been translated as 'betwixt and between' and has been variously attributed to Homer (Bundy, 1999, p. 55) and Plato (Allern, 2001, p. 78). Metaxis implies a *dissonance* in the simultaneous management between the fictional context of the drama and the real context of the participants (O'Toole, 1992). This echoes Vygotsky's (1926/1971) aesthetic theory, particularly Lima's (1995, p. 418) interpretation of Vygotsky's aesthetic experience as "the collision of the contradictory emotions" generated by *form* on *content* (see "Aesthetics in Education" in Chapter 3). It also connects to Davis (2015), as she makes a case for metaxis, aesthetic engagement, and Vygotsky's *perezhivanie* (felt-experience) in process drama. In the example above, tension of metaxis may set in if Sam had experienced, in real life, a situation where he had to choose between being loyal to a friend and winning a competition, particularly *if* in his life Sam went through a circumstance similar to the fictional context of the drama, but acted differently, and *if* the simultaneous management of the two contexts created an emotional reaction that moved him. As seen in the previous chapter, imagining ourselves as other is at the heart of drama and, in L2 contexts, involves interpreting reality from an intercultural perspective. Accordingly, the elements of drama can be infused with, and can infuse, a kind of engagement that is both intercultural and aesthetic. This brings into question the intercultural dimension of the dramatic elements.

3 The Elements of Drama in an Intercultural Perspective

Sam's story functioned as a pre-text in the sense that it afforded inspiration for what was to come. At this point it is important to note that Sam's story has ceased to be *his* story, but it has become the group's story—the group shaped it, extended it and made new meanings from of it, well beyond its initial form. As in this instance the pre-text was a personal story (not always the case), it was essential to seek the storyteller's permission to play with the story. Upon agreement, an important point is that, through the dramatic exploration, the teacher/artist steers the story away from the protagonist, focussing for example on secondary characters in the story, to create a degree of distancing (see "Protecting into Emotion" in Chapter 6). Exploring the storyteller's personal experience within a story is common practice in other dramatic forms, including forum theatre (Boal, 1985), Rainbow of Desire (Boal, 1995) and Playback Theatre (Fox, 2007; Salas, 1996), where the focus is on political and social action, psychological change and community engagement (see "A 4D Map of Dramatic Forms" in Chapter 8). On the other hand, the approach to dramatic form discussed here falls within the domain of process drama in second language education, with attention to the intercultural domain. Below is an overview of a possible train of thoughts that may aid the teacher/artist's choices, to convert the pre-text from oral narration into an embodied experience, looking at the elements of drama from an intercultural perspective.

3.1 Dramatic Situation, Characters and Relationships in an Intercultural Key

Any drama involves a situation and some characters. The characters, in turn, will imply some relationships. Haseman and O'Toole advance

4 The Elements of Drama: An Intercultural Perspective 87

three basic aspects that make up a character. These aspects are *purpose*, *status* and *attitude*, which together form part of the character's *motivation*, that is, "what the character hopes to achieve" (2017, p. 1).

In an intercultural key, considering the *situation*, as well as the purpose, status and attitude within a character's motivation, is fundamental to delineate the *relationships* that will unfold in the rest of the drama. The initial situation depicted in the story is a group of jugglers, juggling in front of a station, with an onlooker gazing in fascination (Sam). This situation also implies characters and relationship. In Sam's story the explicit characters are himself (the storyteller) and the group of jugglers. This action, in its simplicity, is sufficient to bind them into a social role, to denote them as 'jugglers'. Who are the jugglers? Where are they from? We know they are in Italy, but are they *from* Italy? If so, where from in Italy? Multiple tensions are implicit between Northern and Southern Italy, for example—that would give its own spin to a drama. If, perhaps, the teacher's aim is to get the learners to reflect on social issues between North and South of Italy, this could be a good lead. Although we know they are juggling, there are many aspects of their characters left to construe. Thinking about the cultural background of the jugglers is an initial point of entry into the intercultural dimension—it could be left to the students to decide, or it could be a conscious decision of the teacher to connect characters with cultural backgrounds. In terms of the characters' motivations, we could look at the cultural norms of the jugglers—(1) as a social group, whether they fit with the Italian society, and/or the cultural values; (2) as individuals within the jugglers' group.

First, it may be productive to explore the purpose, status and attitude of the jugglers, forming their character motivation, as a social group. In terms of *purpose*: why are they there juggling? Are they promising young athletes from another country, practising while they wait for their coach to attend an important event tomorrow? Or are the jugglers living on the streets, busking for some change to earn their next meal? If so, how much have they raised? When was their last proper meal? Choosing a *purpose* immediately connects to *status*. At first glance, one might say that in the first lot (as athletes), their status is higher than in the second lot (as beggars). But not necessarily so, as status is always negotiated with whom one interacts. For example, in an interaction with passers-by, the beggars could adopt a higher status than the young athletes—the beggars might feel tougher, more street-savvy in the interaction. These choices would send the drama to a particular direction. It would impact on their *attitude*, in terms of language, posture, and so forth. It would also be the beginning point for intercultural discussion: how do homeless youth integrate into the community in Italy? What about in other countries? Any choice related to purpose, attitude and status would immediately set the drama on its own course. Focussing on the social role of the jugglers preparing for a festival would imply other possible characters in the story: the festival's organisers, other artists at the street festival, the audience. All of these nuances would be tainted by an intercultural perspective, dictated by the setting and by the cultural norms associated with it.

Second, it may be useful to explore the purpose, status and attitude of the jugglers, forming their character motivation, as individuals within the group. This immediately sheds light on their intercultural relationships. Who is the leader? Is one of them jealous of the others? Is one of them hot-headed? As we define these relationships, it may be helpful to personalise the roles. Who juggles with what? In Sam's story, one artist was on a mono-cycle, another had four juggling balls, a third one had juggling clubs. Now, to add an intercultural cue: what are their backgrounds? Are they all locals, or is someone from elsewhere? Or are they all from different places, with only one local? We could continue posing questions, or encouraging the students to do so in small groups, to look at the purpose, status and attitudes of each one, and the impact of roles and situation on the intercultural perspective. What has happened here is that, through a flight of the imagination, we have sketched a scenario whereby these characters now have some depth—the *motivation* created by inferring the *purpose*, *status* and *attitudes* of the jugglers, the situation, and the relationships.

3.2 Intercultural Dramatic Focus

Many questions could be asked, and we could have dozens of dramas stemming from them. But we need to focus on one. This is where dramatic focus makes the difference. Just as by adjusting the focus lens of a camera we can see the details in a shot, similarly, adjusting the dramatic focus helps the details of a story to emerge. Clearly setting time, place and physical space helps to focus the drama. *Intercultural dramatic focus*, accordingly, helps to shed light on those issues that can afford a lived experience of the language and culture. A key question we need to consider as teacher/artists is: Does the pre-text hold a clear intercultural focus?

Let us abandon, for the time being, the busking jugglers' story. A better example to illustrate dramatic focus can be offered by the workshop in the previous chapter, *At the Gypsy Camp* (Workshop 2). The pre-text of that workshop, a black and white photograph (Fig. 1 in Chapter 3), holds a sharp intercultural focus, as it throws us into the vivid landscape of a gypsy camp. The intercultural focus starts from the title of the photograph: *Vicolo Savini, Roma* (Savini Road, Rome). In the discussion preceding the launch of the pre-text (Step 1.c), students were anticipating *Vicolo Savini* to be a typical-looking, cobblestoned lane in the centre of Rome. Instead, they found an unpaved car park, with a series of old caravans parked in rows, one with a broken window. This mismatch in the participants' expectations provided an initial intercultural focus.

The pre-text also implies intercultural focus for the *roles*: the teacher taking the role of the gypsy child in the foreground, and the learners taking the role of parents (from an Italian background, from a gypsy background, and other cultural backgrounds) in a pre-school community in Rome (Step 9). Moreover, the pre-text acts as a pivotal point to focus the drama; Step 8 is framed *one week before* the photo was taken; Step 10 is framed *on the same day* the photo was taken, at the bus stop near the camp. The focus here is constructed as a dynamic element inferring movement in time and space across different cultural contexts: the gypsy cultural context (at the camp), the Italian context (the pre-school setting), the culture of the actual participants (Australians and New Zealanders studying Italian language and culture at university).

3.3 Intercultural Dramatic Tension

Tension exists in both narrative and non-narrative forms. *Narrative tension* is generated by the relationships between characters, narrative, language and so forth, as we have explored above. However, the sequence of events, or as Styan (1960) puts it, the "sequence of impressions" (p. 120) in a drama, is given not only by events, but also by non-narrative elements. *Non-narrative tension* is generated by the contrast of darkness/light, silence/sound and stillness/movement, what Heathcote describes as the three spectra of theatre. Most significantly, non-narrative tension is connected to the sensory/affective sphere, as it is a non-tangible manifestation of emotional currents:

- *Non-narrative intercultural tension* is generated by the contrast of music/silence, movement/stillness and light/dark—where culture-specific rhythms, melodies, soundscapes, movement sequences, gestures, rituals and signs are consciously managed. In Workshop 2, degrees of non-narrative intercultural tension were generated by the reading (Step 5), by performing the gypsy poem (Step 7), by dimming the lights and juxtaposing silence and sound through the teacher's narration pauses (Step 10). The aesthetic charge of the poem imbued a strong, intercultural non-narrative tension that permeated the other episodes.
- *Intercultural tension of relationships* relates to the potential tension stemming from different cultural values manifested in roles and situations. In Workshop 2, a degree of intercultural tension of relationships was present in the parent/teacher meeting (Step 9) chaired by the pre-school director (Teacher in Role). Tension between the Italian parents and the parents from different ethnic backgrounds, mediated via the parent/teacher meeting's performative as a social ritual, escalated into an intense debate—singled out by some participants as the highest peak of engagement.
- *Intercultural tension of the task* implies the potential tension of having to accomplish a cross-cultural task, given the different cultural systems associated with it. In Workshop 2, a degree of intercultural tension of the task transpired from the role play between the gypsy child and the Italian parent (Step 8)—the task being to manage to get the €50. The gypsy child's genuine desire to help his friend resulted in the action of begging for change, a cultural norm from his own context that clashed with the cultural norms of the Italian parent.

- *Intercultural tension of surprise* implies the gap between two (or more) cultural worlds, generating a surprise in terms of how an event or circumstance is perceived by different individuals, and how they react to it. Workshop 2 is perhaps not the best example for tension of surprise. An initial degree of tension of surprise was generated between Steps 1.c and Step 2—discussing typical streets in the city of Rome, and then showing the photograph of *Vicolo Savini* being a gypsy camp instead.
- *Intercultural tension of the mystery* implies the gap between two (or more) cultural worlds, creating a mystery in terms of how an event, ritual or circumstance is perceived by different individuals, and how they react to it. In Workshop 2, in Step 4 the teacher (in role as a gypsy child) finally reveals with gravity to be sad because his best friend Nino will be taken to the river. Here a seed of intercultural tension of the mystery is planted. What does that mean? The river, and the cultural meaning attached with 'being taken to a river' seems to be firmly planted in the gypsy child's perception of reality—but not in the students' perception of reality. What does 'being taken to the river' imply? This question is deliberately left unanswered. It is hinted at in Step 7, especially in the third stanza of Usin Kerin's poem:

> I was born, as my mother died
> My old father *bathed me in the river:*
> *Hence* my body is strong today
> And blood runs forcefully within me.
> (My English translation from http://www.assopaceaurunca.altervista.org/4.html)

The intercultural tension of the mystery related to Nino 'being taken to the river' comes back in the second line of this stanza, leading to more questions: is Nino ill? If so, 'being taken to the river' might signify a healing ritual to regain strength. Alternatively, has Nino's mother passed away? In that case, bathing in the river might be interpreted as a grieving ritual. Intercultural tension of the mystery is closely associated with the element of symbol and ritual—it lies in the questions, rather than in the answers, and in the meaning made by the participants.

- *Intercultural tension of metaxis* is generated by a dissonance between the dramatic (play) context and the actual (real) context. In a way, as we have seen, second language students engaged in a process drama are continuously re-negotiating cultural systems. When playing a role, they may experience intercultural tension of metaxis if moved by the disjunction between how they responded in the context of the drama, and how they would normally respond in the context of their first language/culture. In Workshop 2, Step 10 saw a group of adult Australian and New Zealanders, about to graduate in education, linguistics and Italian Studies, interacting in role as gypsy children in Italy. After the improvisation, one participant, Emi, an education student, stated that she was profoundly touched. What moved Emi was how, in the drama, in role as a child, she felt extreme happiness when the school bus did not arrive, as this meant that she could skip school. She was riveted in that state of delight for some time, till after a little while, still in role, the realisation came upon her that she was in fact feeling excited about loitering, instead of going to school. Putting her education hat back on, she felt that this was strongly at odds with her values on children's access to early childhood education. Nevertheless, in the drama, she was very excited at the possibility of loitering all day. She commented on that dissonance, on having experienced a feeling so far-fetched from her own perceived values. Here, a degree of metaxis, and particularly intercultural metaxis, may have triggered Emi's engagement. The construct of metaxis resonates with Taliaferro's (1998) reading of Greene's (1988) discourse on double-consciousness, interpreted as the 'productive tension' held while looking at self from the eyes of the other, discussed in the previous chapter (see "Intercultural Engagement" in Chapter 3).

3.4 Intercultural Time and Place

Kramsch (2009) connects language teaching and the potential of embodied time:

To view the foreign language classroom as a deficient, less than authentic instructional setting is to ignore its potential as a symbolic multilingual environment, where alternative realities can be explored and reflected upon. Language teaching is not just a question of devising the right activities. It has to do with the economy of embodied time. (p. 210)

The main currency of 'an economy of embodied time' in the L2/process drama classroom is a clear management of focus, specifically focussing the dramatic time in which the action is unfolding. Time is truly a potent aesthetic device in drama, which can heighten the intensity of a dramatic moment (O'Neill, 1995). In an intercultural key, focussing *time* might give rise to a reflection on culture and the relationship to time. A whole branch of cross-cultural communication looks at chronemics (the study of the role of time in communication) and how the orientation of time is managed differently across cultures (Hall, 1959). This represents an invaluable source of reflection in process drama, where time is manipulated from one episode to another, and meaning emerges as we encounter the other.

How do different cultural groups perceive time in communication? This can be an interesting dramatic exploration, especially if infused with dramatic tension of the task. In Workshop 2, *At The Gypsy Camp*, the students noted how the perception of time in the drama (while playing roles as gypsy children in the camp) was very different from their own perception of time as undergraduate students attending lectures, seminars, part-time work. Similarly, *place* is essential to allow participants to manifest and visualise the action, with manipulating place in an intercultural key as the backbone of intercultural narration. In Workshop 2, the setting of the Italian pre-school was in opposition to the gypsy camp, the deliberate manipulating between the two being crucial to generate reflection.

3.5   Narrative in an Intercultural Key

Narrative is a universal key element, which humans cling to, perhaps more obviously than other elements, when they relate to stories. It was Aristotle who initially pointed out the 'introduction, middle and end' as the structural points of a story—what has since then been conceptualised as the 'narrative arc': exposition; rising action; climax; falling action; resolution. The danger in this scheme, as Styan (1960) points out, relates to equalling the "sequences of impression" to the plot only (p. 120), losing sight of the other elements. Although he is referring to plays, it is safe to transpose his argument to process drama, where sequences of impression, or episodes, are shaped by focus, tension, time and space and organised into narrative. Looking at narrative as sequences of impression bypasses linearity, opening up to exciting intercultural framings of narrative that can be suggested by the learners. For example, it is interesting to compare how the same event is framed in two different cultures, perhaps an analysis of how events are portrayed by the media in different ways, according to the perspectives that inform our viewpoint.

In process drama, narration is used as a device to connect various dramatic episodes. For instance, in Workshop 2, Step 9, a brief teacher narration introduces the theft incident, focussing the improvisation that immediately follows. Narration by the teacher can incorporate and extend the participants' ideas, or offers, as they emerged through improvised performance in the previous episodes. In this way, the group is effectively co-creating and advancing the storytelling through improvisation. Another possible function of narration is having participants directly react to the narration itself, in role, as seen in Step 10. Here the participants, in role as the children, respond (improvise) based on the teacher's narration, as they wait for a school bus that never arrives.

3.6 Language and Movement in an Intercultural Key

Second language classes are, obviously, a forum to practise the language—ideally with a purpose. Successfully framing a drama through situation, characters, relationship, focus, tension, time and place impacts on the *language* generated. Eliciting the language to frame these elements will be simultaneously a brainstorming on/through the language, what Swain (2006) calls languaging (see "Language Engagement" in Chapter 7) as well as a character-creation exercise. This is because, as language teachers know well, in L2 settings the language is both the vehicle, and the object of learning. Interestingly, while language teachers may direct the focus of a class entirely on language, in drama-based embodied approaches, language emerges spontaneously, triggered by movement, body, imagination. Embodiment is key to such a purpose: in drama we let the body drive, and use language to express what the body is communicating. Language is thus guided by the purpose of an action. Kao and O'Neill point this out as they say: "In a drama context, in order to move the action forward, the students need to activate their language knowledge so that their meaning can get through" (1998, p. 2).

In Workshop 2, this became apparent in the parent/child role play (Step 8) and in the parent/teacher meeting (Step 9). In those instances, some students who were usually shy and introverted in the foreign language became verbose as they put forth their argument. Here, being *inside* the situation by playing a role, fuelled by tension, framed by focus, contributed to activating those students' language knowledge. Such motivation to use the foreign language also stayed strong when they were *outside* that situation. As mentioned above, reflection on experience is as powerful as experience itself. An example here is the discussion on human rights (Step 11), where we examined the regional law that denied access to Italian pre-school to children without Italian residency. This law, later removed, was discussed alongside the *Charter of Fundamental Rights of the European Union* (Article 21) on non-discrimination. Participants were handed out copies (in Italian) of both sets of documentation; the analysis and discussion gave rise to a lively debate on the issue. The debate occurred entirely in the Italian language, and the technical difficulty of the subject matter proved challenging for some students. Their willingness to be involved in the debate, however, was stronger than their self-consciousness as foreign language speakers—resulting, again, in the most taciturn participants making enormous communicative efforts to be part of that conversation.

Movement is perhaps the dramatic element that relates most openly to participants' kinaesthetic experiences in embodied approaches to language learning. Looking at the etymology of the term 'kinaesthetic' itself will illuminate the concept here: from the Greek *kinein* (to move) and *aistesis* (sensation), a kinaesthetic experience is one where, through movement, we undergo a sensory experience. In an intercultural light, experience and reflection can be focussed on kinesics (interpreting body movement as communication) as well as proxemics (interpreting personal space as communication) in different cultural systems, and the meaning made by our movement in space and time. In Workshop 2, reflecting on the body language of the various characters, especially the text and sub-text in the role play between the child and the adult (Step 8), was a useful platform to discuss language and proxemics.

Another fertile development related to movement, in an intercultural key, is exploring rhythm, levels and tempo. Playing with the pace while performing a movement or phrase (a sequence of movements) can generate dramatic tension. After all, deliberately adopting a slow pace in a situation where urgency is expected is the cornerstone of storytelling.

Music, itself a form of language, can also be introduced as a key to creating movement, in an intercultural perspective. Balkan music was a productive way to introduce the short period of relaxation in Step 5, prior to the reading of the biographical account of a child living in a gypsy camp (Adžovic, 2005). This itself might have led to creating a movement sequence, if we'd had more time, perhaps as a closing piece to the drama, using the same music as a stimulus for a stylised choreography. This kind of task, which may initially appear removed from an L2 setting context, is in fact extremely useful: a movement phrase, culminating in a simple choreography, can be the canvas for the practice of verb structures (describing movements sequence using the imperative, or past continuous forms); adverbs (describing the way an individual is moving); spatial prepositions (describing the spatial relationships between individuals); and so forth.

3.7 Intercultural Mood and Symbol

O'Toole (1992) defines *mood* as the "overall emotional climate created by the action" (p. 41). Mood is a delicate construct that is perceived and apprehended in the moment. Dimming the light, projecting a sequence

4 The Elements of Drama: An Intercultural Perspective

of images on the screen, evoking keywords related to a theme, channelling those into a response, reflecting and incorporating those into an abstract movement sequence will create a specific mood. Silence also creates mood. Chanting, playing a tune, facilitating a discussion related to an emerging theme can also create mood. A debate on human rights creates mood. As O'Toole (1992) argues, mood "operates on an intuitive and affective level" (p. 220), and is intimately connected to the aesthetic dimension of process drama.

In L2/process drama, the genesis of intercultural dramatic mood lies in non-narrative tension; it is made explicit by cultivating awareness of, and prompting participants to reflect on, the intercultural tension/s within the drama. Intercultural dramatic mood, it follows, is embedded in the attention to detail in the intercultural aesthetic dimension of a drama. In Workshop 2, intercultural mood was created by a series of details in the drama: quirky details in the nature of the encounter with the gypsy child (Step 4); prosodic details in the students' interpretations of the gypsy poem (Step 7); the vivid details in the biographical passage by Adžovic (Step 5). To mention just one small detail: the *silences* interposing the narration, in Step 10, with each silent pause intensifying the aesthetic mood and the expectations of a bus that did not arrive. This was followed, of course, by the discussion of the law denying access to pre-school education to children without Italian residency in Lombardy. This law, later removed, and the details of the human rights charter, contributed to the mood.

Symbol is another element inextricably connected to the aesthetic domain, as it is through symbols that a story acquires an aesthetic quality. It is interesting to relate symbol to playfulness, which is defined by Neelands and Goode (1995) as: "The basic human instinct to play with the relationships between *symbols* and their orthodox meanings in order to create or express new possibilities of meaning" (p. 85, my emphasis). A 'playful attitude' enables one to reassemble the elements of reality and to transform meanings by creating new symbolic relationships. Courtney (1995) suggests that learning is related to the feelings generated by symbols. He talks about key symbols, which have a social and individual dimension. The social dimension entails symbols that are structured by culture and generate social feelings; the individual dimension entails symbols that can be "strongly felt by an individual because they have a unique relation to imagination" (p. 31).

The intercultural dimension underlying the element of symbol in a performative context opens up endless possibilities of interpretation, drawing on cultural anthropology, literature and performance studies. An intercultural discussion on the symbolic value of a gesture, a token, an invitation, a word spoken—or unspoken (sub-text)—implies reflecting on what a symbol may signify in a given culture, and how the symbolic value may transpose over a different cultural system. Nurturing a productive tension between the two can transform the meaning/s of the symbol itself within the context of the drama.

'Ritual' is closely associated with symbol. Courtney describes rituals as "signifiers that re-present, synthesize and circulate symbols in complex sociocultural felt-meaning" (p. 36). He points to the social and symbolic value of rituals, that is, sequences of actions constructed around symbols. He reminds us that precisely what distinguishes rituals from habits or routine is the use of symbol. Schechner (2013) reaches even further, by defining rituals as "collective memories encoded into action" (p. 52) that enable individuals to deal with hierarchy, power, complex situations, desires, trouble, violations of culturally bound norms. Through play, Schechner notes, we can experience breaking taboos. Exploring the intercultural dimension of ritual is a way of framing intercultural encounters, as ritualised exchanges between what Goffman (1959) calls social actors. In Workshop 2, the main symbol, connected to ritual, emerged in the initial disclosure of the child being sad as his friend was being taken to the river. The river, and being taken to a river, became a symbol—related, in this instance, to the ritual of going to a river as a healing process. The way the river was presented in the poem was open to different interpretations; it could have become a symbol of life (regaining strength) or a symbol of death (mourning).

3.8 Intercultural Dramatic Meaning

In L2 settings our students, eager to understand the meaning of every word, ask over and over again: "What does this mean?". Let us not fall into the trap of confining 'meaning' to issues of translation and back-translation, as 'meaning' is much deeper than that. Meaning is what we make from a process drama experience—what it means to *us*. What we have seen, felt, interpreted and reflected on. In reflecting on her own *Seal Wife* process drama structure, O'Neill (2017) reminds us of this point: "Eventually everyone takes away their own meanings from an aesthetic event, and develops their own responses to the work" (p. 29).

Intercultural meaning relates to students' reflection, to students' questioning of their values. The careful handling and nurturing of the elements of drama, as a symbolic system with attention to the intercultural sphere, opens up endless layers of intercultural meaning-making. These forms of intercultural dramatic meaning may be experienced, in various degrees, during or after a dramatic encounter. The experience itself is important, but not enough; reflection on the experience is vital (Bolton, 1979; Bowell & Heap, 2017; Heathcote, in O'Neill, 2015; O'Neill, 1995; O'Toole & Dunn, 2015). In a performative approach to language teaching, such reflection needs to consider the intercultural dimension through a performative lens, as "questions of embodiment, action, behaviour, and agency are dealt with interculturally" (Schechner, 2013, p. 2). The experience and the reflection upon that experience can generate intercultural aesthetic engagement, as illustrated in the previous chapter (see "Intercultural Aesthetic Engagement" in Chapter 3).

Attention to the intercultural aesthetic dimension also resonates with what Kramsch (2009) calls "symbolic competence" in the context of intercultural education, including:

- An ability to understand the symbolic value of symbolic forms and the different cultural memories evoked by different symbolic systems;
- An ability to draw on the semiotic diversity afforded by multiple languages to reframe ways of seeing familiar events, create alternative realities, and find an appropriate subject position 'between languages';
- An ability to look both *at* and *through* language (p. 201, original emphasis).

These points, and particularly the ability to look both *at* and *through* language, acquire a symbolic meaning in process drama, taking us back to the concept of double masking (Tschurtschenthaler, 2013), that is, the "the experience of the other language from within the other's point of view" (p. 230), when playing a character and then reflecting on the experience it generates. In Workshop 2, the meaning made by each participant transpired through the reflection in-between the episodes, as well as at the end of the drama. Experience and reflection of students' responses to the various elements of drama, prompted by an aesthetically charged pre-text, can enable second language learners to explore their meaning-making.

4   Pre-text and Dramatic Tension

Finally, an important factor impacting on the aesthetic dimension in process drama is the choice of pre-text. At this point, it is important to clarify the differences between a pre-text and a stimulus. As Haseman and O'Toole point out: "A simple stimulus may kindle interest but it is seldom sufficient to launch a drama that opens rich possibilities for groups and audiences to test their own attitudes and beliefs and to extract meanings" (2017, p. xiii). While pre-text and stimulus may be mistakenly taken to be synonyms, they are not. In L2 educational settings, a lesson is often initiated by a stimulus, that is, an icebreaker to create conversation about a certain topic. This could be, for example, an illustration of a market square used to introduce a theme or a topic, and the language related to the semantic area or shopping at a market place. The picture is a stimulus to encourage students to recall their own shopping experiences, to introduce language related to shopping at market places, to elicit expressions that will be practised later. A stimulus introduces the topic and is forgotten; it ushers in the theme, and fades away. A pre-text ushers in the theme and is re-membered, by affording inspiration for what is to come.

Bundy and Dunn (2006) conducted an inquiry on the kinds of pre-texts preferred by drama teachers. They asked a group of drama teachers to choose one pre-text, among many presented to them, that they found inspirational. The pre-texts presented included music, poems, paintings, photographs, objects, articles and a traditional tale. The authors report what the surveyed drama teachers collectively identified as the characteristics of useful pre-texts:

- Inherent tension
- Ability to raise questions for us, e.g. in the unknown
- The mystery, relationships suggested
- The potential for multi-dimensional qualities
- A juxtaposition of the unusual
- Provocation of the emotions and intellect
- Ambiguous or able to be made ambiguous
- Potential for irony
- Sows the seed for forthcoming action, our attention arrested by details not provided and thus questions raised (O'Neill) (sic)
- Open ended
- Creates visual images for us
- Involves, infers a future or a past
- Possibility for many themes emerging
- An impulse to generate action in response is elicited
- A range of scenes, tasks, characters, perspectives are possible
- Relevant to the age group of participants
- Allows for differences in skills, abilities, and interests of the students
- Potential to meet specific curriculum needs (2006, p. 20).

This list can inform us about some of the inherent qualities of a useful pre-text in a process drama. A pre-text must inspire questions 'in the unknown' and provide imagery—in line with age group and curriculum needs. Crucially, it must have the potential for dramatic tension. In fact, dramatic tension is the first item on the list.

Being able to choose a pre-text and knowing tacitly how to work with that pre-text imply understanding the art of making constraints—creating an urge, but then deliberately slowing down the course of action so that participants in role cannot obtain their goal immediately. This basic structuring device is the core of dramatic art. The emotional current created by a pre-text, O'Neill (1995) holds, can evoke an aesthetic mood and can be connected to a theme, feeling or idea. It is the responsibility of the teacher/artist, O'Neill continues, to "find the focus that creates imperative tension and provides a vehicle for the themes and images to be explored" (in Taylor and Warner, 2006, p. 18).

5   Making the Skeleton Dance

As O'Toole notes, "models are chains of ideas linked together and observed at work: skeletons which can be made to dance at the command of the observer" (Walford in O'Toole, 1992, p. 15). In conceptualising the *Dramawise* model, Haseman and O'Toole (2017) introduce the elements as a model, or skeleton, and then refer to "making the skeleton dance" (p. 132). Yet, it is worth pointing out that in the quote above the model does not dance by itself; it is *made to dance*. 'Making the skeleton dance', as Haseman and O'Toole call the active manipulation of the dramatic elements, requires a kind of know-how, which we will explore in the next chapter. However, before concentrating on *making* the skeleton dance, it is important to focus on the skeleton itself, and on the choreography informing the dance. As Haseman and O'Toole (2017) recognise: "Understanding the elements of drama is essential to managing them in order to create your own drama" (p. 163).

Let us come back to Sam's story and the jugglers' adventures. In Workshop 3 (*The Jugglers*) a number of drama strategies are outlined, each implying the elements of drama and their active manipulation. What I have included in the structure below is the skeleton, and choreography of the dance, though we do not see the dance itself. What would such dance look like? Some possibilities have been hinted at throughout this chapter (see "Sam's Story" and "Dramatic Situation, Character and Relationships" in this chapter), and although not all those mentioned occurred in the actual workshop, while those that did occur have not been reported at all. I could have included more information, describing the episodes meticulously as they occurred in that specific drama session. While this might have been helpful to give an example of an L2 drama workshop, it would have run the risk of giving the reader the false perception of process drama as a ready-made set of instructions. This risk is embedded in O'Neill's (2017) comment: "The problem about presenting a drama structure in this way is that the process can easily become a scenario—a fixed structure to be reproduced in the same way" (p. 27). Instead, the drama structure below is deliberately stripped of the details: it focuses on the skeleton, but leaves out the flesh. It hints at the choreography, but omits the dance.

Workshop 3: The Jugglers

Description: This workshop explores issues related to migration, working with language learners new to drama.

Students' Context—Inspiration for the Workshop: The *Cultura e Accoglienza* 2017 project, provided 30 adult asylum seekers and migrants in Padua (Italy) with access to the University of Padova's library, the possibility to audit some modules, a tutor, and access to Italian (L2) classes. As part of this project, in collaboration with Fiona Dalziel, in 2017 we conducted a series of performative language workshops. This particular workshop (The Jugglers) was also open to international students. Participants were a group of male and female migrants from Nigeria, Cameroon and Gambia, as well as three international students from China and Germany. All were learning Italian (L2) at the University of Padua.

Pre-text: A participant's story (with permission from the storyteller).

Educational Aims: Introducing the participants to basic elements of drama; introducing participants to intercultural awareness and reflection.

Level: A2 to B1 (CEFR).

Duration: Three hours.

Workshop 3 The Jugglers

	Drama strategy
Initiation phase	**Step 1. Warm-up:** a. Breathing awareness b. Voice awareness c. *Emotional Palette:* voice, eyes, hands, full body, space, locomotion
Experiential phase	**Step 2. Sharing stories**: In small groups, participants share a personal story related to their first day in Italy. Not all participants have to share a story—only those who volunteer to do so. Write useful language structures and connectors on the board, to help with structuring a story
	Step 3. Pre-text choice: Volunteers share their stories with the rest of the group. As they do, listen carefully to identify one story to work with. Choose a story that is not too raw or personal, and that has potential for *intercultural dramatic tension, focus, roles* and *situation*. Ask the student for permission to play with his/her story. The point is not to *replicate* the story, nor to go deep into it on a psychological level, but to use it as a platform, to *extend* the story beyond its timeline, focussing on a secondary character or setting
	Step 4. Building context: Brainstorm with the student the language related to the story—wherever possible, search online for images to create language and contextual background to the drama. Find a question that holds a degree of *dramatic intercultural tension*
	Step 5. Teacher in Role: Take on the role of one character in the story, connected to the question above. Start *inside* the situation and suddenly stop, hinting at something that prevents you from continuing. Hint at, but do not reveal, building from the participants' improvisation, a mystery or a dilemma for the participants to solve
	Step 6. Tableaux: Invite participants to break into small groups and create a possible explanation, or back story, to the Teacher in Role's main dilemma a. *Create*: Students work in their groups, to physically try out different solutions to embody their key moment in the story—using levels, body language and props b. *Present*: Groups show their interpretation to the others—frozen images with no dialogue c. *Respond*: After each group presents, the others are invited to describe and interpret the body language. Use this discussion as a springboard to reflect on meaning and storytelling. What is happening? What does it evoke?

(continued)

Workshop 3 (continued)

	Drama strategy
Reflective phase	**Step 7. Language revision**: Recap all language structures learned during the session
	Step 8. Final reflection: Reflect on the intercultural dimension of the drama

This chapter has focused on the elements of drama, framed around the process drama literature. The core of the chapter illustrated how the elements of drama can be revisited from an intercultural perspective, and the implications this might have for second language learning. These include intercultural dramatic tension and the relationship between the pre-text and dramatic tension, in structuring process drama. The discussion was presented through a praxial approach that aims to bridge theory and practice. Yet, knowledge of the elements of drama—the coordinates to navigate the aesthetic dimension—is not sufficient; we also need an intuitive decision-making aptitude, to be able to interpret these coordinates in an ocean of possibilities. To address this question, we turn to the artistry of knowing-in-action.

References

Adžović, N. (2005). *Rom. Il popolo invisibile*. Roma: Editore Palombi.
Allern, T.-H. (2001). Myth and metaxy, and the myth of 'metaxis'. In B. Rasmussen & A.-L. Østern (Eds.), *Playing Betwixt and Between: The IDEA dialogues 2001* (pp. 77–85). Bergen: IDEA Publications.
Boal, A. (1985). *Theatre of the oppressed*. New York: Theatre Communications Group.
Boal, A. (1995). *The rainbow of desire: The Boal method of theatre and therapy*. London: Routledge.
Bolton, G. (1979). *Towards a theory of drama in education*. Harlow: Longman.
Bowell, P., & Heap, B. S. (2001). *Planning process drama*. London: David Fulton.
Bowell, P., & Heap, B. S. (2017). *Putting process drama into action: The dynamics of practice*. Abingdon, Oxon: Routledge.

Brecht, B. (1964). *Brecht on theatre: The development of an aesthetic*. London: Methuen.
Bundy, P. (1999). *Dramatic tension: Towards an understanding of 'tension of intimacy'*. (Doctoral dissertation), Retrieved from https://www120.secure.griffith.edu.au/rch/items/dc50533c-7887-47d2-e176-f29d65389cbd/1/.
Bundy, P. (2003). Aesthetic engagement in the drama process. *Research in Drama Education: The Journal of Applied Theatre and Performance, 8*(2), 171–181.
Bundy, P., & Dunn, J. (2006). Pretexts and possibilities. *The Journal of the Queensland Association for Drama in Education: Drama Queensland Says, 29*(2), 19–21.
Courtney, R. (1995). *Drama and feeling: An aesthetic theory*. Montreal: McGill-Queen's University Press.
Davis, S. (2015). *Perezhivanie* and the experience of drama, metaxis and meaning making. *NJ: Drama Australia Journal, 39*(1), 63–75.
Dawson, S. W. (1970). *Drama and the dramatic*. London: Methuen & Co.
Fox, H. (2007). Playback theatre: Inciting dialogue and building community through personal story. *TDR/The Drama Review, 51*(4), 89–105.
Goffman, E. (1959). *The presentation of self in everyday life*. New York: Double Bay Anchor.
Greene, M. (1988). *The dialectic of freedom*. New York: Teachers College Press.
Hall, E. T. (1959). *The silent language* (Vol. 3). New York: Doubleday.
Haseman, B., & O'Toole, J. (2017). *Dramawise reimagined*. Sydney: Currency Press.
Kao, S.-M., & O'Neill, C. (1998). *Words into worlds: Learning a second language through process drama*. London: Ablex Publishing Corporation.
Kramsch, C. (2009). *The multilingual subject*. Oxford: Oxford University Press.
Lima, M. G. (1995). From aesthetics to psychology: Notes on Vygotsky's "Psychology of Art". *Anthropology & Education Quarterly, 26*(4), 410–424.
Morgan, N., & Saxton, J. (1987). *Teaching drama: A mind of many wonders*. Cheltenham: Stanley Thornes.
Neelands, J., & Goode, T. (1995). Playing in the margins of meaning: The ritual aesthetic in community performance. *NJ: Drama Australia Journal, 19*(1), 83–97.
O'Neill, C. (1995). *Drama worlds: A framework for process drama*. Portsmouth: Heinemann.
O'Neill, C. (2015). *Dorothy Heathcote on education and drama: Essential writings*. Abington, Oxfon: Routledge.

O'Neill, C. (2017). Seal Wife—Random observations. *NJ: Drama Australia Journal, 41*(1), 27–29.

O'Toole, J. (1992). *The process of drama: Negotiating art and meaning.* London: Routledge.

O'Toole, J., & Dunn, J. (2015). *Pretending to learn: Teaching drama in the primary and middle years.*

Pheasant, P. (2015). The epiphany in process drama and language learning. *p-e-r-f-o-r-m-a-n-c-e, 2*(1–2), http://p-e-r-f-o-r-m-a-n-c-e.org/?p=919.

Ryle, G. (1949). *The concept of mind.* London: Hutchinson.

Salas, J. (1996). *Improvising real life: Personal story in playback theatre.* Dubuque, Iowa: Kendall/Hunt Publishing Company.

Schechner, R. (2013). *Performance studies: An introduction* (3rd ed.). London: Routledge.

Styan, J. L. (1960). *The elements of drama.* Cambridge: Cambridge University Press.

Swain, M. (2006). Languaging, agency and collaboration in advanced second language proficiency. In H. Byrnes (Ed.), *Advanced language learning: The contribution of Halliday and Vygotsky* (pp. 95–108). New York: Continuum.

Taliaferro, D. M. (1998). Signifying self: Re-presentations of the double-consciousness in the work of Maxine Greene. *The Passionate Mind of Maxine Greene: I "Am–Not Yet"* (pp. 89–121). London: Falmer Press.

Taylor, P., & Warner, C. D. (2006). *Structure and spontaneity: The process drama of Cecily O'Neill.* Sterling, VA: Trentham.

Tschurtschenthaler, H. (2013). *Drama-based foreign language learning: Encounters between self and others.* Munster: Waxmann.

Vygotsky, L. S. (1926/1971). *The psychology of art.* Cambridge, MA: MIT Press.

Wagner, B. J. (1976). *Dorothy Heathcote: Drama as a learning medium.* Washington, DC: National Education Association.

5

Knowing-in-Action

In the previous chapter we have considered the elements of drama as coordinates to navigate the aesthetic dimension. Arguably they are essential elements for drama to be effective. However, it is no use having the coordinates to navigate if we don't have the intuitive know-how to interpret those coordinates. How does the teacher/artist know how to create the conditions for a particular dramatic element to arise? How do we know, for example, what to say (or not say), what to do (or not do), to increase dramatic tension when it is fading away? What does one say, and when, to change the focus, to slow down the pace, or to harness a particular mood? Knowing-in-action, the subject of this chapter, relates to these questions. As Dewey (1925/1981) has it: "Experience, with the Greeks, signified a store of practical wisdom, a fund of insights useful in conducting the affairs of life" (p. 266). The teacher/artist will need to draw from his/her fund of insights, responding to the situation with presence and incisiveness. Yet, how do we build a fund of insights? How do we access it, in real time, when confronted with unique situations embedded in context-specific learning experiences, across two or more languages and cultures?

In *Experience, Nature and Art*, Dewey (1925/1981) discusses experience as a particular way of being in the world, related to active perception and practical wisdom, and the ability to act upon that practical wisdom. Aristotle refers to this concept as *phronesis*, a particular type of wisdom related to practice. Phronesis has been defined and redefined in a number of ways in the literature. I refer to this concept as the "wise practical reasoning in education", that needs to be coupled with teacher artistry—sensibility and the ability to make judgement through a feeling mode, in an educational context (Eisner, 2002, p. 375). It is a form of practical wisdom related to reflection, both tacit and explicit, conveying the relationship between reflection and action, embodied in practice (Kinsella, 2012). To access what Dewey calls our store of practical wisdom, we need to become aware of a mode of knowing that includes, but goes beyond, cognitive knowing. We need to become aware of the pedagogical tact (Van Manen, 2008) that operates tacitly to inform our gestures and intuition in an educational setting, adding a further layer of simplexity (Berthoz, 2012) to the artistry of embodying language in action.

1   The Reflective Practitioner

Reflective practice is a learned conscious process, bringing us to examine our beliefs, attitudes and behaviour in a professional context. With Rokeach (1968), I define 'belief' as "any simple proposition, conscious or unconscious, inferred from what a person says or does". 'Attitudes', on the other hand, are "a relatively enduring organisation of beliefs about an object or situation predisposing one to respond in some preferential manner" (pp. 112–113). Attitudes are therefore a system of beliefs that can be overt, or covert, that influence behaviour. In *How we Think*, Dewey (1910/1998) conceptualises reflection as an essential aim of education. Schön studied and expanded Dewey's work and elaborated his own theory of reflection, following an experiential–intuitive model. He states: "Let us search, instead, for an epistemology of practice implicit in the artistic, intuitive processes which some practitioners do bring to situations of uncertainty, instability, uniqueness, and value conflict" (1983, p. 49).

In his seminal work, *The Reflective Practitioner* (1983), Schön identifies a kind of knowing that is tacit and intrinsic to action: "In our spontaneous, intuitive choices our knowing is tacit, implicit in our pattern of acquisition; our knowing is *in* our action" (1983, p. 49, original emphasis). He believes knowing-in-action to be an essential competence for any professional, in any given field, as a tool to respond to the 'action-present', defined as "a period of time, variable with the context, during which we can still make a difference to the situation at hand— our thinking serves to reshape what we are doing while we are doing it" (1987, p. 26). This knowing-in-action mode involves the implicit decision-making that practitioners bring to unique situations they deal with. It is characterised by those actions, recognitions and judgements that we carry out spontaneously, without premeditation. A peculiar feature of this kind of knowing-in-action, according to Schön, is that we may not be able to pinpoint having learnt the skills that informed a particular action, and are usually "unable to describe the knowing which our action reveals" (1983, p. 54).

To further unpack this construct, Schön recognises two essential features of knowing-in-action: reflection-*in*-action and reflection-*on*-action. Reflection-in-action relates to the kind of inventiveness, flexible decision-making that enables practitioners to respond to challenges in real time. Reflection-on-action refers to reflecting on one's choices after the event has occurred. The difference between the two kinds of reflection is temporal: in the former, one reflects while doing something, reacting in the action-present; in the latter, one reflects after the event has occurred, considering one's actions and their effects to apply those insights in a similar situation. Both kinds of reflection enable practitioners to "cope with the troublesome divergent situations of practice" (p. 62). Schön's point is that these divergent situations are the norm rather than the exception and cannot be passively received. They need to be actively unearthed:

> By placing a great emphasis on problem solving, we ignore problem *setting*, the process by which we define the decision to be made, the ends to be achieved, the means which may be chosen. In real-world practice, problems do not present themselves to the practitioner as givens.

They must be constructed from the materials of problematic situations which are puzzling, troubling and uncertain. (p. 40, original emphasis)

Problematic, puzzling situations afford new solutions to emerge. For this to occur, the reflective practitioner needs to adopt with the client (i.e., the learner) a collaborative relationship of mutual respect, rather than a controlling relationship. Schön synthesises the features of such a relationship by comparing opposite sets of belief systems in what he calls the reflective practitioner's contract (1983, p. 300), as reported in Table 1.

From the first row of Table 1, we see that the reflective contract suggests a teacher/artist operating under a reflective practitioner's paradigm openly accepts that s/he is not the only knowledgeable person in the group. Rather, the participants also inform the ecosystem of the classroom by bringing their experiences, cultures, languages. Acknowledging these is crucial, as they can inform insights into creating tension, mood, focus and other elements of drama, in an intercultural perspective (see Chapter 4). As the second row of Table 1 indicates, the reflective practitioner seeks out connections to tap into the affective dimension of learning. In the third row of Table 1, the teacher/artist operating from Schön's reflective practitioner's model honours an authentic, mutual relationship, based on respect rather than sympathy. Finally, the fourth

Table 1 Reflective practitioners' contract (Schön, 1983, p. 300)

Expert's belief system	Reflective practitioner's belief system
I am presumed to know and must claim to do so, *regardless* of my own uncertainty	I am presumed to know, *but* I am not the only one to have relevant knowledge. My uncertainties are a *source of learning*
I keep my *distance* from the client and hold onto the expert's role	I seek out *connections* to the client's *thoughts* and *feelings*
I give the client a sense of expertise, but convey a feeling of *sympathy* as a 'sweetener'	I allow the client's respect for my knowledge to *emerge* from their discovery of it in the situation
I look for admiration and *status* in the client's response to my professional persona	I look for the sense of freedom and of *real connection* to the client, no *longer needing* to maintain a professional façade

row suggests that the reflective practitioner actively seeks to establish a genuine sense of connection with the students, instead of hiding behind a fabricated 'sage on the stage' façade.

As mentioned in the opening, a belief system is manifested in attitudes that can be overt or covert. It follows that we may or may not be aware of our system of beliefs regulating our behaviour in the classroom unless we deliberately turn our focus towards it. Indeed, just as we hold multiple, fluctuating and contradictory identities (Akkerman & Meijer, 2011), rather than having just one linear belief system, we may uphold several sub-identities and belief systems, fluctuating as we progress through life and, at times, contradicting themselves. We may adhere to a set of beliefs tacitly inherited, and never questioned in childhood. These may be embedded within the particular sub-culture/s we were raised in, and we may consequently come across different sub-cultures, with different belief systems. Bilingual speakers, for example, may be immersed and operate between several belief systems associated with the languages they use. Pavlenko's (2014) research sheds fascinating light onto this territory (see "The Bilingual Reflective Practitioner" in this chapter). Regardless of how many languages we speak, awareness of our belief systems is an important condition for becoming a reflective practitioner.

2   Reflective Practice in Process Drama

Saxton (2015) refers to unexpected moments in drama as moments that "destabilize yet delight us" (p. 255). Her practice appears to be closely aligned with Schön's reflective model. In particular, she reflects on her effort to pay attention to individual students. In order to build a genuine sense of connection with each student, she allocates the first few minutes of her classes to what she named the 'Rialto' activity (from Solanio and Shylock's line "What news from the Rialto?" in *The Merchant of Venice*), that is, students sharing their news and updates, creating a sense of community in the classroom. Anderson (2015) similarly notes this aspect, reflecting on the teacher–student rapport that is created beyond the content of the curriculum: "It came as a revelation that what I had thought of as wasted time was actually crucial for building a trusting relationship" (p. 178). Both practitioners offer examples of reflection-on-action operating from Schön's reflective practitioner contract.

Reflection-in-action and reflection-on-action are vital components of reflective practice in process drama. More than two decades ago, Taylor (1996) suggested that it is the improvisational nature of process drama that *demands* teacher/artists to reflect-in-action, focussing his research on reflective practitioners new to process drama. He identifies openness, receptivity and honesty as the features of a practitioner who reflects in action. Taylor (1998) analyses his relationship with a teacher who participated in his research, noting the teacher "opened up for public scrutiny" and "released himself into a learner role" (p. 215). This notion of 'opening up for public scrutiny' is a decisive feature of reflection-in-action. Neelands (2006) refers to it as reflexivity-in-practice: a practitioner's commitment to make one's practice reflexive, in terms of transparency of the processes that underpin it (p. 19). A good example of such reflexivity-in-practice is Duffy's (2015) edited volume, featuring a wealth of insight from leading practitioners in the field reflecting on action. Reflecting on his early drama practice, Duffy (2015) states:

> I understood the techniques and had the procedural knowledge. What I lacked was the insights and experience of the artist. An artist discerns, discovers, chooses and crafts. I merely executed. An artist sees multiple possibilities and outcomes; I steered lessons towards only one goal – regardless of what was unfolding before me within the drama. (p. 4)

Duffy sets out to investigate the difference between procedural knowledge and artistic insight in his practice, realising that these two modes of knowing are distinct and lead to a difference in quality.

O'Mara's (1999, 2006, 2016) research focuses on the construct of reflection-in-action in process drama. She is fascinated by reflection-in-action, noting its aesthetic, methodological and pedagogical value: "Often in the process of reflection-in-action we invent new forms of drama or experiment with new ways of constructing meaning through unique uses of dramatic form" (2006, p. 42). Her doctoral study attempts to capture the ephemeral nature of her reflection-in-action, by identifying four main factors: (1) Self: recognising the role that one's personal needs play in the teaching; (2) Empathy: being empathically attuned to read the class level engagement; (3) Management: creating a specific atmosphere for dramatic action; and (4) Artistry: focussing on artistry to produce aesthetic moments (1999, pp. 278–286). To examine this further, O'Mara draws on O'Neill's (1995) description of process drama: episodic structure, absence of a script, integral audience, and extended time frame. Table 2 summarises O'Mara's analysis of process drama's integral features, and the kind of reflection-in-action related to each one.

O'Mara (2006) highlights the possibility of reflection-in-action as a research methodology, positioning it "at the most qualitative edge of the spectrum" (p. 43). Her analysis (Table 2) suggests that, in process drama, reflection-in-action occurs on three different planes: within one episode, across several episodes, and across several sessions. Dunn and Stinson (2011) also reflect on the layered nature of reflection-in-action in process drama, recognising two levels: the *macro* and *micro* level. The macro level refers to those decisions made before a drama begins, like selecting the pre-text and preparing a learning sequence. The micro level of reflection-in-action refers to "the 'in the moment' artistry needed to make effective decisions in light of the participants' responses" (p. 619). This distinction significantly influenced my doctoral analysis on reflection-in-action and reflection-on-action, as discussed in Chapter 11.

Table 2 O'Mara (1999) reflection-in-a action (p. 318)

Process drama features (O'Neill, 1995)	Reflection-in-action (O'Mara, 1999)
Episodic structure of process drama	The teacher needs to reflect-in-action as a participant to create the episodes
Absence of script	The teacher needs to reflect-in-action to forward the drama as director
Integral audience	The teacher needs to reflect-in-action to monitor class relationships and participation
Extended time frame	The teacher needs to reflect-in-action between sessions to prepare for future episodes

More recently, O'Mara (2016) extends her research on teachers' reflection-in-action in process drama, analysing the nature of drama teachers' thinking on their feet. In the *Quality Learning through Process Drama* project, she interviewed twenty-five drama teacher educators about the drama strategies they use and how they choose what strategy to use, as they train pre-service teachers. O'Mara discusses four themes emerging from the data: safety, conversion, theory in action and apprenticeship (p. 105). The first theme, 'safety', relates to drama teachers' value in creating a 'safe space' for the drama participants. The second theme, 'conversion' relates to what she describes as the teachers being so passionate about drama that they displayed an "almost evangelistic energy" to the teachers' approach (p. 106). The third theme, 'theory in action' relates to metaxis, the dual state held by process drama participants (see "Intercultural Dramatic Tension" in Chapter 4). O'Mara's findings report of a participant explaining how she navigates through different teachers' functions as "running on a couple of channels" (p. 108), an interesting imagery to describe the kind of reflection-in-action needed to facilitate process drama. Finally, under the theme 'apprenticeship' O'Mara notes that many drama teachers would set up apprenticeship experiences, often in schools for the pre-service teachers to implement process drama pedagogy. This reinforces once more the experiential nature of the form, and the need to provide an embodied experience as well as a theoretical experience. From her findings, O'Mara develops a model that features reflection-in-action, aesthetics, dramatic form, planning, and students' individual classes as central issues, pivoting around the attention of the teacher when working within the dramatic frame (p. 113).

Bowell and Heap (2005, 2017) further analyse reflection-in-action in process drama, focussing on the teacher and students' function. On the one hand, the teacher/artist plays four different roles, or functions: playwright, actor, director and teacher. These functions operate interchangeably, requiring what the authors term Quadripartite Thinking (QT). While facilitating a process drama, the teacher needs to wear these four hats at once, "between two worlds and four functions" (2005, p. 64). Meanwhile, the participants also engage in a Quadripartite Response (QR), functioning as playwright, actor, director and learner. In a recent elaboration, the authors note how each of these functions also interacts with the "self-interactive self" (2017, p. 139), thus adding a layer of introspection to the equation within the four functions. The authors re-phrase these functions as: "self-interacting playwright", "self-interacting director", "self-interacting actor", "self-interacting teacher/learner" (p. 100). Bowell and Heap dedicate a chapter of their book, *Putting Process Drama into Action*, to each function, exploring them great detail. This 'multifaceted spiral' of creative discourse is initiated by the facilitator, and bounces back and forward between the facilitator and the participants in a "reciprocal 'call and response' interchange of ideas, feelings, actions and reactions taking place between teacher and students" (2017, p. 99). A process drama teacher faces the challenge of managing the QT/QR 'call and response' with spontaneity and intuition.

At this point, it may be useful to revisit O'Mara's (1999) early analysis, and to compare it with Bowell and Heap's creative spiral. In Table 3 below, the third column shows the functions, corresponding to specific features of reflection-in-action in process drama, following Bowell and Heap's (2017) most recent classification.

This level of analysis in the different functions related to reflection-in-action in process drama may help the teacher/artist, with time

Table 3 A comparison of the models of O'Neill, O'Mara and Bowell and Heap

Process drama features (O'Neill, 1995)	Reflection-in-action (O'Mara, 1999)	Creative spiral (Bowell & Heap, 2017)
Episodic structure of process drama	The teacher needs to reflect-in-action as a participant to create the episodes	Actor function
Absence of script	The teacher needs to reflect-in-action to forward the drama as director	Director function
Integral audience	The teacher needs to reflect-in-action to monitor class relationships and participation	Teacher function
Extended time frame	The teacher needs to reflect-in-action between sessions to prepare for future episodes	Playwright function

and experience, to have more confidence in the intuitive decision-making process, aiming "to help the teacher to negotiate the *tricky terrain* of the unfolding drama, where choices have consequences" (Bowell & Heap, 2017, p. 7, my emphasis).

Saxton (2015) reflects on this 'tricky terrain', elaborating on the concept of 'failing' and on the implicit learning that comes with the act of failing: "Learning, it seems to me, is an ongoing process of exploration, in which failure is built in" (p. 261). She talks about the 'phronesis of failure' and explores the concept of failing, and what one can learn from failing, in drama. Phronesis, as mentioned in the opening, refers to a particular type of wisdom related to praxis. Saxton engages with reflective work to "untie the complexity of the reflections" on her own failures, "to understand how failure may work in professional growth" (p. 259). Schön also writes about failure, arguing that we usually start reflecting in action when we are stuck or dissatisfied. Teachers are expected to act with confidence and poise; society does not look up to 'failing teachers'. Quite the opposite; failure is a taboo in our culture and especially in the classroom. However, as Saxton reminds us, failing is related to professional growth.

In a way, failing is also part of what Shulman (2004) defines pedagogical content knowledge. This kind of knowledge relates to the most effective teaching strategies—the fruit of engaging with educational theory as well as experience: having failed, having reflected, having developed knowing-in-action related to teaching. Drawing on Shulman, Dunn and Stinson (2011) refer to the 'integrated knowledge' required by the L2/drama teacher as "dual pedagogical content knowledge" (p. 630). The *dual* essence of pedagogical content knowledge entails juggling the aesthetic *and* the educational aspects of the intercultural and dramatic experience, in the target language.

3   Pedagogical Tact

Van Manen (1997, 2008) is interested in investigating the phenomenological experience of reflection-in-action. He argues that "the practical active knowledge that animates teaching is something that belongs phenomenologically more closely to the whole embodied being of the person" (2008, p. 17). He developed the notion of pedagogical tact, intended as "a kind of practical normative intelligence that is governed by insight while relying on feeling" (p. 16). As he puts it:

> My practical knowledge "is" my felt sense of the classroom, my feeling who I am as a teacher, my felt understanding of my students, my felt grasp of the things that I teach, the mood that belongs to my world at school, the hallways, the staffroom, and of course this classroom. (p. 18)

He frames reflection-in-action as lived- and felt-experience of the teacher—that is, reflection as an embodied felt-experience. He describes pedagogical tact as a 'grasped' reflection: "The phenomenology of practice involves a different way of knowing the world. Whereas theory 'thinks' the world, practice 'grasps' the world". This 'grasping' is conceptualised, as a body-centred sensuous knowing. He argues for a kind of 'pathic' understanding, as we "grasp the world pathically" (p. 19). This is an understanding related to the sensuality of body, to personal presence, to relational perceptiveness. He talks about 'active confidence' as a kind of knowing, an immediate and thoughtful pedagogical action within tact, "situated practical knowledge that inheres in the act of tact itself" (p. 14). This confidence is achieved by maintaining presence and by actively listening to the students and other contextual signs, including our own discernment, as we exercise pedagogical tact.

Van Manen identifies that the problem experienced by some teachers is that this kind of reflection is not easily captured in everyday language: "We need a language that can express and communicate these understandings. This language needs to remain oriented to the experiential or lived sensibility of the lifeworld" (p. 19). The arts can provide symbolic forms of expression, oriented towards communicating such lived sensibility. Every teacher will have a unique language of expression. For me, it is poetry.

4   Playing to Be 'Teacher'

In my early years of L2 teaching, I was feeling frustrated by my inability to create meaningful learning experiences for my students. The resources mandated by the curriculum were flat and uninteresting, filled with communicative clichés. I myself fell victim of those clichés, although I 'grasped', to borrow Van Manen's language, that the learning generated was shallow. My frustration is encapsulated well in a poem I wrote on 22 September 2005. On that day, a language inspector came to my class to monitor the standards of my teaching, specifically to check whether it was in line with the institute's teaching philosophy. The institute's director had been warning us of the inspector's visit and we were encouraged to pay particular attention to the planning and facilitation of that class. I had carefully crafted a sequence of activities to showcase the school's commitment to communicative teaching, the institute's teaching approach at the time.

One activity, in particular, included a set of juggling balls that my students had to throw to each other in circles, while practising indirect pronouns. On the outside, it must have looked like a clever activity, as the inspector wrote a glowing report. Students were having fun, learning indirect pronouns in a friendly social environment. Throughout the class I asked the students to read, to write, to speak, to watch a video, to listen, to be active, to interact and to communicate. For the sake of the action-oriented approach, so important in the Common European Framework of Reference for Languages (CEFR), I even asked my students to have language practice games with juggling balls. What could be more action-based than *that*? My class was ticking all the boxes. Or was it? While it may have looked like a fun class, during the lesson I had the dreadful feeling that I was a fraud. I was facilitating a series of disconnected, meaningless exercises. I crammed my classes with a series of activities that the inspector praised, but that I perceived as useless for any significant learning. That hurt. After that class I wrote a poem, in Italian. I include a short extract below, followed by the English translation:

Oggi a lezione,
che tormento, che illusione
Guardare il video senza vedere,
avere voglia di non sapere.
Con gli studenti pieni di sbadigli
e un sorriso stracolmo di insicurezze

giocando a fare l'insegnante
con mille paure sbriciolate in tasca.
[…]

Today's class,
the agony of faking it,
watching without seeing,
with no passion left for knowledge.
Flashing smiles dipped in self-doubt
at my ever-yawning students
playing to be 'teacher'
a thousand fears crumbled in my pockets.
[…]
22/09/2005

The poem captures a series of images that start from the present-moment of the body. An example: on that day I was wearing silk trousers with pockets. During the break I didn't have time to finish an oat bar I had been eating, which I put in my pocket. Later on, back in class as I put my hand into my pocket I felt the texture of the oats crumble. The sensory feeling of the crumbs scratching on the smooth silk pocket lining was anchored with my feeling of angst, in the moment I realised the lack of purpose in the activities. This sensory connection was captured in the poem, in the lines: "Playing to be teacher/a thousand fears *crumbled* in my pockets".

Having put this feeling into words is now enabling me, many years on, to remember that class; to remember that sensation and the feeling associated with it; to reflect on action. The "agony of faking it" and "flashing smiles dipped in self-doubt", related to my frustration in witnessing students disengage with ineffective second language methodologies, while I was unable to engage my "ever-yawning students". I have translated *giocando a fare l'insegnante* as 'playing to be teacher', although it could easily translate as 'pretending to be a teacher' as well as, adopting children's talk, 'playing teacher' as in: 'let's play: I'll be the teacher'. The English translation here can capture only vaguely the nuances of this sentence, which simultaneously expresses self-doubt and lack of confidence, coated in a naïve tone of children's play, with a touch of sarcasm. Going back to Saxton's (2015) discourse on the phronesis of failure, this feeling of failure led me to experiment with different avenues for teaching, researching into the artistry of process drama for language learning. As Brown and Sawyer (2016) suggest: "Reflection is not the product, but the generator of further reflection and new ways to perceive and imagine practice" (p. 3). Interestingly, the process of reflection in more than one language, including the process of translation and back-translation, has now added some depth to that reflective process.

5   The Bilingual Reflective Practitioner

The use of two or more languages is embedded in the everyday life of many L2 teachers. With the exception of those L2 teachers who teach their own language in their own country, as L2 teachers we operate within an intricate mosaic of possibilities. We may teach our first language in a non-native country, to students who speak other languages. We may teach a language we have acquired, to students who speak our first language. We may feel like we have two homes, three homes, four homes, no home; we may feel like we are permanently in-between homes, or belonging to a 'third place' (Kramsch, 1993). Life may also bring us to switch the language/s we teach. We may be teaching our first language for many years, and then having to re-invent ourselves as teachers of an acquired language. This spool of possibilities captures the contextual diversity of L2 teacher educators' backgrounds.

According to linguist Grosjean (2008, 2010), many of the teachers described above would be described as bilingual. He defines bilingual individuals as those who speak more than one language on a daily basis. The proficiency in the language may vary, and the time of having learnt a second language may also vary, but these factors in themselves are not indicators of being bilingual. What defines an individual as bilingual is that s/he lives and operates within two or more languages. Conversely, the term 'bilingual' is subject to several myths (Grosjean, 2010). One is that bilingual individuals do not have an accent in their acquired language. Yet a definite lack of accent will occur only if the two languages were acquired during childhood. If the language/s is learnt after school age (i.e., late bilinguals), a native-speaker accent may be hard to acquire—even though fluency and comprehension may be native-like. Other myths associated with bilingualism, according to Grosjean, relate to bilinguals being also bi-cultural, bilinguals having split personalities, or being able to express their emotions only in their first language.

Often, bilingual individuals write in a language other than their native one, and/or conduct a class in a language other than their mother tongue. The phenomenon of writing across two languages has been variously referred to as translingual writing (Kellman, 2000), flexible bilingualism (Creese & Blackledge, 2011), code meshing (Michael-Luna & Canagarajah, 2007) and heteroglossia (Bailey, 2007). In the last decade, the term *translanguaging* has emerged, both as a conceptual framework and as a pedagogical practice in bilingual studies. Translanguaging has received considerable attention in bilingual education (García & Lin, 2017; García & Wei, 2014; Mazak & Carroll, 2016; Velasco & García, 2014). It refers to the phenomenon of individuals who fluently communicate across more than one language, and whose identity and meaning-making are informed by the different languages they use to communicate. Rather than conceiving of the speaker's L1, L2, L3 as discreet entities, translanguaging theory considers the potential of the practice. Relevant to this discussion, it focuses on the potential that "translanguaging during the writing process—in planning, drafting, and production—is particularly important for bilingual students as they learn to self-regulate their complex linguistic repertoire" (2014, p. 7).

Although bilinguals who engage in translanguaging may be fluent in both languages and well able to communicate their emotions in both languages, the intensity of expression related to those emotions may differ in their use of the two languages. Pavlenko's research on bilingualism, cognition and emotion (2005, 2006, 2011, 2014) investigates bilinguals expressing their emotions in different languages and perceiving their identities differently. In a major study on emotions and identity, Pavlenko (2006) asked 1000 bilingual study participants to reflect on whether they felt like a different 'self' when they spoke a particular language. 675 (65%) participants (65%) responded affirmatively;

266 (26%) responded negatively; 64 (6%) gave an ambiguous response (p. 10). The majority thus indicated that speaking their first language can feel more authentic, natural, while speaking their second language may at times feel artificial.

As Pavlenko argues (2005), often (but not always) a writer's native language is influenced by spontaneous reflexes, resulting in greater expressiveness, emotionality and visceral power, and that writing in an acquired language creates more detachment between the writing and the content itself:

> The 'stepmother tongue' creates a distance between their writing and memories and allows [translingual writers] to gain control of their words, stories, and plots ... The words of the second language, simply speaking, do not feel as real, as tangible, and potentially as hurtful, as those of the first. (Pavlenko, 2005, p. 183)

Drawing on Kellman (2000) Pavlenko defines this writing phenomenon as emancipatory detachment, which gives the non-native writer an edge in terms of being more neutral and detached in her/his reflections (2005, p. 183). Kramsch (2009) also notes how speaking, or writing, in another language triggers alternative ways of apprehending one's reality:

> If language is one symbolic system among many through which our bodies and minds apprehend themselves and the world around them, then speaking or writing another language means using an alternative signifying practice, that orients the body-in-the-mind to alternative ways of perceiving, thinking, remembering the past, and imagining the future. (p. 188)

I have felt this myself on many occasions, as an Italian expat living in English-speaking countries for eighteen years. At times, interacting in an acquired tongue has allowed me to wear an 'emotional raincoat', so to speak, onto which emotions can slide like drops of rain. I can contemplate those drops of rain from the raincoat's thin, transparent layer. I still *see* them, and seeing them affects me. But they do not *soak* me in the same way. Bilingual practitioners may resonate with some of these sensations, and with how reflecting on their practice across languages may slightly shift their perceived sense of reality, emotions and identity.

In my doctoral study I used translanguaging as a method of enquiry to investigate my reflective practice. This unveiled some covert beliefs, which I consciously addressed, resulting in a key finding of the study (see Chapter 11). I followed this up in a later project, where I asked five language teachers to experiment with translanguaging in their reflection-in-action and reflection-on-action. This was the final leg of a seven-year reflective practitioner case study, discussed elsewhere (Piazzoli, 2016). The participating teachers recorded their written and oral reflection in English and in Italian, before, during and after facilitating a process drama. Below I include the structure of that process drama (*High Tide in Venezia*, Workshop 4). Currently there is a lack of methodological guidelines for translanguaging in reflective practice. I hope that this discussion can inspire other reflective practitioners to harness their insights when reflecting across more than one language.

Workshop 4: High Tide in Venezia

Description: This workshop encourages language students to immerse themselves in the target language and culture, looking at the local context from a newly found perspective.

Students' Context—Inspiration for the Workshop: Australian language students of Italian imagined they were Italian residents living in Venice, while their Italian teachers played the role of tourists. The workshop was offered as part of the 2013 Immersion Day event, at the Dante Alighieri Society, in Brisbane, Australia. I co-created and co-facilitated it with a group of language teachers from the Dante Alighieri Society. Participants were approximately fifty adult students of Italian, at different ages and levels of proficiency.

Pre-text: An extract from *Venezia è un Pesce* ('Venice is a Fish'), an evocative guide of the city of Venice by Scarpa (2000), where each chapter is based on exploring the city through a sense (sight, smell, touch, hearing, taste). This passage was used as pre-text:

With less than a metre difference in altitude, many areas are already under water; a serious emergency arises beyond one metre ten. On the terrible night of November 4th 1966, my father swam home from work. The sirens that sounded the alarm during the air raids of the Second World War have been kept on top of the *campanili*. They now announce sea raids, when the *acqua alta* is about to rise; they wake you at five, six in the morning. The sleepy inhabitants fix steel bulkheads to their front doors. (Scarpa, 2008, p. 18)

Educational Aims: Practising the Italian language in a meaningful context; seeing Venice from a different perspective; reflecting on living in Venice as a resident rather than visiting it as tourist.
Levels: B2 to C2 (CEFR).
Duration: Five hours.

Workshop 4 High Tide in Venezia

	Drama Strategies
Initiation phase	**Step 1. Warm-up**. Inner circle/outer circle. Participants, in concentric circles, exchange their names and stories about the city of Venice
	Step 2. Multimodal brainstorming. Compile a visual glossary of key terms related to Venice Watch and comment on videos of high-tide water sirens
	Step 3. Pre-text. Read aloud a passage from *Venezia è un Pesce* (see pre-text)
	Step 4. Total Physical Response (TPR). Imagine living in Venice. What would be your routine, when you hear the high-tide water siren at 5am? Practise the evacuation routine, as the teacher calls out the actions, in two groups: residents and firefighters
	Step. 5. Soundscape. A small groups of students work on a choral re-interpretation of the water sirens, creating a travelling chorus that moves from area to area
	Step 6. Dramatic roles. Participants create a new role as residents of Venice. They are provided role cards that state their family name (typical Venetian) and *sestiere* (area of Venice) and think up their given name and profession as Venetians
	Step 7. Hot seating and map. Participants go in the hot seat to ask each other questions related to their new roles. As they do, they also mark the place of their home and where they work on a large map of Venice hanging on the wall

(continued)

Workshop 4 (continued)

	Drama Strategies
Experiential phase	**Step. 8. Improvisation.** Participants, in role as residents of Venice, improvise a dialogue, in a *cicchetteria* (bar)
	Step 9. Teacher in Role (TiR). The teacher is in role as a tourist from another part of Italy, who is lost in Venice. The students help the tourist (a young girl who has lost her parents in the crowd) to find her way back to her hotel
	Step 10. Animated Tableaux. As the young girl attempts to follow the direction of the residents, the high tide sirens are heard, triggering the [previously rehearsed] evacuation routine, and creating chaos
Reflective phase	**Step 11. Language reflection.** Students write down their reflections on the day and share them with the teacher and each other
	Step 12. Final reflection. What is it like to live in Venice, as opposed to visiting it as a tourist? Discuss

This chapter has focused on knowing-in-action, the reflective practitioner, and pedagogical tact in education, with particular attention to reflective practice in process drama. The discussion has also considered bilingual reflective practice and translanguaging—as a strategy to explore reflection-in-action and reflection-on-action. These themes have been presented through a praxial approach, to bridge reflective practice with research and theory. The chapter concludes Part I of this book. So far, we have considered some key issues needed to navigate the simplex waters of the aesthetic dimension. We now turn to explore *how* teacher/artists can navigate the aesthetic dimension, *to facilitate learning*. Hopefully, we haven't drowned. Hopefully, we yearn for more.

References

Akkerman, S. F., & Meijer, P. C. (2011). A dialogical approach to conceptualizing teacher identity. *Teaching and Teacher Education, 27*(2), 308–319.

Anderson, M. (2015). Encountering the unexpected and extending the horizons of expectation: An autoethnographic exploration of developing through practice. In P. Duffy (Ed.), *A reflective practitioner's guide to (mis) adventures in drama education—Or—What was I thinking?* (pp. 171–182). Bristol: Intellect.

Bailey, B. (2007). Heteroglossia and boundaries. In M. Heller (Ed.), *Bilingualism: A social approach* (pp. 257–274). New York: Palgrave Macmillan.

Berthoz, A. (2012). *Simplexity: Simplifying principles for a complex world* (G. Weiss, Trans.). New Haven: Yale University Press.

Bowell, P., & Heap, B. (2005). Drama on the run: A prelude to mapping the practice of process drama. *Journal of Aesthetic Education, 39*(4), 59–69.

Bowell, P., & Heap, B. (2017). *Putting process drama into action: The dynamics of practice*. London: Routledge.

Brown, H., & Sawyer, R. D. (2016). Dialogic reflection: An exploration of its embodied, imaginative, and reflexive dynamic. In H. Brown, R. D. Sawyer, & J. Norris (Eds.), *Forms of practitioner reflexivity: Critical, conversational, and arts-based approaches*. New York: Palgrave Macmillan.

Creese, A., & Blackledge, A. (2011). Separate and flexible bilingualism in complementary schools: Multiple language practices in interrelationship. *Journal of Pragmatics, 43*(5), 1196–1208.

Dewey, J. (1910/1998). *How we think*. Boston: DC Heath.

Dewey, J. (1925/1981). Nature, life and body-mind. In J. A. Boydston (Ed.), *John Dewey: The Later Works, 1925-1953. Volume I, 1925: Experience and Nature*. Illinois: Southern Illinois University Press.

Duffy, P. (Ed.). (2015). *A reflective practitioner's guide to (mis)adventures in drama education—Or—What was I thinking?* Bristol: Intellect.

Dunn, J., & Stinson, M. (2011). Not without the art!! The importance of teacher artistry when applying drama as pedagogy for additional language learning. *Research in Drama Education: The Journal of Applied Theatre and Performance, 16*(4), 617–633.

Eisner, E. W. (2002). From episteme to phronesis to artistry in the study and improvement of teaching. *Teaching and Teacher Education, 18*(4), 375–385.

García, O., & Lin, A. M. Y. (2017). Translanguaging in bilingual education. In O. García, A. M. Y. Lin, & S. May (Eds.), *Bilingual and multilingual education* (pp. 117–130). Cham: Springer.

García, O., & Wei, L. (2014). *Translanguaging: Language, bilingualism and education*. Cham: Springer.

Grosjean, F. (2008). *Studying bilinguals*. Oxford and New York: Oxford University Press.

Grosjean, F. (2010). *Bilingual: Life and reality*. Cambridge, MA: Harvard University Press.

Kellman, S. G. (2000). *The translingual imagination.* Lincoln: University of Nebraska Press.

Kinsella, E. A. (2012). Practitioner reflection and judgement as phronesis: A continuum of reflections and considerations for phronetic judegement. In E. A. Kinsella & A. Pitman (Eds.), *Phronesis as professional knowledge: Practical wisdom in the professions* (1. Aufl. ed., Vol. 1, pp. 35–54). Rotterdam: Sense Publishers.

Kramsch, C. (1993). *Context and culture in language teaching.* Oxford: Oxford University Press.

Kramsch, C. (2009). *The multilingual subject.* Oxford: Oxford University Press.

Mazak, C. M., & Carroll, K. S. (2016). *Translanguaging in higher education: Beyond monolingual ideologies.* Bristol, UK: Multilingual Matters.

Michael-Luna, S., & Canagarajah, A. S. (2007). Multilingual academic literacies: Pedagogical foundations for code meshing in primary and higher education. *Journal of Applied Linguistics, 4*(1), 55–77.

Neelands, J. (2006). Re-imagining the reflective practitioner: Towards a philosophy of critical praxis. In J. Ackroyd (Ed.), *Research methodologies for drama education* (pp. 15–40). Sterling, VA: Trentham.

O'Mara, J. (1999). *Unravelling the mystery: A study of reflection-in-action in process drama teaching.* (Doctoral dissertation). Retrieved from https://experts.griffith.edu.au/publication/nb554b42fa803302bf51d8588b66d0a33.

O'Mara, J. (2006). Capturing the ephemeral: Reflection-in-action as research. *NJ: Drama Australia Journal, 30*(2), 41–50.

O'Mara, J. (2016). Thinking on your feet: A model for teaching teachers to use process drama. In *Drama and theatre with children: International perspectives* (pp. 98–112). London and New York: Routledge.

O'Neill, C. (1995). *Drama worlds: A framework for process drama.* Portsmouth: Heinemann.

Pavlenko, A. (2005). *Emotions and multilingualism.* Cambridge: Cambridge University Press.

Pavlenko, A. (2006). *Bilingual minds: Emotional experience, expression, and representation* (1st ed., Vol. 56). Buffalo, NY and Clevedon: Multilingual Matters.

Pavlenko, A. (2011). *Thinking and speaking in two languages. Bilingual education & bilingualism.* Bristol: Multilingual Matters.

Pavlenko, A. (2014). *The bilingual mind and what it tells us about language and thought.* Cambridge: Cambridge University Press.

Piazzoli, E. (2016). Mapping an ethnography of change in teachers of Italian (L2) learning process drama. *Teaching Italian Language and Culture Annuals*

(TILCA), 96–114. Retrieved from http://tilca.qc.cuny.edu/wp-content/uploads/2016/12/Piazzoli_Mapping-Finale.pdf.

Rokeach, M. (1968). *Beliefs, attitudes, and values: A theory of organization and change*. San Francisco, CA: Jossey-Bass.

Saxton, J. (2015). Failing better. In P. Duffy (Ed.), *A reflective practitioner's guide to (mis)adventures in drama education—Or—What was I thinking?* (pp. 253–266). Bristol: Intellect.

Scarpa, T. (2000). *Venezia è un pesce*. Milano: Feltrinelli.

Scarpa, T. (2008). *Venice is a fish* (S. Whiteside, Trans.). Milano: Feltrinelli.

Schön, D. (1983). *The reflective practitioner: How professionals think in action*. London: Temple Smith.

Schön, D. (1987). *Educating the reflective practitioner: Toward a new design for teaching and learning the professions*. San Francisco, CA: Jossey-Bass.

Shulman, L. S. (2004). *The wisdom of practice: Essays on teachng, learning and learning to teach*. San Francisco, CA: Jossey-Bass.

Taylor, P. (1996). *Researching drama and arts education: Paradigms and possibilities*. London: Routledge Falmer.

Taylor, P. (1998). *Redcoats and patriots. Reflective practice in drama and social studies*. Portsmouth: Heinemann.

Van Manen, M. (1997). *Researching lived experience: Human science for an action sensitive pedagogy* (2nd ed.). London, ON: The Althouse Press.

Van Manen, M. (2008). Pedagogical sensitivity and teachers practical knowing-in-action. *Peking University Education Review, 6*(1), 1–23.

Velasco, P., & García, O. (2014). Translanguaging and the writing of bilingual learners. *Bilingual Research Journal, 37*(1), 6–23.

Part II: Navigating the Aesthetic Dimension

6

Play, Emotions and Distancing

Shortly after migrating to Australia in 2000, I became a volunteer for The Red Cross Children's Playscheme. Part of my duties involved moving through children's hospital wards with a trolley full of toys, to engage children in play. My English was strong enough for me to move comfortably through everyday life, interacting with the Red Cross Playscheme staff and playing with the children. One day as I was wandering with my trolley around the hospital ward, I noticed a sign pointing to a theatre. I was intrigued. I decided to follow the theatre sign through the maze-like hospital corridors to see what was going on. Little did I know that, in a hospital context, 'theatre' is the equivalent of *sala operatoria* in Italian! I learnt the hard way, as I stumbled into an operating theatre preparing for action. I remember the alarmed look of the theatre nurse who, upon my explanation of the intrusion with the toy-stacked trolley, dismissed me with bewilderment. Never will I forget that, in a hospital setting, 'theatre' means *sala operatoria*.

1   Felt-Experience Across Languages

Reflecting on language and consciousness, Vygotsky (1934/1986) makes a useful distinction between 'word sense' and 'word meaning'. He states: "The dictionary meaning of a word is no more than a stone in the edifice of sense" (p. 245). This differentiation may be helpful to clarify multiple layers of language learning. For example, through the memory I shared above I learnt to reconcile the *sense* of 'theatre' in English, in a hospital context, with its Italian equivalent:

> L2 learners face the challenge of reconciling their developing word sense and word meaning in English with the word sense of the equivalent word in their native language – what that word evokes for them personally. Word meaning in English will predominate over word sense until they develop fluency, until words sound right, until they get a *feeling* for the language. (Mahn & John-Steiner, 2002, p. 56, my emphasis)

How can we get a feeling for a language? How can we develop 'word sense'? Quite simply, emotions and learning are connected. The latest educational neuroscience concurs: "Learning is dynamic, social, and context dependent because *emotions* are, and emotions form a critical piece of how, what, when and why people think, remember and learn" (Immordino-Yang, 2016, p. 17, original emphasis). A strong emotional response helped me to remember that hospital memory, and the word sense associated with it (theatres in a hospital context are off-limit zones for volunteers with toy trolleys). Many years later, I still remember this word sense even though it is now entirely removed from my everyday use.

At the beginning of this book I posed a central question: *How can teachers navigate the aesthetic dimension to facilitate performative language learning?* In Part I we focussed on the first part of the question. Part II we address the second part of the question, looking specifically at process drama. In this chapter we explore the function of play as symbolic mediation, emotions and distancing. To begin, we turn our attention to symbolic mediation, a core concept in sociocultural theory for second language learning.

2   Symbolic Mediation

Sociocultural Theory (SCT) for second language learning takes a Vygotskyan orientation to language development (Lantolf & Poehner, 2014; Lantolf & Thorne, 2006). SCT construes learning as a socially-situated process, occurring through symbolic mediation. As Wertsch (1991) puts it: "A sociocultural approach to mind begins with the assumption that action is *mediated* and that it cannot be separated from the milieu in which it is carried out" (p. 18, my emphasis). In other words, learning does not occur in a vacuum: it is influenced by the cultural artefacts and the social context in which we are entrenched. Lantolf & Thorne (2006) define mediation as "the process through which humans deploy culturally constructed artifacts, concepts and activities to regulate (i.e. gain voluntary control and transform) the material world of their own and each other's social and mental activity" (p. 79). Vygotsky (1930/1978) was interested in the relationship between tools and language, claiming: "The connection between tool use and speech affects several psychological functions: perception, sensory-motor operations, and attention, each of which is part of a dynamic system of behaviour" (p. 31). The source of mediation can be a tool (like a pencil, or a device), a system of symbols (signs, language), or a person in social interaction. Symbolic mediation transforms spontaneous impulses into higher order functions, like voluntary attention, voluntary memory abstraction and meta-cognition. In L2 learning, this includes language learning strategies, as unfocussed learning can become focussed based on *how* the learning is mediated (Donato & MacCormick, 1994).

The notion of *regulation* is linked to mediation. It refers to development being regulated first by an external object (object-regulation) and person (other-regulation), before it can be co-regulated, and finally regulated independently (self-regulation). In L2 settings, the *object*-regulated speaker's utterance would be constrained, limited by a translating software or a phrasal booklet; the *other*-regulated speaker's utterance would be a response regulated by others (the teacher or a more knowledgeable peer) who would model a structure for the learner. The *self*-regulated speaker is able to freely express ideas and feelings in the target language. As Lantolf (2000) states, being an advanced L2 speaker means being self-regulated, that is, able to control one's psychological and social activity *through* the language (p. 6). The transition from *other*-regulation to *self*-regulation develops over time, through the creation of learning affordances that Vygotsky famously termed Zone of Proximal Development (ZPD). These engage learners' mental functions that "have not yet matured but are in the process of maturation"; they are the 'buds' of development rather than 'fruits' of development (Vygotsky, 1930/1978, p. 86).

Within a Vygotskian, sociocultural paradigm, the inseparability of cognition and emotion in second language development is a sine qua non (Swain, 2012). The concept of *perezhivanie*, the unit of embodied felt-experience in the affective, cognitive and social spheres introduced at the beginning of the book (see "Embodiment" in Chapter 2) becomes relevant here. Vygotsky uses the term *perezhivanie*, Russian for felt-experience, to comprehend an individual's affective and cognitive experience in a social environment. Mahn and John-Steiner (2002) describe *perezhivanie* in an L2 context as the affective processes through which interactions in the ZPD are uniquely felt, internalised and represented by the second language learner. To this extent, an important connection is the inter-relationship between *perezhivanie* and play (Ferholt, 2015).

Play, as we will see, is fundamental for learning and development. However, I believe there is considerable confusion about what constitutes play in the L2 classroom, and, importantly, how playing *mediates* language learning. Let us consider L2 classroom settings in relation to the practice of play. It is almost a truism to say that creating a play-based atmosphere is conducive to language learning and most L2 teachers would agree. Yet what does that mean in practice? In many L2 settings, playing is associated with games, although play and games are not necessarily the same. On one level this association may stem from the polysemic ambivalence of the word 'play'. In the English language, 'play' can be both a noun and a verb, each respectively with several meanings. In fact each has so many meanings that one has to specify 'playing a game', as opposed to playing an instrument or playing sport. In languages like Italian, Spanish, French, Portuguese and German, their respective terms *gioco, juego, jeu, jogo* and *spiele* actually mean both 'game' and '[I] play'—leaving a degree of ambiguity when we discuss 'play', 'role play' and/or 'games' in the classroom. But 'play' is not the same concept as 'games' for second language acquisition and development.

Overall, in L2 settings, games and role plays are used for a variety of purposes related to practising language in a relaxed, social environment. Here are some examples for an adult in an intermediate L2 course. At the beginning of term, the teacher may set up a game to help students learn each other's names, to break the ice, to gain an initial feel of students' fluency, personality and learning styles. These ice-breaker games may or may not be based on competition, and usually involve the whole class. Throughout the term, a teacher may use language games to reinforce/practise different aspects of language: from battle-ship type board games to practise numbers, snakes-and-ladders type games to practise conversations bingo type games to reinforce vocabulary in target semantic areas, and domino type games to practise connectors, cause and effect, and so forth. A whole business of L2 commercial games exists, targeted at several levels of proficiency and in several languages. These games are usually based on competition and are conducted in pairs or small groups. Some language games involve simple role plays with instructions written on cards to be drawn from a pile, often involving one-off scenarios like making a complaint, purchasing something, or ordering food. These sorts of games may or may not be based on competition, and often require pair or small-group work. At end of term there may be games to revise content, and language to exchange opinions, again in small groups or with the whole class. This is not to mention thematic games: the Christmas quiz game; the Halloween quiz game, and so forth.

I am not suggesting that L2 classes are based only on these activities, nor that all L2 teachers use games. What I am arguing is that, as far as 'playing' is concerned in L2 settings, it is often associated with games, and these are some of the L2 commercial games available to L2 teachers. While these language games can be successful in assisting teachers with targeted language practice, they often stop at the surface. They may (or may not) encourage participants to engage in 'languaging' (Swain, 2006), that is, producing language to mediate thinking. If these games do, the languaging may be aimed at finding the right answer to satisfy the rules of the game. To return to Vygotsky's quote above, often these games promote language that stops at the 'dictionary' meaning of a word, "no more than a stone in the edifice of sense" (1934/1986, p. 245).

An embodied approach to performative language learning takes 'play' at a different level. Play mediates a felt-experience of learning. It promotes self-regulation in the L2, transforming spontaneous impulses into higher order functions. As mentioned in the opening, from an SCT perspective, language learning is about symbolic mediation. In process drama, the source of mediation is a wider system of symbols, that is, the playful management of the elements of drama (see Chapter 4) including dramatic role, situation, focus, narrative and dramatic tension, to co-create a story. This opens up a much wider array of possibilities for the language to be felt, to be perceived subjectively.

3   Play and Dual Affect

Dual affect is a crucial construct to understand how play mediates learning in process drama. To begin, let us consider play behaviour in children, as it is in children that playing originates. In discussing the phenomenon of children's play, Vygotsky (1933/1976) notes that wherever there is an imaginary play situation, there are rules. This is true across all games, from the simplest forms of games to the most sophisticated abstractions. Even the baby repeatedly dropping an object with the adult picking it up, causing hilarity for the infant—that has an unspoken rule, which is, the adult will continue to pick up the ball and the baby will continue to drop it. The restriction imposed by the rule generates the pleasure. Take, for instance, classic hide-and-seek; what prompts a child to count to fifty with eyes closed, before looking for her playmates? If in this game, finding the children provides the highest source of pleasure, why would the seeker child agree to close her eyes and give her playmates time to hide? According to play theory, what makes discovering the children pleasurable is the constraint imposed by the rules of the game; that is, looking for the children *having given then time to hide,* to then chase them. Since carrying out the rule is *itself* a source of pleasure, it follows that the essential attribute of play is a rule that has become an affect. If the final aim was merely discovering the hiding children, the seeker could just track them down as they search for a hiding spot. But that's not the game.

Why does the child not do what he wants spontaneously at once? Because to observe the rules of the play structure promises much greater pleasure from the game than the gratification of an immediate impulse. In other words, as one investigator puts it in recalling the words of Spinoza: 'An affect can only be overcome by a stronger affect'. Thus, in play a situation is created in which, as Nohl put it, a *dual affective plan* occurs. (Vygotsky, 1933/1976, p. 548, my emphasis)

A dual affective plan, for Vygotsky, is sustained while playing. Affect, in psychological terms, refers to "the feeling tone a person is experiencing at any particular point in time" (Larsen & Prizmic, 2004, p. 40). Dual affect, as described by Vygotsky above, refers to managing two different emotional states at the same time: that of reality, and that of the play state. Imagine a child having fun (real state), squealing in terror (play state) as she is being chased by her dad playing a crocodile. Two counterposed states are occurring simultaneously here: the fun and the terror. As Vygotsky (1933/1976) put it: "The child weeps in play as a patient, but revels as a player" (p. 549).

Vygotsky argues that a child's greatest self-control occurs in play: "Play gives a child a new form of desires, i.e., teaches him to desire by relating his desires to a fictitious 'I'—to his role in the game and its rules" (p. 549). In play, we have seen that affect, or feeling tone, operates across a *dual* affective current. How, we may ask, does this apply to performative language learning? To address this question, it is interesting to re-visit dual affect theory in light of two understandings. These are Tschurtschenthaler's (2013) notion of double masking (see "Aesthetic Engagement in Process Drama" in Chapter 3), as the relationship between the character an L2 learner plays and their sense of self, and Taliaferro's (1998) notion of double-consciousness (see "Intercultural Engagement" in Chapter 3) as looking at self from the eyes of Other. Yet, through dual affect theory, these concepts can evoke a further perspective.

Bolton (1984) was the first to theorise symbolic play in Drama in Education. He offers an insightful critique to Vygotsky's concept of the child 'weeping in play as a patient, but revelling as a player'. To begin with, Bolton finds Vygotsky's theory fundamental but "slightly misleading" (p. 106). While he agrees about the range of contradictory emotions in play (weeping as a patient, revelling as a player), Bolton highlights that it is imprecise to consider the child's crying to be of the same 'order of emotional experience' as the child being a patient in real life. Surely, emotional response in drama may be truly *felt* by a participant, but it is not felt in the same way as in an actual event. In drama emotional expression is a response to abstraction.

To further examine how dual affect and emotions work in drama, Bolton makes a crucial distinction: *first*-order emotions (experienced in the real frame) and *second*-order emotions (experienced in the play frame). He suggests that role plays and drama are deliberately created second-order experiences. However, I may add, not all role plays operate on the same level; differences exist between superficial role plays and role plays as dramatic explorations. To illustrate, in a superficial role play a student may be pretending to buy a coffee (play frame) but actually be insecure about using the target language (real frame). They may be pretending to buy a coffee (play frame) but really be bored about the activity (real frame). They may be pretending to buy a coffee (play frame) and in fact highly enjoying the language practice (real frame).

Whichever the scenario, the student's exploration of meaning in the play frame (buying coffee) will be short-lived. Stereotypical characters, limited dramatic focus, no mood, no symbols, a predictable narrative and no extended time and place will give rise to zero dramatic tension and low commitment to the dramatic encounter. Roles and situations will be likely to reinforce a caricature, rather than inspire the student to explore possibilities. Thus, the domain of second-order emotions will be flat, left unattended. On the other hand, role plays in drama engage second-order emotions in a way that taps into the whole spectrum of emotions. They are not what Heathcote describes as exercises that "have a drive towards ending themselves"; they are "about journeys and not knowing how the journeys may end" (Heathcote, in O'Neill, 2015, p. 53).

Going back to the theory of dual affect, this is central to understand how felt-experience (*perezhivanie*) operates in performative language learning. When intense emotions are felt simultaneously in two contexts, they may, at times, contradict each other. This also echoes the concept of metaxis, a dissonance in responses discussed in previous chapters (see "Intercultural Dramatic Tension" in Chapter 4). As Bolton argues, it is the dialectical relationship between contradicting emotions that defines drama. Precisely, it is the aesthetic dimension of drama that regulates the interplay between the real state and the play state:

> Raw emotion belongs to the actual situation; harnessed, tempered or filtered emotion springs from a dialectic set up between the actual and the fictitious context. Form is made up of the elements that promote and control that interaction. (1979, p. 11)

In this new light, the elements of drama discussed in Chapter 4 may acquire new layers of meaning, as the regulatory mechanism between the real and fictional context in play. Similarly, the tension of *metaxis*, the tension arising from a contradiction between emotions felt in drama and in real life (O'Toole, 1992), may assume new layers of meaning in light of dual affect theory. Understanding this, as teacher/artists, is fundamental to structuring sound emotional experiences for L2 learners engaged in performative language learning. Bateson's (1955/1976) seminal theory casts another layer of simplicity on dual affect in drama. In *A Theory of Play and Fantasy* Bateson holds that the behaviour in play is always characterised by a double paradox, or 'paradoxical frame': the actual behaviour and what it stands for. In his own words: "The playful nip denotes the bite, but it does not denote what would be denoted by the bite" (p. 121). He therefore shifts the focus on the play action (the playful nip) as a signifier of the fact that it is play behaviour. This is at the core of play as mediation in drama.

Bowell and Heap (2017) recognise that the essence of process drama lies in being able to perceive, at the same time, both the real and fictional contexts (weeping as a patient; revelling as a player). More precisely, it is the paradox of tacitly accepting the imaginary context as the 'here and now' in play, but at the same time being fully aware that it is fictional: "At the heart of this paradox, at the point where fiction and reality are in juxtaposition to each other, is the crucible in which both artistic creation and learning are forged" (2017, p. 5). This is what differentiates superficial role plays and role plays as dramatic exploration: in the latter, the dual emotional current will connect felt-experiences to language learning. To do so, a fair amount of what we have called practical knowledge, reflection-in-action, and pedagogical tact (see "Pedagogical Tact" in Chapter 5) is needed to manage the dual affective current in such a way that is conducive to learning.

4   Protecting 'into' Emotion

Above we have argued that emotion and learning are interconnected, and that emotions drive learning. However, we should not throw a blanket over the concept of emotions and learning and simply move on. The relationship between learning and emotions needs further consideration; in its simplicity it has even more to reveal. In Bolton's words:

> As teachers we need to be very sensitive to the emotional demands we make on our students. The notion of 'protection' is not necessarily concerned with protecting participants *from* emotion, for unless there is some kind of emotional engagement nothing can be learned, but rather to protect them *into* emotion. (1984, p. 128)

With these words, Bolton captures the essence of 'protection', a crucial aspect in the management of emotions that has inspired three decades of drama teaching. Although some topics may be painful or controversial, Bolton argues, it does not mean they need to be avoided. Rather, a *direct* handling of them is to be avoided. *Indirect* handling of a topic through drama, on the other hand, can protect participants 'into' emotion. If a topic is handled too directly, Bolton observes, the class "will hastily protect themselves by opting out, fooling around" (p. 129). Another reaction if a topic is handled too directly is that some participants may experience emotions that are too strong—disturbing or even traumatic. This would trigger an emotional black-out, whereby no learning can occur, as an emotive shock inhibits memory retention and other critical functions required in learning. Becoming self-absorbed by emotions to the point of zooming out is arguably not conducive to learning. To deal with a topic *indirectly*, or at an oblique angle, a teacher can place the participants in a role that connects only *obliquely* with the topic. One way to connect obliquely is by adopting an abstract rather than naturalistic approach. An inspiring example of obliqueness through abstraction can be found in Heap's (2015) account of the *Baby Bird* drama, where he works with a dancer in role as a baby bird in a non-naturalistic approach, using a simple, yet powerful narrative to explore delicate issues of mutual dependency between teachers and students with special needs.

Working indirectly helps to regulate aesthetic distance. Eriksson (2007, 2011) explores the concept of distance as a poetic quality operating on a continuum, where degrees of distance regulate our investment in the make-believe; in other words, "the awareness of fiction" (2007, p. 15). Particularly, Eriksson investigates the parallels between Brecht and Heathcote, looking at Brecht's *Verfremdung* (estrangement) and drama in education. In process drama, dramatic episodes involve going in role, followed by reflecting on the role, as well as taking multiple roles – rather than an in-depth exploration to build empathy with one character, more in line with a Stanislavskian approach. This is where envisaging distancing as a continuum (with detachment and empathy on either end) becomes illuminating, as "both points furthest from the middle position lead to loss of distance and consequently *loss of imaginative power*" (2007, p. 20, my emphasis). In an educational context, too much distance produces detachment, leaving the learner unresponsive; too little distance produces an extremely intense emotion, creating affective overload. In this sense, distancing can be construed as a protection mechanism, filtering between the fictitious and the real, that regulates the intensity of emotions. The challenge for the teacher/artist is being able to balance the distancing to emotionally connect, but not to overload. As Morgan and Saxton (1987) put it, "distancing is a means of detouring feeling to arrive at feeling" (p. 136).

Dunn, Bundy, and Stinson (2015) recognise that distancing, and the process drama teacher's awareness of participants' emotional responses across the real and fictional contexts, are critical. To attempt mapping out distancing, they advance a framework based on the constructs of commitment (willingness to engage) and connection (intensity and nature of emotional responses) as two axes of a quadrant, which they propose can be used "to gain insight into how emotions operate in process drama" (p. 10). They apply this framework to planning and facilitating a drama where, as seen above, having too much or too little connection will result in an overwhelming, or detached experience. They use the framework to track down engagement drops due to the planning or facilitation skills of the teacher.

In L2 settings, the process drama teacher who speaks in the target language already starts off with a pronounced degree of distancing, as the participants are experiencing the drama in a foreign language and have an ongoing, underpinning focus on new language items they are being exposed to. Degrees of distancing will vary according to the language level. For L2 beginners it will be more obvious, for more advanced learners less so, but nevertheless a degree of distancing will be in place. This functions as a protective layer between their first-order and second-order emotions (Bolton, 1984) in the second language. Here is where introducing a dramatic context with fictional roles helps to create a felt-experience, *perezhivanie*, in L2 learning. This term, as argued in Chapter 2, also resonates with Stanislavski (1936/1980) and is associated with feeling, experiencing, in other words building empathy. Yet, as seen above, the episodic structure of process drama is such that it manipulates the distance between empathy and detachment, in the make-believe. This is where L2 commercial games flounder; they offer competitive fun, light entertainment, cognitive engagement, but often fail to provide a felt-experience *across* the dual affective plan. Distancing can act as a barrier or a bridge, according to how the teacher/artist structures the drama and how the participants respond to it. In a research project I conducted with Claire Kennedy, we analysed the reactions of undergraduate students of Italian (FL) who experienced process drama as a 'threat' or an 'opportunity' to learn, depending on how teachers and students handled dual affect, protection and distancing (Piazzoli & Kennedy, 2014).

Crutchfield (2015) also discusses using the full spectrum of emotions in the second language classroom, advocating embracing, rather than dismissing or denying painful emotions, whenever they arise. He notes that the teacher has to do this competently, especially if the emotions are particularly intense:

> The challenge for teachers who wish to use an aesthetic approach in their pedagogy is to manage these "negative" emotions in a constructive way, which first and foremost means acknowledging and integrating them consciously, through structured reflection, into the artistic process of which they are necessarily a part. But this in turn means that teachers themselves must be deeply familiar with, and fully competent in, the artistic processes in which they wish to engage their students. They must be fully cognizant of the artistry involved in their own praxis. (pp. 103–104)

Play can afford powerful symbolic mediation, but the teacher/artist needs to be aware of how this operates. For teachers to be "fully cognizant of the artistry in their own praxis", as Crutchfield puts it above, they need to be aware of play as dual affect, protecting 'into' emotion, and distancing. In the rest of the chapter, I illustrate play as mediation through a practical example.

5 Play as Mediation in Context

Lantolf and Poehner (2014) describe praxis orientation as "contingent upon teachers' theoretical classroom activity, that is, their use of theoretical principles to orient classroom practice" (p. 206). To illustrate in practice some aspects of the concept discussed so far, in the second half of this chapter I outline in some detail a project I conducted with primary school children in a public school in Italy, from January to June 2015.

5.1 Content and Language Integrated Learning (CLIL) Pilot Project

The purpose of the project was to evaluate the implementation of Content and Language Integrated Learning (CLIL) in an early primary setting (6–8 year-olds) in an Italian primary school. Content and Language Integrated Learning (CLIL) is a foreign language methodology that involves learning content (science, history, etc.) in/through a second language (Coonan, 2012; Coyle, 2007). While CLIL is common in Italy at secondary level, it is not customary practice in primary years, especially the first two years of primary. I was employed to teach twenty weeks of mathematics, geography, science and music curricula in English, to Italian children, from January to June 2015. Seven classes participated in the project, three Year 1 classes (6–7-year-olds) and four Year 2 classes (7–8-year-olds), totalling approximately 150 children, male and female, of mixed abilities. All of the children were Italian speakers with minimal knowledge of English (for example, colours, numbers, animals). One pre-condition of my employer (a private language centre that supplies CLIL teachers to Italian public schools) was that I would teach all classes exclusively in English, with no Italian spoken at any time in the school. I was to speak no Italian in front of the teachers, children or their parents, throughout the twenty-week long CLIL pilot intervention. The pilot involved no formal assessment, with the Principal more interested in providing the children with a full-immersion learning experience than assessing their English proficiency before and after the intervention.

When asked to undertake this teaching assignment, I agreed on the condition that I would combine the CLIL methodology with performative language teaching. My employer, with a background in performance, accepted enthusiastically. The drama approach combined with the CLIL intervention drew approval from the school Principal and was pitched to the parents through a formal presentation. In fact, the most recent research points to performative approaches in second language education as CLIL (Donnery, 2017). As a starting point to designing the learning experiences for the children, I liaised with the classroom teachers to gather the curricular requirements for each subject and level. I created drama experiences based on six illustrated children's books functioning as pre-texts (O'Neill, 1995) to launch the dramatic world. On average, I used one picture book for up to four weeks, delving into the book's dramatic world to connect with the history, music, maths, geography and science curricula. The books were selected because of their rich imagery, which needed to act as a primary visual support given the language barrier.

An interesting aspect of this teaching experience, which related to the particular nature of my position, was that although in class I could understand the children's Italian conversations, I would speak with them only in English. This resulted in the need to rely on body language like mime as well as visual props and drawings to convey meaning to the children, even though I could understand the children's requests (initially in Italian), which I acknowledged and re-phrase in English. Classes focussed on storytelling, combined with a palette of games targeted to build the vocabulary for the illustrated stories that were to function as pre-text for the drama. I drew on basic drama strategies, including Heathcote's Teacher in Role (Heathcote & Bolton, 1995), still image, drawing in role, and Total Physical Response (TPR) (Asher, 1969). None of the pupils or the classroom teachers had any experience in drama as such, and while the children had an innate ability to engage in play-based pedagogy, the classroom teachers needed an elucidation. For this reason, after three weeks at the school I ran a workshop for all staff. This helped the teachers to understand the pedagogical guidelines underpinning process drama, and to share their curriculum needs so we could co-plan the lessons. However, since most teachers spoke no English and I was bound by the paradoxical nature of my employment to speak only English, in most instances their input was confined to pointing at what syllabus topics I should cover.

5.2 The 'Poisoned Leaf' Process Drama

Here I confine the discussion to one process drama workshop (Workshop 5, *The Poisoned Leaf*) conducted over three one-hour lessons, related to one curriculum subject (science), one grade level (Year 2). I can zoom into one aspect of the syllabus (leaf anatomy). This process drama was created *ad hoc* with no pre-planned structure, and it was later transcribed into a structure for documentation purposes.

The science teacher had been working on leaves, specifically leaf parts (stem, blade, veins, margins) and leaf shapes (lobed, dentate, serrate, entire) and asked if I could teach the children this terminology in English. With this educational objective in mind, my immediate concern was how to make the topic relevant for the children. Why would Italian seven-year-olds care about leaf anatomy, in English? I decided to integrate this topic within the illustrated book we were reading at the time, *The Gruffalo's Child*, by Julia Donaldson (2007). The previous month we had been immersed in Donaldson's bestseller, *The Gruffalo*, using it as a springboard to discuss the landscape of the forest (geography), decimal patterns (maths), past and present sequencing (narrative history). Children had become attached to the habitat, the story, and the characters of *The Gruffalo*, as well as to the accompanying song. They seemed to be intrigued to find out about the book's sequel, *The Gruffalo's Child*—and her mischief. In this story, a child disobeys her father, a boar-like friendly monster. While the Gruffalo is asleep, the child sneaks out of their cave, venturing into a dark forest. After many dangerous adventures she tip-toes back into her father's cave, while he is (seemingly) fast asleep. As the story ends, it appears that the father has not realised the child's night wandering.

The process drama starts as the story ends, precisely from the last page of the illustrated book (Fig. 1), considering the possibility that *The Gruffalo* was not really asleep (see Step 1.c in Workshop 5).

I decided that in the drama, I would take on the role of the Gruffalo's child. To focus the space and to visually anchor the drama, we reproduced the cave of the Gruffalo, using three gym mats, signs, and other props. I stepped into role, telling the children that my name was *Gruffalina* (a name that, through the Italian suffix *ina* evokes a small, friendly character, and would help to carry the idea that I was the Gruffalo's daughter) and I was seven years old (the same age as the children). I made these choices to create a connection between the Teacher in Role and the children. I signalled that I was in role as *Gruffalina* by wearing a hoodie jumper (as it was snowing in the story) and carrying a stick similar to the one she is holding in the picture book. In role as *Gruffalina*, I told the children that I was in trouble, as my father had discovered my misdeed, and was very upset with me. Would the children help me to make up for this mess? I suspected this to be a scenario

Fig. 1 An illustration from the Gruffalo's child

familiar to them; I asked if they had ever been in this situation, and this immediately created empathy for *Gruffalina*. Of course, the children had been in trouble with their parents before, and had many (inventive) suggestions on how to make up for it. This created some connection and identification as the children had experienced in their real frames a similar situation to what we were exploring in the play frame. On the next day, each child was to draw a present, which I, as *Gruffalina*, was going to offer to my father. Note that all of this was in English, 11 weeks into the CLIL intervention, with a class of Italian children who were at beginners' level before the CLIL full-immersion experience. Using props, the illustrations in the book, the narrative of the story, body language, and a lot of guesswork created the conditions for understanding to emerge.

Although this sequence was fun for the children, I was still facing the challenge of integrating the science curriculum into the drama. How would the leaf anatomy come into it? I could sense the sceptical stare of the science teacher, who was in the classroom as I came in and out of role as *Gruffalina*. In line with Heathcotian tradition, my vision was to enrol the children as some kind of experts—with an expertise in leaves. I went back to the original illustrations and noticed that the cave depicted in *The Gruffalo* had a straw mat, with a few leaves on the floor (Fig. 1). We could make a new mat, with more leaves, for *The Gruffalo* to sleep on. We had previously reproduced the cave for learning spatial prepositions, so it lent itself well for further integration into the drama—and the science curriculum. I pointed out that my father slept on a mat made of straw and leaves, but the leaves were wearing out. To sharpen the dramatic context, in the make-believe I suggested that it was going to be his birthday soon. Children had brought in drawings of gifts they wanted me to give to my father, and we practised the handover ritual, with the appropriate expressions related to gift-giving. This personalised their input into the story. Now, the children had brought their own presents, but I as his daughter wanted to make my own. Would the children help me collect as many leaves as possible, to weave a new leafy mat for my father's birthday? Next, I encouraged the children to trace leaf patterns and create their own colour combinations, then to cut out the leaves and place them in a basket for *Gruffalina*.

Let us pause. Let us consider play as mediation and the theory of play as dual affect (Vygotsky, 1933/1976). The language related to the dramatic context (the forest and the animals in the story) was already established, as we had been working on it for months in class (in the real frame). To prepare for the drama (play frame), we resumed the leaf terminology (Fig. 2) already practised in the science curriculum in Italian (real frame). Yet, while we were reviewing the leaf terminology in English (in the real frame), the children sensed that we would soon need this to engage in the drama (play frame). During this phase, play mediated the children's learning about the leaves in English.

This activity was designed to integrate the curriculum subject with the drama. On the surface it was educationally sound. It covered the prescribed science topic, using the English terminology and integrating it within the storytelling. I could see nods from the science teacher sitting at the end of the classroom. Yet, something was missing. By the end of the second lesson the children had cut out many colourful leaves and put them all in a basket for *Gruffalina* to give to her father, but they seemed to be disengaging from the task.

It felt like a source of dramatic tension was lacking, a strong hold to hook their investment into those leaves. As I packed up that lesson, surrounded by hundreds of leaf cut-outs, I tacitly knew the drama had stalled. It precisely was at that time, just before I left the classroom and

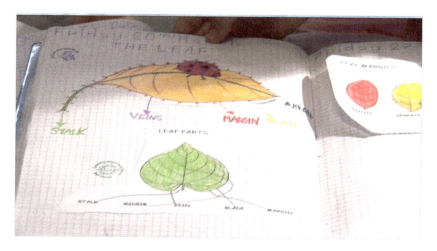

Fig. 2 Work on leaves

6 Play, Emotions and Distancing   151

with my hand on the door handle, that Giacomo (pseudonym) called out: "Miss Erika, watch out for the poisoned leaf!" Giacomo was a very intelligent child. However, his unruly personality earned him the reputation of classroom rascal, so much so that his teachers would push his desk to the front wall to isolate him from other pupils. In that instance, his attitude was playful and provocative and, needless to say, the science teacher disciplined him to be quiet. Yet, his offer provided just the missing element that I was looking for: the poisoned leaf. He spoke in Italian, a language I understood, although I did not speak it in class. I acknowledged his idea by rephrasing it in English, and added, sifting slowly through the leaf cutouts: "Yes, children, one leaf *is* poisoned. I wonder now, *which one* is it?"

In Dunn's (2011) analysis of children's improvisation, Giacomo's offer would classify as "intervening playwright function" (p. 24), that is, advancing the plot by introducing new offers that change focus, status or inject dramatic tension. Dunn argues that these contributions "are crucial for the evolving text, for without them tension will be lost and the experience becomes tedious and repetitive" (p. 24). She describes children able to contribute in this way as children with a "keen intuitive understanding of dramatic tension and rich imaginations" or "master dramatists" (p. 24). Indeed, acknowledging Giacomo's suggestion pushed the drama in a new, unexpected direction. As I stood at the classroom door in a preoccupied mood, sifting through those leaves, the children responded with sighs of worry, mixed with giggles of anticipation, at the prospect of one leaf being poisoned.

The next day, in role as *Gruffalina*, I produced a secret message featuring the drawing of a skull and crossbones, a universal symbol signifying hazard (Fig. 3). The sign, my facial expression, and my body language pointing to the leaves besides me, mediated the children's understanding of 'danger'. The message confirmed Giacomo's guess that, alas, a poisoned leaf had been planted within the lot prepared by my assistants. Unless it was plucked out, the sleeping mat would be lethal for my father *The Gruffalo*. Again, the children responded with sighs of worry and giggles of anticipation. To go back to Bolton's (1984) discourse of emotions in drama, the sighs seemed to indicate concern about the poisoned leaf's effects, and could be described as second-order emotions (felt within the realm of the play frame—the Gruffalo

Fig. 3 Teacher in Role holding the message, next to the leaves prepared by the children

was in danger). Meantime the giggles betrayed the fun of that possible scenario, and would be considered first-order emotions (in the real frame—the children were having fun).

As I outlined the problem of the poisoned leaf to the children, in role, they took this affair with the utmost seriousness, and immediately deliberated that the culprit leaf had to be identified and removed for the safety of *Gruffalina*'s father. The poisoned leaf, the message read, was 'lobed', had 'blue veins', a 'red stem' and a 'yellow blade'. I repeated these instructions a number of times at the children's request. Having worked on leaves with the science teacher in Italian and with myself in English meant that the children had a repertoire of factual knowledge (in the real frame) about leaves, which they could draw from and use towards the play context. *Gruffalina*'s assistants appeared proud and excited to be in a position to help her to identify the poisoned leaf, as *Gruffalina*, regrettably, knew absolutely nothing about leaf anatomy.

The children worked in groups of four to carefully inspect every single leaf. This task was carried out meticulously, until the poisoned leaf was identified (Fig. 4) and, to the delight of the children, destroyed forever.

We proceeded to stuff all the 'safe' leaves in an uncontaminated box, and to place the box inside our cave made by makeshift gym mats. Framing the space in this way provided focus, as each child waited for his/her turn to go inside the cave and place a present and personalised birthday card. These rituals (placing presents and cards) were accompanied by context-related language for offering their gifts, and were peppered by my suggestions to place their cards *inside* the cave, *to the left, to the right*, or *on top* of the leaf-straw mat, and so forth.

Fig. 4 A pupil finds the poisoned leaf

Through these processes, symbolic play mediated their ability to engage in higher order functions, like focus, attention and acquisition of specific terminology related to the science curriculum. By the end of the class the children had practised a range of specific vocabulary, in a context that was meaningful to them. Play and dual affect mediated their learning of the science curriculum, in English.

5.3   CLIL, Process Drama and Play

Overall, the children responded enthusiastically to the synergy between CLIL and embodied drama pedagogy, showing high levels of engagement with the English language, with the curriculum subject, and with the drama approach. After one month (four contact hours per week) their English comprehension appeared to improve significantly, with children showing a basic understanding of the activity instructions, the vocabulary and idiomatic expressions related to the illustrated stories. After twenty weeks, the children appeared to clearly understand my English instructions and made an active attempt to communicate in English, either relying on language structures on the various signs around the classroom (object-regulated), repeating the teacher's prompts (other-regulated), or actively combining given language structures into new meaning (self-regulated), according to developmental levels and abilities. To document the drama activities, a professional filmmaker was hired in Week 12 to film seven hours of classroom activity. This was edited and screened at the end-of-year school celebrations, as a memory of the project for the children and their families. The video recordings present evidence of the children's learning engagement, language comprehension, and motivation to communicate—also noted by the teachers, the parents, and the Principal.

At the end of the six months, the Principal evaluated the intervention as a successful learning experience, and commissioned the language centre (my employer) to continue offering CLIL at early primary. However, as I moved on from that appointment, and the next teacher did not have a drama-based background, the performative aspect of the CLIL intervention was discontinued. Considering that experience, as a reflective practitioner, I noted the growth in language acquisition, and was particularly impressed by the intensity and the amount of children's comments related to their *motivation* to continue learning English. Although no quantitative or qualitative data was collected, my personal observations, based on the quantity of unsolicited children's comments about their experience of learning English, the positive feedback from the classroom teachers and parents, the affirmative feedback from the Principal and director, strongly confirmed my impression that performative language teaching, combined with CLIL methodology, can generate high levels of motivation in early primary settings.

However, two important points must be raised. First, the amount of language preparation needed for the children to be able to engage in a Teacher in Role, in a foreign language, was substantial (see "Teacher in Role and SLA" in Chapter 7). To prepare the children to comprehend and respond to the Teacher in Role, in English, 44 hours of preparation (narrating and working with the text of the stories, TPR, games, drawing and singing activities) were necessary. In fact, this process drama took place in Week 11 of the CLIL intervention. It is imperative to note that a full-length process drama, in English, could not have worked in Week 1, due not only to the language barrier, but also to the (teacher-centred) school culture the children were entrenched in. It took months before they were ready to respond to a full-length process drama, in English.

Moreover, I should reinforce that while I, as the CLIL teacher, spoke no Italian in the classroom, I did understand the children's interactions, in Italian. This was a huge advantage because it gave me immediate feedback in terms of their engagement levels, both within the dramatic frame, and with the curriculum subject. In the example outlined above, it was because I could understand Giacomo's suggestion in his first language (Italian) that I was able to take it on board, and build from it. This may not—likely, could not—have happened in a situation where the CLIL teacher does not understand the first language (L1) of the children (as is often the case). Given the above, my observations point to a synergy between CLIL and process drama in the early years of schooling, but only when process drama was introduced gradually, with ample language preparation, and when the CLIL teacher could understand, and was *willing* to build on, the children's ideas in the L1 for advancing the improvisation.

Finally, it is significant to note that the child who provided the source of dramatic tension for *The Poisoned Leaf* drama was a child usually silenced by other classroom teachers. As I entered that school culture, Giacomo was referred to me as a disruptive element to be disciplined. As *The Poisoned Leaf* drama unfolded, Giacomo was well aware that his suggestion had not only been heard, but had become pivotal. The *dissonance* between his label as rascal in the classroom, and this role in the drama as 'master dramatist' (Dunn, 2011) may have created a significant felt-experience for him, related to his sense of confidence as a young English speaker, as well as a valued member of the classroom community. Being able to identify a source of dramatic tension (in the play context), see it cherished by the teacher (in the real context) and transposed to the play context of the children, was a rich and valuable experience for Giacomo, an instance of play as symbolic mediation.

Workshop 5: The Poisoned Leaf

Description: Three drama classes that explore an aspect of the science curriculum, at early primary level, through drama-based pedagogy, in a Content and Language for Integrated Learning (CLIL) context.

Students' Context—Inspiration for the Workshop: Three CLIL lessons focused on leaf anatomy, aligned with the science syllabus at early primary level, in an Italian primary school. In the class, pupils (7–8-year-olds) engaged with learning leaf anatomy (shapes and parts). We had recently been working on *The Gruffalo* and *The Gruffalo's Child* illustrated stories.

Pre-text: The last page of *The Gruffalo's Child*, a children's book by Julia Donaldson (2007).

Educational Aims: Differentiating types of leaves: serrated, dentated and lobed. Learning to name different parts of a leaf: stem, bud, tip, blade, margin, and veins.

Level: A2 in their 11th week of a full-immersion CLIL intervention.

Duration: Three lessons (one hour each).

Workshop 5 The poisoned leaf

	Lesson 1
Initiation phase	**Step 1. Pre-text:** a. Read aloud *The Gruffalo's Child* b. Browse through the pages to identify characters and situation, finding connections to the prequel (*The Gruffalo*) in terms of narrative and language c. Stop at the final page and shift the attention to a possible sequel to the story. Was the father really asleep? What if he wasn't?
Experiential phase	*Pre-Teacher in Role*: describe the main features of the child in terms of her personality and looks; prepare the children to meet the child
	Step 2. Teacher in Role: Gruffalo's child introduces herself. She shares with the children that her father wasn't asleep, is well aware of her mischief, and she is now in trouble. She asks children for advice
	Post-Teacher in Role: out of role, check the children have comprehended
Reflective phase	**Step 3. Drawing in role**: invite children to think of one item that Gruffalina could give to her father as a gift and to draw it. While they draw, elicit a summary of the drama experience. Finish the drawing at home
	Lesson 2
Initiation phase	**Step 1. Pre-text:** a. Children volunteer to play a role in *The Gruffalo's Child* story b. While the teacher reads out the story, the children in the middle of a circle embody the story, using mimes and direct speech c. Focus on the last page of the story, reminding the children of the previous workshop's Teacher in Role
Experiential phase	*Pre-Teacher in Role*: remind children about their presents to give Gruffalina. Prepare the children for the improvisation that follows, introducing the new key language and ideas
	Step 2. Teacher in Role: ask the children if they have brought their presents, and accept each gift personally. Introduce a new item to the story: it will be the Gruffalo's birthday soon and Gruffalina would like to make a new mat, out of leaves, for her father. Ask if they'd like to help
	Post-Teacher in Role: out of role, check that the children are following

(continued)

Workshop 5 (continued)

	Lesson 1
	Step 3. Art and craft in role: children use pre-made templates to colour different parts of leaves (previously studied in Science, both in Italian and English), cut them out and put them into a basket to make the leaf mat
Reflective phase	**Revision**: revise the terminology related to the leaves, and the story so far
	Lesson 3
Initiation phase	**Step 1. Pre-text**: a. Show images of *The Gruffalo's Child* and get the children to narrate and embody the story b. Resume the situation (the children have prepared leaves to create a leaf mat for the Gruffalo) c. Prepare the leaves so that the Gruffalo can receive his present. Build momentum for the birthday present to be a surprise
	Pre-Teacher in Role: remind children about their presents to give Gruffalina. Prepare the children for the improvisation that follows, introducing the new key language and ideas
Experiential phase	**Step 2. Teacher in Role**: Gruffalina has received a message to say that one of the leaves is poisoned
	Post-Teacher in Role: out of role, check that the children are following
	Step 3. In role task: children work in groups to identify the poisoned leaf according to the specifications indicated. Once the leaf is identified, it is destroyed through a ritual decided by the children
	Step 4. Whole class improvisation: children set up the present for the Gruffalo and position their drawings and birthday cards on the leaf mat, in his cave
Reflective phase	**Step 5. Revision**: retell the story, including the features of the poisoned leaf
	Step 6. Debrief: children do a drawing of the adventure, showing their favourite moment in the story. Use it as a springboard to reinforce the language

This chapter adopted a sociocultural perspective to consider play as symbolic mediation. It introduced dual affect theory—the dual emotional current sustained by individuals engaged in play, and the implications for second language learning. This was further explored in relation to direct and indirect handling and managing the aesthetic distance that regulates these two spheres. In a praxis-oriented move, the second half of the chapter offered a reflective practitioner account of a Content and Language Integrated Learning (CLIL) intervention, at early primary level, drawing on a number of drama-oriented strategies including Teacher in Role. In the next chapter, we explore the Teacher in Role strategy in greater depth, and the kind of engagement it can generate in the second language classroom.

References

Asher, J. J. (1969). The total physical response approach to second language learning. *The Modern Language Journal, 53*(1), 3–17.

Bateson, G. (1955/1976). A theory of play and fantasy. In J. Bruner, A. Jolly, & K. Sylva (Eds.), *Play: Its role in development and evolution*. Harmondsworth, Middlesex: Penguin Books.

Bolton, G. (1979). *Towards a theory of drama in education*. London: Longman.

Bolton, G. (1984). *Drama as education: An argument for placing drama at the centre of the curriculum*. Harlow, Essex: Longman.

Bowell, P., & Heap, B. (2017). *Putting process drama into action: The dynamics of practice*. London: Routledge.

Coonan, C. M. (2012). Affect and motivation in CLIL. In D. Marsh & O. Meyer (Eds.), *Quality interfaces: Examining evidence & exploring solutions in CLIL* (pp. 52–659). Eichstaett: Eichstaett Academic Press.

Coyle, D. (2007). Content and language integrated learning: Towards a connected research agenda for CLIL pedagogies. *International Journal of Bilingual Education and Bilingualism, 10*(5), 543–562.

Crutchfield, J. (2015). Fear and trembling. *Scenario: Journal for Performative Teaching, Learning and Research, 9*(2), 101–114.

Donaldson, J. (2007). *The Gruffalo's child*. London: Macmillan.

Donato, R., & MacCormick, D. (1994). A sociocultural perspective on language learning strategies: The role of mediation. *The Modern Language Journal, 78*(4), 453–464. https://doi.org/10.1111/j.1540-4781.1994.tb02063.x.

Donnery, E. (2017). The intercultural journey: Drama-based practitioners in JFL in North America and JSL and EFL in Japan. In J. Crutchfield &

M. Schewe (Eds.), *Going performative in intercultural education: International contexts, theoretical perspectives and models of practice* (pp. 233–240). Bristol: Multilingual Matters.

Dunn, J. (2011). Analysing dramatic structures within improvised forms—The extended playwright function framework. *NJ: Drama Australia Journal, 34*(1), 21–34.

Dunn, J., Bundy, P., & Stinson, M. (2015). Connection and commitment: Exploring the generation and experience of emotion in a participatory drama. *International Journal of Education & the Arts, 16*(6), n6.

Eriksson, S. (2007). Distance and awareness of fiction: Exploring the concepts. *NJ: Drama Australia Journal, 31*(1), 5–22.

Eriksson, S. (2011). Distancing. In S. Schonmann (Ed.), *Key concepts in theatre/drama education* (pp. 65–72). Rotterdam: Sense Publishers.

Ferholt, B. (2015). *Perezhivanie* in researching playworlds: Applying the concept of *perezhivanie* in the study of play. In S. Davis, B. Ferholt, H. Grainger Clemson, S. Jansson, & A. Marjanovic-Shane (Eds.), *Dramatic interactions in education: Vygotskian and sociocultural approaches to drama, education and research* (pp. 57–78). London: Bloomsbury.

Heap, B. (2015). The aesthetics of becoming: Applied theatre and the quest for cultural certitude. In G. White (Ed.), *Applied theatre: Aesthetics*. London: Bloomsbury.

Heathcote, D., & Bolton, G. (1995). *Drama for learning: Dorothy Heathcote's mantle of the expert approach to education*. Portsmouth: Pearson Education.

Immordino-Yang, M. H. (2016). *Emotions, learning, and the brain: Exploring the educational implications of affective neuroscience*. New York: W. W. Norton.

Lantolf, J. P. (Ed.). (2000). *Sociocultural theory and second language learning*. Oxford: Oxford University Press.

Lantolf, J. P., & Poehner, M. E. (2014). *Sociocultural theory and the pedagogical imperative in L2 education: Vygotskian praxis and the research/practice divide*. Oxfordshire and New York: Routledge.

Lantolf, J. P., & Thorne, S. L. (2006). *Sociocultural theory and the genesis of second language development*. New York: Oxford University Press.

Larsen, R. J., & Prizmic, Z. (2004). Affect regulation. In R. F. Baumeister & K. D. Vohs (Eds.), *Handbook of self-regulation: Research, theory, and applications* (pp. 40–61). New York: Guilford Press.

Mahn, H., & John-Steiner, V. (2002). The gift of confidence: A Vygotskyan view of emotions. In G. Wells & G. Claxton (Eds.), *Learning for life in the*

21st century: Sociocultural perspectives on the future of education. Malden, MA: Blackwell.

Morgan, N., & Saxton, J. (1987). *Teaching drama: A mind of many wonders.* Cheltenham: Stanley Thornes.

O'Neill, C. (1995). *Drama worlds: A framework for process drama.* Portsmouth: Heinemann.

O'Neill, C. (2015). *Dorothy Heathcote on education and drama: Essential writings.* Abington, Oxfon: Routledge.

O'Toole, J. (1992). *The process of drama: Negotiating art and meaning.* London: Routledge.

Piazzoli, E., & Kennedy, C. (2014). Drama: Threat or opportunity? Managing the 'dual affect' in process drama. *Scenario: Journal for Performative Teaching, Learning and Research, 8*(1), 52–61.

Stanislavski, K. (1936/1980). *An actor prepares.* London: Eyre Methuen.

Swain, M. (2006). Languaging, agency and collaboration in advanced second language proficiency. In H. Byrnes (Ed.), *Advanced language learning: The contribution of Halliday and Vygotsky* (pp. 95–108). New York: Continuum.

Swain, M. (2012). The inseparability of cognition and emotion in second language learning. *Language Teaching, 46*(2), 1–13. https://doi.org/10.1017/S0261444811000486.

Taliaferro, D. M. (1998). Signifying self: Re-presentations of the double-consciousness in the work of Maxine Greene. In W. Pinar (Ed.), *The passionate mind of Maxine Greene: "I am—not yet"* (pp. 89–121). Routledge: Taylor & Francis.

Tschurtschenthaler, H. (2013). *Drama-based foreign language learning: Encounters between self and others.* Munster: Waxmann.

Vygotsky, L. (1933/1976). Play and its role in the mental development of the child. In J. Bruner, A. Jolly, & K. Sylva (Eds.), *Play: Its role in development and evolution* (pp. 537–554). Harmondsworth, Middlesex: Penguin.

Vygotsky, L. S. (1930/1978). *Mind in society: The development of higher psychological processes.* Cambridge, MA: Harvard University Press.

Vygotsky, L. S. (1934/1986). *Thought and language.* Cambridge, MA: MIT Press.

Wertsch, J. V. (1991). *Voices of the mind: A sociological approach to mediated action.* London: Harvester Wheatsheaf.

7

Language Engagement and Teacher in Role

After having considered the role of emotions and play in language learning, we now turn to language engagement as, in a sociocultural key, dialogic mediation informs the learning process. In line with sociocultural theory (SCT), "the relationship of learning to development hinges on dialogic mediation" (Thorne & Hellermann, 2015, p. 292). How does dialogic mediation work in process drama? In addressing this question, we subscribe to the view that second language learning occurs in context, through 'collaborative dialogue' or "language use mediating language learning" (Swain, 2000, p. 97). Also described as 'languaging' (Swain, 2006; Swain, Lapkin, Knouzi, Suzuki, & Brooks, 2009), collaborative dialogue refers to the active process of making meaning through language. It is the language used by the students to solve a problem, to create ideas, to make meaning (Swain, 2006, p. 96). In this chapter we consider the kind of collaborative dialogue that can be generated by Teacher in Role, a cornerstone strategy in process drama. If, from an SCT perspective, languaging is key to the learning process, it becomes essential to consider more carefully the dialogue created between the teacher and the students in a process drama, and the kind of language engagement it generates.

1 Engagement with Language

Describing a process drama activity with American high school students in a Spanish language class, Kao and O'Neill write: "The tension of the drama, and the need to overcome obstacles and to accomplish their mission produced commitment to the activity and a degree of fluency that *surprised* the students themselves" (1998, p. 15, my emphasis). It is the nature of this engagement with language that "surprised" the students, which is of outmost interest to us here. Surprise can afford self-regulation. As we saw in the previous chapter (see "Symbolic Mediation" in Chapter 6), in the sociocultural literature, self-regulation is associated with being able to freely express oneself—that is, to exercise agency (Lantolf & Poehner, 2014, p. 158). So what exactly is agency, and how does it manifest in the language engagement process? As Lantolf and Thorne suggest, agency entails "the ability to assign relevance and significance to things and events" (2006, p. 143); in other words, to make meaning.

Swain (2006) uses the notion of 'languaging' to describe a state of being actively producing language, to problem-solve about language, to mediate cognition, to make meaning (p. 97). In essence, then, we can safely argue that languaging is a form of exercising agency. Van Lier (2008) provides a broad definition of agency as "the socioculturally mediated capacity to act" (p. 112). More specifically, he identifies three qualities of agency:

1. Agency involves initiative or self-regulation by the learner (or group);
2. Agency is interdependent, that is, it mediates and is mediated by the sociocultural context;
3. Agency includes an awareness of the responsibility for one's own actions vis-à-vis the environment, including affected others. (2008, p. 172)

Van Lier proposes an agency scale, to track learners' initiative in an L2 classroom from 'passive' to 'committed'. His scale of agency encompasses six levels:

Level (1)   Learners are unresponsive or minimally responsive;
Level (2)   Learners carry out instructions given by the teachers;
Level (3)   Learners volunteer answers to teachers' questions;

Level (4) Learners voluntarily ask questions;
Level (5) Learners volunteer to assist, or instruct other learners and create a collaborative agency event;
Level (6) Learners voluntarily enter into debate with one another, and create a collaborative agency event. (2008, pp. 169–170)

For van Lier (2007), meaning is made through an active relationship, or engagement, with the environment, entailing *perception* and *action*. Drawing on Vygotsky and Luria (1934/1994), who describe the developmental process of learning in the child as a "newly born unity of perception, speech and action" (p. 109), van Lier argues that second language learning requires an active perception, or "perception-in-action" (p. 97). Engagement with language becomes more intense as a result of this active cycle of "perception-in-action" (p. 54), encompassing both *other*-perception and *self*-perception. Interestingly, this notion resonates with perception as a creative act, as observed in Dewey (1934/1980) and Vygotsky's (1926/1971) work (see "Aesthetic Engagement" in Chapter 3) as well as Taliaferro's (1998) discourse of self and Other, or double-consciousness, and Byram's (1997) suspension of disbelief (see "Intercultural Engagement" in Chapter 3). What emerges is a thread uniting aesthetic, intercultural and language engagement, where agency is a key construct encompassing the affective, embodied, aesthetic, social and cognitive realms of learning.

Van Lier makes a clear connection between perception-in-action, engagement, and agency, as he states: "Second Language development is the development of *agency* through the second language" (2008, p. 178, my emphasis). In an earlier work, Van Lier (1996) offers a more in-depth explanation of the process of engagement with language. He argues that language *exposure* is the first step necessary in learning a language. To go from language exposure to language engagement, the learner needs to become receptive. He defines receptivity as "a state of mind, permanent or temporary, open to the experience of becoming a speaker of another language" (p. 157). He considers receptivity an active state, which is not dissimilar from Dewey's (1934/1980) concept of active receptivity, involving affect and cognition, in the aesthetic experience. Van Lier (1996) links receptivity to a spirit of exploration, curiosity and play. When good quality exposure to language and receptivity are present, the speaker can attend to the language, with various degrees of attention. This may lead the learner to experience the rare state of *vigilance*: an intense, all-absorbing state whereby the speaker is alert and "ready to act on partly predictable, partly novel stimuli" (p. 52). In a vigilant state, the L2 learner processes language through a cognitive, emotional, physical and social investment. As exposure is the first condition for language engagement to occur, let us turn our gaze to the kinds of language exposure available in L2 discourse.

2   Teacher Talk in L2 Settings

Teacher Talk (TT) is a practice used in L2 settings to communicate classroom instruction in the target language, in a way that facilitates comprehension. Generally speaking, TT refers to a particular aspect within teachers' pedagogical knowledge typical in L2 settings, which includes slowing down the pace and over-emphasising for clarity. While specific L2 approaches and methods (Richards & Rodgers, 2014) will influence the degree of TT, to some extent most L2 teaching instructors tend to adjust their speech in class. TT includes over-emphasising articulation, paraphrasing sentences and/or repeating sentences frequently to allow learners to process what is being said. It is also used for re-phrasing and modelling correct language structures. In this sense, it is an important form of other-regulation (Lantolf & Thorne, 2006) that can be useful at beginner level.

In the *Longman Dictionary of Language Teaching and Applied Linguistics,* TT is described as: "Used by teachers when they are in the process of teaching. In trying to communicate with learners, teachers often simplify their speech, giving it many of the characteristics of *foreigner talk* and other simplified styles of speech." (Richards & Schmidt, 2010, p. 588, original emphasis). In turn, 'foreigner talk' refers to a linguistic phenomenon observed in individuals who, when interacting with foreigners, slow down their speech, raise their volume, over-rely on gesticulation and simplify syntax to convey meaning. However, while foreigner talk is sometimes characterised by deliberate mistakes, as in 'me-Tarzan-you-Jane', the idea of TT is of a more sophisticated speech vpattern adopted by language professionals for a purpose, with a simplified, yet accurate linguistic register.

It goes without saying that while these TT features are exaggerated in the L2 beginners' class, they are meant to be phased out as learners' ability advances. Yet, by professional default, to some degree the TT features may always linger in L2 teachers' speech patterns, unless conversing with a bilingual student or with a native speaker. By its very nature, TT speech is not natural; it is an acquired speech pattern. As two decades of research suggest, TT speech is not always that helpful and may actually become an obstacle to learning opportunities (Gharbavi & Iravani, 2014). It can facilitate comprehension, but when too artificial it does not reflect the vibrancy of language used outside the classroom. At its most helpful, TT is a subtle balance between two extremes: the nervous teacher who mumbles or speaks too quickly, using slang or regional idiomatic expressions, and the teacher who speaks too slowly, producing sugar-coated conversations entirely removed from the sociolinguistic richness of the language and culture. Both scenarios are, arguably, not the quality exposure that van Lier (1996) recognises as the first condition to enable language engagement. However, it would be misleading to condense TT into a single behavioural pattern. TT speech pattern is composed of a wide spectrum of different aspects, some more useful than others, including—according to Van Lier's (1996, p. 132) classification: form (prosody, rate, redundancy, vocabulary, syntax); content (familiar topics, current topics, reduced vocabulary, simple grammar, increased examples, visual back-ups, support structures); and interaction (Initiation Response Feedback exchange, error correction, wait times, control of turns).

Here let us focus discussion on one particular aspect of TT: the Initiation Response Feedback (IRF) exchange, which is one of the features most associated with TT (Clifton, 2006). Teacher–student interaction was initially studied in a 1966 classroom study by Bellack, Kliebard, Hyman and Smith. Sinclair and Coulthard (1975) first coined the IRF exchange to identify the three-part exchange that characterises the teacher–student pattern of interaction. Fifty years on, research suggests that the IRF pattern is still ubiquitous in most classroom settings (Lee, 2016). An obvious reason may be that it enables the teacher to maintain control; the teacher usually knows the answer in advance, opening and closing the IRF interaction, therefore keeping the floor, and with it, status and control. However, the IRF pattern is a double-edge sword; while allowing for orderly turn-taking, it inhibits the natural flow of communication.

Van Lier (1996) recommends that L2 teachers become aware of their speech patterns and use them selectively, rather than as an unquestioned modus operandi. Reflecting on my own practice, I remember when I started my training as a pre-service L2 teacher in 2000, I had to undertake a semester of observation and noted a senior colleague's TT. In trepidation, I wondered whether I would ever be able to talk as professionally, as elegantly as my colleague. At that stage I did not realise that TT is a learnt behaviour, and I felt unsure whether I could match that level of professionalism. Six months into my teacher training, I started practising my own TT pattern, which initially felt artificial, but contributed to shaping my newly formed identity as an L2 teacher. After a couple of years of L2 teaching practice, TT became a tacit feature of my pedagogical knowledge, automatically activated as I stepped into the classroom. It sort of merged with my persona in the L2 classroom and 'fused' with my teacher identity. After several years of L2 teaching, I came across van Lier's analysis of TT above; I became aware of my TT pattern having become automatic, and I tried to monitor its use, including my use of IRF exchanges. This was not easy; I found it challenging to become aware that my L2 persona was a social role that I was playing in the classroom. Particularly, I realised that I needed to monitor my tendency to over-use TT when playing Teacher in Role (TiR) in a process drama. After fifteen years of L2 teaching, I started to appreciate that 'TT mode' can be modulated, using it only as needed.

Now, eighteen years on, I see the range of TT patterns not only as a useful strategy to facilitate comprehension at beginners' level, but also as a 'distancing' device (see "Protecting into Emotion" in Chapter 6). TT can be used intentionally in process drama to reduce or amplify aesthetic distance (Eriksson, 2011), reflecting on meta-linguistic awareness. This holds true especially before or after an improvisation in role, while an inconsiderate use *during* an improvisation in role would be overkill. As we will see below, awareness of one's TT pattern before, during and after TiR is an important component of performative language teaching.

3   Teacher in Role and SLA

Eight years ago I was commissioned to run an intensive professional development workshop for Italian (FL) teachers at The University of the Sunshine Coast (Australia). As part of the practical process drama experience, I took the role of the local mayor, trying to persuade the participants, in role as town residents, to take action to solve a matter. In an unexpected twist of fate, during this TiR a professional film crew from Italian public broadcasting company, *Radiotelevisione Italiana* (RAI) *International* trotted into my classroom. The RAI film crew had been invited by the director of the institution to capture a series of Italian events for a documentary about teaching Italian in Australia. I had not been informed of the possible visit of a film crew and they certainly took me by surprise as they rocked into the classroom while I, in role as town mayor, was urging fellow residents to keep an issue confidential *before it reached the media*. As the RAI crew crashed the party we continued to improvise, taking the 'real frame' into the 'play frame' and responding to what was afforded by the context in that moment. "The news has leaked!" I called out, pointing to the film crew. I then lowered my tone, whispering to the participants: "Who was the whistle-blower?" This drew heightened attention, adding layers of tension of relationship among the group. After that improvisation ended, we paused the drama and addressed the film crew who, needless to say, was totally bamboozled by our behaviour. They were expecting to come into a static event and instead they ran into a highly dynamic scene, in which they were unknowingly bestowed a role within a drama, as evidence that someone had betrayed the town council.

TiR is a powerful strategy to create engagement, impacting on L2 classroom discourse in unique ways. As noted in Chapter 1, TiR originates from Heathcote's pioneering practice, as illustrated by Wagner (1976) and Johnson and O'Neill (1991). More recently, O'Neill (2015) features a spectrum of examples of Heathcote's TiR practice (pp. 57–60). Heathcote crystallised this practice in the Mantle of the Expert system (Heathcote & Bolton, 1995), thoroughly documented by a number of scholars, as well as in a comprehensive archive of her work (http://www.mantleoftheexpert.com/). TiR can generate high levels of productive tension which, as Heathcote says, "create the binding circumstances that hold the group in the fictional world at a level of attraction that catches their interest" (in O'Neill, 2015, p. 57). While I have discussed the relevance of Heathcote's notion of 'authenticity' in L2 learning elsewhere (Piazzoli, 2014), in this chapter I focus on the function of TiR to support SLA, considering different phases of TiR in L2 contexts.

Kao and O' Neill (1998) write: "Students do not merely play roles but create roles and *transcend* them" (p. 17, my emphasis). They do indeed, and so does the teacher. This statement encapsulates precisely the essence of how TiR supports L2 learning. The attentive reader might have noticed that in the drama structure provided at the end of the previous chapter (see "The Poisoned Leaf" in Chapter 6), each step that featured a TiR was preceded, and followed, by a pre and post TiR activity (Workshop 5, Step 2, Lessons 1, 2, 3). These preparation phases occur naturally in all L2/process drama exchanges. They have not been mentioned so far, nor were they written down in the other drama structures, as they would normally not be written down on paper—they fall under what Dewey (1925/1981) refers to as the "fund of insights" (p. 266), or what Van Manen (2008) calls 'pedagogical tact'. In Workshop 5, I deliberately wrote them down, so as to be able to place the reader's attention upon these phases. Let us now turn our conscious attention to these pre and post TiR phases, zooming into an L2/TiR improvisation.

3.1 Pre-teacher in Role Phase

First, a word of caution: if using TiR for the *very* first time, it is essential to communicate clearly to the students how TiR works before anyone goes in role, rather than surprising students by going in role and they cannot understand what's happening (O'Toole & Dunn, 2015). The pre-TiR phase described here refers to instances where students have already experienced, at least once, how TiR works. In second language pedagogy, it was Renee Marschke (2004) who first integrated the task-based L2 methodology notion of pre-task, during task and post-task into L2/process drama planning, advancing the notion of 'mid-episode': an in-between step, between episodes, to cater for the needs of a second language learner.

In this light, a necessary phase before going in role, particularly with lower language levels, is preparing the students to improvise within the context. This may mean, according to the language level: introducing some key words that are relevant to what will be said; recapping the narrative up to that moment, discussing pros and cons on the language register to use (formal or informal register) when addressing the TiR; brainstorming both the kinds of questions that the students may want to ask when in role, and how to best phrase them, in line with the dramatic context. Here the teacher is effectively using the pre-TiR phase to invite the students into the 'languaging' process (Swain, 2006), discussing in the target language how to use language in the drama. With lower language levels, it will be very helpful to use the white board as a visual scaffold, writing suggestions as they emerge from the group. The teacher may be using an instructional mode (as appropriate to the language level), which may include some TT features. This phase directly influences the improvisation, as it creates the pre-conditions for language receptivity and vigilance, and therefore for the quality of language engagement arising during the TiR. It can support the improvised dialogue, and encourage the less talkative students to participate.

3.2 During Teacher in Role

During TiR, when the teacher is playing a role, TT gives way to a more natural, context-specific register of language, in line with the sociolinguistic background of the role being played. For example, when I was playing the town mayor, my register resembled the jargon that a mayor may use in a town meeting situation. As Kao and O'Neill (1998) point out, TiR is not a display of acting skills, but an invitation to engage into a co-created dramatic frame, "an act of conscious self-representation" (p. 26). The idea is to take on a role whose attitude, status and purpose within the drama provoke the students' reactions. This may occur by sharing (often hinting at sharing, but not sharing in full) important/confidential information—that is, by creating degrees of dramatic tension.

As Bowell (2015) reflects, "being in role requires not only a deliberate stepping out of teacher behaviour and talk, but also a deliberate stepping into the talk and behaviour of the role" (p. 51). During TiR in L2 settings, the idea is to improvise, without stopping the flow of the conversation to correct students' mistakes, or to supply vocabulary. As Kao and O'Neill point out, it is not recommended to stop the improvisation every time a student stumbles or hesitates, "unless the obstacles are fatal to the continuation of the drama" (1998, p. 118). This is not a clear-cut line, and every L2 teacher will make her/his own evaluation of how far s/he can push the students. An important point to keep in mind is that, during a TiR, the teacher is also monitoring the new language emerging, and students' reactions to it, so to then revise it during the post-TiR phase.

3.3 Post-teacher in Role Phase

After coming out of role, in the post-TiR phase the teacher needs to make sure that L2 learners have understood what has emerged in the improvisation. This of course will not be consistent, as groups are never homogeneous. Each student may have understood an aspect, or may need clarification on some developments. Disregarding this phase may cause frustration amongst learners, especially when dramatic tension is high and learners did not catch some crucial key words or sentences connected to specific information; thus, lingering on the group's comprehension is an important step before advancing the narrative. Here TT may be re-introduced (if appropriate), with the teacher eliciting key words, idioms, ideas that have emerged. Rather than the teacher *telling* what was being said, the idea is that the group reconstructs what occurred, making sense of the language through collaborative dialogue.

To sum up, TiR in L2 contexts implies a preparation phase and a revision phase. The deliberate, purposeful fluctuation between these modes of exposure allows students to experience and to reflect on the languaging experience—while entrenched in the dramatic context. These phases are geared towards the dramatic exploration of meaning and language; their smooth transition is negotiated by the teacher through an artful use of questioning.

4 The Art of Questioning

It is important to note that while process drama *can* generate high degrees of tension, facilitating a process drama does not guarantee high levels of tension at all. This is precisely what brought Kao to pinpoint the role of dramatic tension in SLA. In Kao's (1995) research, when analysing different process drama activities it appeared that one activity was *less* successful in encouraging students' participation. Upon further investigation, Kao realised that this activity carried less intrinsic tension (p. 99). Her study thus concludes that a key factor provoking students' active participation was the dramatic tension generated by the theme in specific activities.

The presence or absence of dramatic tension and the degree of its intensity if present can vary greatly, based on the kinds of *questions* that are asked. Kao and O'Neill define 'questioning' in drama as a "useful strategy available to the teacher to help set up the parameters of the fictional world" (1998, p. 21). The art of questioning can help to gauge students' attitudes, to create mood, to establish dramatic roles, to interrogate a pre-text, to advance the narrative, to change direction, to focus the action, and to prompt for reflection. Put this way, it sounds like questioning is all-important; truthfully, it is. As Kao, Carkin, and Hsu (2011) note, drama teachers ask questions "to shape the story, unveil the details, sequence the scenes, create a beneficial linguistic environment to elicit student output and promote meaning negotiation in the target language" (p. 489). Kao et al. (2011) differentiate between display questions (questions to which the answer is known in advance) and referential questions (questions to which the answer is not known). Their findings suggest that in using drama, L2 teachers in their study asked more referential questions than display questions, and that the status of the teacher, either *in* role or *out* of role, determined the use and the distribution of question functions in the activities (p. 90). These findings go arm in arm with Kao's (1995) early findings that, through process drama, L2 classroom discourse can break free of the unnatural IRF interaction exchange.

Questioning is tightly connected with the creation of dramatic tension in a drama. Accordingly, it is important to note the difference between 'tension' and 'conflict' in improvisation. As Heathcote argues:

> Productive tension is quite different from conflict. It is the key to deepening the exploration of motive that influences the action and therefore the journey. Conflict is a shallower concept, for it tends to lock people into negative repetitive responses during the interactive process and prevents more subtle exploration. (In O'Neill, 2015, p. 56)

For example, in the drama workshop I discussed above, the question that I posed when the RAI television crew entered the class was: "Who was the whistle-blower?" This question planted a seed of tension (of relationships) between the town residents: one of the town citizens had betrayed us. In this way, a potential external distraction (a television crew rocking into an intimate improvisation) deepened the inner tension and motives. Going for conflict, on the other hand, like questioning the crew in role, would have resulted in a shallower response, as the film crew was not part of the drama and wouldn't have been able to sustain the make-believe. In Bolton's (1979) words: "The tension is there because the conflict might be around the corner" (p. 76).

In *Asking Better Questions*, Morgan and Saxton (2006) propose a classification of questions by general function: Category A, Eliciting information; Category B, Shaping understanding; Category C, Pressing for reflection. Questions from Category A include: questions that teachers ask to establish rules, set up procedures, to manage behaviour and that draw out information that is already known about experience. Questions from Category B include: questions that allow participants to pause, reflect and express how they are thinking about the material. Questions from Category C demand a cognitive and affective commitment, challenging the participants to answer by thinking critically and creatively (2006, p. 45). Morgan and Saxton report specific directions and examples for each question, under the three categories (see pp. 46–54). Their work is a useful contribution to developing the art of questioning in ways that challenge classroom discourse far beyond IRF exchanges.

Evidently, questioning can occur in-role and out of role, with different purposes. In both instances, questioning can increase layers of tension, relationships, roles and situations, focus, mood and dramatic meaning (see Chapter 4). However, equally important to being able to ask fine questions is *listening* to the students' questioning, as well as to their answers, and being able to weave these contributions into the drama structure. As Bowell and Heap (2017) suggest, crafting "enabling questions" (p. 70) in the drama is not enough—the *answers* also need to be acknowledged:

> No matter how fine-tuned your questions are and no matter how well-intentioned, they will fall flat if you do not remember that having elicited the students' responses you do have to act on them. (pp. 69–70)

Listening is a key feature of questioning. The very art of questioning relates to listening, while being acutely aware of the interplay between the real context and the play context (see "Play and Dual Affect" in Chapter 6), and realising that the questions asked can resonate on multiple levels.

5   Make-Believe and Make Belief

In performance studies, Schechner (2013) makes a distinction between make-believe and make belief. On the one hand, in make-*believe*, the boundary between what is real and what is imagined is clear, like children playing crocodile, or actors on stage (children know they are playing—that there is no real crocodile in the room; the audience know the actors are acting). On the other hand, the performances of everyday life make *belief*; that is, professional roles, status and gender influence situations to "create the very social realities they enact" (p. 42). Thus, in make belief the boundary between what is real and what is enacted is blurred.

Improvisation in process drama, including TiR, is structured around what Schechner defines as make-believe: both the teacher and the students know that the exchange is playful. The boundary between the real context and the play context is very clear to both. Conversely, a teacher-centred L2 lesson, typically involving strings of Initiation Response Feedback (IRF) exchanges between teacher and students, implies a degree of *make belief*. Learners and teacher can be positioned as social actors, in a sociological perspective (Goffman, 1959). In this sense, arguably, the role of the teacher usually denotes a higher status than that of the student: the teacher is one who knows the right answer; the one who is knowledgeable, and fluent, in the target language; the one who passes/fails the student—with all that means for the individual. The teacher may or may not consciously register this; same for the student. This may be felt at a tacit level though, generating a degree of authority or confidence in the teacher's tone, and hesitation or insecurity in the student's answer. Alternatively, the student may answer with satisfaction (if s/he knows the answer), or provocation (if s/he wants to challenge the teacher). These dynamics of power and status create the social reality of the IRF exchange in many classrooms.

While we have focused on IRF exchanges, this is of course applicable to other contexts, extending beyond the IRF pattern. Discussing classroom communication, Sawyer (2004) points out that, in educational settings, the entire classroom is improvising together, engaged in unscripted communication. Yet, as the students interact in a class, are they actually aware that they are improvising? How clear are the boundaries between what is real and what is enacted? According to the principles of improvisation, for a story to be improvised, players need to 'accept' each other's offers. If the *offer* is the main currency in improvisation, 'accepting an offer' is like making a transaction. Becoming aware of these dynamics when engaged in a drama improvisation (make-believe) context will also benefit the students' communication as they make belief.

In the classic *Impro for Storytellers*, Johnstone (1999) describes improvisation referring to the opposite of accepting, that is, 'blocking'. In improvisation, blocking refers to not accepting an idea offered by another, in favour of one's own. Blocking is related to fear and determination to be in control, which harm the improvising process. Johnstone identifies many categories of blocking—a particularly defiant one is 'gagging' that is, laughing at the expense of the story, a classic mechanism that can sabotage aesthetic mood in a drama. These dynamics can be present both in drama improvisation, when students deliberately play a role, and a traditional class. Whenever gagging behaviour arises, it can be insightful to reflect with the group on these power issues. This may not always be possible, depending on the level of language comprehension, age and contextual factors. However, whenever appropriate, it is interesting to highlight the power and status factors informing the classroom's make-believe and make belief.

This recently occurred in a class I facilitated, with a group of student-teachers enrolled in a Master's programme at Trinity College Dublin. My aim in that workshop (see Workshop 6, *Pygmalion*), was using Ovid's myth of Pygmalion as pre-text to discuss power and agency, specifically connecting these issues with the play *Pygmalion* by George Bernard Shaw. This is a drama structure I designed and it was the third year I facilitated it as part of that module. I felt confident about the drama structure, though alas, I did not know those students at all. Yet, before we could even get to the pre-text, the participants appeared restless, fighting in vain to repress bouts of laughter, for no apparent reason (a painful position for any teacher to be in). In a neat departure from the planned structure, I addressed the giggles, first by facilitating a set of yoga laughter exercises, then discussing make belief (Schechner, 2013) and power dynamics in classroom communication.

This potentially tense start became the platform for the exploration that followed. It served us well to re-focus the workshop, leading into the myth of Pygmalion, and the issues of power and control inscribed within it. We performed Ovid's myth through voice and movement (Steps 2–3), which enabled us to embody the theme of shaping and being shaped, in a metaphorical sense. Exploring Shaw's play in the experiential phase (Steps 5–9) allowed us to deal with the topic indirectly, with the *make-believe* generating some aesthetic distance (see "Protecting into Emotion" in Chapter 6). In the final discussion (Steps 10–11), we consciously shifted our attention back to the *make belief*, with reference to the blocking and sabotaging dynamics that had occurred at the start of the class. This generated insights into power and agency in the classroom, a heartfelt topic for those pre-service teachers. As Professor Higgins says to Eliza in Act 5: "I can't turn your soul on. Leave me those feelings; and you can take away the voice and the face. They are not you."

Workshop 6: Pygmalion

Description: This workshop investigates the connection between teacher and learner; artist and the work of art; power and agency.

Students' context—inspiration for the Workshop: This is a drama workshop I designed for Irish postgraduate students of education. These student-teachers were on a teaching placement and the inspiration came when looking at their English students' textbook, in particular the extract taken from their textbook featuring a passage from *Pygmalion*, Act 2.

Educational aims: Familiarising the student–teachers with the use of process drama to teach English.

Pre-text: *Pygmalion*, by George Bernard Shaw and Ovid's myth from *The Metamorphosis*.

Level: Native speakers.

Duration: Three hours.

Workshop 6   Pygmalion

	Drama strategy
Initiation phase	**Step 1. Warm-up**: a. Breathing awareness b. Emotional Palette: voice, eyes, hands, full body, space, locomotion c. From posture to still image—introduction to tableaux d. Using volume, rhythm and emotions to interpret a text e. Reflection **Step 2. Soundscape**: • Students, in groups, consider an extract from the myth of Pygmalion by Ovid, *The Metamorphosis* • They prepare a vocal interpretation of one extract from the legend (groups working on different segments, six lines of text each) • Groups perform their extracts using emotions, rhythm, volume. The teacher asks permission to audio record the extracts **Step 3. Tableaux**: • In the same groups, students prepare a tableau to capture the essence of their segments • They present their tableaux and invite feedback, observations, questions • They present again, adding music and/or their audio recordings from Step 2 **Step 4. Discussion**: Engage the group in a discussion on how these activities can enable a different perspective on the text. Introduce *Pygmalion* by George Bernard Shaw

(continued)

Workshop 6 (continued)

	Drama strategy
Experiential phase	**Step 5. Teacher in Role**: Eliza's now running a flower business. A best friend from her past applies for a job, but is rejected. Feeling sad and betrayed, Eliza's best friend fears that her friend has changed **Step 6. Role plays**: A role play between Eliza walking in the street with her new 'upper class' friends, running into an old friend **Step 7. [Open]**: Find out in what direction the participants are interested to take the drama and follow up, as appropriate **Step 8. In-role writing**: We hear Eliza's point of view. Eliza has now left London. *After ten years*, she writes to her best friend **Step 9. Voice collage**: Ask participants to read their extracts, in pairs. Ask volunteers to read their extracts to the group
Reflection phase	**Step 10. Discussion**: Here the focus on language shifts back to the educational experience. How can student-teachers use these strategies with their own students? Discuss, if relevant, the 'Pygmalion effect' in educational research, also known as the 'Rosenthal effect' **Step 11. Debrief**: Ask students how they felt in the drama classroom, how was it to use their body, voice, imagination. What challenges, related to power and control, can they anticipate with their own students? What about the benefits?

This chapter considered the kinds of classroom discourse generated by performative language teaching approaches, particularly process drama. It introduced the constructs of learner engagement, agency, and perception-in-action. It examined the practice of Teacher Talk (TT) and some of its typical features in the second language classroom, including the Initiation Response Feedback (IRF) exchange. It juxtaposed TT with TiR, a core pedagogical strategy in process drama. It discussed pre-TiR and post-TiR phases, and how awareness of TT features can support or hinder language engagement. The chapter also discussed the art of questioning and the difference between make-believe and make belief in classroom dynamics.

References

Bolton, G. (1979). *Towards a theory of drama in education*. London: Longman.

Bowell, P. (2015). Teaching in role: Just another name is never enough. In P. Duffy (Ed.), *A reflective practitioner's guide to (mis)adventures in drama education—Or—What was I thinking?* (pp. 43–58). Bristol: Intellect.

Bowell, P., & Heap, B. (2017). *Putting process drama into action: The dynamics of practice*. London: Routledge.

Byram, M. (1997). *Teaching and assessing intercultural communicative competence*. Clevedon: Multilingual Matters.

Clifton, J. (2006). Facilitator talk. *ELT Journal, 60*(2), 142–150. https://doi.org/10.1093/elt/cci101.

Dewey, J. (1925/1981). Nature, life and body-mind. In J. A. Boydston (Ed.), *John Dewey: The Later Works, 1925–1953. Volume I, 1925: Experience and Nature*. Illinois: Southern Illinois University Press.

Dewey, J. (1934/1980). *Art as experience*. New York: Perigee.

Eriksson, S. (2011). Distancing. In S. Schonmann (Ed.), *Key concepts in theatre/drama education* (pp. 65–72). Rotterdam: Sense Publishers.

Gharbavi, A., & Iravani, H. (2014). Is teacher talk pernicious to students? A discourse analysis of teacher talk. *Procedia—Social and Behavioral Sciences, 98,* 552–561. https://doi.org/10.1016/j.sbspro.2014.03.451.

Goffman, E. (1959). *The presentation of self in everyday life*. New York: Double Bay Anchor.

Heathcote, D., & Bolton, G. (1995). *Drama for learning: Dorothy Heathcote's mantle of the expert approach to education*. Portsmouth: Pearson Education.

Johnson, L., & O'Neill, C. (Eds.). (1991). *Collected writings on education and drama: Dorothy Heathcote*. London: Hutchinson Publications.

Johnstone, K. (1999). *Impro for storytellers*. New York: Routeledge Theatre Arts Books.

Kao, S.-M., & O'Neill, C. (1998). *Words into worlds: Learning a second language through process drama*. London: Ablex Publishing Corporation.

Kao, S.-M. (1995). From script to impromptu: Learning a second language through process drama. In P. Taylor & C. Hoepper (Eds.), *Selected readings in drama and theatre education: The IDEA '95 papers*. NADIE Research Monograph Series, 3 (pp. 88–101). Brisbane: IDEA Publications.

Kao, S.-M., Carkin, G., & Hsu, L. F. (2011). Questioning techniques for promoting language learning with students of limited L2 oral proficiency in a drama-oriented language classroom. *Research in Drama Education: The Journal of Applied Theatre and Performance, 16*(4), 489–515.

Lantolf, J. P., & Thorne, S. L. (2006). *Sociocultural theory and the genesis of second language development*. New York: Oxford University Press.

Lantolf, J. P., Poehner, M. E., & ebrary, I. (2014). *Sociocultural theory and the pedagogical imperative in L2 education: Vygotskian praxis and the research/practice divide*. Oxfordshire, England; New York, NY: Routledge.

Lee, J. (2016). Teacher entries into second turn positions: IRFs in collaborative teaching. *Journal of Pragmatics, 95,* 1–15.

Marschke, R. (2004). *Creating Context, Characters and Communications: Foreign Language Teaching and Process Drama*. (Master's Thesis), Retrieved from https://eprints.qut.edu.au/16104/.

Morgan, N., & Saxton, J. (2006). *Asking better questions* (2nd ed.). Markham, ON: Pembroke Publishers.

O'Neill, C. (2015). *Dorothy Heathcote on education and drama: Essential writings*. Abingdon, Oxon: Routledge.

O'Toole, J., & Dunn, J. (2015). *Pretending to learn: Teaching drama in the primary and middle years*.

Piazzoli, E. (2014). The 'authentic teacher': Heathcote's notion of 'authenticity' in second language teaching and learning. *Drama Research Journal: International Journal of Drama in Education, 5*(1), 2–19.

Richards, J. C., & Rodgers, T. S. (2014). *Approaches and methods in language teaching*. Cambridge: Cambridge University Press.

Richards, J. C., & Smith, D. (2010). *Dictionary of language teaching and applied linguistics*. London: Longman.

Sawyer, R. K. (2004). Creative teaching: Collaborative discussion as disciplined improvisation. *Educational Researcher, 33*(2), 12–20.

Schechner, R. (2013). *Performance studies: An introduction* (3rd ed.). London: Routledge.

Sinclair, J. M., & Coulthard, M. (1975). *Towards an analysis of discourse: The English used by teachers and pupils*. Oxford: Oxford University Press.

Swain, M. (2000). The output hypothesis and beyond: Mediating acquisition through collaborative dialogue. In J. P. Lantolf (Ed.), *Sociocultural theory and second language learning*. Oxford: Oxford University Press.

Swain, M. (2006). Languaging, agency and collaboration in advanced second language proficiency. In H. Byrnes (Ed.), *Advanced language learning: The contribution of Halliday and Vygotsky* (pp. 95–108). New York: Continuum.

Swain, M., Lapkin, S., Knouzi, I., Suzuki, W., & Brooks, L. (2009). Languaging: University students learn the grammatical concept of voice in French. *The Modern Language Journal, 93*(1), 5–29. https://doi.org/10.1111/j.1540-4781.2009.00825.x.

Taliaferro, D. M. (1998). Signifying self: Re-presentations of the double-consciousness in the work of Maxine Greene. In W. Pinar (Ed.), *The passionate mind of Maxine Greene: "I am—not yet"* (pp. 89–121). London: Falmer Press.

Thorne, S. L., & Hellermann, J. (2015). Sociocultural approaches to expert–novice relationships in second language interaction. In *The handbook of classroom discourse and interaction* (pp. 281–297). Oxford: Wiley-Blackwell.

Van Lier, L. (1996). *Interaction in the language curriculum: Awareness, autonomy, and authenticity*. London: Longman.

Van Lier, L. (2007). Action-based teaching, autonomy and identity. *Innovation in language teaching and learning, 1*(1), 46–65.

Van Lier, L. (2008). Agency in the classroom. In J. P. Lantolf & M. E. Poehner (Eds.), *Sociocultural theory and the teaching of second languages*. London: Equinox.

Van Manen, M. (2008). Pedagogical sensitivity and teachers practical knowing-in-action. *Peking University Education Review*, 1–23.

Vygotsky, L. S. (1926/1971). *The psychology of art*. Cambridge, MA: The MIT Press.

Vygotsky, L. S., & Luria, A. (1934/1994). Tool and symbol in child development. In R. Van Der Veer & J. Valsiner (Eds.), *The Vygotsky reader* (pp. 99–105). Oxford: Blackwell.

Wagner, B. J. (1976). *Dorothy Heathcote: Drama as a learning medium*. Washington: National Education Association.

8

Navigating Performative Language Pedagogy

Recently I attended a Music and Drama Education event in London. As part of the two-day programme, there were several 'teach meet' sessions: informal meetings for teachers interested in specific topics. I was attracted to the topic 'Drama and Students with Special Educational Needs and Disabilities'. As I arrived the session had just started. Here was a group of teachers of drama (secondary), all English, all based in England. Although drama and students with Special Needs was the topic of the session, almost immediately after I joined, the discussion shifted to teaching drama and English as Additional Language (EAL) students. More than dealing with those who are generally classified as Special Needs students, these teachers found dealing with non-English speakers in their classroom to be a real issue. One teacher, who had been teaching drama in the same suburban school for seventeen years, said she was struggling with her EAL pupils. "They're in second year and they still refuse to speak English!" she complained. "They keep to their Spanish and Greek circle of friends."

Up to that moment, I had remained silent. After all I am a shy, taciturn person. My heart raced as I butted in: "It's like they're resisting their new identity as English speakers, isn't it?" Everyone turned in my direction. As I spoke, I heard my non-British accent leap out of my mouth; it hit the walls, pulled their attention, and came back to me. I introduced myself. No one had shared their names or affiliations. I mentioned that I worked in the area of drama and language education. I perceived a hostile, intangible mood, which I dismissed as my own self-consciousness. I asked the drama teacher how she was dealing with the issue, in practice. She replied that she would do extra work to translate the PowerPoint slides from English into Spanish, and into Greek, for her EAL pupils. She would do this outside her extra school hours, to support them. The other drama teachers were impressed. The problem, this drama teacher believed, was the EAL Department in her school: they were not supporting her. Other teachers agreed that it was a real problem. I didn't want to sound presumptuous; I politely suggested that, perhaps, translating the slides was not the only solution. There were other approaches. "They just don't have the urgency to speak English!" another teacher lamented. I continued: "Through drama, the very subject we are teaching, we can create that urgency to communicate!"

I was very deliberate in using 'we'. After all, *we* were all drama teachers; *we* were all colleagues, weren't we? I had their attention. "Like what? Can you give us some examples?" Another teacher intervened: "I'll give you a practical example. When I'm working with one particular script, I abridge the script for my EALs—I have recently abridged the abridged version of the script!" But how much could one abridge, she wondered, before losing the aesthetic value of the work. Another teacher suggested: "Perhaps you could get *them* to abridge it; this would encourage independent learning!" This suggestion was met with general approval. I, however, was still trying to make my case. I thought that getting students to abridge a script wasn't the only possible way to deal with language learners in a drama classroom. There were other ways. The group now all faced me. "Like what? Can you give us an example?" At that point I felt I had pushed myself into a corner. I offered one or two examples, without going into too much detail. I felt under pressure. I mentioned I worked with L2 language teachers and students, and (disastrously) I said I had a Ph.D. in this area. This is when I started to feel I was losing the floor. "I am really passionate about the topic", I pleaded. "Let's stay in contact! I could forward you more examples of practice." An awkward silence followed. I looked around the room and scribbled in my diary: "No smiles."

The conversation went back to the inefficiency of their EAL Departments, and moved on to what scripts they were using that year. Shortly after, the session ended, bringing an end to my embarrassment. No one said goodbye as the group dismissed. In that session I learned little about drama and students with Special Educational Needs and Disabilities. What I learnt was more about how drama teaching means different things to different people; that translating is still mistaken for language pedagogy in some contexts and that there are EAL Departments that don't support drama teachers. With my best intentions, I tried to make a point, but I failed. Once again, the phronesis of failure (Saxton, 2015) comes to mind here, as I was unable to even remotely address the gap between that drama teacher's pedagogical approach and her students' disengagement. The purpose of this book—and of this chapter in particular—is to attempt to address this gap.

1   The Trap of an Instrumental Agenda

Needless to say, I believe that speaking more than one language is not a deficiency, but richness. Being a language learner is not the same as being a learner with Special Needs—generally understood as having a physical disability, learning disability or intellectual disability. While in the second part of this chapter I focus on L2 learners with intellectual disabilities, unless otherwise specified—in this book and in society at large—L2 learners are usually understood as physically and intellectually able individuals. This is worth pointing out, as occasionally I sense a subtle confusion related to the Special Needs 'label', as was perhaps the case at the London 'teach meet' session I discussed above. A notable example of this subtle confusion can be found in the edited volume *Key Concepts in Drama Education* (Schonmann, 2011), which organises fifty-seven chapters into ten thematic sections. Section V, titled *Different Populations and Their Needs*, includes four chapters: 'Drama and the education of young people with special needs', 'What dramatic literature teaches about disability', 'Drama education for individuals on the Autistic Spectrum', and 'Drama and English Language Learners'. Arguably, the fourth chapter in this section is the odd one out; it might have fitted into other sections, like Section III, *Identity, Culture and Community*, or Section VI, *Narrative and Pedagogy*. The book is a superb collection of chapters from state-of-the-art international drama practitioners. The actual chapter on drama and English language learners is by a respected researcher and practitioner, who worked extensively on L2/drama and embodiment (Yaman Ntelioglu, 2011). Positioning this chapter in Section V reinforces a subtle narrative subscribing to an *instrumental* agenda in drama-based language education.

Recently, Coleman (2017) critiques the work of two L2/drama practitioners who used O'Neill's pre-text the *Seal Wife* (1995) for L2 teaching purposes. Coleman analyses the two workshops, mainly focussing on the steps in which they diverge from O'Neill's structure. Responding to that analysis, O'Neill (2017) comments:

> I was surprised that the structure was used in L2 classrooms. It can be an intense and problematic drama to undertake and may not be particularly useful if the leader has precise *instrumental* purposes. It contains episodes which depend for their effect on the constraints on speech when there's a secret to be hidden – a sophisticated notion, difficult to implement where language capacity is limited. (p. 27, my emphasis)

O'Neill makes a vital point here, one that is worth expanding: the episodes' effect depends on "constraints on speech when there's a secret to be hidden". With this sharp statement, O'Neill brings us back to dramatic tension, the cornerstone of dramatic form, involving constraints related to withholding information. Process drama is difficult to implement, O'Neill continues, wherever the leader has precise *instrumental* purposes. I concur; if the purpose of a process drama is instrumental only, one can hardly call it a process drama. As Crutchfield (2015) argues, discussing the aesthetic dimension of performative language teaching:

> In other words, the desire to "instrumentalize" aesthetic processes for purposes of education is constantly in danger of throwing the baby out with the bathwater. We want the pleasure without the pain, forgetting that the pleasure without the pain is a different pleasure, a lesser pleasure, because part of the soul is being left out. And once that omission has been made, we're no longer in the realm of art, but of mere entertainment. (p. 103)

Here Crutchfield is reflecting on the importance of teacher/artists not shying away from painful emotions or themes, whenever they arise, but developing the competence to manage emotions in the classroom. This point resonates with Bolton's (1984) discourse on protection and distancing in process drama (see "Protecting into Emotion" in Chapter 6).

In reflecting on her *Seal Wife* process drama, O'Neill (2017) focusses on the pre-text's mythic nature as affording a degree of aesthetic distance: "This distance will allow the participants to engage with powerful and possibly *painful* themes" (p. 28, my emphasis). O'Neill reinforces how painful, intense emotions can arise in that drama and be powerful activators for aesthetic engagement. This, she notes, can be "difficult to implement where language capacity is limited" (p. 27). On the one hand, I agree with O'Neill that the *Seal Wife* is not a suitable process drama for language beginners. It can be done, but the instrumental agenda may become a trap. It reminds me, in a way, about the drama teacher mentioned above 'abridging the abridged' script—process drama being an improvised script, abridged to a point where dramatic depth is lost. On the other hand, O'Neill's comment throws a blanket over L2 learners, as if *all* learners were unable to capture the nuances of constraints in the language. This is not the case.

When a drama is conducted in a second language, it becomes imperative to design learning experiences that are dramatically engaging, but that are not so linguistically challenging to discourage L2 learners. This is not an easy task, resulting in many L2 resources being overly simplified, not only in terms of language but also in terms of content, providing dull (but easily comprehensible) scenarios. Thus, the L2 learner may understand the language, but disengage from the content. On the other hand, offering highly intricate narratives may confuse or overwhelm the L2 learner. Where does this leave us? An effective drama structure does not need to be too intricate. It needs attention to the elements of drama, including dramatic tension; it needs the teacher/artist being attentive to reflect-in-action, harnessing the potential to evoke a connection (Bundy, 2003) in the learners. The second half of this chapter offers an example, in practice, of a simple, yet potent drama structure. The structure started from a visual pre-text that culminated in a role play based on concrete language (in line with A1 level), charged with a felt-experience, possibly evoking some painful themes. This worked only because, in that specific context, English (L1) was used as the medium of instruction and Italian (L2) was used for the improvisation. It couldn't have worked in a full-immersion mode, as at A1 level, learners are not yet able to comprehend sophisticated instructions in the target language. At this point it may be useful to consider the different levels of proficiency related to comprehending and voicing abstract concepts in a second language.

2   CEFR Level Descriptors and Drama

The Common European Framework of Reference for Languages (CEFR) has been referenced various times in this book. However, no in-depth discussion so far has explored the issue of proficiency, leaving room for a degree of ambiguity on the alignment of process drama at various levels.

The CEFR framework plays a fundamental role in specifying progressive mastery of language skills, in Europe and beyond. Published by the Council of Europe in 2001, the most recent version is a companion volume with new descriptors, released in 2018. The CEFR aims to: "Promote and facilitate *co-operation* among educational institutions in different countries"; "Provide a sound basis for the *mutual recognition* of language qualifications"; and "Assist learners, teachers, course designers, examining bodies and educational administrators to *situate and co-ordinate* their efforts" (2018, p. 25, original emphasis). We are, I feel, in great need of assistance in coordinating our efforts between learners, teachers, and educational administrators, when an EAL Department in a UK school fails to provide effective pedagogical support to a drama teacher, as I learnt at the 'teach meet' I describe at the onset of this chapter.

In the CEFR, language learners are positioned as social agents "acting in the social world and exerting agency in the learning process" (2018, p. 26). It calls for a paradigm shift, with teaching and planning carried out in such a way as to promote learner engagement and autonomy. This is in full alignment with a performative approach to language teaching, though never explicitly making this connection. Interestingly, the notions of performativity and language as performance are embedded in the CEFR's definition of language proficiency: "In the CEFR,

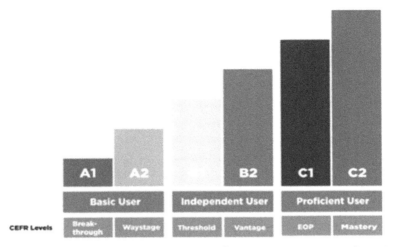

Fig. 1 CEFR Levels Global Scale. Adapted from https://www.eaquals.org/our-expertise/cefr/

'proficiency' is a term encompassing the ability to *perform* communicative language activities [...] and activating appropriate communicative strategies" (2018, pp. 32–33, my emphasis).

The CEFR categorises language proficiency into six common reference levels, from A1 to A2 (Basic User), B1 to B2 (Independent User), C1 to C2 (Proficient User), as per Fig. 1. For each threshold level, CEFR recognises that competence is activated in the *performance* of various activities and strategies, related to: (1) Reception, (2) Production, (3) Interaction, and (4) Mediation.[1] Mapping each one across a series of descriptors helps to create a proficiency profile for learners, "to capture the complex reality of communication" (2018, p. 30). Specifically, zooming into (3) Interaction, several sub-categories are identified, grouped under Overall Spoken Interaction, Overall Written Interaction and Online Interaction, as well as Interaction Strategies (turn-taking, cooperating, asking for clarification). Each activity and strategy is set out in discrete components,

---

[1] The concept of mediation, as put forward in CEFR (2018), refers to mediating meaning within/across languages: "In mediation, the user/learner acts as a social agent who creates bridges and helps to construct or convey meaning, sometimes within the same language, sometimes from one language to another (cross-linguistic mediation)" (p. 105). This notion of mediation does not conceptually align with the construct of symbolic mediation in sociocultural theory.

for which illustrative descriptors from pre-A1 to C2 levels are available. Table 1 outlines the illustrative descriptor for 'Overall Spoken Interaction'.

Many other illustrative descriptors appear under (3) Interaction. Refer to CEFR (2018) for a more comprehensive overview of those, as well as all the other descriptors for Reception, Production and Mediation. A thorough review of each descriptor is well beyond the scope of this chapter. My point in choosing to zoom into one indicator, Interaction, and particularly 'Overall Spoken Interaction', is not to suggest that performative language teaching can only be useful for spoken interaction skills; far from it. It can beneficial for reception and production skills (oral and written), as well as interaction and mediation skills. My chosen example has simply served to give an indication of the range and the depth of the various levels. The six-scale CEFR proficiency classification has been highly influential, as well as controversial (Figueras, 2012). It has resulted, in the last two decades, in an industry proliferation of certified testing systems, instrumental to the fact that particular entry levels are required to access higher education, and sometimes employment, across Europe.

A point of clarification: process drama, as well as other approaches belonging to the performative language teaching family, is *not* to be seen as an instrumental training to take an L2 learner from, say, A1 to A2 certified level. Those who hope for a quick fix will be disappointed. Embodied, drama-based approaches to learning may be integrated with L2 language courses in an infinite number of ways. They can be integral to, or the main mode of teaching, but they can never be reproduced *exactly*, and they always need to be denoted by a sense of the art form, as Dunn and Stinson (2011) have argued convincingly.

As Table 1 indicates, abstraction in the second language is handled in different degrees by L2 users, with articulation of abstract ideas in the target language starting from an intermediate level upward. With this in mind, let us go us back to our discussion on process drama.

How can an embodied, performative language teaching approach be integrated within the various CEFR levels? Can drama stand alone as an approach to teach languages? And, crucially: from what level can process drama be used in a full-immersion setting? Here we need to be highly aware of the trap of becoming locked into an instrumental agenda. A

Table 1 Overall spoken interaction (CEFR, 2018, p. 85)

C2	Has a good command of idiomatic expressions and colloquialisms with awareness of connotative levels of meaning. Can convey finer shades of meaning precisely by using, with reasonable accuracy, a wide range of modification devices. Can backtrack and restructure around a difficulty so smoothly the interlocutor is hardly aware of it
C1	Can express him/herself fluently and spontaneously, almost effortlessly. Has a good command of a broad lexical repertoire allowing gaps to be readily overcome with circumlocutions. There is little obvious searching for expressions or avoidance strategies; only a conceptually difficult subject can hinder a natural, smooth flow of language
B2	Can use the language fluently, accurately and effectively on a wide range of general, academic, vocational or leisure topics, marking clearly the relationships between ideas. Can communicate spontaneously with good grammatical control without much sign of having to restrict what he/she wants to say, adopting a level of formality appropriate to the circumstances
	Can interact with a degree of fluency and spontaneity that makes regular interaction, and sustained relationships with speakers of the target language quite possible without imposing strain on either party. Can highlight the personal significance of events and experiences, account for and sustain views clearly by providing relevant explanations and arguments
B1	Can communicate with some confidence on familiar routine and non-routine matters related to his/her interests and professional field. Can exchange, check and confirm information, deal with less routine situations and explain why something is a problem. Can express thoughts on more abstract, cultural topics such as films, books, music etc
	Can exploit a wide range of simple language to deal with most situations likely to arise whilst travelling. Can enter unprepared into conversation of familiar topics, express personal opinions and exchange information on topics that are familiar, of personal interest or pertinent to everyday life (e.g., family, hobbies, work, travel and current events)
A2	Can interact with reasonable ease in structured situations and short conversations, provided the other person helps if necessary. Can manage simple, routine exchanges without undue effort; can ask and answer questions and exchange ideas and information on familiar topics in predictable everyday situations
	Can communicate in simple and routine tasks requiring a simple and direct exchange of information on familiar and routine matters to do with work and free time. Can handle very short social exchanges but is rarely able to understand enough to keep conversation going of his/her own accord

(continued)

Table 1 (continued)

A1	Can interact in a simple way but communication is totally dependent on repetition at a slower rate of speech, rephrasing and repair. Can ask and answer simple questions, initiate and respond to simple statements in areas of immediate need or on very familiar topics
Pre-A1	Can ask and answer questions about him/herself and daily routines, using short, formulaic expressions and relying on gestures to reinforce the information

sophisticated process drama like the *Seal Wife*, to go back to O'Neill's (2017) response to Coleman (2017) above, works well if the language proficiency of the students is advanced (C1–C2), to the point where they can express, and comprehend, the abstract concepts evoked by the myth (pre-text). In particular, it can work very well, I believe, with those L2 advanced students who have a vast language repertoire but who lack a motivating context to unlock their expressiveness, or who are self-conscious, inhibited by foreign language anxiety (MacIntyre, 2017), or other affective factors. A process drama like the *Seal Wife* can also work well with receptive teacher/artists approaching the field of L2 teacher education. Yet, while a simple process drama structure can work well with a B2 level, the nuances in an oral narration like the *Seal Wife* myth may be too abstract for intermediate levels. In other words, the lower the student's L2 language level, the more immediate the pre-text needs to be. Ideally, a visual pre-text works better with intermediate levels, using sign and symbol to launch the dramatic world.

On the other hand, as O'Neill rightly remarks, L2 learners whose language proficiency is lower (A1–B1) may not be ready to embark on a full-length process drama like the *Seal Wife*. Carkin's L2 process drama, as described by Coleman (2017), generated questions like: "Where's the woman? Does she have long hair or short?" (p. 33) in response to launching the *Seal Wife* pre-text—clear examples of concrete questions, aligned with A2–B1 levels. For L2 learners with a low level of proficiency, such a process drama may not be appropriate, especially if a full-immersion approach is used. This is a crucial point (about full-immersion), to which we come back later. The choice of whether to use full-immersion may not be up to the teacher; it is often dictated by the educational guidelines of the institution s/he is working within. In this regard, a long debate has populated linguistics textbooks since the 1970s, with the pendulum swinging back and forth.

At this point, I will state the obvious: all language levels, as discreet categories, are "conventional, socially constructed concepts", as recognised in the CEFR itself (2018, p. 34). Levels are not fixed; L2 development occurs over time, with learners evolving and growing in competence every day. Furthermore, even if we accept the CEFR differentiation in proficiency levels, an L2 classroom will never be uniform. A student's 'declared' A2 level may be in fact A1 or B2—not to mention that levels very often are further subdivided into lower and upper categories, such as B2.1 and B2.2, and so forth. Applying a 'label' to a group's language proficiency does not automatically mean that the set of competences associated with that level has actually been mastered—by all or by any of them. I have yet to find an L2 class where all students homogeneously fit under the CEFR's classification.

However, in Europe, CEFR is the reality on which L2 classes are organised. Exercising a degree of pedagogical tact (Van Manen, 2008), a teacher would know whether participants are ready for a particular process drama experience. This tact becomes vital at intermediate levels, as working with a B2 group may mean, in practice, having L2 students whose ability to articulate abstraction in the second language varies greatly. Going back to Coleman's (2017) account of the *Seal Wife* process drama, specifically in the first workshop she describes, her brief outline of Carkin's workshop suggests the students may not have been ready to grasp the level of abstraction afforded by the pre-text and dramatic elsewhere of the mythical world of the *Seal Wife*. I'm cautious, however, about taking Coleman's analysis of Carkin and scrutinising his practice, as it is mediated by the perspective of Coleman's eye.

Above I have argued that a full-length process drama, based on a spoken pre-text like the *Seal Wife* legend, better suits an upper-intermediate to advanced level of proficiency. Yet, crucially, the level of abstraction does not preclude lower language levels from engaging in performative language learning. They can, but with a different focus. Though A1–B1 language learners do not comprehend instructions, and cannot (yet) express abstract concepts *in the second language*, they are able to comprehend it *in their first language*, and express it through body language. Here lies the very potency of embodied approaches. L2 learners are able to invest meaning, to imagine, to express intense emotions through non-verbal behaviour. This is what Kramsch (2009) describes as symbolic competence, what Rothwell (2011) calls the kinaesthetic dimension of language learning through drama—through which bodies become a springboard for language learning: "By using *bodies* as a visible, tangible springboard for language this class became engrossed in each other's work, copying and re-creating verbal and kinaesthetic interactions to rehearse familiar utterances and develop new" (Rothwell, 2011, p. 582, my emphasis).

Voice work, breathing, movement, image theatre, tableaux and the kinds of language activities I describe in the second chapter of the book (see "Embodiment in Practice" in Chapter 2) can attune (Lutzker, 2016) the L2 beginner to the non-verbal abstraction in the language. Lutzker (2007) sees the gestural dimension of language as composed of "thousands of overlapping micro-kinesic movements accompanying all speech and speech perception" (p. 374). A level of abstraction therefore is present, but at paralinguistic level. L2 learners at A1 level can express themselves by infusing gestures and key sentences with emotions, giving life to simple yet potent storytelling. This is the very strength of performative language teaching, as opposed to some of the commercial L2 classroom games (see "Symbolic Mediation" in Chapter 6). Basic drama strategies described in introductory L2/drama workshops *Names and Identity* (Workshop 1) and *The Jugglers* (Workshop 3) are also effective in mediating language development at A2–B1 levels. Furnished with this layered understanding, let us delve a bit further into the depth of performative language teaching, looking at small-scale forms and large-scale forms.

3 Across the 4 Dimensions of Performative Language Pedagogy

Performative language teaching is an embodied approach to teaching second languages that encompasses a rich variety of dramatic forms. As noted in Chapter 2, under this umbrella term Schewe (2013) identifies small-scale forms and large-scale forms. The former includes a range of theatre games, as well as strategies and conventions associated with the Drama in Education (DiE) tradition; the latter includes longer forms aimed at theatrical productions, as well as Theatre in Education (TiE). See Bolton (2007) for a historical and contextual overview of how DiE and TiE have evolved. Before continuing, however, a brief detour is needed. Both small-scale forms and large-scale forms within a performative language teaching approach refer to the use of DiE and TiE, drama and theatre *in education*.

In contrast, drama for therapeutical purposes, or drama therapy (Emunah, 1994), is a cognate field, whereby drama therapists are trained as, or work alongside, counsellors, psychologists or psychiatrists. Understanding the distinction between drama for educational purposes and drama for therapeutical purposes is paramount, as second language teachers are not therapists, and have a responsibility to relate to their participants as teachers relate to students, not as psychologists relate to clients. It is important to know where we stand, as educators. Within this textured landscape, the term Applied Theatre has gained momentum in the last two decades, to describe an inter-disciplinary field of practice conducted in settings like prisons, mental health, military veteran centres, respite centres, refugee centres (Prentki, 2013; Thompson, 2006). Applied theatre practitioners work in a variety of contexts; the facilitator's purpose can be aesthetic as well as therapeutical, educational, social, political—often a combination, according to the project and the practitioner's background. This book, as it will be clear, is about the aesthetic dimension of drama for *educational* purposes, specifically in second language education.

Having clarified this point, we come back to performative language teaching, encompassing a great variety of embodied approaches to facilitate L2 learning, including, but not limited to, the DiE and TiE traditions. How do the CEFR levels fit it? How do we attend to the aesthetic dimension, without losing sight of the educational? Much relies on the tacit knowing of the practitioner, based on the uniqueness of the context. This takes us back to the Introduction, where I stated that the genius in teaching lies in the act of listening: listening to our students, listening to our pedagogical hunches, listening to the context, listening to the responses they generate. Still, as much as we can carefully listen to these factors, it is useful to have an idea of the choices before us, as we modulate between various dramatic forms, strategies, techniques, with different age groups, language levels, abilities.

To visually anchor the discussion, I find Motos's (2016) contribution to the field enlightening. Motos maps out a variety of existing dramatic forms on three axes, inter-connected into a 3D cube (Fig. 2). On the vertical axis Motos positions the process/product continuum; on the horizontal axis he positions the participation/non-participation continuum; on the diagonal axis, the play/performance continuum.

Process, *play* and *participation* converge into one vertex on the bottom left corner of the cube. From this vertex, each dimension takes off in a different way (vertical, diagonal, horizontal) culminating in *product*, *performance* and *non-participation*. Motos draws on the cube to map out a number of forms, including improvisation, process drama, role play, dramatic play, simulation, forum theatre, readers' theatre, *perf mis* (from Pavis (2013) concept of "*mise en perf*" or performise [p. 47]), playwriting and theatre production. This book is focussed on the process drama tradition; other dramatic forms have been

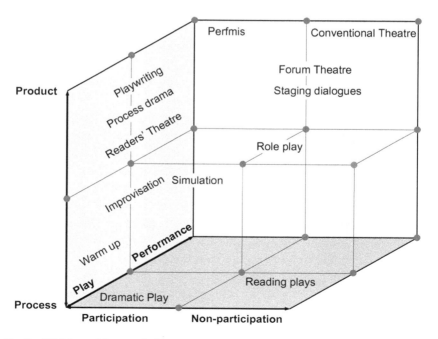

Fig. 2 3D Map of Dramatic forms. Motos (2016)

comprehensively described elsewhere (Blatner, 2007; Jackson & Vine, 2013; Menegale, 2016; Prendergast & Saxton, 2010; Prentki, 2013). In process drama alone, a plethora of dramatic strategies (conventions) exists, each of which would fluctuate on different points of Motos's cube. How do we, as teacher/artists, know what dramatic form, what strategy to use, with different groups of L2 learners?

Clearly, Motos's cube diagram is intended as a tool to graphically represent the richness of the field, rather than as a precise scientific instrument. Any point in the area within the cube may be closer or further away, but is it still contained within the area. This is why holding on to an antagonistic vision of theatre and drama, as in the 1980s drama/theatre divide (see "Theatre and Drama" in Chapter 2), is flawed. Trying to argue that dramatic play is more or less connected to performance is nonsensical, like a fish swimming freely across the depth of the ocean, sometimes moving closer to the bottom, sometimes coming right up to the surface, but still very much immersed in the volume of water. This huge volume of water is not static, of course; it moves, it has currents within it. Similarly, the dramatic forms represented on the cube are not static points; the boundaries between these forms are fluid, often overlapping, with teacher/artists navigating the cube, uniquely drawing on their "fund of insights" (Dewey, 1925/1981, p. 226) to inform their practice, based on their experience, as well as on the group of learners before them.

Correspondingly, L2 learners' language competence is neither static, nor fixed; language learning develops *over time*. In a Vygotskian perspective, development occurs in the interaction between the learner and a more knowledgeable other: in the gap between the actual developmental level, and the potential developmental level of a learner, creating Zones of Proximal Development (ZPDs). In sociocultural terms, the ZPD is negotiated through the dialogic interaction occurring in 'collaborative dialogue' (Swain, 2006). What is the ZPD, if not a spatial metaphor to describe L2 development over time, embedded in a social environment?

Hence, I propose to introduce a fourth dimension to the cube: time. By imagining Motos's cube with this extra dimension, we obtain a hyper cube, that is, a four-dimensional cube – a concept I have attempted to capture in Fig. 3. The fourth dimension, together with the other three dimensions, creates what is known as *space-time*. In

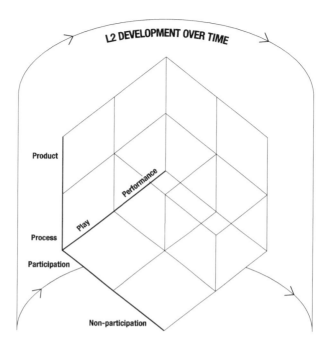

Fig. 3 Hyper Cube: Four Dimensions in Performative Language Teaching and Learning

philosophy, space-time has been traditionally associated with intuition, and this may be helpful to grasp how L2 development over time relates to teacher artistry in performative language learning. In this context, we can see *space-time* as the teacher/artist's intuitive knowing in choosing what dramatic form, strategy, technique (within the play/performance, process/product, participation/non-participation axes) best allows for the creation of collective ZPDs, according to the learners' needs and group dynamics. Thus, space-time can be seen to metaphorically represent the knowing-in-action (see Chapter 5) needed to navigate the aesthetic dimension of performative language teaching.

In proposing a fourth dimension to the cube, my point is to underline the importance of grasping performative language teaching through a fourth-dimensional model that considers L2 development over time, and knowing-in-action, rather than a linear model (like progression from A1 to B2, for example). Based on this model, we can orientate ourselves within the rich territory of performative language pedagogy, both large-scale forms and small-scale forms, at different levels of proficiency.

Large-scale forms encompass voice and body warm-ups (Berry, 2011; Linklater, 2006; Rodenburg, 2015); impro theatre games (Johnstone, 1999; Spolin, 1986); L2/drama exercises (Maley & Duff, 2005); action-oriented language games—notably the Total Physical Response (TPR) method (Asher, 1969); drama games, image theatre and forum theatre (Boal, 1992, 1985). These forms can be channelled towards devising, or towards staging plays. Here a huge range of traditions exists including, to name a few, Barba (2002); Stanislavski's (1936/1980) system and methods inspired by the system, like method acting (Strasberg, 1988); the Suzuki method (2015); and several others (see Hodge, 2000), towards the creation of full-scale productions. These traditions can afford invaluable experiences for L2 learners. Clearly, large-scale forms fluctuate across the *process/product* continuum, as they are extensive processes that lead to a product. In devising or staging a play, both aspects are valuable for L2 learning; as Almond (2005) remarks, when using a script "there is an element of performance or end product which brings its own benefits, but the emphasis is much more on the process and on how language skill development can be integrated" (pp. 10–12). Large-scale forms operate within the *participation/non-participation* continuum, as the intensive preparation work and rehearsal stages occur with the whole group participating, while the play is watched by an audience. They can also be positioned within the *play/performance* continuum, with the very notion of performance defined by Schechner as 'ritualised behaviour conditioned and/or permeated by play (p. 52). They reverberate across the four dimensions, within *space-time*, as the level of language abstraction in theatrical text can vary considerably, allowing for great flexibility, from absolute beginners (pre-A1) to advanced language competence (C2). In fact, working with text is very useful for beginners, who initially do not have *any* language at their disposal, and therefore benefit immensely from working with a script, a text conceived to be spoken.

Small-scale forms in performative language approaches encompass: warmups, impro theatre games; L2/drama games; action-oriented language games (TPR); forum theatre; the DiE tradition, including Mantle of the Expert system (Heathcote & Bolton, 1995); and process drama (O'Neill, 1995). The last of these in particular, a focus in this book, draws on a wide range of dramatic strategies (dramatic conventions). Neelands (2013) identifies forty-three conventions in his A–Z glossary (pp. 93–98); Neelands and Goode (2015) compile a compendium of one hundred conventions, organised as: context-building action, narrative action, poetic action, reflective action. Different conventions imply various degrees of L2 verbal abstraction, for example 'narrative action' conventions may require more verbal abstraction than 'poetic action' conventions. Nevertheless, they all require a basic L2 comprehension for the instructions, as they are not used in isolation, but are structured to explore the dramatic world of a pre-text (O'Neill, 1995). Complex process drama structures, as argued above, are best suited to advanced levels, while simpler structures can be used at intermediate levels—in line with the contextual features. At the most basic level of non-verbal abstraction, for both large-scale and small-scale forms, we have the *breath*. Work on breath is grounded; voice work, body and movement, infusing simple key words/sentences with emotion, can work on all language levels.

At a surface level, small-scale forms seem to fluctuate towards 'participation', in the *participation/non-participation* continuum of Motos's cube, as the group is involved simultaneously as actors and spectators, what Boal (1992) famously terms 'spect-actor'. Yet, according to the specific game, exercise, technique, dramatic convention in use, participants may be actively creating, or actively observing, or both—alone, in pairs or in groups. This means that the participatory involvement necessarily changes, whether in a strategy like 'collective role'—where all participants are in role, improvising as the same character—or hot seat, when one participant is sitting in the hot-seat, the other/s asking questions, or while working out of role to create tableaux. The level of fluctuation on the participatory continuum is essential to keep in mind when evaluating L2 students' responses in process drama.

Small-scale forms can also oscillate on the *process/product continuum*. This applies to all performative language forms, including 'process' drama. While in the past I tended to conceive process drama as based on process, rather than being a product, I am now moving away from this dichotomy. With Fleming (2016), I am not convinced it is useful to construe process drama through an either/or antonymic operation, as this distinction draws artificial boundaries. Schewe (2013) is helpful here as he reflects on how, in process drama, the short episodic units interconnected by temporal and spatial links can be seen as interconnected products in an over-arching process, as "a continuous output in the shape of tangible creations" (2013, p. 12). In effect, although dramatic conventions tend to create drama work that is *process*-oriented, some conventions can be *product*-oriented—if we conceive of an episodic unit as a product in an over-arching process. This is important to keep in mind when assessing L2 students in process drama.

As we have seen in Chapter 4, the elements of drama operate structurally to generate dramatic meaning, in *both* small-scale and large-scale forms, with the teacher/artist relying on knowing-in-action to 'make the skeleton dance' (Haseman & O'Toole, 2017). In doing so, the elements of drama operate on the *participation/non-participation*, *process/product* and *play/performance* axes whereby tension, role, focus and the other elements mediate dramatic meaning. As the authors state: "When performed for an audience, this becomes *theatre*" (p. i). The point I am making here is that, whether the teacher/artist chooses to draw on large-scale forms (long processes leading to a product) or small-scale forms (shorter units within an overarching process) to facilitate second language learning, the crucial aspect to be aware of is the fourth dimension, leading us into the aesthetic domain—to embody language in action.

4 Assessment in Embodied Pedagogy

It is time to face the elephant in the room: how can performative, embodied learning be assessed? To begin with, a myth to debunk is that process drama cannot be assessed, or that to assess process drama we have to assess students' abilities to plan a process drama, as highlighted by Dunn (2016). "Rather", she continues, "we should be assessing our students' dramatic responses within and reflections following it" (p. 138). As Dunn notes, what is central in process drama is to assess the students' *responses* within the drama, and the reflections generated by it. This is an important premise to establish before reflecting on assessment in performative language teaching, where the students' responses in the drama are in a second language.

Moreover, are we considering the students' responses related to their language proficiency, or are we considering their responses related to drama as a curriculum subject? Or to another subject taught through a drama-based approach? This is a key question to ask, one that will dictate the discussion on assessment. The drama teachers at the London 'teach meet' session I described in the opening seemed to be concerned with the responses to drama as a curriculum subject in their schools, and saw their EAL pupils as falling behind on that basis. Placing the effort on translating the content of the slides denotes a focus on the verbal content, a focus that, we have seen, does not align with L2 learners' lower levels of proficiency. In that context, it also appeared that motivation played a major role in those students' language disengagement. In L2/drama settings, some key questions related to assessment and evaluation can be posed. One such question is, as I argue in a paper with Marrucci, are we discussing 'assessment', from Latin *assessus*, past participle of *assidere*, meaning 'sitting by', historically related to a tax collector sitting beside a person to assess the amount of tax owing—or are we discussing 'evaluation', from French *évaluer*, 'to find the value of'? This is often referred to as summative and formative assessment, although I would argue that evaluation and formative assessment are again different. The roots of 'assessment' and 'evaluation', related to the what (product) or the how (process) in the learning (Marrucci & Piazzoli, 2017), can help us focus on different aspects of students' responses in an L2/drama context.

Second, the question that we need to ask is: what kind of evaluation/assessment? Clearly, teachers operate within contexts whereby predetermined objectives exist, dictated by guidelines and policies. In Europe, the CEFR has been conceived as an actual resource for assessment/evaluation, and focusses a considerable amount of typology of assessment, from self-assessment, continuous assessment, direct and indirect assessment, peer assessment, teacher assessment, and so forth. Currently the CEFR identifies twenty-six types of assessment. The alignment of the CEFR objectives, including assessment, and performative language teaching was investigated in a number of major studies (Berdal-Masuy & Renard, 2015; Cornaz & Fonio, 2014; Fonio & Genicot, 2011).

From a sociocultural perspective, Dynamic Assessment (DA) aims to overcome the traditional distinction between formative and summative assessment (Poehner, Davin, & Lantolf, 2017), and has gained credibility through a large number of studies, in different contexts (Davin & Donato, 2013; Davin, Herazo, & Sagre, 2016; Hidri, 2014; Mehri & Amerian, 2015). As Poehner (2008) argues, DA bypasses traditional SLA testing, which divorces real life situations from the test. DA seems particularly suitable for drama-based, embodied approaches, as it looks at the teacher engaging cooperatively with the learners. Raquel's (2013) study considers DA and performative language teaching, with attention to large-scale forms in an L2 education tertiary setting in Hong Kong. For what concerns small-scale forms, including process drama, to date there is little, if any, research on L2 DA. Future research in this direction can yield interesting perspectives on teacher–learner collaboration. The DA approach may be conducive to explore key conventions of process drama, looking at, for example, how collaborative dialogue (Swain, 2006) and play mediate learning during pre-Teacher in Role, Teacher in Role, and post-Teacher in Role phases (see "Teacher in Role and SLA" in Chapter 7).

What kinds of forms of evaluation and assessment exist, in practice, to monitor language development in performative language teaching? Alongside traditional formats for evaluation and assessment, we can focus embodied approaches—according to criteria in line with the language course's objectives. Teacher/artists can assess oral and written reception and production by engaging learners in a variety of tasks, drawing on a pre-text used during the drama, to stimulate recall. This may involve setting up a teacher–student role play related to a specific pre-text used in the drama, group improvisations (without the teacher) related to a previously considered pre-text, in-role writing connected to a dramatic encounter, a new pre-text introduced as part of a newly discussed theme. They can also set up structured reflection through reflective journals, blogs, wikis and discussion forums, where participants interact and reflect on their experiences stemming from a dramatic experience, in either their L1 or L2, depending on language proficiency, literacy, age group and ability. In this view, evaluation and assessment become a tool for experiencing and reflecting on growth.

Above I have argued that a sophisticated process drama structure, as a "complex encounter" (O'Neill, 1995, p. viii), would be suitable for advanced levels of proficiency, while a basic structure can be used with intermediate levels. This, however, is arbitrary as it holds true only when operating within a full-immersion setting. In the second half of this chapter I take a different angle, illustrating drama work with students at A1 level, where I alternated between using the students' L1 and L2, within the unique context of the project—navigating across the four dimensions of performative language pedagogy.

5   Embodying Language: A Case Study on the Effects of Embodiment on L2 Learning Processes of Adult Students with Intellectual Disabilities

This project entailed the design, facilitation and analysis of a language module, with a group of Irish students with intellectual disabilities, absolute beginners of Italian. First, a myth I wish to debunk in relation to this project is that students with disabilities are not able to learn a second language, and that students with learning disabilities are prone to fail, or withdraw from foreign language courses (Sparks, 2016, p. 255). With Sparks, I believe that this is a misconception that, certainly in this project, was proven to be tenuous. The students in this project not only were motivated to learn, but thrived at the opportunity to speak the Italian language.

5.1   Context of the Project

This research project was conducted between January and April 2017 with colleague John Kubiak at Trinity College Dublin. The setting for the project was the Trinity Centre for People with Intellectual Disabilities (TCPID), and particularly a group of Irish male and female adult students with a range of intellectual disabilities, who were studying Italian at beginner level. The spectrum of disabilities of the participants included Autistic Spectrum Disorder (ASD), dyspraxia, Down Syndrome as well as learning disabilities like dysgraphia, dyscalculia and dyslexia.

The students were enrolled in the Arts, Science and Inclusive Applied Practice (ASIAP) programme, a two-year tertiary programme we launched in 2016 at the TCPID. One of the elective modules on the ASIAP programme is *Italian for Beginners*. Another elective is *Exploring Arts*, coordinated by colleague John Kubiak. When we were designing the new ASIAP programme structure, in 2015, we were expecting to have a larger cohort of students and therefore envisaged the possibility of running two elective modules. Unforeseen circumstances brought the 2016/2017 cohort to be restricted to six students only. Thus, in their second term of studies, when the students had to choose their elective (*Italian for Beginners* or *Exploring Arts*) we asked the whole group to choose either one or the other. As it happened, three students wanted to do one module, and three wanted the other—so we decided to combine the syllabi.

On the one hand, the *Exploring Arts* module aimed at exploring key developments in Western art between 1600 to the present day, from Pieter Bruegel the Elder, to Albrecht Dürer, Leonardo da Vinci, Raphael, Michelangelo, Caravaggio, Claude Monet, Édouard Manet, Van Gogh, Dali, Picasso and Frida Kahlo. On the other hand, the *Italian for Beginners* module aimed at introducing the language at beginner level. This includes greetings, expressing identity, expressing basic needs and expressing likes and dislikes. It was decided that the arts curriculum would create the context for the language content, thus the Italian language was taught using the art work as contextual background.

The embodied drama approach used to facilitate learning encompassed voice work inspired by Linklater (2006), Rodenburg (2015) and Berry (2011), language practice games inspired by the TPR method, and drama games (in Italian); basic process drama strategies (with instructions given in English) and targeted role plays (in Italian). The art curriculum was taught by John in English, and the assessment of the module was based on the arts content only. Throughout the project, spanning twelve weeks for a total of 16 hours contact, we documented the experience through three student focus groups, photographs and filming of the workshops, and by recording our observations on reflective practitioners' journals. Half-way through the term we planned a visit to a Caravaggio exhibition at the National Gallery of Ireland, which, as discussed below, proved inspiring to elucidate the influence of embodying language in action.

5.2 Breath, Voice, Gesture

As the project started, the group had just finished Term 1 module *Expressive Arts*, a creative/writing storytelling course where I incorporated voice work, basic process drama strategies and storytelling, in English. Having already worked for a term using an embodied approach in English was a huge advantage, as the students were familiar with routines and breathing exercises in their first language.

In the spirit of a praxial approach to research, below I share some of my reflective notes related to the breath routine, and how I drew on my knowing-in-action to navigate across the four dimensions of performative language pedagogy. For the voice-work part of the course, I used the target language (Italian) only. This was not decided a priori, but came through an intuitive mode on knowing, on the first day of the course. On the day we started, sitting down in a circle, it seemed just natural to address the group in Italian, being an Italian language module. This was not so obvious in the TCPID context, especially as the course was co-taught with John, who spoke no Italian, and I had previously worked with that group, speaking English only. Moreover, from my previous experience starting A1 courses with absolute beginners, I understood that launching in full-immersion mode from day one is not always well-received by adults; it can generate degrees of anxiety and defensiveness. With the TCPID students this might have been even more pronounced, as some of them were prone to severe anxiety.

I greeted the students, and proceeded to do our voice breathing routine, as we had previously done in English (in Term 1), but this time in Italian. After a minute or so of leading the voice exercise in Italian, I noted that participants had naturally accepted the Italian mode of instruction. Shortly after, I invited them to stand up, and we continued with some warm-up exercises. While some Teacher Talk features informed my speech (see "Teacher Talk in L2 Settings" in Chapter 7),

I attempted to speak as 'naturally' as possible. As I did, I was well aware that a full-immersion mode could generate unease in those students whose threshold of tolerating ambiguity varied greatly. At that moment, as I facilitated the breath routine, their body movements and their breathing responses to my instructions tacitly confirmed that I should proceed. As described in my logbook:

> We start off with the usual routine, *inspiriamo* [breathing in] *espiriamo* [breathing out] and counting. This time, though, it's all in Italian. As we roll down the spine, they cannot see me model the action of breathing in. I call out *inspiriamo* [breathing in] and they can't see me, but I hear the intake of air and this is feedback to me that they understand the instructions in Italian. Here the sound of their breath intake is evidence to me that they comprehend the Italian instructions. (Logbook 1, p. 11)

The breath intake I describe was particularly loud, louder than a normal breath, as well as the sigh of relief (Linklater, 2006) that followed. This was done in a position where they could not see me, as they were rolling down their spine. The progression of the voice exercises thus became a symbolic system, which mediated their understanding of the actions as they transitioned to the target language instruction mode.

Quite frankly, I did not know whether addressing them in Italian for fifteen minutes, with no English, would work. Arguably, FL anxiety is a real obstacle to SLA (MacIntyre, 2017), and particularly so for L2 learners with specific disabilities (Kormos, 2017). My decision-making process in that moment was based on what Van Manen described as 'pathic' knowledge, that is, tacit and experiential knowledge: "Teacher practical knowledge is pathic to the extent that the act of practice depends on the sense and sensuality of the body, personal presence, relational perceptiveness", referring to aspects of knowledge that are in part "pre-reflective, pretheoretic, pre-linguistic" (p. 19). This kind of tacit knowing (See Chapter 5, "Pedagogical Tact"), guided my responses through each exercise, strategy, game, affording new layers to the integration of Italian and the visual arts curriculum.

Each class consisted of an embodied series of activities, which I conducted in Italian, followed by a visual arts lecture, taught by John (in English), and ending in an Italian TPR-oriented language practice game.

Occasionally the visual arts lecture was peppered by tableaux, or other basic drama strategies. In one particular class, we had a full-length process drama. The TPR-inspired language practice games aimed to anchor body movement with language practice (spatial prepositions; like/dislike; colours; action verbs; numbers) in Italian. This seemed particularly successful as specific gestures were anchored as signifiers for meaning. An example is 'thumbs up' for *mi piace* (I like it) and thumbs down for *non mi piace* (I don't like it). This was accompanied not only by the gestures, but also by marked facial expressions related to an elated mood (*mi piace*) and a deflated mood (*non mi piace*). As I noted in my logbook:

> I introduce *mi piace/non mi piace*, using thumbs up/down first, then voice, body language and image theatre. They respond to what I do naturally/there is great trust from everyone (even Dylan). I then ask them to walk around the space, and as I call out *mi piace/non mi piace* they physically embody that in the way they walk and talk. They are enthusiastic about jumping off their seats, and follow me around the space.

The introduction of language to express like/dislike was supported by many examples and visual prompts, which students had to colour, cut and hang around the room, using them as reference points to embody and to vocalise the actions. The following extract is taken from my journal, in the second week of the project:

> As I arrive Amy calls out *mi piace!* and puts her thumbs up. That is, she's anchored the gesture with the phrase and remembers it – from last week. It is seven days later, with no Italian class since then, and she remembers it. (Logbook 1, p. 4)

For these students, even though living in Ireland in a context where the language is not used, *mi piace*/thumbs up and *non mi piace*/thumbs down gestures soon became a natural routine. Given the arts-based content of the (English-taught) curriculum, expressing like/dislike in Italian became an important vehicle for them to express their opinion related to the art material. This is worthy of remark as, in other situations, these students appeared to be more passive-like. Throughout the weeks, the *mi piace/non mi piace* expression was internalised (always in association with the thumbs up/down and elated/deflated facial and body posture) to the point where it became integrated in the culture of the course, even when speaking English:

> MI PIACE/NON MI PIACE, associated with the iconic gesture, has become a common phrasing, its communicative value is now at equal status as English for both the students and John. For example, I quote John saying: The French *Académie des Beaux Arts* rejected those subjects related to still life as they were considered lower: "in other words, *non mi piace*". When that happened, the students, unprompted, repeated *non mi piace* aloud, in an exaggerated tone, with thumbs down. It's becoming a leitmotif. (Logbook 1, p. 9)

John then proceeded to show different subjects (still life, portraits, nature, religious scenes) related to French Impressionism. Students, unprompted, called out *mi piace! non mi piace!* as well as *così così!* (so and so), again anchoring the iconic gesture and language expressions.

This became more obvious during the mid-term visit to the Caravaggio exhibition at the National Gallery of Ireland. In that instance, our group was greeted by a volunteer gallery tour guide, who accompanied us through the exhibition. The guide was particularly interactive and instead of just regurgitating facts like some art guides sometimes do, was attentive to engage our students and seek their opinion on the art work. The guide was Irish, and spoke no Italian. Needless to say, when he asked the students whether they liked the first painting on display, the students vigorously replied calling out: *Mi piace!*, physically embodying the associated gesture and expression. The students were quick (and proud) to explain that they were learning Italian at college. In that instance, their reactions suggested that the links between theme, language and embodiment (art work, expressing personal opinions in Italian) were stronger than the new social context (having left the classroom and now talking to an Irish tour guide).

5.3 Overcoming Defensiveness

As mentioned above, we documented the project through teacher observation notes, filming, and focus groups. The research question guiding the study was: What effects does embodiment have on the L2 learning process of a group of adult students with intellectual disabilities? The analysis revealed that, while at the onset of the project some participants manifested a degree of defensiveness towards embodied pedagogy, the symbolic mediation afforded by the pre-text, and mediated by the elements of drama, contributed to overcome such resistance. To elucidate this claim, I focus on one student, Dylan, and his responses within the drama. At the onset of the project, Dylan openly manifested a degree of defensiveness towards the embodied approach. He was notified that his participation was voluntary, that he could withdraw at any time and that there would be no formal assessment on the Italian component of the module. After giving it some thought, he grudgingly agreed to participate. His defensiveness is documented in his comments during the initial session, in the first focus group, in my logbook, and is also evidenced in various photographs revealing a closed body posture. A self-proclaimed 'I'm-not-creative' type, Dylan had a vast factual knowledge related to military training, war combat and the army, with a passionate fixation for these themes, as typical of some individuals on the ASD. While his participation in the drama games and TPR activities was initially limited to sitting back with crossed arms, across the course, a gradual shift in his attitudes became apparent.

This culminated in an intense performance on the last week of the project, when Dylan volunteered to play the main role in the process drama *David and Goliath* (Workshop 7). In this drama, we drew on Caravaggio's *David with the Head of Goliath* as the pre-text, and explored the everyday life of David and his struggle before building up to the fight. What I believe was crucial in enabling Dylan to overcome defensiveness and engage in the language and drama work, was to find a connection between the pre-text (art work), his everyday context, and his interest in war and combat. In my logbook, I note:

> Dylan was in role as David and Ross as the giant Goliath. I was struck by Dylan's interpretation and *intensity of the role*, and by his transformation in the course. At the beginning Dylan didn't even want to be involved in the drama; now he volunteered for this tableau and he seemed really committed to the role. In the focus group that followed, he also made this point explicit. (Logbook 1, p. 14, original emphasis)

To contextualise the argument, I briefly discuss *David and Goliath* (Workshop 7), a dramatic encounter that was created spontaneously from the pre-text, with no drama structure, and put into writing later for documentation purposes. To open the session, after the voice warm-up in Italian, I asked students who was their favourite artist. I asked this in Italian as they were familiar with the like/dislike structure. This phase took ten minutes, and was useful to reinforce previous language. They referred to Caravaggio's *David with the Head of Goliath*, a painting we had seen at the National Gallery of Ireland. At that point, I had a variety of choices before me, in terms of navigating performative pedagogy to embody language in action. I decided to use the painting as pre-text for a process drama.

In the next phase we switched to English, as the students' language proficiency (A1) was too low for effective manipulation of the elements of drama (see Chapter 4) in the target language. As a group, we reconstructed the Bible story, focussing on the *narrative* in the storyline and on the *characters* in the story: David, the giant and the villagers. Some students pointed to the emotional charge of David's expression in Caravaggio's painting, as he is holding the giant's head. This in itself is a very important skill to work on for people with disabilities, in terms of practising reading emotional responses. As the students noted the intensity of the emotions in the painting, I harnessed it to manipulate *dramatic focus*, related to time and place. Through focussed questioning (see "The Art of Questioning" in Chapter 7) we framed the story of David and Goliath on the conversation that David may have had with his parents on the day of the fight, just before leaving his home to face Goliath. Here dramatic focus, time, place, roles and situations were framed towards a role play between the parents and their teenage son. The character of David, constructed by the students as the underdog, was that of an everyday young man, with limited strength, who had big dreams about facing the problems in his community. Yet nobody trusted him, as he was lacking confidence.

I felt that David's *status*, *purpose* and *attitude*, that is, his motivation (see "Dramatic Situation, Characters and Relationships in an Intercultural Key" in Chapter 4), connected with the students on an affective plane. Each of these students had worked hard to gain a place on the ASIAP programme. In a recent oral presentation they had conducted as part of the programme, many students had stated in front of a big audience that they felt proud to be a college student. Ross (who was playing the giant in the tableaux) particularly made an impact statement in his presentation, declaring that for all his life he had been sent to special schools and he felt that 'he had been denied a proper education'. He stated that he was incredibly proud to show to his mother, father and friends that he was now a college student. A Down Syndrome student, Ross was very excited to participate in the embodied language Italian and Art project. He was also actively involved in a drama group outside college and was highly engaged in the drama.

This was in stark opposition to Dylan, who did not initially manifest enthusiasm for the drama-based work. All students seemed to identify strongly with David, the underdog, treated like a child by his parents and the villagers. The parents in this situation would be over-protective, the students admitted, telling David that he wasn't strong enough to face the giant. It was for his own good, to care for him, the students recognised, but at the same time, they said, David needed to do it, he could not live under his parents' protection for ever. It appeared to me, although this was not openly mentioned, that the parents' rhetoric these adult students were describing was referring not only to the story in the Bible; I sensed in that moment a degree of what Bundy (2003) calls connection to an idea at a metaphoric level, a quality of aesthetic engagement.

This emotional connection to the status, purpose and attitudes, that is, to the *motivation* of the character of David, impacted on the dramatic tension in the role play that followed. It informed the tone of *language* that they chose to use, just as David announced to his parents that he would go against their advice, and try to fight the giant. While the instructions phase was in English, this role play took place in Italian, a simple conversation, highly intense in expressiveness. The language in the role plays consisted of a basic exchange between parents and son, related to pleading, giving/defying orders, and saying goodbye. Here, while the Italian at the students' disposal was concrete, aligned to their A1 level, the expressiveness and emotional depth behind their words was deeply felt. Abstraction was rendered through paralanguage, fuelled by the metaphorical connection they had with the theme of being an underdog, craving to prove to their parents (and the community) that he could face 'the giant'. Beheading the giant became a *symbol*, for them, and this gave rise to a particular *mood*. After the role plays, in groups of three (parents and son), we all came back as one group to create a tableau of David and his parents, just before, and after, beheading the giant. Dylan's knowledge of combat and war proved useful here to illustrate the various techniques to fight the giant that informed the body posture in the tableau.

Dylan's interpretation of David was so moving for me that I annotated in my logbook: "I was struck by Dylan's interpretation and *intensity of the role*" (as quoted above). Dylan's attitude in willingly volunteering for the tableau, and his intensity of expression in the role, was followed by this comment, in the focus after the class:

> Dylan: So now that I know a bit of Italian I might be able to translate into English for my parents. Because I'm learning Italian so it's interesting to know so when I go to Italy I can understand what people are saying. Or what's written on something; I can translate it into English for my mum and dad. (Focus Group 3, 6.50')

Dylan's perception of his own ability, rather than dis-ability, related to the target language, is noteworthy. His perception of having learned Italian is related to speaking the language for a purpose, embedded in a socially-oriented perspective (understanding the signs; translating for his parents) and context-situated (projecting to a future in which he will travel to Italy). Through his comment, he is actively constructing himself as an L2 speaker, in a social context, revealing a healthy self-esteem and academic self-efficacy, particularly important in the L2 processes of learners with specific learning difficulties, including ASD (see Kormos, 2017). Significantly, although the students in this project had learning and intellectual disabilities, this did not preclude their language development–a misconception widespread in the past, now challenged by contemporary research (Kormos & Smith, 2012; Kormos, 2017). These findings align with Sparks (2016) in debunking this myth and instead suggesting that, despite these students having intellectual and learning disabilities, they were just as able to learn a second language as any other student. They wholeheartedly embraced the target language use, whenever Italian was used, at beginners' level, demonstrating enthusiasm that embodied their language in action. Their responses support van Lier's view of language learning:

> Learning is not a matter of changes to the workings of the brain (through information processing), rather it is a whole-person, body and mind, socially situated process. […] Language learning is physical as well as cognitive, individual and social, multisensory and situated activity. (Van Lier, 2000, p. 180)

Further details of the study have been presented elsewhere (Piazzoli & Kubiak, 2017). Being a pilot study, much more research is needed to evaluate the embodied language learning of students with intellectual disabilities, paving the way for future research. Yet, what the analysis seems to be suggesting is that these students responded well, acquiring basic language skills over the course of one term. The overall findings of this pilot project also support ample literature on drama-based approaches for people with learning difficulties and special needs (Peter, 1995; Cattanach, 1996), drama and people with ASD (Kempe & Tissot, 2012; O'Sullivan, 2015, 2017; Ramamoorthi & Nelson, 2011) and the value of embodied learning for second language acquisition (Ntelioglou, 2016; Rothwell, 2014).

Workshop 7. David and Goliath

Description: This workshop explores the tension between parents and son, community and personal achievement.

Students' Context—Inspiration for the workshop: This L2/drama workshop was conducted with a group of male and female adult students with intellectual disabilities, enrolled in an introductory Italian and visual arts module at the Trinity Centre for People with Intellectual Disabilities in Dublin. As we had just attended an exhibition at the National Gallery of Ireland on Caravaggio's works, the students were particularly attracted to Caravaggio's art work.

Educational Aims: Practising basic Italian language skills, including negotiating permission in informal discussion (family context); building emotional and spatial awareness; building social skills; expressing feelings and opinions related to art work.

Pre-text: *David with the Head of Goliath*, by Caravaggio.
Level: A1 (CEFR).
Duration: Two hours.

8 Navigating Performative Language Pedagogy

Workshop 7 David and Goliath

	Drama Strategy
Initiation phase	**Step 1. Warm-up**: a. Breathing awareness b. Voice awareness c. Spatial awareness
	Step 2. Choosing the pre-text: Ask students who was their favourite artist, and what was their favourite artwork. Describe the artwork in terms of: a. Colours and shapes b. Feelings evoked c. The style of the painting
	Step 3. Storytelling: As a group, the students reconstruct the story of David and Goliath. Through focussed questioning, depict: a. The everyday life of David in the village b. How people in the village saw David c. His relationship with his mother and father
Experiential phase	**Step 4. Still images**: Engage the group in a discussion: How do you think David felt as he decided he would face the giant? Create, and share, still images of his feelings
	Step 5. Role plays: How do you think David broke the news to his parents that he would face the giant? Form two groups and: a. Step 5a. Discuss David's options b. Step 5b. Engage in a role play of the family c. Step 5c. After each group presents, the others are invited to reflect and comment. How did it go? Why did his parents agree/disagree with David's choice? Why would he disobey them?
	Step 6. Tableaux (before and after): In the same groups, ask students to imagine what might have happened five minutes before the fight, and five minutes after the fight a. Create the tableaux (before and after) b. Present the two tableaux to each other c. Comment on and discuss the various choices
Reflective phase	**Step 7. Debrief**: Asking students how they felt to be in David's shoes—an ordinary boy, proving to the community he was stronger than he looked
	Step 8. Language revision: Students are asked to recap all language structures learned during the session
	Step 9. Final reflection: What is it like to learn a language through drama?

This chapter advanced a four-dimensional model to navigate performative language pedagogy, considering L2 development over time and knowing-in-action. It opened with a brief overview of the Common European Framework of Reference for Languages (CEFR) levels, and alignment with various dramatic forms in performative language learning, both large-scale and small-scale. It also contemplated language assessment in process drama from a variety of perspectives. The second half of the chapter illustrated a pilot case study on teaching Italian at beginner level, working with adult L2 students with intellectual disabilities. The case study was intended as a praxial example to integrate the discussion on navigating the four dimensions of performative language pedagogy.

This chapter concludes Part II of the book. So far, we have considered the question: *How can teacher/artists navigate the aesthetic dimension to facilitate performative language learning?* We looked at some key concepts in aesthetic and intercultural engagement (Part I), as well as play, protection, distancing, and navigating the aesthetic dimension (Part II). In Part III we turn to performative research, grounding these themes in a research-based discussion. The next chapter offers an overview of the unique methodological challenges that I encountered during my doctoral study.

References

Almond, M. (2005). *Teaching English with Drama. How to use drama and plays when teaching – for the professional language teacher.* Hove: Keyways Publishing.

Asher, J. J. (1969). The total physical response approach to second language learning. *The Modern Language Journal, 53*(1), 3–17.

Barba, E. (2002). The essence of theatre. *TDR/The Drama Review, 46*(3), 12–30.

Berdal-Masuy, F., & Renard, C. (2015). Comment évaluer l'impact des pratiques théâtrales sur les progrès en langue cible? Vers un nouveau dispositif d'évaluation de l'oral en FLE. *Lidil. Revue de linguistique et de didactique des langues, 52,* 153–174.

Berry, C. (2011). *Voice and the actor.* New York: Random House.

Blatner, A. (2007). *Interactive and improvisational drama: Varieties of applied theatre and performance.* Lincoln, NE: iUniverse.

Boal, A. (1985). *Theatre of the oppressed.* New York: Theatre Communications Group.

Boal, A. (1992). *Games for actors and non-actors.* London: Routledge.

Bolton, G. (1984). *Drama as education: An argument for placing drama at the centre of the curriculum.* Essex: Longman.

Bolton, G. (2007). A history of drama education: A search for substance. *International Handbook of Research in Arts Education, 45–66.*

Bundy, P. (2003). Aesthetic engagement in the drama process. *Research in Drama Education: The Journal of Applied Theatre and Performance, 8*(2), 171–181.

Cattanach, A. (1996). *Drama for people with special needs* (2nd ed.). London: A&C Black Publishers.

Coleman, C. (2017). Precarious repurposing: Learning languages through the Seal Wife. *NJ: Drama Australia Journal, 41*(1), 30–43.

Cornaz, S., & Fonio, F. (2014). Présentation et premiers résultats de la conception d'un référentiel de compétences en pratiques artistiques et apprentissage des langues. *Editions du CRINI, 6,* 32.

Council of Europe. (2018). *Common European framework of reference for languages: Learning, teaching, assessment: Companion volume with new descriptors.* Strasburg. Retrieved from https://rm.coe.int/cefr-companion-volume-with-new-descriptors-2018/1680787989.

Crutchfield, J. (2015). Fear and trembling. *Scenario: Journal for Performative Teaching, Learning and Research, 9*(2), 101–114.

Davin, K. J., & Donato, R. (2013). Student collaboration and teacher-directed classroom dynamic assessment: A complementary pairing. *Foreign Language Annals, 46*(1), 5–22.

Davin, K. J., Herazo, J. D., & Sagre, A. (2016). Learning to mediate: Teacher appropriation of dynamic assessment. *Language Teaching Research, 21*(5), 632–651.

Dewey, J. (1925/1981). Nature, life and body-mind. In J. A. Boydston (Ed.), *John Dewey: The Later Works, 1925–1953. Volume I, 1925: Experience and Nature,* Illinois: Southern Illinois University Press.

Dunn, J. (2016). Demystifying process drama: Exploring the why, what, and how. *NJ: Drama Australia Journal, 40*(2), 127–140.

Dunn, J., & Stinson, M. (2011). Not without the art!! The importance of teacher artistry when applying drama as pedagogy for additional language learning. *Research in Drama Education: The Journal of Applied Theatre and Performance, 16*(4), 617–633.

Emunah, R. (1994). *Acting for real: Drama therapy process, technique, and performance.* New York and London: Brunner-Routledge.

Figueras, N. (2012). The impact of the CEFR. *ELT Journal, 66*(4), 477–485.

Fleming, M. (2016). Exploring the concept of performative teaching and learning. In S. Even & M. Schewe (Eds.), *Performative teaching, learning, research—performatives Lehren, Lernen, Forschen* (pp. 189–205). Berlin: Schibri Verlag.

Fonio, F., & Genicot, G. (2011). The compatibility of drama language teaching and CEFR objectives–observations on a rationale for an artistic approach to foreign language teaching at an academic level. *Scenario: Journal for Performative Teaching, Learning and Research, 2011*(2), 75–89.

Haseman, B., & O'Toole, J. (2017). *Dramawise reimagined.* Sydney: Currency Press.

Heathcote, D., & Bolton, G. (1995). *Drama for learning: Dorothy Heathcote's mantle of the expert approach to education.* Portsmouth: Pearson Education.

Hidri, S. (2014). Developing and evaluating a dynamic assessment of listening comprehension in an EFL context. *Language Testing in Asia, 4*(1), 4.

Hodge, A. (2000). (Ed.), *Twentieth Century actor training* (2nd ed.). London: Routledge.

Jackson, A., & Vine, C. (2013). *Learning through theatre: The changing face of theatre in education.* London: Routledge.

Johnstone, K. (1999). *Impro for storytellers.* New York: Routledge Theatre Arts Books.

Kormos, J. (2017). *The second language learning processes of students with specific learning difficulties.* New York and London: Taylor and Francis.

Kormos, J., & Smith, A. M. (2012). *Teaching languages to students with specific learning differences.* Multilingual matters.

Kempe, A., & Tissot, C. (2012). The use of drama to teach social skills in a special school setting for students with autism. *Support for Learning, 27*(3), 97–102.

Kramsch, C. (2009). *The multilingual subject.* Oxford: Oxford University Press.

Linklater, K. (2006). *Freeing the natural voice: Imagery and art in the practice of voice and language.* Hollywood, CA: Drama Publishers.

Lutzker, P. (2007). *The art of foreign language teaching: Improvisation and drama in teacher development and language learning.* Tübingen: Francke Verlag.

Lutzker, P. (2016). The Recovery of Experience in Foreign Language Learning and Teaching. In S. Even & M. Schewe (Eds.), *Performative Teaching,*

Learning, Research – Performatives Lehren, Lernen, Forschen (pp. 222–239). Berlin: Schibri Verlag.

MacIntyre, P. D. (2017). An overview of language anxiety research and trends in its development. In C. Gkonou, M. Daubney, & J.-M. Dewaele (Eds.), *New insights into language anxiety: Theory, research and educational implications* (pp. 11–30). Bristol: Multilingual Matters.

Maley, A., & Duff, A. (2005). *Drama techniques in language learning* (3rd ed.). Cambridge: Cambridge University Press.

Marrucci, L., & Piazzoli, E. (2017). *Evaluating learner engagement in arts education: Perspectives from music and drama in education*. 3rd International Conference on Higher Education Advances, HEAd '17 Universitat Politecnica de Valencia, Val`encia, 2017. DOI: http://dx.doi.org/10.4995/HEAd17.2017.5516.

Mehri, E., & Amerian, M. (2015). Group dynamic assessment (G-DA): The case for the development of control over the past tense. *International Journal of Applied Linguistics and English Literature, 4*(5), 11–20.

Menegale, M. (Ed.). (2016, [2015]). *Drama and CLIL: A new challenge to the teaching approaches in bilingual education* (p. 170), S. Nicolás Román & J. J. Torres Núñez (Eds.). Bern: Peter Lang. ISBN: 978-3-0343-1629-3.

Motos, T. (2016, April). ¿Lo tuyo es "puro" teatro? (Juego dramático versus performance) [Is yours "pure" theatre? (Dramatic play versus performance)]. Paper presented at the 2 Congreso Internacional de Glotodidáctica Teatral en España: Fundamentos teóricos, metodología y prácticas de la Glotodidáctica teatral [2nd International Conference of Second Language Learning through Drama in Spain: Theoretical foundations, methodology and practice], Madrid.

Neelands, J. (2013). *Beginning drama 11–14* (2nd ed.). London and New York: Routledge.

Neelands, J., & Goode, T. (2015). *Structuring drama work: 100 key conventions for theatre and drama* (3rd ed.). Cambridge: Cambridge University Press.

Ntelioglou, B. Y. (2016). Embodied multimodality framework: Examining language and literacy practices of English language learners in drama classrooms. In M. Perry & C. L. Medina (Eds.), *Methodologies of embodiment: Inscribing bodies in qualitative research* (pp. 86–101). New York: Routledge.

O'Neill, C. (1995). *Drama worlds: A framework for process drama*. Portsmouth: Heinemann.

O'Neill, C. (2017). Seal wife—Random observations. *NJ: Drama Australia Journal, 41*(1), 27–29.

O'Sullivan, C. (2015). The day that Shrek was almost rescued: Doing process drama with children with an Autism Spectrum Disorder. In P. Duffy (Ed.), *A reflective practitioner's guide to (mis)adventures in drama education—Or—What was I thinking?* (pp. 229–252). Bristol: Intellect.

O'Sullivan, C. (2017). *The 'social drama' model for children and young people with autism spectrum disorder.* iBook version. www.apple.com/itunes.

Pavis, P. (2013). *Contemporary Mise en Scène: Staging Theatre Today.* London and New York: Routledge.

Peter, M. (1995). *Making drama special: Developing drama practice to meet special educational needs.* London: David Fulton.

Piazzoli, E. & Kubiak, J. (2017, May). *Embodying language: A case study on students with intellectual disabilities learning Italian (FL) through Visual Arts and Drama.* Paper presented at the Scenario Forum Conference: Performative spaces in literature, language and culture education, University College Cork, Ireland.

Poehner, M. E. (2008). *Dynamic assessment: A Vygotskian approach to understanding and promoting L2 development* (Vol. 9). New York: Springer.

Poehner, M. E., Davin, K. J., & Lantolf, J. P. (2017). Dynamic assessment. In E. Shohamy, I. Or, & S. May (Eds.), *Language Testing and Assessment, Encyclopedia of Language and Education*, 243–256. Cham: Springer.

Prendergast, M., & Saxton, J. (Eds.). (2010). *Applied theatre: International case studies and challenges for practice.* Bristol: Intellect.

Prentki, T. (2013). *The applied theatre reader.* London: Routledge.

Ramamoorthi, P., & Nelson, A. (2011). Drama education for individuals on the autism spectrum. In S. Schonmann (Ed.), *Key concepts in theatre/drama education* (pp. 177–181). Rotterdam: Sense Publishers.

Raquel, M. R. (2013). Towards a framework for assessing second language through drama: A Dynamic Assessment approach [Special Issue]. *Asia Pacific Journal for Arts Education*, 11(7), 159–183.

Rodenburg, P. (2015). *The right to speak: Working with the voice.* London: Bloomsbury.

Rothwell, J. (2011). *Second language learning through drama: Practical techniques and applications*, J. Winston (Ed.). London: Routledge.

Rothwell, J. (2014). Let's eat the captain? Thinking, feeling, doing: Intercultural language learning through process drama. *TESOL in Context*, 24(2), 10–12.

Saxton, J. (2015). Failing better. In P. Duffy (Ed.), *A reflective practitioner's guide to (mis)adventures in drama education—or—What was i thinking?* (pp. 253–266). Bristol: Intellect.

Schewe, M. (2013). Taking stock and looking ahead: Drama pedagogy as a gateway to a performative teaching and learning culture. *Scenario: Journal for Performative Teaching, Learning and Research, 8*(1), 5–23.

Schonmann, S. (2011). *Key concepts in theatre/drama education.* Rotterdam: Sense Publishers.

Sparks, R. L. (2016). Myths about foreign language learning and learning disabilities. *Foreign Language Annals, 49*(2), 252–270. https://doi.org/10.1111/flan.12196.

Spolin, V. (1986). *Theater games for the classroom: A teacher's handbook.* Evanston, IL: Northwestern University Press.

Stanislavski, K. (1936/1980). *An actor prepares.* London: Eyre Methuen.

Strasberg, L. (1988). *A dream of passion: The development of the method.* New York: Penguin Books.

Suzuki, T. (2015). *Culture is the body.* New York: Theatre Communications Group.

Swain, M. (2006). Languaging, agency and collaboration in advanced second language proficiency. In H. Byrnes (Ed.), *Advanced language learning: The contribution of Halliday and Vygotsky* (pp. 95–108). New York: Continuum.

Thompson, J. (2006). *Applied theatre.* Oxford: Peter Lang.

Van Lier, L. (2000). From input to affordance: Social-interactive learning rom an ecological perspective. In J. P. Lantolf (Ed.), *Sociocultural theory and second language learning* (pp. 245–260). Oxford: Oxford University Press.

Van Manen, M. (2008). Pedagogical sensitivity and teachers practical knowing-in-action. *Peking University Education Review, 6*(1), 1–23.

Yaman Ntelioglu, B. (2011). Drama and English language learners. In S. Shonmann (Ed.), *Key concepts in theatre/drama education.* Rotterdam: Sense Publishers.

Part III: Researching the Aesthetic Dimension

9

Performative Research: Methodology and Methods

Reflective practice, as discussed in Chapter 5, relates to a conscious effort to become aware of our practice and reflect on it, through reflection-in-action and reflection-on-action (Schön, 1983). This is particularly relevant to process drama practice, as the spontaneity intrinsic to the form requires the practitioner to continuously adjust to the context, operating through what Kershaw and Nicholson (2011) call the "mysteries of *reflexive unpredictability* in drama" (p. 10, original emphasis). However, reflective practice is not only a philosophy of teaching; it is also a methodological stance, an approach to conducting research and to analysing data.

In this chapter, I draw on my doctoral research, based on investigating the aesthetic dimension of process drama in second language learning. Rather than offering a set of methodological guidelines, I discuss performative research through the unique lens of the study, in line with reflective practitioner methodology. The research was conducted between 2009 and 2013; in the account that follows, I reflect on it with a critical eye, as time and practice have now enabled me to acquire some distance from the study. Reflecting on action on my juggling roles as researcher, teacher and artist, five years after its completion, it becomes evident that a reflective practitioner stance characterised not only the practice-led intervention, but also the conceptualisation, research design and analysis. Below I reflect on how knowing-in-action informed and shaped the various phases of the research.

1 The Research Metaphor

The first encounter with my doctoral research topic was through a metaphor that I quickly endorsed, and slowly transformed. This metaphor became the spine of the research design. In *Into the Labyrinth: Theory and Research in Drama*, O'Neill (1996) puts forth a metaphor of the researcher venturing inside a Greek labyrinth, a valiant Theseus looking for the Minotaur:

> At the dead centre of the labyrinth lurks our research topic, the monster, its jaws dripping with the gore of scholars it has already consumed. It may pounce upon us and destroy us too, immediately or slowly. The battle may be long drawn out with neither side yielding victory […] Take your vorpal swords in hands, and go forth… (p. 145)

I resonated with the idea of research being a labyrinth of scholarship, and adopted the metaphor to make sense of my venturing in. I envisaged entering a labyrinth where a cacophony of sounds and voices surrounded me. In the metaphor, the researcher is looking for the research topic, the Minotaur. Thus, one of my initial preoccupations as I began the doctorate was to attempt visualising the Minotaur that I was going to slay. I reviewed many visual representations of the Minotaur, but found inspiration in none. I gradually realised that 'slaying a monster' did not fit my idea of research. Rather, what I was envisaging finding in the labyrinth was a mythical creature, sitting at the crossroads of forked paths, whose voice could help me find my way through the maze.

In Greek mythology, Hecate is a three-headed goddess of crossroads, who uses her heads to guard a three-way crossing. Also known as the goddess of fertility, she is associated with foretelling the future and witchcraft in the Shakespearian tradition: Hecate appears in *Macbeth* and is also mentioned in *Hamlet*, *King Lear* and *A Midsummer Night's*

Dream. At the time, Hecate seemed particularly apt for guiding my study. Again, I started searching for visual representations of Hecate. I was struck by contemporary artist Patricia Ariel's artwork of Hecate, a watercolour and graphite painted on illustration board (Fig. 1).

An intangible quality of this artwork captured my imagination. Perhaps it was the vibrant transparency of the watercolour, the seriousness of the three women's gaze, the contrast of the cold gazes and sensual curves, the wolf resting on the hip of the central figure. Whatever it was, an instinctual pull towards the work established a solid connection

Fig. 1 Hecate, Patricia Ariel (2008)

between O'Neill's labyrinth metaphor, the character of Hecate, and that painting. I used this imagery as a visual anchor to make sense of my research, in several aspects: in structuring the Research Questions, in conceptualising the literature review, in designing the research methods, in presenting my analysis, in making sense of the findings, and in the thesis structure (main title, title of the chapters).

Reflecting on action in this aspect of my research process, it occurs to me how important I felt it was to look for a metaphor in the first place; to appropriate it, not only to give explicit form to an abstract topic, but also to interpret this abstraction into new symbolic meanings. As Haseman (2006) puts it, this process can provide focus in performative research:

> Attending to the symbolic form of particular artworks provides a powerful focus for the performative researcher (and their audience) as each symbol functions as a means to conceptualise ideas about aspects of reality, and also as a means of communicating what is known to others. (p. 105)

My research topic, the aesthetic dimension of process drama in second language learning, was a complex area that needed to be communicated clearly. The concept of 'simplexity' (Berthoz, 2012) applied to education, research and praxis (Sibilio, 2015) becomes relevant here, as it allows for complex ideas to be explored in 'simplex' ways. In this case, the metaphor allowed for that simplex process to emerge. Visualising Hecate as a three-headed creature felt particularly apt, as I realised that my research topic was also informed by three heads, or domains: Second Language Acquisition (SLA); Intercultural Education; Aesthetic Learning. These domains merge into one interdisciplinary body—process drama in second language teaching and learning. In the same year I completed the doctoral research, Schewe (2013) published a seminal article calling for this interdisciplinary field to be framed as performative language teaching. I now see that I framed Hecate's imagery as a metaphor for performative language teaching and research, with each head as one of the informing domains.

This phase of my research, from the quest for a suitable metaphor, to its adaptation into a visual identity of that metaphor, represented not only a cognitive effort to conceptualise the research, but my aesthetic engagement with the process of research itself, to make sense of, and to create new meanings through, symbol and form. These premises, as well as the practice-led approach embedded in the fieldwork, echo a performative research paradigm.

2   Performative Research

In *A Manifesto for Performative Research*, Haseman (2006) advocates for a performative paradigm to research, insisting on the importance of practice: "The 'practice' in 'practice-led research' is primary—it is not an optional extra; it is the necessary pre-condition of engagement in performative research" (p. 103). He proposes that practice-led research aims at "new epistemologies of practice distilled from the insider's understandings of action in context" (p. 100). He situates performative research as practice-led research, defined, with Gray (1996), as:

> Firstly, research which is initiated in practice, where questions, problems, challenges are identified and formed by the needs of practice and practitioners; and secondly, that the research strategy is carried out through practice, using predominantly methodologies and specific methods familiar to us as practitioners. (1996, p. 3)

My research was practice-based, in the sense that it involved the design of three process dramas, and forty-five hours of drama practice, conducted with thirty-four student-participants, and observed by fourteen teacher-participants, across multiple case studies (Stake, 2013). Specifically, the research was concerned with my developing understanding of the aesthetic dimension of process drama for second language learning, with reference to two main constructs: *engagement* and *artistry*. Through the metaphor of the three-headed Hecate, I broke down engagement into three fields: SLA, Intercultural Education and Aesthetic Learning. This perspective was further articulated into two Research Questions:

- What is the nature of engagement in process drama within the Second Language Acquisition, Intercultural and Aesthetic domains?

- How can a Second Language teacher develop and harness process drama artistry to facilitate engagement?

These questions were explored through a practice-led approach to research, but were not just confined to practice. As Freire states:

> Without practice, there's no knowledge. At least it's difficult to know without practice. We have to have a certain *theoretical kind of practice* in order to know also. But practice in itself is not its theory. It creates knowledge, but it is not its own theory. (in Horton & Freire, 1990, p. 98, my emphasis)

I see this 'theoretical kind of practice' as the bridge between practice and theory, rendered by practice-based methodologies. Haseman (2007) argues that performative research embraces methodologies like reflective practitioner, participatory research and action research. I chose to explore my research aims through reflective practitioner methodology. Before going further, a brief account of the context of the study will help to focus the discussion.

The thirty-four student-participants in the study were adult international students, studying Italian as a Second Language (L2) in Milan, Italy. In Case Study One, student-participants were sixteen international students, enrolled in a second year Linguistics course, in a Cultural Mediation undergraduate degree at a public university. They came from different provinces of mainland China, except for one from Tibet. They were aged between 21 and 25, and were enrolled in the university's exchange programme. In Case Study Two, they were nine female learners of Italian (L2), enrolled in a private language school, ranging from 20 to 50 years old. They came from various countries, including Russia, the United States, Japan and Taiwan. In Case Study Three, nine female student-participants were enrolled in a private school of Italian (L2). Their ages ranged from 23 to 51, and they came from Brazil, German-speaking Switzerland, Iran, Taiwan and Russia. On paper, their proficiency was aligned with B2 level. But their actual levels spanned from B1 to C1. Two Brazilian students' proficiency was aligned with A1 level. None of these students had heard of process drama before our introductory meeting.

The fourteen teacher-participants in the study were all native Italian speakers, either pre-service or accredited teachers of Italian (L2). The three teacher-participants in Case Study One were pre-service teachers enrolled in a Teacher Education (L2) Master Degree at the same university. All three teacher-participants observed each drama workshop continuously. The teacher-participants in Case Study Two were three accredited teachers and one pre-service teacher. Their participation in the project was voluntary, offered by the school as a 15-hour in-service, embedded in their teaching roster. Not all of them observed continuously. Teacher-participants in Case Study Three were seven accredited teachers. Their participation was voluntary, offered by the school as a 15-hour in-service, outside their teaching roster. Five teachers observed some workshops, in rotation, while two (including the school director) observed each workshop, continuously. No more than four teachers observed one workshop at the same time. None of these teachers had heard of process drama before our introductory meeting.

3 Problem-setting

In discussing performative research, Haseman (2006) points to "enthusiasm of practice" as opposed to "narrow problem-setting", as the researcher's main attitude:

> Many practice-led researchers do not commence a research project with a sense of 'a problem'. Indeed, they may be led by what is best described as 'an enthusiasm of practice' — something which is exciting, something which may be unruly [...] This is not to say that these researchers work without larger agendas or emancipatory aspirations, but they eschew the *constraints of narrow problem-setting* and rigid methodological requirements at the outset of a project. (2006, p. 100, my emphasis)

During the research methods design, that is, before carrying out the practice-based fieldwork, I was often faced with methodological dilemmas. My "enthusiasm of practice", as Haseman put it, deeply craved methodological clarity to thrive in action. Surely, I eschewed the constraints of 'narrow problem-setting'. However, at the same time, I embraced the constraints of *productive* problem-setting, which, with Schön (1983), can guide reflective practitioners in situations that are unique and unpredictable.

Constraints, as storytellers know, create productive tension, and I followed this through. This tension, as we will see below, led me into new territories, on an ontological quest for the essence of aesthetic engagement in second language education. Below I reflect on some problem-setting that I encountered in the methods design, and on how a reflective practitioner approach gave rise to a number of creative solutions—some disastrous, resulting in the discarding of data, and some exciting, resulting in new methodological developments.

3.1 Creating Descriptors

- Problem-setting: Research tools needed to allow participants to express their perception of the given phenomenon. These research tools needed to be framed concisely, to allow participants to reflect on their engagement as clearly as possible. 'Learner engagement' is too broad a construct for this.

The first Research Question was about my understanding of the aesthetic dimension of process related to learner engagement. In order to create effective research tools, I needed to clearly frame the concept of engagement, which was not that easy a task, as engagement can be defined in several ways (Alred, Byram, & Fleming, 2003; Bundy, 2003; Kress, 2009; Platt & Brooks, 2002; Svalberg, 2009; Van Lier, 1996, 2004). At that point, the visual metaphor of Hecate proved strategic to initiate the design of research tools. For each of Hecate's three faces (SLA, Intercultural, Aesthetic Learning) I associated an orientation to engagement, as shown in the diagram (Fig. 2). This unravelled some initial knots.

To initially visualise ways that would enable participants to reflect on their self-perceived engagement, I broke down 'engagement' into three indicators, corresponding to Hecate's sets of eyes: (a) engagement with

9 Performative Research: Methodology and Methods

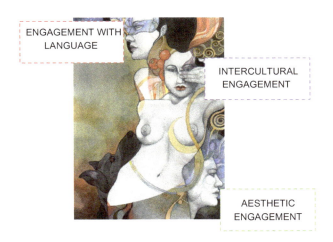

Fig. 2 Breaking down the construct of learner engagement

language; (b) intercultural engagement; and (c) aesthetic engagement. Engagement with language was informed by van Lier's (1996, 2004) discourse on perception-in-action (see "Language Engagement" in Chapter 7). Intercultural engagement was informed by Byram's (1997) 'dual operation' in readiness to suspend disbelief and willingness to suspend beliefs about cultural meanings (see "Intercultural Engagement" in Chapter 3). Aesthetic engagement drew on Dewey (1934/1980) and Vygotsky's (1926/1971) notions of active and creative perception (see "Aesthetic Engagement" in Chapter 3), and the collision of contradictory emotions generated by form on content (see "Aesthetics in Education" in Chapter 3). While I was positive about being able to draw on qualitative interviews and questionnaires to investigate the first two indicators, I felt the third indicator was still too abstract to be clearly articulated in an interview question or questionnaire item. I knew that in order to design a method to investigate aesthetic learning, the third gaze of Hecate needed further breaking down.

The paradigm of simplexity lends itself well to this operation. Lost in a particularly complex nook of the labyrinth, I needed to make some sense of this complexity, and to communicate it as efficiently, as clearly, as concisely as possible, through the research methods instructions to my research participants. Sibilio (2015) discusses the simplicity paradigm in education, recognising "the constant attempt to resolve the tension between simple and complex, theory and practice, descriptive models and praxis exigencies" (p. 488). I took this one step further, using simplexity to make sense of reflective practitioner research. The task at hand was simplexifying the construct of 'aesthetic engagement', in order to enable the research participants to make sense of it, and to articulate their experience of it.

3.2   Simplexifying 'Aesthetics'

- Problem-setting: Research tools needed simple instructions. These tools needed to align with the needs of research participants. The research participants—foreign language speakers—needed basic language to understand the instructions. Aesthetics is too complex a concept.

The problem-setting I faced in designing the architecture for the methods was that 'aesthetic engagement' was too difficult to explain to my student-participants, for a number of reasons. The student-participants' level of Italian, as mentioned above, ranged from lower-intermediate to advanced. 'Aesthetics', as we have seen in Chapter 3, is certainly not a basic concept. Arguably, it is a complex concept to convey to native speakers over the course of a series of philosophy lectures, let alone to second language learners. Moreover, student-participants came from a wide spectrum of age groups, education, ethnic and cultural backgrounds, each of which would have its own interpretation of aesthetic engagement. A direct question on a questionnaire, like 'rate your aesthetic engagement' would have been a leap in the dark. Expecting a homogeneous understanding of a concept such as 'aesthetics' would be unrealistic even with educated native speakers from the same background, as the depth of this concept can be associated with various philosophical traditions. In the case of the research participants, not all of them, if any, were educated in philosophy. Filling this gap, in a foreign language, at B2 level, was well beyond my remit.

As if the semantic complexity of the term wasn't enough, a semiotic complication prevented me from using the term. In contemporary Italian, the term 'aesthetic' has been hijacked by the beauty industry, and often appears on the front house signs of beauty parlour centres, commonly found around the research venues. Beauty centres abound in the city centre, with *centro estetico* (literally: 'aesthetic centre') being such a common sighting in central Milan that the opportunities for misinterpretation were served on a silver platter.

Thus, the third indicator (aesthetic engagement) was broken down into three indicators: (c.i) affective engagement, and (c.ii) engagement with the art form (perceiving), and (c.iii) engagement with the art form (creating). My understanding of these indicators was informed by theories of dual affect and play, and the Vygotskyan connection between emotion and cognition. Engagement with the art form (perceiving and creating) was informed by Dewey (1934/1980) and Vygotsky's (1926/1971)'s notions of aesthetic engagement, as well as Bolton (1979), Bundy (2003) and Gallagher's (2005) notion of aesthetic engagement in process drama (see "Aesthetic Engagement in Process Drama" in Chapter 3) (Fig. 3).

This operation enabled me to conceive of a number of methods to capture the various gazes: questionnaires for the student-participants, observation templates for the teacher-participants, interviews for both cohorts.

The questionnaire tool invited the student-participants to evaluate their own learner engagement in a *specific moment* of the drama. This attention to specificity was mandated by Bundy's (2005) discourse on working within a specific moment. The questionnaire was conceived to be a tool for self-evaluation, where student-participants could reflect on a specific moment of the drama, immediately after the workshop had finished. The questionnaire aimed to get students to reflect on three indicators: (a) engagement with language, (b) intercultural engagement, and (c.i) affective engagement. These indicators were then crystallised into descriptors, resulting in three clear statements, as close as possible to students' classroom culture. They were statements that the students could identify with, or refuse, on a scale from one to ten:

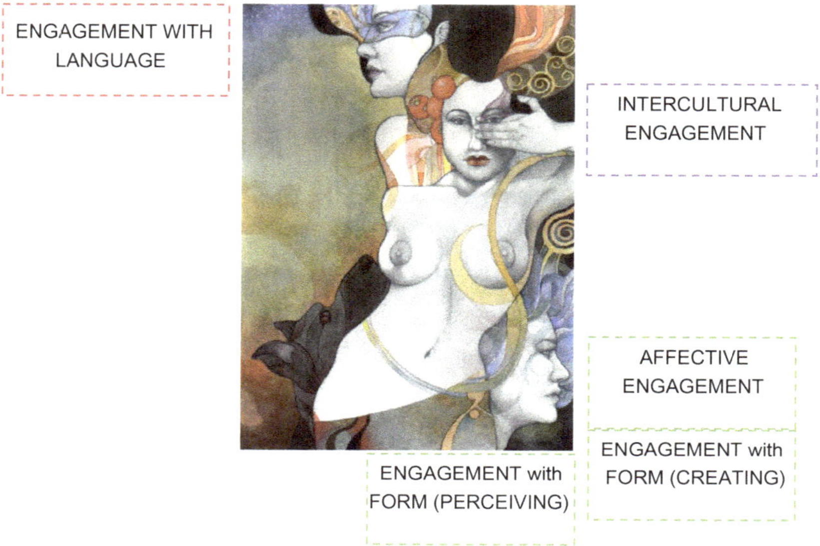

Fig. 3 Aesthetic engagement indicators

(a) In [specific moment of the drama]: I wanted to speak in Italian a lot/I did not feel like speaking in Italian at all;
(b) [Specific moment of the drama] made me reflect a lot on my culture, in relationship to the Italian culture/did not make me reflect on any culture at all;
(c) [Specific moment] made me feel powerful emotions/did not make me feel any emotion at all.

The questionnaire (Fig. 4) was a graphic representation of the scales on which to gauge these statements. Statements were placed at the top and bottom of three large arrows, taking over an entire A4 page, which student-participants had to cross at the point they felt most appropriate. The purpose of the questionnaires being as graphic as possible, rather than descriptive, was to bypass the language barrier (students were not required to write anything; just to tick), but at the same time to start them thinking about these issues so that, in the follow-up interview, we would have a graphic platform for discussion. In that, the self-evaluation

9 Performative Research: Methodology and Methods   237

COME TI SEI SENTITO OGGI IN CLASSE DURANTE __SUL TRENO__ [MOMENTO SPECIFICO]?
INDICALO CON UN PICCOLO SEGNO SULLE FRECCE

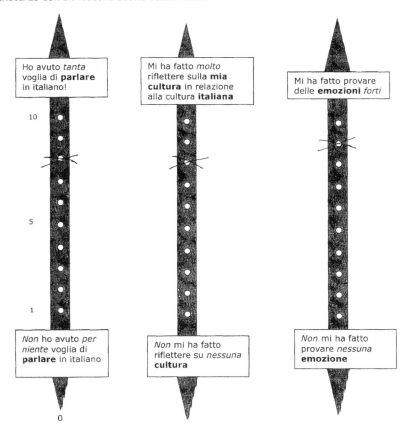

Fig. 4 Engagement questionnaire template

questionnaire was conceived as a support for the collection of qualitative data, rather than an instrument to generate data for quantitative analysis.

On the other hand, the interviews aimed to get students to follow up on their self-perception of: (a) language engagement, (b) intercultural engagement, (c.i) affective engagement, and importantly to reflect on the other two indicators in the 'aesthetic engagement' category; (c.ii) engagement with dramatic form (perceiving); and (c.iii) engagement with dramatic form (creating). Specific interview questions were designed to solicit their impressions of engagement with their emotions, and with dramatic form, in terms of both perception and creation. Besides seeking demographic information, the student-interview questions included:

(1) What was your *favourite/least favourite* part of the workshop? Why?
(2) What moment do you remember *most vividly* from today's workshop?
(3) How did you feel in that specific moment?
(4) What did you learn today about [intercultural topic]?
(5) What did you find most *challenging*? Why?
(6) What did you learn today about *yourself* as an *L2 learner*?
(7) What did you learn today about your *cultural* background?
(8) What about the *other learners'* backgrounds?
(9) What did you learn today about your *relationship to Italian culture*?
(10) They say process drama is an *art form*. Did it seem like an art form to *you*?
(11) If so, did you feel like an artist?
    [Discuss Engagement Questionnaire]

These indicators of engagement were also used to evaluate the teacher-participants' *perception* of students' engagement. The teachers were asked to observe, and take notes, of the student-participants' engagement in terms of the three indicators (a), (b), and (c.i). Thus, the teacher-participants' observation template required them to observe and record specific moments of the drama, and specific students, breaking down their observation according to communicative, intercultural, and affective engagement. The word choice of 'communicative engagement', rather than 'engagement with language' was made in an effort to get closer to the teachers' classroom culture, as 'communicative' is a term widely understood by L2 professionals (all teacher-participants identified with the communicative approach).

The teacher-participants were also interviewed, once, immediately before the observation, and immediately after. In the pre-observation questionnaire, I aimed to gather information on the teachers' pedagogical approach and their beliefs about teaching and learning, previous experience with drama pedagogy, expectations of the workshop. In post-observation interviews, teacher-participants were asked to follow-up, using the template that they had used for the observations (with the three indicators) as a springboard for discussion. Besides demographic information, the post-observation teacher-interview questions included:

1. What did you think? Tell me your overall impressions;
2. How is this approach different to the way you usually teach?
3. Discuss their observation sheet—refer to their notes and comment;
4. What do you think was the *most* effective part of the lesson plan
    a. From *your* point of view?
    b. From *the students'* point of view? Why?
5. What was the *least* effective part of the lesson plan
    a. From *your* point of view?
    b. From *the students'* point of view? Why?
6. What do you think about process drama, from what you've experienced so far?
7. They say process drama is an *art form*. Did it seem an art form to *you*? In what way?

While the interviews occurred throughout the drama practice, the focus groups (see "Kinaesthetic Focus Groups" in this Chapter) were conducted at the end of the drama experience. Similarly, the focus groups aimed to gather participants' perceptions of all of the various indicators of engagement.

To sum up, the first Research Question gave rise to some problem-setting propositions, inherent to the specificity of the context. This resulted in the aesthetic dimension of learner engagement in L2/process drama being expanded into a series of descriptors, captured by a number of methods (questionnaires, observations, interviews and focus groups) as represented by Fig. 5.

While these research tools were aimed to bring forth the perceptions of participants, it was also my intent to capture the process drama practice through the 'objective' eye of a video camera, in order to later

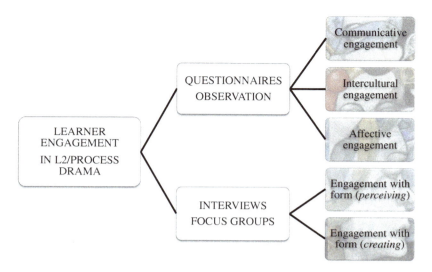

Fig. 5 Research methods, research question one

cross-reference the subjective participants' voices with filmed sequences. This proved to be the next problem-setting challenge in the journey, as I ventured deeper in the labyrinth of research.

3.3 Ethnographic Filming

- Problem-setting: The research called for an ethnographic stance to recording classroom fieldwork. Ethnographic filming entails capturing the action *as it is*. Filming a process drama entails filming dynamic frames that continuously change in the space of the classroom, and multiple groups of participants operating simultaneously. The definition of ethnographic filming needed to be revisited for effective film-making.

With process drama being an unscripted, improvised collective form, from the outset I felt that capturing it on camera was essential to later analyse it. Using film in educational research is an established practice.

However, often in educational research, filming is carried out without a clear rationale of the attitude to film-making that the researcher adopts, as if filming were a neutral operation. Far from it, filming is a conscious representation of a portion of reality, which deserves closer attention.

Before the first workshop of Case Study One, the course coordinator suggested that the process drama take place in a television studio, newly built within their institute, where a professional team of operators would manage the filming. In a meeting prior to the commencement of the practice, the television studio director insisted on applying a lapel microphone to me, as the teacher, but not to the students. I was coming from an ethnographic stance, with filming for research purposes intended as a faithful record of a participatory practice and therefore I insisted that all participants needed to be equipped with lapel microphones. The television studio director was operating from a different stance, envisaging a teacher-centred approach whereby only the teacher needed to be heard. In my researcher's eyes, I saw this attempt to devoice the student-participants as a methodological flaw. As my view was ill-received, the agreement was called off. We therefore proceeded to conduct the process dramas in a classroom, renouncing the glory of high-tech equipment and relying instead on my personal handy camera on a tripod.

As Thompson and Hall (2016) point out: "Analysis has already begun the moment the camera is turned on, and the researcher begins to make decisions on what to shoot" (p. 118). In order to film in the least obtrusive way possible without interfering with the unfolding of improvised events, I set the camera on a wide angle, recording in one long take, and refrained from doing any major editing in post-production. This was my initial attitude, informed by my theoretical understanding of visual ethnography. However, the practice-led intervention brought about unexpected challenges. Soon after we began the process drama, I was forced to revise my stance: it was not always possible to keep the camera in one position only and record through a long take, as in process drama the action keeps unfolding, and the dynamic use of space necessitates constant re-framing of the camera. Attention to filming could potentially have become an extra layer of my reflection-in-action, one which would distract me from my main focus.

As Heider (2009) suggests, ethnography embodies the fusion of anthropology and cinematography, warning that "ethnographic filmmaking is useless, unless it is transmuted by filming imagination" (p. 57). It was not feasible for me to attend to my filmic imagination in those circumstances, as my imagination was focused on the 'here and now' of the L2/drama practice, and on the research layer that encompassed it. Yet, as Heider puts it, "films that are cinematographically incompetent are also ethnographically incompetent (even when made by an ethnographer)" (pp. 3–4), and filming the drama was an important channel of data collection for me. The situation forced me to quickly reassess my stance on the camera being set on a wide angle, recording through long takes. I asked one of the observing teachers to look after the filming.

This created a new set of implications, as the filming was now managed by a teacher-participant, thus showing her view of the dramatic action. Throughout the process, I was aware that video capturing devices can offer merely one representation of the action unfolding; that visual ethnography is a subjective construction (Pink, 2013) and "subjective understandings will have implications for the knowledge that is produced from the ethnographic encounter" (p. 37). As I briefed the teacher-participant/camera operator not to come too close to the intimacy of the groups, it was not always possible to record the spoken interactions of the student-participants' improvised language in independent group work. Thus, the videos are a conscious construction of the teacher-participants' filmic imagination, a limitation that I acknowledge.

The purpose of filming the intervention was twofold. On the one hand, it allowed for later access to the dramatic action and languaging (Swain, 2006), enabling coding, transcription and analysis. On the other hand, it allowed for Video-Stimulated Recall (VSR), a method for stimulating memory and discussion. This technique involves showing participants a replay of their actions, and using it as a prompt for discussion. It has been largely documented in educational research, in the last two decades, as a way to prompt participants' cognitive and affective mechanisms related to their behaviour and beliefs (Airey, 2015; Ethel & McMeniman, 2000). I selected to use VSR cross-referencing the specific moments that student-participants had rated on their questionnaires, and teacher-participants had noted down on their observation templates, and in the interviews. Both student-participant and teacher-participant cohorts enjoyed watching a replay of their L2/drama experiences and, in doing so, freely commented on what they saw, affording me access to their perceptions of engagement.

3.4   Interviewing in a Foreign Language

- Problem-setting: Research interviews needed to be conducted without leading questions. Using a foreign language as a vehicle to conduct interviews may put the interviewer in a position to paraphrase, to an extent that the question becomes leading.

My purpose in interviewing the student-participants was to explore learners' engagement. As student-participants came from a variety of backgrounds that could not be anticipated in advance, it was difficult for me to organise interpreters. Instead, the participants were interviewed in Italian (L2), the target language they were studying.

In linguistics, the kind of language produced by an L2 learner at a given point during the learning process is referred to as his/her interlanguage (Selinker, 1972), that is, the language used by an L2 learner that may still retain some interference from the first language. Most student-participants were interviewed in their interlanguage (Italian), except for four who were more comfortable to be interviewed in English (L2), and two who were native speakers of English (L1). While conducting the interviews in Italian (L2) or English (L2), my focus was therefore to use simple language structures to try to ensure the interviewees could comprehend. Despite my efforts to paraphrase, to avoid direct questioning, and to use basic vocabulary, at times the interview questions proved too complex for some student-participants' interlanguage, as described in Piazzoli (2015). In those times, I became a victim of my own Teacher Talk (see "Teacher Talk in L2 Settings" in Chapter 7); in attempting to over-simplify the language of the interview questions, I effectively produced leading questions.

'Interlanguage interviewing', as I have described it, is a practice not to be recommended in qualitative research, as it jeopardises the voice of the participant, compromising the trustworthiness of the research. At times student-participants appeared to be frustrated at not understanding, or not being able to fully express a concept. In several interviews, especially with those participants whose actual proficiency was lower, the communication tended to break down. For this reason, some student-participant interviews were ultimately discarded from the data analysis. The interview extracts shared in the next chapter are only those whose participants' voices maintained integrity, despite the language barrier. The interviews that remained methodologically sound needed to be translated from Italian into English, proving to be the next methodological riddle.

3.5   Translating Interlanguage

- Problem-setting: Interview transcripts in Italian (L2) needed to be translated into English. Translating interlanguage interviews injects a further layer of distance between the speaker's intended meaning, and the reader's perceived meaning.

Translating is an operation that decodes and re-codes meaning across different language systems. Translating sentences uttered by a foreign language speaker, where meaning may be approximated due to interlanguage, containing syntactic, morphological, lexical errors, can further break down the original intended meaning of the speaker, producing flawed data. The interlanguage interviews that were considered valid were transcribed verbatim in Italian, then translated into English.

Translating in 'cross-language research', that is, research involving the collection of data in more than one language (Temple, 2002) is a delicate operation, vulnerable to a series of methodological pitfalls. Marshall and Rossman (2006) call for more transparency in cross-language research. When translating data in qualitative research, some considerations need to be openly addressed: acknowledging that the data has been translated, acknowledging whether the translator is the researcher or someone external, and acknowledging whether the translator was involved in the analysis.

The translation of the research instruments (interview questions, instructions for the questionnaires, and observation templates) was conducted by myself, overseen by an accredited translator (English–Italian) who was also a lecturer in Italian (L2), and piloted with a group of Italian L2 teachers. The raw data (interview transcripts, classroom interaction) was translated by myself and overseen by my research supervisor, an accredited translator (Italian–English). I have discussed elsewhere some methodological implications related to translation in this research (Piazzoli, 2015); here, suffice to say, the pitfalls varied according to the kind of text: translating research instruments' instructions, translating L2 transcripts with L2 students in role and out of role, transcribing interviews by native speakers (teacher-participants), and translating interviews by foreign language speakers whose level of proficiency was too low for meaning to be articulated clearly (student-participants' interlanguage).

While methodological rigour was sought in the translating process from all kinds of texts, the final category (interlanguage translating where participants were at a low level of proficiency) was considered to be flawed. In the next chapter, when reporting interviewees' translated comments, I include only utterances that were considered comprehensible enough to be translated. In some instances, I have included the original version in footnotes. An implication of this development is that, like all kinds of 'relay' translation—the translation of a translation (St. André, 2011)—interlanguage interviewing is to be frowned upon, calling for high transparency in the translation process. In this case, juggling the roles of L2 teacher, researcher, interviewer and translator proved to be an uncompromising match.

3.6 Translanguaging as Method

- Problem-setting: The drama practice was conducted in Italian. The research needed to be written up in English. If I tried to write my reflection-in-action notes in English, while teaching in Italian, I would become unfocussed during class.

In Chapter 5, I define myself as a bilingual researcher (see "The Bilingual Reflective Practitioner" in Chapter 5) fluent in two languages: Italian, my native language, and English, my acquired language. *Translanguaging* refers to the practice of bilingual individuals who draw from two (or more) languages to construe meaning (García & Lin, 2017; Mazak & Carroll, 2016; Velasco & García, 2014). During the data collection phase of my research, I found it difficult to keep to English only (the official language in which the research was to be disseminated), as the process drama practice was conducted entirely in the target language (Italian). Accordingly, the logbook compiled during the drama practice, and in-between sessions, was written mainly in Italian; my reflective journal, written systematically after workshops, was in English. This translanguaging pattern emerged out of a natural call to follow the language within which I was immersed at the time. This also meant that, while conversing with the observing teachers in Italian, I would reflect on those conversations in English.

At the end of the first of the three case studies, I unveiled a tacit dissonance in my attitudes through the comparison of my Italian comments and my English comments. I decided to deliberately engage in translanguaging as a self-regulated practice of inquiry. My reflection-in-action (mostly in Italian) and reflection-on-action (mostly in English) entries were later coded and analysed, looking for the insights that emerged from the translanguaging reflective practice (see Chapter 11).

As Pavlenko's (2006) research suggests, bilingual individuals may feel like a different 'self' when speaking in another language. In my circumstances, the think-aloud conversations with the Italian teacher-participants brought out my Italian self, not just in terms of the language I was speaking, but also in terms of the baggage of culturally-bound beliefs related to teaching and learning. Similarly, the Italian notes taken in my logbook were spontaneous, on the spot comments in-between teaching strategies. On the one hand, the Italian reflections captured some raw emotions. On the other hand, the English reflections were more analytical and detached. This writing phenomenon, referred to as "emancipatory detachment" (Pavlenko, 2005, p. 183) became pivotal in my reflective practitioner analysis of two data sets: reflection-in-action (in Italian) and reflection-on-action (in English). Engaging in translanguaging practice as a method of inquiry thus triggered the analysis related to the second Research Question.

3.7 On Kinaesthetic Focus Groups

- Problem-setting: Using the foreign language as a vehicle to conduct interviews had proven to be flawed. Focus groups needed to elicit memories about the drama, somehow bypassing the language barrier and without producing leading questions.

Interlanguage interviewing had proven unreliable as an interviewing strategy, resulting in discarding some of the interview data. For this reason, in the final focus group with the student-participants I attempted to bypass the language barrier by making the focus groups as *experiential* as possible, drawing on participants' kinaesthetic perception. Besides using VSR, discussed above, I set up kinaesthetic focus groups, presenting the student-participants with items used during the drama, namely, props and costumes (hats, scarves, glasses, etc.), asking them to comment and elaborate on what these remind them of, and how they made them feel.

Using realia in the L2 classroom (Campbell, 2017) can be helpful in providing kinaesthetic anchors to previous experience. Similarly, in the L2 focus groups, the objects shown to the student-participants (mostly related to the Teacher in Role) opened a visual, tactile channel through which to remember their drama experience. A kinaesthetic approach to focus groups has been documented before, particularly in relation to research with children (Sanz, 2008) and embodied empathy in arts therapy (Rova, 2017). Drawing on this technique in an L2 process drama context was beneficial to stimulate memory and elicit the language related to the drama. Overall, I found that kinaesthetic approaches to focus groups are under-researched and underdeveloped in performative language research. A clear absence of methodological guidelines echoes Haseman's (2006) words: "[Practice-led researchers] tend to 'dive in', to commence practising to see what emerges" (p. 100). In this study, the kinaesthetic focus group technique emerged as I 'dived in' responding to a limitation of the research, and unexpectedly proving to be a rich avenue to gather data about participants' experiences.

4 Limitations as Openings

The design of the study featured a number of limitations. First, being a qualitative reflective practitioner study, informed by three small case studies, no overall generalisations can be made. Second, limited contact time (five three-hour workshops) with the participants, who were new to embodied pedagogy, may not have been enough time for them to become acquainted with dramatic form. Third, the lack of individual microphones, and technical issues related to audio-recording with one camera only, prevented me from clearly recording and transcribing the utterances of L2 speakers doing pair work and group work, a major limitation that restricted the analysis of (verbal) interaction to whole class drama, and whole class discussion.

Some limitations of reflective practitioner methodology also need to be considered before proceeding—namely subjectivity and consistency. Of particular interest, my efforts to overcome these limitations gave rise to new openings in the development of the research. The first limitation is subjectivity. Undeniably, reflective practice is subjective, as data comes from the researcher's personal reflections. This drives the research forward but, alas, puts the reflective practitioner in the risky position of ultimately producing findings that can be exposed to criticism for being biased. To overcome this limitation, I chose to inform my reflective practitioner's stance with a number of outsiders' voices that were, respectively, participating in, and observing, my L2/process drama practice. The drama was filmed, and key moments were transcribed and re-played to the participants for further prompting. I used NVIVO qualitative analysis software to create memos, to code my reflections, to source emerging themes and to query the data for patterns. Thus, in an effort to *overcome* subjectivity, I created an opening for a choreography of voices to emerge.

The second limitation is consistency. Arguably, it is difficult to be consistent when recording reflective practitioner's data, especially if collecting reflective data while teaching (Van Manen, 2008). I realised that soon enough, as I was attempting to keep a logbook with my reflection-in-action (during teaching) as a support to my reflective journal (compiled before and after teaching). The logbook entries during teaching were sketchy, often made by jotting down key words, rather than full sentences. If I were to record my reflection-in-action while improvising, this could not be done through writing. My response to overcome this drawback was to use think-aloud protocol: whenever possible, in-between drama strategies, I would openly discuss my decision-making processes with the teacher-participants sitting at the side, who had been invited to observe. During the observations, as well as in the interviews that followed, I shared with the teachers my pedagogical dilemmas, reflecting in action and on action with them. My collaborative attitude towards the teacher-participants was effectively an open window into my internal decision-making processes.

As I claimed in the opening of this chapter, a reflective practitioner stance characterised not only the practice-led intervention of this research, but also the conceptualisation, research design and analysis of this research. This pattern, taking limitations as openings in performative research, has given rise to the colourful developments described in this chapter. The final limitation as opening that I discuss here relates to the generation of the pre-text, and the subsequent process drama structure, in Case Study One.

5   The Researcher's Aesthetic Engagement

In discussing the aesthetic experience in performative language teaching, Schewe (2017) talks about routine experiences or 'unproblematic perception' as opposed to an 'aesthetic experience'—concerned with feeling, the senses and imagination. At the edge, or the boundary, of aesthetic experience, he positions irritation. A state of irritation, he argues, can sometimes be productive for aesthetic engagement. In the account below, I reflect on what led me to design the process drama that I used for my first case study practice. This, in hindsight, originated from a spark of irritation that triggered an aesthetic response.

Although having clearly stated that, in line with ethics protocols, the students' participation was to be voluntary, free of charge and not assessed, one week before Case Study One I was informed that, anticipating difficulties in recruiting student-participants during exam period, the project had been promoted to the students by telling them that, if they participated in my research, they could study *one less chapter* in their textbook for their linguistics exam. This incident, what I have called 'the bargaining deal' deserves attention, as it represents the source of irritation that sparked my aesthetic response. The assessment system at university level in Italy is traditionally based on the accumulation of knowledge, tested through oral exams, where students study several texts from a reading list. Negotiating the amount of texts in the reading list is standard routine between lecturer and students leading up to the exam. In other words, these kinds of bargaining deals are not an unusual negotiation between students and lecturers in Italian academic contexts. As I discovered that my research sampling had been mediated by this bargaining deal, I experienced conflicting responses. Perceiving the circumstance through my Italian persona allowed me to understand the context of such arrangement. At the same time, perceiving it through my Australian persona was irritating, as I interpreted it as an incentive drawing on the extrinsic, rather than intrinsic motivation of my participants. I also saw it as divorcing theory from practice, specifically devaluing practice by offering process drama as a somewhat easier solution to studying a linguistics chapter.

This source of productive irritation propelled me to act: I proceeded to source the specific chapter that students could avoid, titled *La Lingua dei Quotidiani* ('The Language of Newspapers') by Bonomi (2003), and I used it to source the inspiration for the process drama structure. The Teacher in Role, dramatic focus and dramatic context of the drama, as well as the source of dramatic of tension, were directly related to that chapter's content. 'The Language of Newspaper' chapter focuses on the role of online journalism, arguing that the traditional role of 'chief editor' is gradually disappearing, threatened by newspapers' online presence. In the drama, I took on the role of a disenchanted Chief Editor, who had a compulsive aversion for technology in general, and specifically for that chapter. Yet, within the chapter itself there was a series of guidelines related to editing that he *expected* his editorial team to know. In an ironic twist, I turned the very chapter that students had skipped by participating in my research into the 'dramatic world' of the drama, with its main points as the source of dramatic tension.

As Haseman (2006) holds, "practice-led researchers construct experiential starting points from which practice follows" (p. 100). This incident proved to be an experiential starting point for me, through which I initiated my practice, resulting in a lived felt-experience of 'The Language of Newspaper' chapter for the participants. Haseman describes performative research drawing on Austin's (1962) notion of performativity, with 'performatives' as utterances that actively *do*, rather than describe, an action. Haseman notes that, in performative research, practice itself takes a performative function (in Austin's sense). Rather than relying on words or numbers, practice thus acts as a performative:

> But how can presentational forms be understood as research? What makes a dance, a novel, a contemporary performance the outcome of research? One clue is provided by J.L. Austin's (1962) notion of performativity. For Austin, performative speech acts are utterances that accomplish, by their very enunciation, an action that generates effects. (Haseman, 2006, p. 102)

Haseman argues that "symbolic data work performatively" as they "not only express the research, but *in that expression* become the research itself" (p. 102). In a way, *The Journalists* process drama (Workshop 8) became a 'performative' act in itself, as it embodied how I responded, through *practice*, to what I perceived as irritation, waving dramatic irony from the context of the research, to the context of the drama. As Kramsch argues (2009): "No teaching can be meaningful if it doesn't enlist, beyond rational and well-thought-out lesson plans, also emotions and feelings, that is, teacher subjectivity" (p. 208).

In closing, my response to the bargaining deal—understanding it through my Italian and through Australian lenses, can also be interpreted as my bilingual reflective practitioner response to the unique idiosyncracies of cross-cultural educational research. Moreover, we could argue that this practice-led intervention, which saw the students immersed in a dramatic world inspired by the chapter on journalism, was my own aesthetic response to perceiving practice devalued over theory. As such, the practice thus assumed a performative function, in Austin's (1962) sense, as it filled that very gap between theory and practice through the dramatic world it generated. This stance reinforces the symbolic function of practice as a performative text (Haseman, 2006) within a performative research paradigm. As Seitz (2016) puts it, performative research "aspires to be one with practice, to activate tacit knowledge, and generate new insights [...] Processes can 'speak for themselves', as it were" (p. 307). In the account below, I recount the drama in narration form, letting the process speak for itself.

Workshop 8: The Journalists

Description: The workshop was inspired by the content of a chapter titled La Lingua dei Quotidiani ('The Language of Newspapers'), a university textbook by Bonomi (2003). It aimed to immerse the students in a dramatic world based on this chapter, getting the students to experience, to apprehend the content of the chapter.

Students' Context—Inspiration for the Workshop: The drama sessions explored issues related to how Chinese journalists may perceive the Italian culture. They were conducted with sixteen international students of Italian (L2) from China and Tibet, with an interest in business, media communication, and the Italian culture, enrolled in an exchange programme in a public university in Milan, Italy. The drama was created as part of Case Study One of my PhD research (2009/2013), supervised by Julie Dunn and Claire Kennedy, at Griffith University (Brisbane). The overview is deliberately presented in narrative form, focussing on the storyline, rather than in its typical drama structure, to support an argument advanced in Chapter 11.

Pre-text: A job offer (fictional) issued by the Italo-Chinese Chamber of Commerce (Fig. 6)

Educational Aims: Understanding the various parts of a newspaper article; conducting an interview for a newspaper article; writing a newspaper article; presenting the content of a newspaper article, in Italian (L2).

Level: B1 to B2 (CEFR).

Duration: Twelve hours (four three-hour sessions).

```
JOB OPPORTUNITY WITH POSSIBILITY OF PERMANENT POSITION

Once again, we are looking for graduates for a journalistic
collaboration, with the possibility of permanent position, at the
Italian Chamber of Commerce in China.

This is an opportunity to work in our Shanghai branch; the job will
involve working in the Editorial Quaderno - the CCIC trimestral
magazine coordinated by Editor-in-chief Dr Righello.

Applicants must have an excellent knowledge of the Italian language
and culture and must be willing to work alongside Dr Righello.
```

Fig. 6 Pre-text (case study one)

Workshop 8   The Journalists

Initiation phase	We read the pre-text (Fig. 6) through a soundscape of voices. I told the students to imagine it was *five years into the future*. They were graduates looking for a job in Shanghai at the Italo-Chinese Chamber of Commerce. Having spent many years in Italy, they were more advantaged than other Chinese applicants as they were 'experts' in the Italian language and culture. In the drama, most Chinese participants chose to play the role of *Italians* in China. Initially, the candidates were greeted by the Vice President of the Chamber (Teacher in Role), who announced they had passed the first selection criteria and officially started their one-week trial to be hired by the Chamber. The Vice President hinted that, to get this job, they would need to *cope* with the Chief Editor, who would be their boss. The Editor, she confided, had been behaving strangely lately. He was obsessed with counting stationery, and felt strongly threatened by technology. In particular, he hated a seminal book, *The Language of Newspapers*, which should *never* be mentioned—for their own sakes
Experiential phase	Candidates then met the obsessive-compulsive Editor, Mr. Righello (Italian for 'ruler', as in the stationary item), a rather peculiar figure, mostly preoccupied with sticking post-it notes around the space to remember futile errands. The Editor (Teacher in Role) divided the journalists into four teams and gave them a task to carry out for their job trial: writing a *feature article* for the bulletin of the Chamber. This involved a series of sub-tasks: browsing (real) newspapers to choose a topic of interest for the readership of the Editorial; identifying a key theme and a potential interviewee for the feature article; drafting five questions for the interview. Once their ideas were presented to the Editor, the candidates could fly from Shanghai to Rome, courtesy of the Chamber, to conduct the interview, and write the feature article for the Editor to appraise. The quality of the article, in terms of depth of intercultural relevance for the Chinese readership of the Italo-Chinese Chamber of Commerce, would determine whether the candidates would be hired as full-time journalists

(continued)

Workshop 8 (continued)

As the editor mentioned flying to Italy "courtesy of the Chamber", he started shaking and behaving more strangely than usual. This pattern was noted, but left unresolved. As the secretary had been fired by the temperamental Editor, the candidates had to book their own accommodation and negotiate deals for flights, hotels, and so forth. Just before they left for Italy, Mr. Righello announced that *only one team* would be hired. This injected tension of relationships, setting up competition between the teams. Each team plotted a 'secret strategy' to prevail over the others. Rumours of secret strategies were spread at the airport, on the bus, and at the train station in Rome. On the train journey from Rome to Milan, the journalists discovered that the train tickets they were issued were *fake* and the journalists were accused of international fraud. They pleaded their innocence with the Train Ticket Inspector (Teacher in Role), but were nevertheless arrested, due to a previous connection between the Chamber and international fraud. When the charges were dropped, the journalists resumed their journey, but had *only one hour* to conduct the interview, before flying back to China

The interviews were conducted in teams. Interviewers were briefed separately, advised to ask *succinct* questions, take notes of verbal and non-verbal responses. Interviewees were also briefed separately, advised to answer *vaguely*, and continually praise *technology*. This was, of course, the Editor's taboo, which placed the journalists in a difficult position over how to report the outcome of the interviews. Once back in Shanghai, the Vice President (Teacher in Role) expected to see the finished articles. Instead, she had to listen to the journalists' misadventures. She warned them not to mention the word 'prison' as this evoked *uneasy past memories* in the Editor. She suggested they write the article before the Editor arrived, providing them with *detailed guidelines* on how to write a journalistic piece (from the 'forbidden' textbook chapter). The teams wrote their articles, using their notes from the interviews. After presenting the articles, the Editor dismissed the first two teams, concentrating on the third team, his favourite. This team, however, demanded an explanation about the fraudulent tickets, provoking an impulsive reaction, and as a result all were fired

(continued)

Workshop 8 (continued)

Reflective phase	To conclude the drama, the Vice President hired the candidates as 'business consultants' for the Chamber. They provided advice on how to improve the business, including with the firing of Mr. Righello. They explored a series of dreams that Mr. Righello could have had that night

This chapter has presented a reflexive exploration of my doctoral research methodology and methods. The chapter opened with the appropriation of a conceptual metaphor to make sense of the research problem, and its transformation into a visual metaphor to crystallise the research design. In a reflexive gesture, seven methodological challenges were outlined, framed as 'problem-setting' scenarios emerging from the study, problematised within the unique context of the research. The chapter ends with a reflection on the researcher's aesthetic engagement, which provoked an active response and infused the practice with a performative function—bridging the contexts of the research and the context of the drama. The next chapter presents the research analysis and findings related to this doctoral study.

References

Airey, J. (2015). From stimulated recall to disciplinary literacy: Summarising ten years of research of teaching and learning in English. In D. Slobodanka, A. Hultgren, & C. Jensen (Eds.), *English-medium instruction in European higher education: English* (pp. 157–176). Boston: De Gruyter.

Alred, G., Byram, M., & Fleming, M. (Eds.). (2003). *Intercultural experience and education*. Clevedon: Multilingual Matters.

Austin, J. L. (1962). *How to do things with words*. Oxford: Clarendon Press.

Berthoz, A. (2012). *Simplexity: Simplifying principles for a complex world* (G. Weiss, Trans.). New Haven: Yale University Press.

Bolton, G. (1979). *Towards a theory of drama in education*. London: Longman.

Bonomi, I. (2003). La lingua dei quotidiani. In I. Bonomi, A. Masini, & S. Morgana (Eds.), *La lingua italiana e i mass media* (pp. 127–164). Roma: Carocci.

Bundy, P. (2003). Aesthetic engagement in the drama process. *Research in Drama Education: The Journal of Applied Theatre and Performance, 8*(2), 171–181.

Bundy, P. (2005). Asking the right questions: Accessing children's experience of aesthetic engagement. *Applied Theatre Researcher, 12*(6), 1–21.

Byram, M. (1997). *Teaching and assessing intercultural communicative competence.* Clevedon: Multilingual Matters.

Campbell, L. (2017). Technoparticipation: The use of digital realia in arts education. *Spark: UAL Creative Teaching and Learning Journal, 2*(3), 176–178.

Dewey, J. (1934/1980). *Art as experience.* New York: Perigee.

Ethel, R. G., & McMeniman, M. M. (2000). Unlocking the knowledge in action of an expert practitioner. *Journal of Teacher Education, 51*(2), 87–101.

Gallagher, K. (2005). The aesthetics of representation: Dramatic texts and dramatic engagement. *Journal of Aesthetic Education, 39*(4), 82–94.

García, O., & Lin, A. M. Y. (2017). Translanguaging in bilingual education. In O. García, A. M. Y. Lin, & May, S. (Eds.), *Bilingual and multilingual education* (pp. 117–130). London: Springer.

Gray, C. (1996). *Inquiry through practice: Developing appropriate research strategies.* www.rgu.ac.uk/criad/cgpapers/ngnm/ngnm.htm.

Haseman, B. C. (2006). A manifesto for performative research. *Media International Australia Incorporating Culture and Policy, 118*(1), 98–106.

Haseman, B. C. (2007). Rupture and recognition: Identifying the performative research paradigm. In *Practice as research: Approaches to creative arts enquiry* (pp. 147–157). London: IB Tauris.

Heider, K. G. (2009). *Ethnographic film: Revised edition.* Austin: University of Texas Press.

Horton, M., & Freire, P. (1990). *We make the road by walking: Conversations on education and social change.* Philadelphia: Temple University Press.

Kershaw, B., & Nicholson, H. (2011). *Research methods in theatre and performance.* Edinburgh: Edinburgh University Press.

Kramsch, C. (2009). *The multilingual subject.* Oxford: Oxford University Press.

Kress, G. (2009). Assessment in the perspective of a social semiotic theory of multimedial teaching and learning. In C. Wyatt-Smith & J. Cummings (Eds.), *Educational assessment in the 21st century.* London: Springer.

Marshall, C., & Rossman, G. B. (2006). *Designing qualitative research.* Thousands Oaks, CA: Sage.

Mazak, C. M., & Carroll, K. S. (2016). *Translanguaging in higher education: Beyond monolingual ideologies.* Bristol, UK: Multilingual Matters.

O'Neill, C. (1996). Into the labyrinth: Theory and research in drama. In P. Taylor (Ed.), *Researching drama and arts education: Paradigms and possibilities* (pp. 135–146). London: RoutledgeFalmer.

Pavlenko, A. (2005). *Emotions and multilingualism*. Cambridge: Cambridge University Press.

Pavlenko, A. (2006). *Bilingual minds: Emotional experience, expression, and representation* (1st ed., Vol. 56). Buffalo, NY and Clevedon, England: Multilingual Matters.

Piazzoli, E. (2015). Translation in cross-language qualitative research: Pitfalls and opportunities. *Translation and Translanguaging in Multilingual Contexts, 1*(1), 80–102.

Pink, S. (2013). *Doing visual ethnography*. London: Sage.

Platt, E., & Brooks, F. B. (2002). Task engagement: A turning point in foreign language development. *Language Learning, 52*(2), 365–400.

Rova, M. (2017). Embodying kinaesthetic empathy through interdisciplinary practice-based research. *The Arts in Psychotherapy, 55*, 164–173.

Sanz, E. J. (2008). Creating opportunities for expression: Interactive games in children's focus groups. In D. J. Trakas (Ed.), *Focus groups revisited: Lessons from qualitative research with children* (pp. 101–114). Berlin: LIT Verlag.

Schewe, M. (2013). Taking stock and looking ahead: Drama pedagogy as a gateway to a performative teaching and learning culture. *Scenario: Journal for Performative Teaching, Learning and Research, 8*(1), 5–23.

Schewe, M. (2017, September). *The state of the art*. Key note address at the University of Padova Summer School: The role of drama in higher and adult language education – from theory to practice. Padova, Italy.

Schön, D. (1983). *The reflective practitioner: How professionals think in action*. London: Temple Smith.

Seitz, H. (2016). Performative Research. In S. Even & M. Schewe (Eds.), *Performative Teaching, Learning, Research – Performatives Lehren, Lernen, Forschen* (pp. 301–321). Berlin: Schibri Verlag.

Selinker, L. (1972). Interlanguage. *International Review of Applied Linguistics in Language Teaching (IRAL), 10*(3), 209–231.

Sibilio, M. (2015). Simplex didactics: A non-linear trajectory for research in education. *Revue de Synthèse, 136*(3–4), 477–493.

St. André, J. (2011). Relay. In M. Baker & G. Saldanha (Eds.), *Routledge encyclopedia of translation studies*. London: Routledge.

Stake, R. E. (2013). *Multiple case study analysis*. New York and London: The Guilford Press.

Svalberg, A. M.-L. (2009). Engagement with language: Interrogating a construct. *Language Awareness, 18*(3–4), 242–258.

Swain, M. (2006). Languaging, agency and collaboration in advanced second language proficiency. In H. Byrnes (Ed.), *Advanced language learning: The contribution of Halliday and Vygotsky* (pp. 95–108). New York: Continuum.

Temple, B. (2002). Crossed wires: Interpreters, translators, and bilingual workers in cross-language research. *Qualitative Health Research, 12*(6), 844–854. https://doi.org/10.1177/104973230201200610.

Thomson, P., & Hall, C. (2016). Using film to show and tell: Studying/changing pedagogical practices. In J. Moss & B. Pini (Eds.), *Visual research methods in educational research* (pp. 116–132). New York: Palgrave Macmillan.

Van Lier, L. (1996). *Interaction in the language curriculum: Awareness, autonomy, and authenticity.* London: Longman.

Van Lier, L. (2004). *The ecology and semiotics of language learning: A sociocultural perspective.* Norwell, MA: Kluwer Academic.

Van Manen, M. (2008). Pedagogical sensitivity and teachers practical knowing-in-action. *Peking University Education Review, 6*(1), 1–23.

Velasco, P., & García, O. (2014). Translanguaging and the writing of bilingual learners. *Bilingual Research Journal, 37*(1), 6–23.

Vygotsky, L. S. (1926/1971). *The psychology of art.* Cambridge, MA: The MIT Press.

10

Learner Engagement

In this chapter, I discuss the findings on learner engagement, based on my doctoral research on process drama in second language education. In 2009, I had a peculiar telephone conversation with my father, which I report below, as it was recorded in my reflective memo at the time.

1 A Conversation with My Father

Erika: [Talking about the *International Drama in Education Research Institute* 2009 conference] Oh, dad, and I loved the IDIERI conference! I met other researchers, we exchanged ideas …

Papà: Oh yes; the researchers. And… what would they be searching for?

Erika: Well, everyone is researching a different topic … within Drama in Education.

Papà: Yes, yes, but what are they *searching* for? I wonder. I can picture these researchers, I picture them walking, wandering about with their heads low, like an image from Hades in the Odyssey, or in Dante's Inferno. I see the researchers condemned to look for something on the ground, aimlessly carrying on with their search.

They are looking for something to feed them. They are hungry. What are they *searching* for?

Erika: [Giggles] Dad, I like your imagery, very poetic but you're wrong! First of all, Drama in Education researchers don't just aimlessly look for something they don't know; they are guided by a research question, they have an idea of what they are looking for; also, they don't wander about, they follow a research design, a trajectory based on their design and methodology.

Papà: Aha. I've changed my vision now. I see the researcher sitting on a chair now. There's a chair. Searching. On a chair. Waiting.

Erika: But researchers don't just search for research's sake! They have a plan, and purpose. It might be to expand the literature in the field, to share knowledge with other practitioners, to improve or better understand the practices in their disciplines …

Papà: Aha. They have purpose. I see them on a chair, with a plate of *risotto* in front of them. They have a purpose! They are eating it. Tasting it. Mmm good! I can hear the metal spoon clicking on their teeth [tink tink] as they eat it. Good chef! The researcher sits comfortably in his chair, then looks up at me and says: What are you looking at?

My father, a master electrician by trade, a humourist by calling, has always fed me philosophical pearls with a sense of grounded irony. He is the least academic person I have ever met; yet his comments on research were illuminating, if a master electrician may excuse the pun. His provocation, right at the time of beginning my doctoral study, spurred me on to question my own vision of the researcher: not damned in hell aimlessly wandering about, but guided by a sense of purpose and a trajectory. It is interesting to note that he equals 'having a research design' to having a chair to sit on, and 'having a research purpose' with eating nourishing food. The researcher with purpose, in the final image, operates through the senses (tasting the risotto) and makes a judgement ("Good chef!"). In the last image the researcher, as the storytelling self, throws a direct provocation at the narrator ("What are you looking at?"), piercing through the suspension of disbelief. In an act of meta-reflection, breaking the fourth wall, the researcher becomes conscious of being.

2   Hecate's Voices: Engagement

In this chapter, I share my analysis and research findings related to Research Question One: What is the nature of engagement in process drama within Second Language Acquisition, intercultural and aesthetic domains? In the previous chapter, I discussed the metaphor of research as a labyrinth of scholarship, echoing with a cacophony of voices, with Hecate, a three-headed creature, as the research topic within the maze. In answering the research question, I consider Hecate's three voices separately first, then I take a step back and appraise them as a whole.

The data analysis spanned over two years. After transcribing and translating the data, I employed NVIVO software to annotate the video-recordings of the drama. I generated several nodes, through which I coded raw data in each case study. I exported the populated coding tree and I compiled three detailed case study reports, letting the rich data find its own voice. I then took the reports and sifted through them, colour coding to extract emerging themes. From this new layer a key pattern emerged, including the presence of three significant Specific Moments. These were scrutinised, frame by frame, through microgenetic inquiry, noting verbal and non-verbal cues in the process as it unfolded, to "grasp the process in flight" (Vygotsky, 1930/1978, p. 68). Microgenesis allowed me to capture the "unfolding of a single psychological act (for instance, an act of perception), often over the course of milliseconds" (Wertsch, 1991, p. 23). The microgenetic inquiry culminated in a final layer of analysis, which was elaborated into key findings. Below I offer a brief flavour of the findings. Let's take a seat, so to speak, and taste the risotto.

2.1   Second Language Acquisition

In attending to the first voice of Hecate (Fig. 1), I was influenced by a sociocultural framework of language learning, including task engagement (Platt & Brooks, 2002), embodiment as gesture and self-regulation (Platt & Brooks, 2008), and perception-in-action (Van Lier, 2007). I construed second language engagement in process drama through

Fig. 1   Hecate, Patricia Ariel (2008). Detail, first voice

Van Lier's (2004) theories of language engagement. As discussed in the second part of the book (see "Language Engagement" in Chapter 7), for Van Lier the pre-conditions of L2 engagement are exposure and receptivity, from which different degrees of attention may culminate in the rare state of vigilance. The microgenetic analysis revealed that engagement with language manifested as an active process of perception-in-action, through which dramatic action provided quality exposure to language.

Van Lier refers to quality exposure as language indexed to a context. This condition, coupled with the receptivity of the learners, triggered a state of vigilance which, in turn, promoted learners' agency. I refer to this active process as perception-in-action (Van Lier, 2007). Learners' agency manifested as playfulness with language and with the elements of drama; indeed, this active process was mediated by the elements of drama (see also Piazzoli, 2014). To support and illustrate this key finding, I draw on excerpts from classroom improvisation, my reflective journal, student-participants' and teacher-participants' voices. These data sets help to illuminate, in practice, how receptivity, vigilance and agency manifested as self-regulation and playfulness in dialogic interaction, creating collective Zones of Proximal Development (ZPDs), and how this process was mediated by the elements of drama.

I begin with a Teacher in Role sequence from Case Study One (for participants' background see "Performative Research" in Chapter 9). Particularly, the extract quoted below is the closing improvisation of *The Journalists* (described in Chapter 9, Workshop 8). In this final episode the student-participants, in role as apprentice journalists at the Italo-Chinese Chamber of Commerce, get their hard-earned revenge over Editor Mr. Righello, their lunatic boss, who has subjected them to misadventures. In the extract reported below, the Vice President (Teacher in Role) has just hired them as business consultants, and is seeking their expertise to improve the efficiency of the Italo-Chinese Chamber of Commerce.

1   Vice President: … any other suggestions?
2   [Viola whispers something to Flora and laughs]
3   Vice President [to Viola]: Doctor, would you have some advice?
4   Viola: to delete [laughs] … Righello!
5   Mara: to change Righello!
6   Teodoro: to fire Righello!
7   Vice President: to fire Mr Righello? Are you sure?
8   Everyone: yes!
    (1.3.5, 31:55)

In this extract (translated into English), Chinese students Viola, Mara and Teodoro interact together, in Italian, offering suggestions for the appropriate verb to suit the context (to delete; to change; to fire). Their exchange denotes their receptivity to the drama (T 4), to the language (T 5–6), and to each other (T 6). I reinforce the appropriate verb (T 7), which they have found as a group, through dialogic interaction, creating a ZPD that forms "something of a collective expert" (Lantolf & Thorne, 2006, p. 283). This exchange also shows a degree of alertness to each other, in the improvisational context. In my Reflective Journal, I comment:

1   It struck me how all students are collaborating together to communicate one idea
2   across (sacking the editor), trying different options until they find the correct one.
    (RJ, pp. 43–44)

Dramatic tension in connection to the Editor was infused throughout the drama, in terms of tension of the mystery (related to the Chamber); tension of relationships (between the teams' secret strategies); tension of surprise (getting arrested for fraud); tension of the task (completing the interviews, despite the arrest); and potential tension of metaxis (a dissonance between how they responded in the drama as they got arrested 'as Italians', and how they would have responded in real life to this situation). These forms of tension, and the participants' responses to them, were thoroughly analysed in the filmed sequences, coded in the NVIVO nodes, and cross-referenced in the questionnaires, interviews and teacher-participants' observations. These forms of tension, the evidence shows, contributed to the L2 speakers becoming more alert in the dialogic interaction described above. Dramatic role, focus, narrative, the use of time and space, movement and symbol further imbued that interaction with dramatic meaning, creating vigilance, an all-absorbing state through which the speaker is "ready to act on partly predictable, partly novel stimuli" (Van Lier, 1996, p. 52).

Process drama, a participatory improvised form, afforded these students the opportunity to create collective ZPDs. In the extract above, the group is collaborating to create a string of sentences, but rather than subscribing to the Initiation Response Feedback (IRF) pattern (see "Teacher Talk in L2 Settings" in Chapter 7), this interaction entailed an Initiation in role, followed by a student's response, shared with another student (T 2), a second response by the teacher, followed by a string of responses, in role. The Feedback provided by the teacher in Turn 7 to close the exchange, reinforces the correct verb choice ('to fire'), importantly, *without breaking the drama improvisation*. This pattern is a typical example of L2/process drama discourse, as emerged from the analysis, where dramatic tension is high, with or without the mediation of the Teacher in Role. In the example quoted above, the improvisation moved on and the Teacher in Role asked for more tips for dealing with the Chamber's business structure. In my Journal, I note:

1 They keep offering suggestions, and the Vice President embraces all of them. Finally
2 she gets back to the idea of sacking Righello (which was left unresolved): "To fire
3 Righello … but I wouldn't know how! He's been working here for 50 years!" Flora

4   looks shocked to hear that. Tommaso quickly jumps in: "He needs to retire!". Alessia
5   suggests to send him to Africa (for the soccer World Cup, Giorgio adds). The Vice
6   President accepts, and congratulates them on their new position.
    (RJ, pp. 55–57)

Here the student-participants are demonstrating not only receptivity, but also agency as self-regulation. On one level, Tommaso's contribution (line 4) denotes self-regulation as he does not feed off the teacher's language (for example, by saying "I know how"), but creating his own sentence ("He needs to retire"). This contribution, again, indicates *vigilance*, as he is responding to novel stimuli (a solution to the Editor's long service) in the target language. Moreover, agency here manifests as self-regulation in playfulness with the elements of drama, and playfulness with dramatic role: Tommaso is ironically using his newly found status, in his position of power as expert business consultant, to sack the offending Editor.

As O'Neill argues, dramatic irony consists in asserting the opposite of what is taken for granted socially. Through this process, irony can provoke an "active response" (in Taylor & Warner, 2006, p. 148). Tommaso's irony certainly provokes an active response, as illustrated in lines 5 and 6. Alessia suggests going to Africa, with Giorgio adding, for the World Cup. Both contributions are examples of self-regulation with language, indexed to the context of the drama (as the World Cup was to be in South Africa that year, one of the teams interviewed a World Cup champion). Alessia and Giorgio saying that the Editor should go to Africa implies a degree of playfulness in context in the drama. A text is ironic, Pavis (1998) holds, when, in addition to its primary, obvious sense, it reveals a deeper, different, perhaps even opposite meaning, or antiphrasis. Here the participants are pretending to offer a professional consultation to the naïve Vice President, suggesting the Editor retires to Africa to follow the sporting event, when they are obviously trying to get rid of him.

For van Lier, the kind of quality exposure needed to trigger engagement is an exposure to language that is indexed to a context. This feature emerges from the student-participants' comments, across all case studies. For example, Olga, below (interviewed in English) states that process drama generates a language that is "more connected to real life":

```
1   Olga: the teaching approach of other teachers is more like … standard, maybe,
2   normal? Let's call it this way. Where … we train … like grammar skills, for
3   example, in normal activity like … exercises. But here it's kind of … hidden, in
4   some way … though at the same time we are learning, through the game, through
5   drama, so it's not that obvious and probably it's also like … more connected to …
6   real life, because these situations … can happen.
7   Erika: uh uh
8   Olga: and while you're studying with … just text or exercises you are not like … I
9   don't know, put into a real situation!
    (Olga, interview, p. 1:23–29)
```

Olga, a Russian student from Case Study Two, believes that process drama can place the L2 speaker in a "real situation". Yoriko, Japanese, also from Case Study Two (interviewed in Italian) comes to the same conclusion:

```
1    Yoriko: This for me was a new experience because usually first I think: if the teacher
2    asks me something, I think a lot, I arrange [the thoughts] in my head and then speak.
3    Erika: sure.
4    Yoriko: but during the meeting and … I couldn't think, it was like a live
5    conversation!
6    […]
7    Erika: but in [a traditional] classroom it didn't … it didn't happen that often?
8    Yoriko: yes yes, it happened but … like sure, this is different … [process drama] is
9    like at home, in the street, very reality[1]
10   Erika: yes; and what about in the classroom, isn't that like 'at home'?
11   Yoriko: mmm … not really. Each… sometimes it is, like [when we are] chatting
12   together, during the break
13   Erika: but during class?
14   Yoriko: in this moment I speak spontaneously.
     (Yoriko, p. 3:3–22)
```

I find this concept fascinating; Yoriko identifies the language generated by process drama as the kind of conversation that would happen at school "during the break" (T 10–11), therefore a type of natural, spontaneous conversation. Some teacher-participants expressed a similar concept, in that the language generated by process drama is not like the usual L2 discourse, but is comparable to "someone relaxed, like friends in a café" (Rossana and Giovanni, FG, 20:35). Paradoxically, in both situations, the discourse generated by process drama is described as a kind of communication occurring

---

[1] Original: *molto realtà*.

in the real context, rather than a play context (the break; chatting in a café), although it is produced during the make-believe.

Catherine, an American student (interviewed in English) on the other hand, points out that process drama is helpful to "dig deeper", as well as for promoting fluency:

1 I haven't taken many classes like this one ... my other courses, they do a lot of work
2 for you ... in terms of [...] the verb we need to conjugate, they're giving us the verb,
3 setting a stage of the conversation we're gonna have, whereas this class ... you really
4 have to ... dig deep and maybe ripen your level of vocabulary, create what you want
5 to say, so I think it's helpful in terms of ... fluency.
(Catherine, p. 1:42–47)

Catherine's comments, in lines 4–5, also hint at the notion of agency ("create what you want to say"), echoing the main theme emerging from the teacher-participants' voices. Simone, a teacher-participant from Case Study Two, makes a remark about the language revision phase, observing the student-participants attitudes as "alert" (T 5):

1 Simone: what I really liked is ... I think the idea of the journey within this type of
2 technique emerges quite strongly ... and it's very useful ... how can I put it ...
3 precisely, for the communicative side of learning. What I really liked yesterday ...
4 curiously enough, was ... the last part, when they put together ... let's call it the
5 language revision [...] Because ... I noticed they were really alert.
6 Erika: yes
7 Simone: I noticed that they had been taking notes; they were interested to explore the
8 vocabulary that emerged ... I liked it, because ... it actually means that it worked, in
9 that moment for me as a teacher it was evidence that it worked.
(Simone, p. 3:9–23)

As Simone notes, agency manifested not only in the improvisations, but also in the reflection.

In the analysis, I monitored agency across the case studies using Van Lier's (2008) agency scale (see "Language Engagement" in Chapter 7), going from at Level (1) to Level (6). The analysis indicates that the student-participants reached different levels of agency, from Level (3) to Level (6). Significantly, the case studies differed in agency levels: Case Study One spanned between Levels (3) and (4); Case Study Two between (4) and (5); Case Study Three agency oscillated between (5) and (6).

On the one hand, this shows that L2 classroom discourse engendered by process drama has an *agentic* quality, as there were no instances of communication below Level (3). On the other hand, potential reasons behind these differences in agency levels may relate to the case study contexts, with the first cohort being monolingual (Chinese) and the other two cohorts being multilingual. Another explanation could be that the increase in agency was influenced by my progressive letting go of a tacit attitude to control the process drama improvisation, a pattern I discuss in the next chapter.

2.2   Intercultural Education

Analysing engagement through Hecate's intercultural voice (Fig. 2), I was influenced by Alred, Byram, and Fleming's (2003) being intercultural, Byram's (1997, 2008, 2009) model of the intercultural speaker, and gesture studies in embodiment (McCafferty & Stam, 2008). Alred, Byram and Fleming discuss 'being intercultural' as an active experience triggering awareness, and analysis of such awareness (meta-reflection), leading the individual to act upon those insights, towards a "heightened awareness" of one's identity—a psychological shift that might lead to

Fig. 2   Hecate, Patricia Ariel (2008). Second voice, detail

a more integrated sense of 'self' and confidence in being 'in-between', socially and culturally (p. 4). The notion of intercultural speaker relates to "being able to take an 'external' perspective on oneself as one interacts with others" (Byram, 2008, p. 60). Being an intercultural speaker is an active involvement to understand one's own language and culture, and another's language and culture. It relates to de-centring from one's own cultural codes, a "willingness to suspend disbelief in one's meaning and behaviours" (Byram, 1997, p. 34).

The analysis focussed on engagement as an active process originated in a drama experience, creating a degree of intercultural dramatic tension (see "Intercultural Dramatic Tension" in Chapter 4), triggering various degrees of intercultural awareness, and resulting in engagement as intercultural meaning-making. The concept of intercultural dramatic tension, as described in Chapter 4, relates to the potential dramatic tension that engages one at an intercultural level and operates within the gap existing between two (or more) cultural systems. A distinct pattern that emerged in the cross-case analysis of the data is that the *explicit* or *implicit* presence of intercultural dramatic tension in the pre-text influenced the degree to which participants were able to articulate their intercultural meaning-making. An example of how the intercultural dramatic tension manifested across the three case studies has been reported elsewhere (Piazzoli, 2017). Instead, here I focus on intercultural dramatic tension and its relationship to intercultural meaning-making, to pave the way for a connection between the L2/drama structure and the aesthetic dimension. To illustrate this key finding, I cross-reference Case Study One with data from Case Study Two and Case Study Three.

The data from Case Study One, from both the microgenetic analysis of the Specific Moment, and analysis of participants' interviews and focus groups, is rich with instances of intercultural engagement triggered by an intercultural experience, creating awareness and intercultural meaning-making. This generated a quality of engagement aligned with Byram's (2008) notion of the intercultural speaker, evidenced in comments such as those of Alessia, a Chinese student-participant (interviewed in Italian) who after fifteen hours of process drama stated:

1   Alessia: My mother tells me, in any given moment, you must be a gentle, elegant
2   girl. All these regulations [laughs] and so [through process drama] you make me
3   become another girl, a bit different.
4   […]
5   Alessia: I found out … that I have a lot of energy inside that I don't understand … I
6   mean, before maybe I didn't know myself! Now I've come to know myself anew.[2] I
7   mean, I opened … a bit different, maybe I can be … a real journalist, or someone
8   doing a traineeship … it makes me learn … discover some new things, which is not
9   only what I studied, learnt … in terms of vocabulary, grammar … it's not! Not just
10 that; I find myself really … something unique!
11 Erika: Is this a new discovery for you?
12 Alessia: Exactly, exactly … about myself, as if there were truly a mirror in front of
13 me: [surprised] Oh! That's what Alessia's really like! I mean, you are playing
14 another person but really, it's really the aspects … aspects different [quietly] from
15 yourself.
    (Alessia, pp. 4:6-10–5:12–24)

These comments (translated from Italian) and others of a similar nature by the student-participants of Case Study One resonate with what Alred et al. (2003) describe as a "heightened awareness" of one's identity, a psychological shift that might lead to a more integrated sense of 'self' and confidence in being 'in-between', socially and culturally (p. 4).

The findings point to this engagement process being mediated by the intercultural dramatic tension in the pre-text of the drama. This intercultural dramatic tension in the pre-text was harnessed and manipulated, generating a strong intercultural dramatic context, as well as scope for some intercultural reflection. From this I advanced a connection between the pre-text, the intercultural dramatic context, intercultural roles, and intercultural dramatic tension in process drama. In Piazzoli (2017), I refer to this framework as the intercultural dramatic structure in process drama, encompassing: (1) intercultural dramatic tension in the pre-text, (2) manipulation of intercultural elements in the drama structure, and (3) the scope and breath of the intercultural reflection generated by the drama (pp. 190–191).

In the cross-case analysis of the process drama, I note that while in Case Study One the intercultural tension in the pre-text was *explicit*, in the pre-text of Case Study Two and Three the intercultural element in

---

[2]Original: *adesso ho riconosciuto a me stessa!* See Piazzoli (2015, p. 89) for a methodological discussion on 'dynamic equivalence' in the translation of this line, and the challenges related to 'inter-language interviewing'.

the pre-text was *implicit*. This gave life to important findings related to the explicit or implicit presence of the intercultural dimension of the pre-text, and its impact on intercultural engagement. Going back to my Journal's notes on Case Study Two:

> 1 There was absolutely no intercultural dimension to the drama today. Why? I don't
> 2 know. I somehow left this dimension totally unattended today. The pre-text itself did
> 3 not hold any intercultural tension (my mistake) and the roles/situations I created did
> 4 not allow for an (obvious) intercultural gap. Next time I look for a pre-text this is
> 5 imperative! The pre-text must hold intrinsic intercultural tension. Now it's too late to
> 6 change the pre-text of course, so I need to correct this oversight by injecting
> 7 intercultural tension through role and/or situation.
> (RJ, p. 46:38–43)

From this entry, which at the time of writing (29 June 2010) was still raw, eight years have passed. In meta-reflection, I see that at the time of journaling, I *initially thought*—or at least I initially wrote—that I 'didn't know why' there was no intercultural dimension (lines 1–2). I recognise now that when I wrote that, rather than not knowing why, I *thought I couldn't articulate* why. This exemplifies knowing-in-action as a kind of knowing, what Schön frames as being "unable to describe the knowing which our action reveals" (1983, p. 54). In fact I followed in lines 2–4 with what I understood to be those very reasons: the pre-text was without intercultural tension (line 3), and the roles/situations I created did not allow for an (obvious) intercultural gap (line 4). I now appreciate that I immediately tried to articulate why—to "describe the knowing which our action reveals" (p. 54)—to help identify my tacit knowing related to the presence of intercultural dramatic tension.

In my later writing, on the same day, I refer to these concepts as the *implicit* or *explicit* presence of intercultural tension in the pre-text:

> 1 INTERCULTURAL REFLECTION: this was shorter than the linguistic reflection. It
> 2 was like a recap of what we had discussed. I think the biggest fault of this drama (as
> 3 the teachers identified in their observation sheet) lies in the lack of depth of the
> 4 intercultural dimension. Yes, we spoke about mental health being taboo in Italy and
> 5 we resumed the discussion on Italian families pushing to represent a perfect image in
> 6 society. […] *the intercultural dimension wasn't as explicit and the reflections*
> 7 *themselves were not as in-depth. This is because the pre-text and the whole drama*
> 8 *lacked intercultural tension.*
> (p. 48:23–34, original emphasis)

In Case Study Two, my approach to facilitating the intercultural discussion seemed to be more like a box to be ticked, rather than a quality of the mood to be made explicit through reflection. Truth be told, a level of *implicit* intercultural tension was always present in the case studies, because of the student-participants' real context (second language speakers, outsiders to the Italian cultural system, engaging with otherness) as well as my own context (a native speaker, who had been away from my own country for ten years). While these circumstances informed to some extent our experience of the real context, the structure of the drama, in Case Study Two, did not particularly lend itself to any explicit intercultural exploration in the play context.

Conversely, an explicit degree of intercultural tension was present in Case Study One, as identified in the pre-text, and saturated the narrative structure of the process drama. As this tension was high in the pre-text, it became embedded in roles and situations, and permeated to the other elements of drama, making the discussions much richer—as observed by the teacher-participants, and the quality of the reflection more in-depth, as found in the interviews of the student-participants. Through the course of Case Study Two process drama, I paid close attention to the intercultural dramatic structure, during both the practice-based intervention and the data analysis. I noted that the intercultural dimension was present, but 'stayed in the background'; the meaning-making remained implicit. An example can be found in the comment below from Catherine, an American Case Study Two student-participant (interviewed in English):

```
1  I would define [process drama] as a technique ... that allows the students to approach
2  a language and leave their sort of cultural baggage ... put it up to the side for a
3  moment which can allow you to sort of ... take in what you're learning ... in a less
4  filtered way. I would describe it as that.
   (Catherine, pp. 3–4: 49–4)
```

Catherine's comments seem to denote that her experience of process drama is related to what Byram (1997) called de-centring from one's own cultural codes, a "willingness to suspend disbelief in one's meaning and behaviours" (p. 34). Her self-evaluation questionnaires scored high in intercultural engagement, averaging 8/10 and affective engagement 9.5/10 (very high). However, when Catherine was asked to further articulate any meaning-making, she could point to a dramatic encounter in the drama, but not to any intercultural meaning generated through it—adding that she "did not feel surprised" (p. 3:28) by the intercultural dimension. In stark opposition to Case Study One, none of the Case Study Two student-participants were able to articulate any intercultural meaning-making, despite intercultural engagement as self-regulation emerging as a theme in the microgenetic analysis of their gesturing, in role.

In Case Study Three I kept the same pre-text as in Case Study Two, but made more effort to infuse the story with intercultural roles and situations. Yet, intercultural engagement was still perceived as weak. A teacher-participant from Case Study Three comments in a post-observation interview:

1 Towards the end, they needed to be spoon-fed again, in the intercultural reflection,
2 ehm ... I don't think it was working very well because... it's not... it's not like it
3 didn't work, but there wasn't that kind of debate that a teacher always hopes for at
4 the end of a class. [...] Really, I saw them, they didn't look into each other's eyes,
5 but ... like they would turn towards you and reply to your question.
(Rossana, p. 13:22–27)

Being spoon-fed, as Rossana argues (line 1), is arguably the opposite of engaging in an active process of intercultural engagement. Similarly, according to teacher-participant Giovanni's written observation notes, reflection in Case Study Three was somewhat stilted:

1 In the last phase, the intercultural reflection, everyone replied individually to the
2 teacher, and more because they were asked to, rather than because they really needed
3 to talk about it.
(Giovanni, OBS, p. 1:46–48)

In a similar trend, the student-participants from Case Study Three described process drama as a potentially useful tool to engage interculturally, but when asked questions related to intercultural awareness, they could not articulate any intercultural meaning-making. Compared with some Case Study One participants' comments, this is striking.

My first instinct was to re-assess the trustworthiness of the interviews, wondering if the issue was related to interlanguage interviewing (see "Interviewing in a Foreign Language" in Chapter 9). Interestingly, however, the participants who could not articulate intercultural meaning-making were either interviewed in English (as their first language), or were proficient Italian speakers. Thus, interlanguage interviewing was not the main cause of this apparent lack of articulation in intercultural meaning-making. The language level of participants from Case Study One was paradoxically lower, but they were well able to articulate intercultural meaning-making, albeit using simpler language. Here I offer one short example, from Ariel, a Swiss student-participant, interviewed in Italian (advanced level of proficiency):

1 Erika: … and what about your perception of Italian culture?
2 Ariel: perception?
3 Erika: on your idea of Italian, of Italian culture?
4 Ariel: oh. I haven't changed a lot.
   (Ariel, p. 3:19–22)

From Ariel's snappy answer, it may appear that she did not engage in intercultural meaning-making. Yet, in the same interview, she also states that the intercultural discussions were her favourite part, as she engaged in a lot of thinking "to contrast and compare cultures" (p. 2:7–11). She hints at generating some meaning, but she is not able to articulate it (at the time of the interview). Her questionnaire further indicates that she perceived her intercultural engagement as very high (9/10). Thus, her self-evaluation indicates a high engagement in the experience, but she does not articulate it through explicit intercultural meaning-making. I connect this trend, occurring throughout Case Study Two and Three, to the intercultural dimension of the elements of drama being less incisive, carrying less explicit intercultural dramatic tension.

2.3   Aesthetic Learning

In attending to the third voice of Hecate (Fig. 3), I was inspired by Vygotsky's (1926/1971) notion of aesthetic engagement. This is an active

Fig. 3 Hecate, Patricia Ariel (2008). Third voice, detail

process beginning with a sensation, entailing a 'creating perception' followed by a 'delayed reaction' where the feeling is overcome, culminating in a higher awareness that propels one to act, in a social context. In Lima's (1995) analysis of Vygotsky's aesthetic theory, he frames aesthetic experience as "the *collision* of the *contradictory* emotions" generated by form on content.

The analysis revealed that both teacher-participants and student-participants experienced various degrees of aesthetic engagement, and that the manipulation of aesthetic distance (Eriksson, 2011) influenced the quality of engagement. Distance was manipulated extensively across the case studies, resulting in profound differences, as monitored in my Reflective Journal. Specifically, a cross-case analysis revealed that in Case Study Three the affective engagement was particularly intense, and that, in some episodes, the emotional charge in the real context became *too* intense. At one point, when it became too close to the participants' lives, it caused some participants to disconnect from the group. During two specific episodes, participants were not "protected into emotion", as Bolton (1984, p. 128) would have it, and were thus thrust into a fictional context that they found too raw (see "Protecting into Emotion" in Chapter 6). This resulted into different responses: participants becoming highly involved in the improvisation, but not able (or not willing) to reflect on their meaning-making; becoming highly involved in the improvisation, but remaining aloof in the group discussions; participants acting on their own accord, and then fighting with the group; or one participant dropping out altogether.

I illustrate this argument through a praxial approach, interweaving the drama practice, the data, and the literature on aesthetic learning. I start by contextualising a specific drama episode, to then discuss the reactions of three participants. In the *Mirrors* process drama (Workshop 9), student-participants were in role as psychologists, each with their own professional expertise, employed to solve the bizarre case of an L2 teacher ('the subject') who refused to communicate. The pre-text (a silent clip of a middle-aged man seeing his double in the mirror) was the same as in Case Study Two. At the onset of the drama, 'the subject' had been found squatting in a lift. His last words spoken, before ceasing to communicate, were: 'Today I am not very communicative'. This was followed by a further message, written on a strip of paper: 'Mirrors should stop reflecting'. The psychologists had to solve this riddle, find a strategy to remove 'the subject' from the lift, and interrogate his family and friends to understand what had happened. In the development of the drama, the man, who initially was in a catatonic state, was persuaded to leave the lift and go into hospital, but consequently escaped, to take refuge in a mirror-maze at Luna Park. He was found and hypnotised by the psychologists, to investigate into his own double—a delusion he saw in the mirror. In the final episode of the drama, the psychologists presented this case at a conference.

Initially, the group engaged with the dramatic world with a sense of playfulness. In the third workshop, I noted a marked shift in aesthetic mood when, in Specific Moment Three, student-participant Agate volunteered to be in role as 'the subject' stuck in the lift and, through a long, improvised animated tableaux sequence, she finally came out of the lift (Step 6, Workshop 9). After this intense performance, I asked Agate how she was feeling, as a means to de-brief. Though we all had come out of the improvisation, when Agate responded she was still in role:

1   I experience some relief, because I have been … been* in this situation for too long,
2   I'm still tired, hungry and afraid … but [voice breaking] I have some relief because I
3   feel [heavy gasping] that I can trust … the doctor.
    (3.3.5, 20:15)

The (*) in Turn 1 here denotes Agate's auto-correction, in the Italian original transcript, from the feminine to the masculine form (*sono stata; sono stato*). This change is significant, as it shows that Agate was speaking in character, as 'the subject' (a male), rather than as herself. The paralinguistic features in her speech, like her voice breaking and heavy gasping (lines 2, 3), suggest a strong affective engagement, also confirmed by her self-engagement questionnaire value of 10/10 for that Specific Moment. During the interview that followed, conducted in English, Agate (bilingual English/Portuguese), described her experience as a unity of feeling, thinking, movement and language:

1   That time when I was coming out of the lift, I could feel that … there was …
2   consistency … in the [way] I was feeling, I was thinking, I was moving, I was
3   communicating.
    (Agate, p. 4:32–33)

Agate also added that she felt she was an artist—it was an artistic experience for her. These comments resonate with Vygotsky's (1934/1994) notion of *perezhivanie*, Russian for intensely lived felt-experience, whereby we apprehend an experience cognitively, affectively and socially—as introduced in the first part of the book (see "Embodiment" in Chapter 2).

The analysis indicates that, in that Specific Moment, not only Agate, but also the other participants—both students and teachers who were observing—experienced various degrees of engagement. As I showed the replay of that sequence to the teacher-participants during the focus group Video-Stimulated Recall (VSR), Linda yelled: "Amazing tension; I really felt it here!" (39:05). Linda recalled how this was a moment of transition for her, when she "stopped feeling like an observer, entered the situation as a participant" (39:14). She added: "Honestly, I felt sick, like, in a good way! I was really inside the scene, because they were, too."

Her next comment echoes Scully's (2017) concept of the 'groupness of the group' in a drama process, binding the participants in an aesthetic, social and deep learning engagement: "Here you can tell how there isn't anymore … there isn't Herminia; there isn't Ariel; there isn't Marika [student-participants]. They really were… also touched, I think. I was" (39:48). Linda here was suggesting that, as she was observing the action unfold, she was no longer seeing her own students, whom she taught during the day. She was able to transcend that, becoming in tune with the drama. Teacher-participant Rossana added that, in that same moment, she stopped taking notes because it was "a moment to watch", where the students "really let themselves go … a lot" (40:55). Teacher-participant Renato, director of the school, agreed that there was a deep level of engagement, commenting about the four observing teachers: "We were holding our breath to see what would happen" (43:53). He observed the student-participants were "completely engaged, they were willing to run risks […] they did what they felt, and they were all engaged" (44:30). Student-participants, Renato noted, lost self-consciousness, forgetting about being observed by four teachers, fully giving in to the improvisation. He spoke about a "theatrical moment, of great intensity". He finished: "Very… strong moment, really" (3:06).

I noticed the word 'strong' was used so often in that focus group, that it prompted me to run an NVIVO text-frequency search of all data sources for the adjective 'strong' in Case Study Three. It revealed that in the interviews the student-participants used it eighteen times and teacher-participants used it fourteen times, and I used it ten times in my Journal. Teachers also noted they found it very hard to go back to their usual teaching routine after witnessing the drama improvisation. This episode was arguably highly engaging. What impact did it have on the learning?

The transcript below reports a classroom improvisation, on the following day, as the student-participants recalled that same Specific Moment (removal of 'the subject' from the lift) to recapitulate the situation to fellow classmate Yelena, who had been absent:

```
1   Erika/coordinator [addressing Yelena]: We decided to make an inspection, that is, we
2   decided to go and meet the subject to try to remove him from the lift. [To the others] How
3   did that go?
4   Carme/psychologist: the first time … [shakes her head, gravely]
5   Eduarda/psychologist: we've tried three times
6   Erika: uh uh
7   Eduarda/psychologist: the first time [looks over at Agate]
8   Agate/psychologist [mumbling]: We have obtained
9   Carme/psychologist: nothing!
10  Erika: Dr. Ivanova
11  [Carme nods]
12  Erika: has tried to convince him
```

13   [Eduarda mimes hitting her head to Agate; Marika, Eduarda, Agate laugh]
14   Carme/psychologist: the sweet voice, not convince him! [Shakes her head]
15   Erika: but … Paolo remained in the lift
16   Agate/psychologist [sarcastic]: Doctor of Communication, right?
17   Erika: but, unfortunately, this time, the sweet voice … of Ivanova … didn't work.
18   Carme/psychologist: he was very *amargo* (bitter)
19   Erika: he was very embittered!
20   Carme/psychologist: he doesn't like him … the sweet
21   [General laughter]
22   Marika/psychologist: bitter!
23   [Laughter; Jun drops her head down, from laughter]
24   Erika: he wasn't ready! [Smiling] He wasn't ready; too embittered.
25   Eduarda/psychologist: too embittered.
     (3.4.1, 34:20)

Note here how the strong dramatic engagement, in the recollection of the previous day's events, supports the language learning. For example, when Carme uses the Portuguese adjective for 'bitter' (T 18) and I, in role, weave my feedback into the improvisation, it is picked up again by Eduarda (T 25). This process of perception-in-action (see "Second Language Acquisition" in this chapter) was characterised by receptivity, vigilance, agency and playfulness, including bouts of laughter (T 13, 21, 23) and a sense of irony, related to Carme's 'sweet voice' pun—an ongoing joke in the drama, in that Carme was a very talkative woman (in the real context) as well as an expert in communication (in the play context), but she failed in removing 'the subject' from the lift with her sweet talking (T 14–16). A sense of collaboration in the improvised discourse is described by the observing participants as "being in tune" (Renato, p. 3) and being "close-knit" (Rossana, OBS, p. 35:1). In the following episode, however, the intensity of emotions started to escalate, causing some of the participants to disengage. To support this claim, I take as examples three student-participants' responses: one who stayed aloof (Eduarda), one who went against the group (Yelena), and one who dropped out in the final session (Carme). These dynamics, I believe, arose as the emotions caused by the drama context were too raw, too close, to the actual context.

In the intercultural discussion that followed the Specific Moment Three, Eduarda, a 34-year-old Brazilian, remained completely aloof.

During the VSR, while watching the replay of that video sequence, Eduarda whispered that that session 'made her think a lot'. Eduarda did not comment further, despite my prompt that followed. Only in the individual interview did she disclose that the topic was too close to home, related to a personal issue. In this instance the aesthetic experience was under-distanced, creating an affective overload.

Another interesting case is Yelena, Russian, 27 years old (interviewed in Italian; high level of proficiency), who during the hypnosis session appeared to have a powerful insight, as I noted in my Journal:

```
1  The tension of relationship was high as we were interviewing the hypnotised version
2  of the subject. Just before Yelena was going into her role, she looked at me with
3  feverish eyes saying: "Tomorrow, when you interview me, I have to tell you
4  something! I understood something!" She was visibly animated and wanted to tell me
5  straight away but couldn't. (RJ, p. 58:39–43)
```

During that very same improvisation, although the psychologists had agreed on a tactic to interview the subject under hypnosis, Yelena took a different approach, causing confusion in the group and, after the improvisation finished, resulting in a confrontation with the others (in the target language). The group's confrontation, which was noted by the observing teacher-participants as a peak of communicative engagement, ended with Yelena apologising to the group and a loud, releasing group laughter. For the rest of the drama, I was careful to structure episodes that re-framed the focus, and balanced the aesthetic distance.

In the interview the following day, Yelena went back to the moment that lead her to disconnect from the group:

```
1   Yelena: I remember most vividly … mmm … day before yesterday … when we
2   almost finished class, it was a sentence that the niece … helped the subject to run
3   away from hospital and that she brought him to the Luna Park, in the mirror room, I
4   had goose bumps … yes, goose bumps, really!
5   Erika: Yes. Me too.
6   Yelena: Because I imagined what can happen in this room, I imagined his reaction,
7   and this was a strongest action for me. […] This classes, the day before yesterday and
8   two days ago, when we had them, I really felt I understood this, this hypothesis,
9    because I truly entered in the subject's body and also in his double's body, I'm been
10   like them, I no longer exist.
     (Yelena, p. 1:32–39, p. 2:3–5)
```

Her affective engagement was so intense, that she paradoxically disconnected from the group. Her self-evaluation scores, for affective and communicative engagement, were rated as 10/10. Yelena added, in writing: "Emotional; I had goose bumps at the end of the class"—also reiterated above (T 4). As the interview continued, she went on to say that she understood the power of being in the moment; after the incident, she reflected on the importance of the collectiveness of the group, which she described as "the sun and its rays" which converge into the nucleus (p. 4:33). The experience was so strong, the reported, that she almost transcended it, with the rest of the interview seeing Yelena get lost in highly metaphysical matters, like time being an illusion. Insofar as these insights are fascinating, the reality of the matter is that, at the time, they caused her to disconnect. What emerges is an intensely-lived situation, but aesthetic distance being so reduced that it caused disconnection—in this case a social disconnection. Being able to then discuss it, as a group, and experiencing a series of episodes where the aesthetic distance was re-adjusted, helped Yelena, and the others, to re-engage as a group and experience even higher levels of agency, in the target language.

Finally, Carme, a 46-year-old Brazilian, fully participated up to and including the third workshop, but appeared to gradually disengage in the fourth workshop and dropped out in the fifth. She came back for the individual interview, where she disclosed her aversion to dwelling in a drama about mental illness, strongly voicing that she would have preferred a lighter theme. She was interviewed in Italian, and her proficiency was low—hence some interference from Portuguese—but she made herself understood:

1 Carme: Because psychology, mental disorders, *todo* (everything) of that thing, the
2 drama for… learning another language [shouting] for me, at this moment… I don't
3 like it!
4 Erika: Sure, I see.
5 Carme: If it was another… another topic: it's all good, alright? […] Psychology
6 topic, mental disorders… all of that [shouting] it's not my moment!
(Carme, pp. 4:17–36)

In my analysis, I relate Carme's disengagement to managing aesthetic distance, as well as to managing the element of *mood* generated by the pre-text. Setting the dramatic world in a hospital and dealing with mental illness was, for Carme, a threatening context. Thus, the mood generated might have been disturbing for her. As a result, she disengaged. Besides these three examples of disengagement, the other five participants in Case Study Three remained engaged, exercising agency and highly receptive to the drama and the language. In the interviews, they were all able to reflect on the aesthetic *form* of drama, on how intense it was, and on how a performative approach impacted on the learning. However, the lack of aesthetic distance at times was such that they were not able (or were unwilling) to disclose whether they were touched by the influence of the *form* on *content*. It is also possible, of course, that they needed more time to process their experience as, with Vygotsky (1926/1971), creative perception is followed by a delayed reaction, where the feeling needs to be overcome.

In Case Study One, on the other hand, the pre-text was related to graduates applying for a job as journalists in China; this might have been, in the real life of the participants, a desirable context, connected to their sense of high-achievement and business-oriented attitude; thus, the *mood* associated might have been one of 'accomplishment', aligning with, and validating their motivation to learn the language. The analysis of Case Study One's participants points to a level of aesthetic engagement related to the influence of aesthetic *form* on *content*, resulting in a heightened awareness about their identity, self and other, made possible by playing a dramatic role. For example, Tommaso, Chinese, 23 years old, disclosed a heightened sense of awareness related to his newly found identity as a speaker of Italian, playing a role in the drama, and operating between both Chinese and Italian cultures. Similarly, Viola, Chinese, 23 years old (interviewed in Italian, intermediate level of proficiency) reflected on her experience of getting used to a performative approach, and gradually embracing it, once she realised it helped her to 'feel' the Italian language and culture:

1   Erika: What did you find most difficult, in the class?
2   Viola: ehm at first we didn't understand what this is, what is the reason … to do this
3   performance, that performance, so … we didn't understand very well; so we don't

```
4    know how – how to do it. This is a bit hard.
5    E: so you're talking about the first class, at the beginning? So you found it hard
6    because you didn't understand how to do it … or because you didn't understand why
7    we do it?
8    Viola: why we do it.
9    Erika: why you do it.
10   Viola: yes yes!
11   Erika: and now do you understand why?
12   Viola: mmm yes [smiles]
13   Erika: you understood a bit more
14   Viola: yes
15   Erika: why do we do it?
16   Viola: ahhh… to help us … to … feel… the Italian language, more.
     (Viola, p. 3:31–45)
```

Viola here captured the felt-experience (*perezhivanie*) dimension of the language, and, in the same interview, related it to the art form of process drama:

```
1    [Process drama] is an art form in order to … show others. Yes for us as well,
2    ourselves. I think that it's a [laughs] it's an art form to feel the culture and the
3    language, that's it.³ (Viola, p. 4:39–40)
```

Viola's comment can be seen to support a social experience process drama, understood as a participatory form ("for us, as well"). They point to performative approaches to language learning being able to tap into a felt-experience of the target language, what Mahn and John-Steiner refer to as "getting a feeling for the language" (2002, p. 56).

Another thread emerging from the analysis of Case Study One is aesthetic learning in process drama connected to a sense of beauty. An example is Huifang's answer below. During the interview, conducted in Italian (upper intermediate), I asked a question that prompted her to reflect on her notion of beauty in an educational context:

```
1    Erika: in what way can it be defined as an art form?
2    Huifang: this class?
3    Erika: yes
```

---

³Original: […] *É un'arte per sentire la cultura e la lingua, è così*. See Piazzoli (2015, pp. 97–98) for methodological considerations related to the translation of this passage.

```
4    Huifang: that … firstly, art has to be beautiful.
5    Erika: okay
6    Huifang: for me this class is … really beautiful! I mean, I've seen that … it's
7    different from … the other classes. In first year … now I'm started a year, in first
8    year I never went to class, I just did exams … but this class your class … I want to
9    attend it, because it's beautiful.
10   Erika: in what way is it 'beautiful'?
11   Huifang: I like it [smiles]
12   Erika: what do you mean by 'beautiful'? Do you mean beautiful on a superficial
13   level, or on an internal level? I mean what … what do you mean by …? Because
14   'beautiful' … for example, we can say that a girl is beautiful; but we can say that she
15   is beautiful outside … or inside. Which one did you mean?
16   Huifang: I would say: outside, also inside …
17   Erika: outside and also inside
18   Huifang: yes.
19   Erika: and how can we say that this class is beautiful, what is 'beautiful' about it?
20   Huifang: I mean we do things together … and then given that… you are trying to
21   make us talk … this makes us work so hard! That there are the teachers that … lazy
22   … they don't get the kids to work … and then they sleep or … they leave early
23   Erika: mmm
24   Huifang: then, in this class we do everything altogether …
25   Erika: so, when you say 'beautiful' you mean …
26   Huifang: that I like it.
     (Huifang, p. 5:8–31)
```

I am fascinated by Huifang's notion of beauty in process drama. She connected beauty to "doing things together"—a concept she repeated twice (T 20, 24); as well as motivation: "I want to attend" (T 8) and liveliness, as well as structuring activities that promote active communication (T 20–21). Huifang described her understanding of 'beauty' in process drama using the example of something opposite to it, discussing students' non-heightened responses as in "sleeping and leaving early" (T 22). Her remarks on beauty echo Winston's (2010) argument of the value of beauty in education, a profound, yet underestimated endeavour, as mentioned in the Introduction of the book.

The notion of beauty was mentioned by student-participants across the three case studies. Gianni (Tibetan, 25 years old) connected the idea of 'beauty' to feeling 'lively':

```
1    Erika: how was it for you, the experience to learn Italian though drama?
2    Gianni: I feel beautiful! Yes, yes.
```

3   Erika: yes? What do you mean?
4   Gianni: when I attended this drama class … I feel very lively. I like it a lot, it's not
5   like other classes – a bit boring, a bit tired
    (Gianni, p. 2:12–16)

Similarly to Huifang above, Gianni (interviewed in Italian, lower intermediate) explained himself by contrasts, by stating that which is not: it is *not* like feeling tired or bored (T 5); it is connected to a feeling of invigoration, to a lively sensation (T 4). This goes back to Alessia's interview, as mentioned in the previous section (see "Intercultural Education" in this chapter) in which she discussed an enhanced self-awareness of her identity as a Chinese young woman, now living in Italy, a new sense of freedom that through her role she realised she is embodying—as if there was a mirror through which she found herself anew. Maxine Greene (1995) comes to mind here, and her definition of aesthetic education as a mode of countering the 'anaesthetic', a way of awakening people to the awareness of life's richness. According to Greene, the purpose of aesthetic education is to arouse students to become more than passive onlookers; to be willing to engage. Greene defines imagination as the power to conceptualise things "as they could be otherwise" (p. 10); to bring the 'as if' into being. Engaging in a make-believe in a second language, then, brought a dimension in the 'as if' of these learners into being.

3   A Polyphony of Voices

After tuning into Hecate's voices separately, let us attend to the polyphony they have created (Fig. 4).

Doing process drama in a second language implies being immersed in a situation that starts off with a degree of distancing in place, as the very language being used is not the participants' mother tongue. This can be seen as a 'mask' that the learner, as a social actor, wears in the make *belief* of the classroom (see "Make-Believe and Make Belief" in Chapter 7). The language used in the L2 classroom may or may not be *fully* comprehensible to the learner. If the language isn't comprehensible at all, frustration may set in and the learner may disengage, or engage

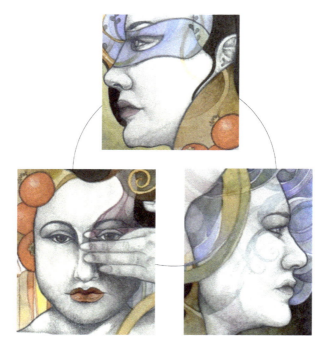

Fig. 4 Hecate, Patricia Ariel (2008). A polyphony of voices, my interpretation

elsewhere (see my account of watching a German play without understanding the language, in the Foreword). On the other hand, if the language is partly or fully comprehensible to them, their initial cognitive response may be to analyse the language.

Even when a language becomes less foreign, and more familiar, the L2 learner may focus on the linguistic, sociolinguistic, or pragmatic aspects, resulting in an implicit cognitive detachment that prevents the 'sense' of the words, *á là* Vygotsky (1934/1986), to directly reach their core emotions. To engage L2 learners' subjectivity in a second language, L2 teacher/artists need to find strategies to harness this detachment. In other words, individuals interacting in a second language adopt a role as L2 learners. As such, they wear a *first* mask; the mask is present—it cannot be taken off, but it can be acknowledged into the texture of engagement, through careful management of the elements of drama. By playing a role in a process drama, the L2 learner engages in make-believe, what Schechner calls a playful exchange between the real context and the play context. In the make-believe, L2 learners wear a *second* mask—that of a dramatic role. Awareness of this phenomenon is what Tschurtschenthaler (2013) calls "mask-upon-a-mask" (p. 230) or double masking: the degree of integration of the foreign language with one's role (see "Aesthetic Engagement in Process Drama" in Chapter 3).

The participants of the research study, particularly from Case Study One and Case Study Two, suggested that the double masking within the make-believe allowed them to imagine they were outside an L2 classroom, into a real context, producing language that was more similar to everyday life. Some participants equated it to real-life conversation, like relaxed chatting in a café. Thus, paradoxically, the double masking effect of the make-believe brought the learners closer to real-life communication. The nature of engagement with language was analysed and construed as an active process of perception-in-action, entailing receptivity and vigilance, mediated by dramatic tension, and manifesting as agency and playfulness. However, at times, particularly during Case Study Three, the aesthetic experience was under-distanced. Whenever this happened, the emotions became too intense for participants to dwell in the make-believe of the drama as well as in the real context of the learning. Both masks were dropped. This confirms that management of aesthetic distance, and protection 'into' emotion (Bolton, 1984) are vital to support learner engagement.

With attention to the intercultural dimension, in Taliaferro's (1998) reading of Maxine Greene's work, holding a double-consciousness refers to being able to see oneself through the eyes of the other, made possible by the faculty of imagination. In Taliaferro's words: "The dialogic nature of the human mind is manifested in the relationship between the Self and the Other, and it is through the imagination that they dialogue" (p. 94). Imagination is framed as the dialogical pathway between self and other—a relationship sustained by a *productive tension*. Looking at the findings of this study from an intercultural perspective, it was observed that whenever intercultural dramatic tension saturated the drama structure, it enabled the teacher/artist, and participants as co-artists, to sharpen the dramatic elements' intercultural perspective, and to harness the engagement of these elements into ongoing intercultural reflection—in a dialogue between self and other. O'Neill (1995) also elaborates on role negotiation in process drama as "exploiting the *tensions* between appearance and reality, *mask* and *face*, and *role* and *identity* that lie at the heart of the theatrical experience" (p. 85, my emphasis). Yet identity, as we have seen, is far from a linear construct: it is multifaceted, composed of different sub-identities that are at times contradictory (Akkerman & Meijer, 2011) and each with potentially its own stance, or I-position. Wearing a mask, or mask-upon-a-mask in the case of L2/process drama, can resonate with different aspects of identity as if, paradoxically, by wearing a double mask an inner dialogue can be activated with multiple sub-identities. This was made possible by the faculty of imagination, playing a dramatic role, framed by dramatic focus and sustained by tension, and the other elements of drama—in an intercultural key.

For this to occur, the pre-text needed to hold enough intercultural 'kick' to infuse intercultural dramatic tension into the elements of drama and, consequently, into the percipients' responses. What the analysis revealed is that, while the pre-text in Case Study One carried a degree of *explicit* intercultural dramatic tension, the pre-texts for Case Study Two and Case Study Three did not. Conversely, not all participants were able to *elaborate* on their intercultural engagement as double-consciousness, particularly whenever the intercultural dramatic tension in the drama was not strong enough to rouse an intercultural dialogue between self and other. This suggests that intercultural dramatic tension is a vital element to support intercultural aesthetic engagement.

Notwithstanding the different degrees of aesthetic engagement reached by the participants, the findings suggest that some of them went through an intensely lived felt-experience, *perezhivanie*, in the second language. I situate *perezhivanie* within aesthetic engagement, endorsing O'Neill's (1995) argument that the purpose of process drama is to embody meaning, expanding the participants' capacity to perceive—to "arrest attention" and "extend perception" in order to "invite interpretation" (p. 127). Most student-participants were able to reflect on the *form* of drama. Others could also reflect on the influence of the *form* on the *content* of the drama. Some experienced a collision, or dissonance, between their responses in the drama, and how they would have responded in the real context. Whenever this happened, the nature of metaxis afforded an aesthetic experience *in* the second language, and/or *of* the second language, resulting in insights into identity, self and other.

In that, I agree with Tschurtschenthaler (2013) as she states: "Drama-based foreign language learning, consequently, becomes an aesthetic process which integrates the constitution of the language learner's self" (p. 245). For L2 speakers engaged in a process drama, the intercultural experience of their identity, mediated by role and tension through play, can trigger potent intercultural insights. If intercultural dramatic tension is harnessed in the pre-text, it can then flow into the context of the drama, be explored by the teacher and the participants as recipients of an aesthetic experience, and permeate into the context of the learning. Intercultural dramatic tension can thus channel the dialogic imagination that fuels our double-consciousness.

Workshop 9: Mirrors

Description: This workshop aimed to investigate the relationship between students and teachers, communication and schizophrenia.

Students' Context—Inspiration for the Workshop: In this workshop, participants played the role of psychologists trying to help an L2 language teacher who stopped talking. The two drama structures reported below were designed as part of a scheme of five workshops, created for Case Study Three of my Ph.D. research, supervised by Julie Dunn and Claire Kennedy, at Griffith University (Brisbane). The workshops were conducted in an adult school of Italian (L2) in Milan, Italy.

Educational Aims: Reflecting on mental illness as taboo in Italy and in other cultures; learning and practising language related to psychology in Italian.

Pre-text: The short video *Buongiorno*, directed by Melo Prino, featuring a man who wakes up to see his own delusion in the mirror, over and over, to the soundtrack of Ennio Morricone https://www.youtube.com/watch?v=3W5V2bM0G-w.

Level: A2 to C1 (CEFR).

Duration: Two three-hour sessions.

Workshop 9 Mirrors

	Drama strategy
Initiation phase	**Step 1. Warm-up**: a. Names and emotions b. Vocal warm-up c. Mirror exercise: mirror each other, in pairs; after several minutes instruct the mirrored image to slightly switch, then 'misbehave' **Step 2. Pre-text**: a. Watch the short film again https://www.youtube.com/watch?v=3W5V2bM0G-w b. Improvise the dialogues in selected still frames from the video c. Write, in pairs, the lines of each personality (the delusions in the mirror) d. Individual feedback from the teacher on the written texts e. Vocal interpretation **Step 3. Dramatic roles and situation**: a. The group recaps the drama (roles/situations) from the previous day b. Each participant briefly re-introduces herself, in role **Step 4. Improvisation**: The police have given us another clue: the subject has written a note [show the note, handling it with care]: 'Mirrors should stop reflecting'. What can we do? What can we deduce? Improvise
Experiential phase	**Step 5. Role play**: a. In pairs, psychologists interview the neighbour; two colleagues and the school director b. All together recap the situation and what we have discovered **Step 6. Animated tableau**: The team of psychologists decides to go to the lift to meet the subject. Create an animated tableau vivent that represents how that encounter went and then re-present it through three tableaux **Step 7. Improvisation**: Report the operation to the psychologists' coordinator, who was absent. Decide, as a team, which members of the family need to be contacted **Step 8. In-role writing**: a. Write a letter to a member of Paolo's family to inform him/her of the situation and ask for a meeting b. Individual language feedback c. Read the letters aloud
Reflective phase	**Step 9. Linguistic revision**: What new language have we learnt today? **Step 10. Intercultural discussion**: Mental illness as taboo

This chapter addressed findings of my doctoral research, related to learner engagement in process drama for second language learning. Learner engagement was analysed across three domains, in line with the Hecate metaphor. Within the domain of Second Language Acquisition, language engagement was construed as an active process of perception-in-action. Within the domain of Intercultural Education, intercultural dramatic tension emerged as a vital element to sustain intercultural meaning-making. Within the domain Aesthetic Learning, heightened awareness was related to insights on identity, language learning, and intercultural awareness on self and other. By contemplating the three domains together, some conclusions were made as to the nature of intercultural aesthetic engagement, and undergoing a felt-experience in a second language. The next chapter presents the second part of the research analysis and findings related to this doctoral study.

References

Ariel, P. (2008). *Hecate: Watercolor and pencil on illustration board*.
Akkerman, S. F., & Meijer, P. C. (2011). A dialogical approach to conceptualizing teacher identity. *Teaching and Teacher Education, 27*(2), 308–319.
Alred, G., Byram, M., & Fleming, M. (Eds.). (2003). *Intercultural experience and education*. Clevedon: Multilingual Matters.
Bolton, G. (1984). *Drama as education: An argument for placing drama at the centre of the curriculum*. Harlow, Essex: Longman.
Byram, M. (1997). *Teaching and assessing intercultural communicative competence*. Clevedon: Multilingual Matters.
Byram, M. (2008). *From foreign language education to education for intercultural citizenship: Essays and reflections* (Vol. 17). Bristol: Multilingual Matters.
Byram, M. (2009). Intercultural competence in foreign languages. In D. K. Deardorff (Ed.), *The Sage handbook of intercultural competence* (pp. 321–331). Thousand Oaks, CA: Sage.
Eriksson, S. (2011). Distancing. In S. Schonmann (Ed.), *Key concepts in theatre/drama education* (pp. 65–72). Rotterdam: Sense Publishers.
Greene, M. (1995). *Releasing the imagination: Essays on education, the arts, and social change*. San Francisco: Jossey-Bass Publishers.

Lantolf, J. P., & Thorne, S. L. (2006). *Sociocultural theory and the genesis of second language development*. New York: Oxford University Press.

Lima, M. G. (1995). From aesthetics to psychology: Notes on Vygotsky's "Psychology of Art". *Anthropology & Education Quarterly, 26*(4), 410–424.

Mahn, H., & John-Steiner, V. (2002). The gift of confidence: A Vygotskyan view of emotions. In G. Wells & G. Claxton (Eds.), *Learning for life in the 21st century: Sociocultural perspectives on the future of education*. Malden, MA: Blackwell.

McCafferty, S. G., & Stam, G. (2008). *Gesture: Second language acquisition and classroom research*. New York: Routledge.

O'Neill, C. (1995). *Drama worlds: A framework for process drama*. Portsmouth: Heinemann.

Pavis, P. (1998). *Dictionary of the theatre: Terms, concepts and analysis*. Toronto: University of Toronto Press.

Piazzoli, E. (2014). Engagement as perception-in-action in process drama for teaching and learning Italian as a second language. *International Journal of Language Studies, 8*(2), 91–116.

Piazzoli, E. (2015). Translation in cross-language qualitative research: Pitfalls and opportunities. *Translation and Translanguaging in Multilingual Contexts, 1*(1), 80–102.

Piazzoli, E. (2017). Intercultural/Dramatic Tension and the Nature of Intercultural Engagement. In J. Crutchfield & M. Schewe (Eds.), *Going performative in intercultural education: International contexts, theoretical perspectives and models of practice* (pp. 172–197). Bristol: Multilingual Matters.

Platt, E., & Brooks, F. B. (2002). Task engagement: A turning point in foreign language development. *Language Learning, 52*(2), 365–400.

Platt, E., & Brooks, F. B. (2008). Embodiment as self-regulation in L2 task performance. In S. G. McCafferty & G. Stam (Eds.), *Gesture: Second language acquisition and classroom research* (pp. 66–87). New York: Routledge.

Schön, D. (1983). *The reflective practitioner: How professionals think in action*. London: Temple Smith.

Scully, G. (2017, May). *From performance to the periphery and beyond: Group devised theatre for additional language acquisition*. Paper presented at the Scenario Forum Conference: Performative spaces in literature, language and culture education, University College Cork, Ireland.

Taliaferro, D. M. (1998). Signifying self: Re-presentations of the double-consciousness in the work of Maxine Greene. In W. Pinar (Ed.), *The passionate mind of Maxine Greene: "I am—not yet"* (pp. 89–121). London: Falmer Press.

Taylor, P., & Warner, C. D. (2006). *Structure and spontaneity: The process drama of Cecily O'Neill.* Sterling, VA: Trentham.

Tschurtschenthaler, H. (2013). *Drama-based foreign language learning: Encounters between self and others.* Munster: Waxmann.

Van Lier, L. (1996). *Interaction in the language curriculum: Awareness, autonomy, and authenticity.* London: Longman.

Van Lier, L. (2004). *The ecology and semiotics of language learning: A sociocultural perspective.* Norwell, MA: Kluwer Academic.

Van Lier, L. (2007). Action-based Teaching, Autonomy and Identity. *Innovation in Language Learning and Teaching, 1*(1), 46–65.

Van Lier, L. (2008). Agency in the classroom. In J. P. Lantolf & M. E. Poehner (Eds.), *Sociocultural theory and the teaching of second languages.* London: Equinox.

Vygotsky, L. (1933/1976). Play and its role in the mental development of the child. In J. Bruner, A. Jolly, & K. Sylva (Eds.), *Play: Its role in development and evolution* (pp. 537–554). Harmondsworth, Middlesex: Penguin.

Vygostky, L. (1934/1994). The problem of the environment. In R. Van Der Veer & J. Valsiner (Eds.), *The Vygotsky Reader* (pp. 338–354). Oxford, UK: Blackwell.

Vygotsky, L. S. (1926/1971). *The psychology of art.* Cambridge, MA: The MIT Press.

Vygotsky, L. S. (1930/1978). *Mind in society: The development of higher psychological processes.* Cambridge, MA: Harvard University Press.

Vygotsky, L. S. (1934/1986). *Thought and language.* Cambridge, MA: MIT Press.

Wertsch, J. V. (1991). *Voices of the mind: A sociological approach to mediated action.* London: Harvester Wheatsheaf.

Winston, J. (2010). *Beauty and education.* London: Routledge.

11

Teacher Artistry

In this chapter, I report findings on teacher artistry, based on my doctoral research on process drama in second language education. How do we, as teacher/artists, strike a balance between careful planning and managing the dual affect as the drama unfolds? As we have seen in the previous chapter, managing either of these aspects has direct consequences for learners' engagement and disengagement. In discussing L2 teaching, Kramsch (2009) talks about '(un)predictability by design':

> A good lesson plan has an organic rhythm, it is both ritualistic and spontaneous; it has no more than one or two themes with multiple variations. It has enough predictability to keep the theme going, and enough unpredictability to make the students curious about the next variation – a kind of (un)predictability by design, that both calms the body, and stimulates the mind. (p. 203)

Calming the body and stimulating the mind; mastering unpredictability by design; performing ritualistic and spontaneous classes. Kramsch's words are enchanting, but how do we get there, in practice? To attempt to address this question, in my doctoral analysis I scrutinised my own teaching style, attitudes and beliefs, through reflective practitioner methodology (Schön, 1983). A key finding was that I needed to reconsider my tacit values and beliefs about teaching and learning. My steepest learning curve was realising, through translanguaging (García, 2014) in reflective practice (see "Translanguaging as Method" in Chapter 9), that some tacit convictions emerging from my behaviour clashed with what I thought were the values I upheld.

1   The Competence Ladder

Analysing my comments in the think-aloud exchanges with the teacher-participants, and cross-referencing those with my reflective writing unearthed surprising results—particularly, as mentioned above, a clash between the values and behaviour I aspired to and my actual behaviour—in action. This discovery originated in a specific incident, which I call, with Dunn, a "category three mistake" (2015, p. 189). This kind of mistake involves process drama facilitators privileging their agenda, in spite of the participants' creative suggestions. Having identified my propensity to take control in this situation, I chose to change my behaviour, to mindfully stop effecting this tacit control over the workshop and students. To better understand my disposition, I carried out a systematic analysis, through which I kept track of my conscious letting go of this power-related issue.

I saw my relinquishing of this disposition as a competence. The competence ladder is a model used in psychology to map the transition from incompetence to competence when learning a new competence. I was particularly attracted to Underhill's (1992) adaptation of the model in teacher education. This model maps out four stages of awareness and competence in a teacher's growth:

Stage 1   Un*conscious* in*competence*. I am not aware of what I am not doing well.
Stage 2   *Conscious* in*competence*. I become aware of what I am not doing well.
Stage 3   *Conscious competence*. I am aware of doing it more competently.

Stage 4   Un*conscious competence*. My new competence becomes second nature.

(p. 76, my emphasis)

As Underhill suggests that the stages are cyclical, I chose to use the golden spiral to graphically represent them. In Fig. 1, I visualise the four stages in a spiralling growth, with each quadrant representing a stage, from stage 1 (un*conscious* in*competence*) to stage 4 (un*conscious competence*).

The spiral (Fig. 1) tracked my ongoing progression related to thinking on my feet, as I facilitated the drama. This was done with attention to my macro planning (the choices made before starting a drama) and micro reflection-in-action (in-the-moment-artistry choices taken as the drama unfolds), following Dunn and Stinson's (2011) terminology. I discovered through the analysis that although I welcomed participants improvising *within* each episode, initially I resisted letting them join the dots *between* episodes.

To make sense of these differences, which are related to managing reflection-in-action at the micro level, I needed to differentiate between

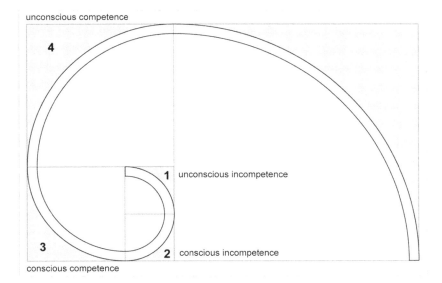

Fig. 1   Underhill's (1992) teacher development model

intra-episode reflection-in-action and *inter*-episode reflection-in-action: the former referring to reflecting in action *within* one episode; the latter to reflecting in action *across* episodes. Specifically, I found that my *inter*-episode reflection-in-action shifted from *un*conscious *in*competence (at the onset of Case Study One), to conscious *in*competence (between Case Study One and Case Study Two), to conscious competence (at the end of Case Study Two), to fluctuate towards a glimmer of *un*conscious competence, by the end of Case Study Three. Across the three case studies, I adopted a reflexive attitude to map my competence as it shifted from *un*conscious *in*competence to *un*conscious competence. I identified three stages that I termed 'addiction to plot', feeling 'trapped by the plot', to finally glimpse towards what O'Neill terms 'structuring for spontaneity' (in Taylor & Warner, 2006).

2 Addiction to Plot

In *Reading for the Plot*, Brooks (1984) draws on Barthes' (1966) concept of 'narrative impulse' (*la passion du sense*) challenging the Aristotelian sense of plot, and advocating instead for the relationship between plot and meaning. In discussing Brook's theory, Stewart (1986) laments the modern trend in literature as an "addiction to plot" (p. 107). In my data analysis I endorsed this phrasing, and analysed, in some depth, my tacit addiction to plot.

Before undertaking my doctoral research, my sense of identity related to being an improviser, a storyteller and a creative writer. Storytelling—in the form of plays, children's stories, novels, short stories, screenplays, as well as poetry—has always been a prominent part of who I am. Before starting my doctorate, I found great pleasure (and I still do) in creative writing. Yet, I had never questioned the origins, and beliefs, informing my passion for pouring words onto paper. The roots of my creative writing were embedded in an Aristotelian plot sense (beginning, middle; end). They dated back to my childhood when, as an only child, I used to spend afternoons writing short stories, with five siblings as the recurring characters, to keep me company after school. This storytelling consolidated through my undergraduate training in creative writing, and in a decade of work as a children's playgroup leader and drama practitioner. As I became accustomed to the process drama genre, I abandoned prose and started conceiving stories in episodes as part of a dramatic structure. These, as O'Neill (1995) reveals, are linked with each other in a web of meaning. Due to my inclination for storytelling, I have always favoured creating my own process drama structures, rather than relying on pre-existing drama templates.

I gained the above insights by reflecting-on-action during the course of Case Study One, precisely as I pondered over this passage that I wrote spontaneously after a drama workshop:

1   I have realised that what I really love is engaging with the creative process,
2   especially writing the process drama. This is what I absolutely love, it is the source of
3   my own aesthetic engagement that motivates me and commits me to the work. This is
4   my ultimate truth.
    (RJ, p. 11:4–7)

I wrote this entry directly in English. In lines 2 and 3 what clearly transpires is a passion for the creative process relating to the playwright's function. I had created a drama structure much like a playwright would, for the students to animate. In discussing the playwright function, O'Neill (1995) suggests that as a process drama unfolds, the teacher/artist is supposed to negotiate the process with the participants, as co-artists.

What I discovered through my analysis was that I was not willing to share the playwright function with the participants. For example: to create tension of surprise, the journalists had to be arrested while on the train (See Workshop 8, *The Journalists*). In the drama, they tried to *resist* being arrested, fighting back the accusations of fraud with all the verbal and non-verbal means at their disposal within the dramatic context. Participants, in role, orchestrated a 'conspiracy theory' to rebel against the arrest. I reacted to it, in role, by overruling their idea and sending them off to jail. As I've signalled above, this response echoes what Dunn calls a "category three mistake", that is, facilitators privileging their agenda over the participants' creative suggestions (2015, p. 189). My unwillingness to share the playwright function, made explicit in the 'category three' incident, does not align with process drama philosophy. Indeed, as Bowell and Heap (2017) suggest:

"The framework does not drive the course of the drama; the course of the drama drives the shape of the framework" (p. 22).

In truth, the negotiation of the train arrest episode induced high levels of engagement among participants. Nevertheless, during the final Video-Stimulated Recall (VSR) focus group with the teacher-participants, as we watched the video I emphatically stated that it was "the worst moment of my entire career" as I wanted to persuade them to get off that train, but I failed to do so. This was painful, I continued, as I acknowledged that "I am a terrible actress" (FG, 1:07:43). These comments, uttered in Italian to three teacher-participants, are important to the analysis as they uncover my propensity to assume control over the process drama. By appraising that moment in terms of what I claimed to be my flawed persuasion skills, I was revealing my disposition to take control over the improvisation. Stating that "I failed" reinforced this point. Failed what? Though engagement levels hit the roof, at that time I focussed on my persuasion skills failing.

Beyond my recognition at the time, what I really meant by failing, alas, seemed to refer to my inability to take control over the students, in role. I failed to persuade them and, therefore, I opined, I was a terrible actress. If anyone had tried to tell me at the time that a will to control the participants was embedded in my actions I would have vehemently denied it. I would have countered that process drama is "emphatically not about giving a display of acting", but about provoking into action, in line with Kao and O'Neill's argument (1998, p. 26). If anyone had asked me at the time, I would have sworn that I was endorsing this in my teaching. In fact I wasn't—as my liberating but painful awakening later revealed to me.

While writing an NVIVO reflective memo I realised that, while some aspects of process drama improvisation came naturally to me, like reflecting in action to improvise *within* an episode (intra-episode), what did not come naturally was to re-structure *between* episodes (inter-episode). As I was unsure how to re-structure, thinking on my feet, aspiring to ad hoc episodes that could inject tension, I clung to the structure. Reflecting on this aspect at the time, I noted that "for me this is still a cognitive task (to inject tension), not a spontaneous, second-nature task" (NV Reflective Memo). I decided the journalists would get arrested, and I was not going to let them get away with it—as evidenced in my think-aloud exchanges with the teacher-participants. I was unable to re-negotiate a new episode, following the participants' offer about the conspiracy theory. While Heathcote's stance is 'evoke, not direct' drama (Wagner, 1976), I was unwittingly doing the opposite – directing, not evoking. This represents the departure point of the analysis, that is, *un*conscious *in*competence at inter-episode level of micro reflection-in-action (Fig. 2).

It was by analysing some impromptu comments, in Italian, with three pre-service L2 teachers, that disposition of mine was made explicit. As research on identity and bilingualism suggests, bilingual individuals may feel like a slightly different person when switching over to a different language (Dewaele, 2010; Pavlenko, 2006). In my case, on the one hand my Italian teacher identity appeared to cling to a more controlling style. On the other hand, my Australian teacher identity aspired to adopt a more flexible style of facilitation, one aligned with the principles

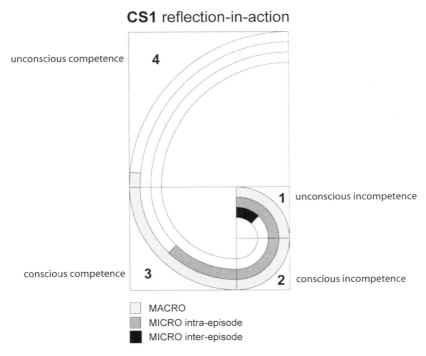

Fig. 2 Unconscious incompetence in micro reflection-in-action (inter-episode level)

of process drama. The teacher-participants, being Italian, evoked and appealed to my Italian sense of self. In our friendly conversations, motivated by a reflexive attitude, I made myself vulnerable by letting my inner beliefs come to the surface. I am grateful to them, as those eerie remarks would have never surfaced in an English conversation with a process drama colleague. Those exchanges granted an access point into my tacit system of beliefs related to improvisation and Teacher in Role.

My inner beliefs also came to the surface in my personal writings, in Italian. The day Case Study One ended, I sat down in a café and wrote a long entry in my logbook, looking for a sense of closure with the case study. Below is an extract from it:

1   I finished the first case study!!!!!!!! It went really well, I guess: surely it's the best process
2   drama I've ever written […] The only thing that didn't go well, I suppose, is the student
3   focus group and the very last tableau (the dream) as opposed to the language and
4   intercultural reflections. What was I thinking?!?!?!?!?!!? The tableau was fun for them, but
5   they didn't turn their language from implicit to explicit. It was as if I was thinking: ah-ah. It's
6   all over (i.e. the story is complete), <u>but</u> actually the last workshop is the most important; the
7   reflection must take much more time. We ended in silly mode, not in reflective mode. *Ouch*.
(LG, 23/06/2010)

My emotional investment transpires from the colourful use of punctuation, expressiveness and figurative words. A naïve enthusiasm, rooted in a playwright's stance, emerges in lines 1–2 ("the best…I've ever written"). However, an internal dialectic between my *un*conscious *in*competence and my conscious *in*competence emerges notably in line 4, in the "What was I thinking?" followed by a string of question marks and exclamation marks. My tendency to cling to Aristotelian sense of plot is evidenced in lines 5–6, when I clarify that by "it's all over" I mean that "the story is complete". Most interestingly, the emphasis then falls on the conjunction 'but' (underlined in the original), which ushers in a contrastive clause, with a newly found insight (lines 6–7). Right then, in the very act of writing, I was processing what happened, and coming to terms with reflection being more important than finishing the story, unveiling my addiction to plot.

This was my way of debriefing from the intense experience that was my first case study. In a way, my need to gain a sense of closure can be interpreted in terms of what has been referred to as 'teacher melancholia'

(Gallagher, Freeman, & Wessels, 2010). The authors differentiate between 'mourning'—intended as: "The process by which the lost object or person is 'let go' and there is a break with it so that the new can begin", as opposed to 'melancholia': "Avoidance of this mourning process, and subsequent 'letting go'. It is a taking of the lost object into the ego where it turns on itself and becomes hyper-judgemental" (2010, p. 6). They use the term 'teacher melancholia', in a drama education context, when what is lost is not an object or person, but an *ideal*, in a process that sees the loss of ideals accompanied by a hyper-judgement of the self. The authors apply this discourse to shed light on a comment by one of the teachers in their drama research, who stated that her students' performance "could have been so much better" (p. 6). That teacher, they argued, seemed to be appealing to a lost ideal, an aesthetic judgement referring to the performance, rather than the learning engagement.

My logbook entry, charged with intense emotions, marked a turning point in my inter-episode reflection-in-action, from unconscious incompetence to conscious incompetence, as illustrated in Fig. 3.

This is evident in the few days that followed, as my awareness shifted to a position where I was aware that my controlling tendency was a problem. Reflecting on the concluding episode of Case Study One, I write:

1   I feel really humiliated and upset at myself for not wrapping up the case study
2   properly. Remorse is eating me up. What an idiot! What can I learn from this?
    (RF, p. 49:35–39)

Here rampant teacher melancholia (Gallagher et al., 2010) is evident in my becoming hyper-judgemental and in lamenting "not wrapping the case study properly" (line 1). What I am referring to here is that, at the end of Case Study One, I mismanaged my time and failed to harness the newly acquired language in a comprehensive language review. Rather than doing a longer language revision and intercultural reflection, I focussed on in-role writing, followed by an animated tableau of Mr. Righello's and the journalist's dreams. The tableaux were the very final episode and, not surprisingly, student-participants used them playfully, to give their own sense of closure to the story, orchestrating mission-impossible-style spin-offs of Mr. Righello's escape. In doing so,

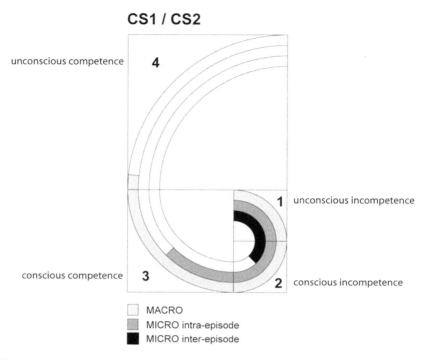

Fig. 3 Conscious incompetence in micro reflection-in-action (inter-episode level)

they had crafted an ending for the story, but did not have time for an ending to the workshop: we ran out of time for the language revision, arguably one of the most important components of L2/drama.

Surely, I had hit conscious *in*competence, a (painful) phase that Underhill identifies as the most critical stage of teacher change, especially for experienced teachers. It can be anxiety-provoking for teachers to acknowledge their *in*competence, especially if their own self-image is that of competent educators. Indeed, a few days later, straight after the introductory session of Case Study Two, I was filled with angst. In my Journal I write:

1 Sad and tired. I feel like I am full of nothingness. Void of meaning. Am I just tired?
2 Once again starting from zero, taking risks, being observed and trying to do my

3   work. Did I fail to inject tension into the story? What is causing this melancholy
4   tonight, this feeling of nothingness? I feel like a total failure.
    (RJ, p. 5:39–44)

In retrospect, I do think that that 'feeling of nothingness' (line 1) goes back to the fact that I felt the drama did not work at its best, and this made me feel depressed. In line 3 my conscious *in*competence ("Did I fail to inject tension into the story?") stung bitterly. It proved even more painful as, in the second day of Case Study Two, the numbers dropped from eighteen students to nine. As it turned out, the students had not been informed that their daily classes would change to drama for one week; not all of them were prepared to trust an outsider doing drama work, with four of their teachers observing and taking notes. At the time, I spent a great deal of time reflecting on the introductory session of Case Study Two, resulting in an analysis of the student/teacher collaboration in Teacher in Role, as documented in Piazzoli (2012). Halfway through Case Study Two, this weakness, favouring a sense of plot over structure, started to feel less like a tacit addiction, and more like a trap from which I wanted to break free.

3   Trapped by the Plot

In a 2011 keynote address at the *National Drama International Conference* at Swansea University (Wales), O'Neill (2011) suggested that a drama teacher should start a process drama only with the first three episodes pre-planned; everything else should arise spontaneously out of the structure. This keynote was an eye-opener for me; eight months on from my drama-led intervention, it profoundly challenged my understanding of the form. The message it brought home was that process drama is constructed around moments of tension, and decisions based around it, rather than a drama structure with a pre-planned string of episodes.

In my analysis of the raw data in Case Study Two, my struggle to break free from an obsession with plot emerges strongly. If, following O'Neill (2011), one was to prepare only three episodes of a process drama, it would mean that, to some extent, the tension-building connection between one episode and the next had to be the fruit of reflection-in-action. During Case Study Two this became obvious in workshop three, as my perceived drive to cling to the plot came to the foreground. The students, in role as psychologists, had gone to meet 'the subject' inside the lift and, through a combination of colour and music therapy, persuaded him to come out from the lift. I comment:

> 1 This was the opposite of what I had envisaged, and surely disrupted my plans for the
> 2 next episodes. I needed the subject to stay in a crisis to continue the drama; if the
> 3 problem is resolved, the drama ends.
> (RJ, p. 25–26:51-1)

My comment here exposes my tendency to adhere to my pre-defined structure; it reveals an obsession with Aristotelian plot, rather than an open attitude to moments of tension. As O'Neill (1995) points out, process drama episodes do not "merely succeed one another in a straightforward chronological sequence" but each unit of action generates the next (1995, p. 48). In an interview immediately following this workshop with teacher-participant Simone, I comment on the same episode, discussing Johnstone's (1999) principle of 'accepting' and 'blocking' in improvisation:

> 1   Erika: Improvisation, the principle of improvisation, holds that if someone … creates
> 2   a situation, or simply has an idea, you cannot block them, you cannot say: 'Let's not
> 3   do this, let's do that!'
> 4   Simone: okay
> 5   Erika: this is very important, for example, when you did the tableaux vivent, the
> 6   students … in your group decided
> 7   Simone: yes
> 8   Erika: they had the idea … to get him [the subject] to come out
> 9   Simone: yes
> 10 Erika: I was very torn, actually [laughs] I even did some writing to try to [laughs]
> 11 externalise my … my concerns, because I didn't want him to get out, he didn't have
> 12 to get out! Because if he did, the story would have finished, but we have two more
> 13 days … he's got to … I mean, it [the story] has to keep going
> 14 Simone: keep being sick!
> 15 Erika: otherwise it would have been … the happy ending … so … I thought to
> 16 myself: What do I do now? Do I block … I mean, do I force him to stay in the lift? I
> 17 can't, because they have to create whatever they want to … and then I realised that I
> 18 could do, this idea of trying twice, the first time it didn't work, and the second time
> 19 around it worked, but then we carried him to the hospital and he has a drawback.

20   This in-between step was a compromise between doing what I wanted to do, *my*
21   drama, and *the students'* drama, giving the students agency to interpret, according to
22   what they prefer.
      (Simone, interview, p. 8:12–34)

My words in this teacher-interview passage are insightful. I expose my tacit attitude and my inner struggle to deal with it. Turns 11–12 indicate a binary opposition between plot vs. structure in my thinking aloud, unveiling a (covert) adherence to a linear, plot-based form ("if he got out, the story would have finished"). Yet, ironically, in the very same passage, this state of affairs is at odds with my overt knowledge of improvisation in Turns 1 and 2: "I thought to myself: what do I do now? Do I block … I mean, do I force him to stay in the lift? I can't." In other words, this passage exposes two contradictory sides of my sub-identities.

As discussed in the Introduction *(The Teacher/Artist, 1.2)*, the construct of identity is not linear: at times we can hold multiple, contradictory sub-identities (Akkerman & Meijer, 2011), each with potentially its own stance, or I-position, which may, at times, contradict each other in the dialogical landscape of the human mind (p. 311). At the end of the interview extract, as I chat to Simone, we gain access to my knowing-in-action, to how I resolve my inner dialogue (T 17–22). My solution there refers to a micro, inter-episode reflection-in-action strategy that allowed the student-participants an opportunity to exercise the playwright function, as they wished. At this stage, I argue, I tentatively moved from conscious *in*competence to conscious competence, in Underhill's (1992) competence ladder model.

Conscious competence (Fig. 4) is a particularly thorny phase, especially in an improvised form like process drama, where spontaneity is an asset and thinking about one's spontaneity can be debilitating. To this extent I found Barthes' (1977) discourse on "the death of the author" inspiring; Barthes argues for a shift of focus from the *auteur*, at the centre of the piece, to the *scripteur*, as 'somebody who writes'. Barthes suggests that a work of literature is constantly re-interpreted, or re-written, in the mind of the reader. He therefore shifts the spotlight from the author to the reader. The "death of the author" he argues, has an immediate and liberating consequence: the birth of the reader (p. 148).

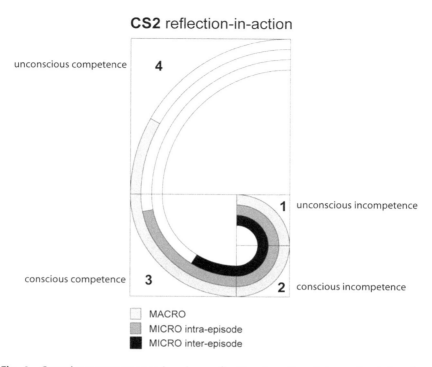

Fig. 4 Conscious competence in micro reflection-in-action (inter-episode level)

I adapted this discourse at this phase of the process drama reflective practice analysis, arguing that the 'death' of my plot-driven, playwright identity had an immediate, liberating effect on the student-participants' agency in exercising the playwright's function.

4 Structuring for Spontaneity

As O'Neill states: "Leaders have to structure for spontaneity. But such structuring will always be informed by the teachers' theoretical perspective and by the aesthetic and pedagogical principles that they believe are truly transformative" (in Taylor & Warner, 2006, p. 117). As I became more aware of my tacit attitude to cling to the plot, and consciously attempted to release it, my approach gradually changed. Johnson and O'Neill (1991) define the improvised text as "an animating current" (p. 148), arguing that every process drama is different because of the participants' unique input. In effect, from this moment on, the participants' improvisation was like a current that took over, taking agency levels to unexpected thresholds. However, this also meant that at times, in my willingness to release control the animating current overflew, resulting in under-distanced aesthetic experiences (see "Aesthetic Learning" in Chapter 10). This proved to be the next challenge: managing the dual affect, without controlling the drama.

Scrutinising the raw data from the video recordings, as well as my think-aloud comments during and after class and my reflective writing, I came to realise that what had shifted was my approach to creating sources of tension in the drama. Previously I relied on the structure, as I was aware of the plot furnishing points of tension. What I progressively started doing was letting these points of tension emerge *from* the group. In other words, the tension-bearing episodes were no longer decided a priori and imposed on the group. The groupness of the group (Scully, 2017) took over the playwright function. The genesis of the tension-generating constraints was created in action, as I harnessed the participants' offers in the improvisation. These were even more authentic than the ones I had planned, as they were indexed to the 'here and now' of the drama, unique to the group. Thus, I took a step back and responded to, rather than always initiated, the exchange that Bowell and Heap (2017) define as QT/QR in process drama (see "Reflective Practice in Process Drama" in Chapter 5). This manifested as a decreased preoccupation to control the sequencing of the drama, and an increased agency in the participants' spontaneity. "To lead the way", O'Neill says, "while walking backwards" (in Taylor & Warner, 2006, p. 26).

Yet, alas, when you walk backwards you do not know what you're going to stumble into—not unless you develop a refined sense of your peripheral vision. It took some time, and adjusting, to realise that participants' ideas related to structuring episodes needed to be filtered in terms of managing the dual affect (Vygotsky, 1933/1976). As discussed in a previous chapter (see "Aesthetic Learning" in Chapter 10), the drama structure in Workshop 4 led to experiences that were too close to the real context for some participants, causing them to disconnect. This, undoubtedly, qualifies as an incident towards my phronesis of failure (Saxton, 2015). However, as for all failures, when examined in praxis they bring forth some growth. While in the fourth workshop the drama became particularly intense, I realised, reflecting-on-action, that it was also my *responsibility* to modulate participants' offers in such a way that a degree of distancing protected them 'into' emotion (Bolton, 1984). Between the fourth and fifth workshop, I decided to use a piece of literature as a distancing device:

1   Last night, as I was reading Herman Hesse's "Steppenwolf" I came across a beautiful
2   passage which, I thought, could be read aloud after a relaxation. So I led a very short
3   relaxation (breathing and shaking) and then I asked them to close their eyes and read out
4   Hesse's text. I put a lot of expression into the passage and I took care to change every
5   verb from the past perfect to the present tense (for two reasons: (1) Immediacy, (2)
6   Simplicity).
(RJ, p. 132:19–26)

This journal entry shows a different attitude, where I have become more conscious of aesthetic distancing, in terms of both the literary piece by Hesse, and a focus on the linguistic features of the class, to channel the students' engagement, without creating affective overload.

This re-adjustment in terms of aesthetic distancing was the fruit of my reflection-in-action and reflection-on-action, as evidenced by my writing at the time, peppered by expressions like: 'intuitively'; 'It occurred to me…'; 'I don't know why, but' and 'I felt', as well as 'having no fear' to let the group take the lead—expressions that are entirely missing from my commentary of Case Study One.

Finally, the shift from feeling trapped by the plot towards structuring for spontaneity approach is also evident in comparing the written style of the three process drama structures across the case studies. Compared to the previous two case studies, Case Study Three's drama structure is less discursive. Note, for example Workshop 10 (discussed below) compared to my re-elaboration of the drama in narrative form (Chapter 9, Workshop 8). That is, in my recollection of the drama I was thinking of it *as* a narrative. This completely changed in Case Study

Three, where I saw the drama as episodes or, quoting Styan (1960), as 'sequences of impressions' connected between them by tension-bearing constraints. Analysing my own progress over the course of the three case studies, drawing on Underhill's model, my competence went through a progression from *un*conscious *in*competence towards a degree of *un*conscious competence (Figs. 4 and 5).

This analysis has addressed Research Question Two, focussed on a reflective practitioner's inquiry into how I developed and harnessed process drama artistry—researching the challenges related to what Kramsch (2009) describes as crafting "(un)predictability by design" (p. 203). We now leave the reflective practitioner's stance, to consider the two research questions together.

5 Obuchenie: Teachers and Learners' Artistry and Engagement

Adopting a Vygotskian perspective, it is essential to contemplate the findings from learner engagement (Chapter 10) and teacher artistry (This Chapter) together, in the teaching-learning collaborative relationship

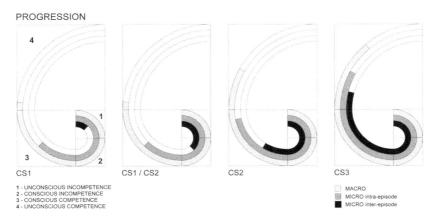

Fig. 5 Progression of reflection-in-action from unconscious incompetence to unconscious competence

expressed by the Vygotskian concept *obuchenie*. This term, which does not directly translate into English, entails both teaching and learning intended as a two-way process, where "the teacher is constantly the learner who is trying to understand the consequences of the teaching practice" (Daniels, 2016, p. 26). In doing so, my aim is to integrate the research findings from multiple angles, considering the influence of the artistry on engagement, and engagement on artistry, from the teachers' *and* the learners' experiences. This discussion is informed by a performative view of teaching and learning, as Eisner (2002) puts it, guided by "a conception of human action rooted in artistry and guided by the feel, the aesthetics of experience" (p. 383).

Overall, thirty-two student-participants agreed that process drama could be described as an art form, while two stated that rather than an art form, they saw process drama as a new approach to language teaching, and a technique to de-centre from stereotypes. The remaining student-participants, who agreed that it could be considered an art form, described the aesthetic dimension of process drama in terms of: taking on a dramatic role (Tommaso; Rebecca; Catherine; Yoriko); creating (Herminia, Carme, Alessia, Yoriko); expressiveness (Agate, Mara); feeling the language (Viola, Tommaso); performing (Alessia, Mara); perceiving (Alessia); interpreting (Jun); increasing understanding (Irina); using the imagination (Hiro, Flora; Olga; Maggie); collaboration between students and teacher (Alessia, Yelena, Yoriko); beauty (Alessia, Gianni; Hiro; Jun).

All fourteen teacher-participants noted that process drama can be considered an art form, in terms of: stepping into another world (Valeria); improvisation and its roots to theatre (Paola, Sabina); improvisation and heightening of the senses (Marisole); the performative dimension (Alfonso); triggering students' creativity (Stefano, Sabina, Simone). Some teacher-participants also described process drama as an approach countering the 'anaesthetic'. Particularly, some teacher-participants were surprised that process drama could work so well because usually, in their classes, the very students they had observed were not perceived as active. In describing the same students' behaviour in traditional L2 classes, several teachers (across all case studies) reported their students as being passive, dull, having to be spoon-fed, and being "without much imagination" (FG, 8:28). Teacher-participant Rossana states:

1 Rossana: my teaching approach? Well, as communicative as possible! Let's say that
2 you try as much as possible to get them to speak, basically, to get them to practice.
3 This is always the intention, then ... hey, sometimes you get zombie-like classes so
4 you have to try really hard.
(Rossana, p. 1:27–31)

Being 'zombie-like' (line 3), I suppose, is the perfect aphorism for the *opposite* of having an aesthetic experience. Zombies are dead but move nevertheless; their trance-like status is not alert, nor heightened. Teacher-participants also complained that traditional role plays did not work for them, as their students would quickly run out of ideas in a role play situation:

1 Rossana: sometimes I find it difficult to do role plays in class because there
2 are some people who quickly exchange two lines
3 Renato: yes, and then
4 Rossana: they just carry out the function of what they have to say, you know, those
5 who are real succinct.
(Rossana & Renato, p. 14:36–40)

The same issue was mentioned in the teacher-participants' focus group, with agreement that teachers should "overcome their fear of role plays not being enough" (FG, 8:28). When watching the replay of one of the drama sequences, a teacher-participant sighed: "Well, this is really incredible, considering the scarcity of imagination that we face in the classroom! [All teachers laugh]". Usually, he continued, "you always have to give them the details, to force them to speak. But here they... created." (FG, 51:33). Learner agency, then, is what stood out for this teacher watching the process drama sequence. Further prompting revealed that the teachers' approach in that cohort consisted of quickly setting up a role play exchange, then leaving the students to it; therefore, unsupported, the students would run out of ideas, denoting "scarcity of imagination", and were construed as 'zombie-like'. Yet, those teacher-participants did not appear to be aware of their own agency in crafting playful role-play experiences. As Eisner (2002) holds: "Teachers craft experience by shaping the environment that both students and teachers share". These, he continues, are "qualitative matters that are informed in part by theory, but in the context of action played out also by feel, in real time on the spot. When it goes well, we call it aesthetic." (pp. 382–383).

The teacher-participants mentioned above were referring to a kind of role play not founded on a clearly defined dramatic context. As Vygotsky (1933/1976) states: "If play, then, were structured in such a way that there were no imaginary situation, what would remain? The rules would remain." (p. 542). Hence all that remained, for those teacher-participants' students, were the rules in the actual context—in that case, practicing a particular language function. This, in itself, was not enough to create the conditions for agency. As Olga, a Russian student-participant commented:

1 Erika: in your experience of process drama, how is it an art form? What makes it art,
2 if anything?
3 Olga: Because it's not like... catered, the activities are not catered, you need to create
4 the class yourself. Everything ... like, it's all about your imagination and things you
5 want to say, want to ... show and when you are going to a standard class we're just
6 kind of following the rules. Here you choose the direction yourself
(Olga, 3:3–17).

Olga here also mentions 'following the rules'. These are prescribed rules that make the activities of a standard class be perceived as 'catered' (line 3). Indeed, student-participants across different case studies voiced that at the beginning of the drama they were looking for the 'correct' answer, and that as the drama progressed, they realised it was more about exploration of meaning, rather than "getting it right" (FG, 26:53). In other words, at the beginning they positioned themselves as having to guess what the right answer was, while through the intervention they developed a sense as agency, self-regulating their own learning. Once they could make this re-adjustment, the performative mode fuelled agency into playfulness.

Now, importantly, the students were not on their own in this quest; I was also there, engaging in a playful exploration—embodying different roles in the drama, and in the research. It was the relationship between the teacher and the students that validated the playful exploration. Playfulness thus coloured the Vygotskian teacher–learner relationship, *obuchenie*. My attitude towards the reflective practice was also characterised by an agentic exploration, a gradual shift towards playfulness, as I engaged in translanguaging to question my own beliefs in teaching, learning, and improvisation. In closing, a crucial finding emerging from this research is that engagement and artistry were characterised by a sense of agency and playfulness, *both* mine *and* the participants'. Agency as playfulness emerges as the aesthetic thread connecting artistry and engagement. On a philosophical level, this key understanding resonates with Schiller's (1795/1965) aesthetic principle of the 'play instinct' (Spieltrieb) as a fundamental instinct to realise the full potential of human development.

To go back to my father's conversation (see "A Conversation with My Father" in Chapter 10) our task as performative researchers and teacher/artists, it turns out, is not only to *taste* the risotto as such; it is to apprehend how it was cooked, and to be playful with the recipe as we adjust it to an ever-shifting menu, to the seasons, and the diners' unique needs.

Workshop 10: The Secret Strategy

Description: This was the third process drama workshop, in a cycle of five that I used as part of Case Study One in my doctoral research.

Students' Context—Inspiration for the Workshop: This was the third process drama workshop, in a cycle of five that I used as part of Case Study One in my PhD research (2009/2013), supervised by Julie Dunn and Claire Kennedy, at Griffith University (Brisbane). The students were a group of Chinese international exchange students who had been living in Italy for two years, enrolled in a public university in Milan, Italy.

Educational Aims: Familiarising the student-participants with the use of Italian language related to journalism and the media.

Pre-text: job announcement (see Fig. 6 in Chapter 9).

Level: B1 to B2 (CEFR).

Duration: Three hours.

Workshop 10 The secret strategy

	Drama strategy
Initiation phase	**Step 1. Warm-up**: a. Breathing awareness b. Laughing exercises c. Voice warm up
	Step 2. Pre-text: Re-visit the pre-text seen the previous day. What more do we know now?
	Step 3. Dramatic Roles and Hot seat: Hand out role cards and invite students to fill them out. Those who were there for the previous session can add more details—new students just enter the basic details. Hot seating in pairs, and then as a whole group
	Step 4. Teacher Narration: Imagine you are in role as the apprentice journalist. You are at home, with your family. Imagine yourself *in the very moment you tell your parents* that you have been accepted for a trial at the Italian Chamber of Commerce. Now look around: in what part of the house are you? What are your parents saying? Paint a picture in your head, imagine as many details as possible. In pairs: What did the parents say?
Experiential phase	**Step 5. Teacher in Role**: The candidates brief the new group members on the project. After a short time, Mr. Righello arrives to say that the interviews have been arranged for this Friday at 10.30 a.m. The Chamber has already purchased a plane ticket in their name, but the plane flies into Rome, instead of Milan (secretary's fault). Hand out train tickets from Rome to Milan
	Step 6. Role play: Hotel booking: Give separate instructions to the two groups (journalists and operators) **Step 6a**: Operators: prepare a script like: Welcome to Italy-booking, your national booking service. For restaurant bookings, press 1/for car bookings, press 2/for tour guides, press 3/for museums, press 4/for hotels, press 5/Welcome to hotel booking: for 5 star hotels, press 1 etc. Until finally they can talk to the customer! **Step 6b**: Journalists: they need to follow the rules and press the right number before speaking. They need to book the cheapest hotel possible in Milan, for seven nights, from 17–24 June Start role plays. In pairs, journalist and operator *back to back*
	Step 7. Teacher in Role: The secret strategy: Mr. Righello returns and announces that, unfortunately, not all of them will be able to get hired after this project: he will hire only one team, the best team. They will need to have a secret weapon, a winning strategy to succeed
	Step 8. Whole group improvisation: **At Rome International Airport.** As they arrive, they line up and show their passport at Customs. The officer asks for some details before stamping their passports

(continued)

Workshop 10 (continued)

	Drama strategy
	Step 9. Whole group improvisation **On the Airport shuttle**: On the shuttle from the airport to the train station: the three teams chat among themselves about what they are thinking in terms of their winning strategy to get the job. At the same time, they try to eavesdrop on the others
	Step 10. Whole group improvisation **At the train station**: the journalists mill around as they gossip about other teams' 'secret weapons' and wait for the train to Milan
Reflective phase	**Step 11. Debrief**: Ask students how they felt in the drama classroom; how was it to use their body, voice, imagination?
	Step 12. Language revision: Ask students to recap some of the language structured learnt during the session
	Step 13. Final reflection: Competition and competitiveness in Italy and China

This chapter addressed findings of my doctoral research, related to developing and harnessing teacher artistry in process drama for second language learning. Translanguaging reflective practice enabled me to unveil a tacit dissonance in my overt and covert attitudes, related to reflecting in action when structuring process drama. Through the analysis, I tracked a progression from my 'unconscious incompetence' to my 'unconscious competence', across three case studies, taking a reflexive attitude to scrutinise my practice. The chapter also considered the teacher–learner relationship, looking at engagement and artistry, and at imagination as an aesthetic key to awaken participants' sense of agency and playfulness. The next chapter closes the book, calling for a sense of community in performative language teaching and research.

References

Akkerman, S. F., & Meijer, P. C. (2011). A dialogical approach to conceptualizing teacher identity. *Teaching and Teacher Education, 27*(2), 308–319.
Barthes, R. (1966). *Introduction to the structural analysis of the narrative.* Birmingham: Centre for Contemporary Cultural Studies, University of Birmingham.

Barthes, R. (1977). *Image, music, text*. London: Flamingo.
Bolton, G. (1984). *Drama as education: An argument for placing drama at the centre of the curriculum*. Essex: Longman.
Bowell, P., & Heap, B. (2017). *Putting process drama into action: The dynamics of practice*. London: Routledge.
Brooks, P. (1984). *Reading for the plot: Design and intention in narrative* (1st ed.). New York: A. A. Knopf.
Daniels, H. (2016). Vygotsky and dialogic pedagogy. In D. Skidmore & K. Murakami, (Eds.), *Dialogic pedagogy: The importance of dialogue teaching and learning* (pp. 34–50). Bristol: Multilingual Matters.
Dewaele, J. (2010). *Emotions in multiple languages*. New York: Palgrave Macmillan.
Dunn, J. (2015). Democracy over-ruled or how to deny young children's agency and voice thorugh drama. In P. Duffy (Ed.), *A reflective practitioner's guide to (mis)adventures in drama education—Or—What was I thinking?* Intellect: Bristol.
Dunn, J., & Stinson, M. (2011). Not without the art!! The importance of teacher artistry when applying drama as pedagogy for additional language learning. *Research in Drama Education: The Journal of Applied Theatre and Performance, 16*(4), 617–633. https://doi.org/10.1080/13569783.2011.617110.
Eisner, E. W. (2002). From episteme to phronesis to artistry in the study and improvement of teaching. *Teaching and Teacher Education, 18*(4), 375–385.
Gallagher, K., Freeman, B., & Wessells, A. (2010). 'It could have been so much better': The aesthetic and social work of theatre. *Research in Drama Education: The Journal of Applied Theatre and Performance, 15*(1), 5–27. https://doi.org/10.1080/13569780903480971.
García, O., & Wei, L. (2014). *Translanguaging: Language, bilingualism and education*. Cham: Springer.
Johnson, L., & O'Neill, C. (Eds.). (1991). *Collected writings on education and drama: Dorothy Heathcote*. London: Hutchinson Publications.
Johnstone, K. (1999). *Impro for storytellers*. New York: Routeledge Theatre Arts Books.
Kramsch, C. (2009). *The multilingual subject*. Oxford: Oxford University Press.
O'Neill, C. (1995). *Drama worlds: A framework for process drama*. Portsmouth: Heinemann.
O'Neill, C. (2011). *Keynote address*. Paper presented at the drama: Same difference, National Drama Conference, Swansea University (Wales).

Pavlenko, A. (2006). *Bilingual minds: Emotional experience, expression, and representation* (1st ed., Vol. 56). Buffalo, NY and Clevedon: Multilingual Matters.

Piazzoli, E. (2012). Engage or entertain? The nature of teacher/participant collaboration in process drama for additional language teaching. *Scenario: Journal for Performative Teaching, Learning and Research*, (2), 28–46.

Saxton, J. (2015). Failing better. In P. Duffy (Ed.), *A reflective practitioner's guide to (mis)adventures in drama education—Or—What was I thinking?* (pp. 253–266). Bristol: Intellect.

Schiller, F. (1795/1965). *On the aesthetic education of man: In a series of letters* (R. Snell, Trans.). New York: F. Ungar Pub. Co.

Schön, D. (1983). *The reflective practitioner: How professionals think in action*. London: Temple Smith.

Scully, G. (2017, May). *From performance to the periphery and beyond: Group devised theatre for additional language acquisition*. Paper presented at the Scenario Forum Conference: Performative spaces in literature, language and culture education, University College Cork, Ireland.

Stewart, G. (1986). Reading for the plot: Design and intention in narrative. Peter Brooks. *Nineteenth-Century Literature, 41*(1), 100–108.

Styan, J. L. (1960). *The elements of drama*. Cambridge: Cambridge University Press.

Taylor, P., & Warner, C. D. (2006). *Structure and spontaneity: The process drama of Cecily O'Neill*. Sterling, VA: Trentham.

Underhill, A. (1992). The role of groups in developing teacher self-awareness. *ELT Journal, 46*(1), 71–80.

Vygotsky, L. (1933/1976). Play and its role in the mental development of the child. In J. Bruner, A. Jolly, & K. Sylva (Eds.), *Play: Its role in development and evolution* (pp. 537–554). Middlesex: Penguin.

Wagner, B. J. (1976). *Dorothy Heathcote: Drama as a learning medium*. Washington, DC: National Education Association.

12

Conclusion: Embodying Language in Action

In April 2016, I participated in an *Arts in Education* conference jointly hosted by the Irish Education Department and the Department of Arts, Heritage and the *Gaeltacht* at the Irish Museum of Modern Art. It was the launch of the Arts in Education portal initiative, an important national event. Upon arrival at the registration desk I was greeted by one of the organisers who, after handing out my name badge, asked: "Are you a teacher or an artist?" They needed to know as they were monitoring attendance, keeping track of how many teachers and how many artists were there. That query threw me off guard; I was aghast at my inability to properly address the question. Feeling somewhat lost, I mumbled that I was both and suggested they draw a third box in the middle. The remark, in my Italo-Australian accent, drew the Irish quizzical, proverbial stare in return. As I walked in, I felt that stinging, yet familiar feeling of non-belonging, or rather to belonging to an in-between space—a third, invisible box on that list. Was I a teacher or an artist? The truth is, in performative language teaching, we are both. Had I felt more confident, I would have loved to better explain myself at that registration desk. *Had I.*

1 Embodiment in Second Language Learning

Teacher/artists may have a hard time articulating their dual identity, just like I did in that situation. Through this book I have attempted to articulate this tacit knowing, to argue that drama-based processes can afford opportunities to embody language in action. Embodiment is understood as a way of constructing knowledge through direct engagement in bodily experiences, "inhabiting one's body through a felt sense of being-in-the-world" (Freiler, 2008, p. 40). Accordingly, performative language learning is an embodied experience based on the *simplex* premise 'we feel, therefore we learn', as put forth by educational neuroscientists Immordino-Yang and Damasio (2016, p. 27). Rather than being a theoretical assumption, or a point of arrival, 'we feel therefore we learn' must represent a point of departure for teacher/artists, with attention to the role of emotion in learning, distancing and dual affect, as seen in Chapter 6. As Perry and Medina (2011) poignantly state: "Embodiment isn't simply an interesting possibility for education, nor is it an alternative practice or method: embodiment *is*" (p. 63, original emphasis). Embodiment *is*—in the sense that teaching and learning, whether we choose to acknowledge it or not, is an embodied activity, with teachers and students bringing their bodies into a mutual space, interacting and responding to each other in various ways, determined by the pedagogical approach.

Two decades ago, Kao and O'Neill (1998) defined process drama as an innovative approach to language teaching, that could neutralise the unequal interactional relationship between student and teacher in the classroom. They pointed out that in many L2 settings the work remains short-term, teacher-controlled and exercise-based, and that, as a result, "the potential for learning is diminished" (p. 3). In many contexts, this is still the case. Now more than ever, it is timely to advocate for embodied approaches in second language education. In Maley and Duff's rationale for using drama in the L2 classroom, they make the point that drama succeeds in "bringing together both mind and body, and restoring the balance between physical and intellectual aspects of learning" (2005, p. i). In the 1982 edition of the same volume, they argue:

Words, other people's words, which have been mechanically memorized, can turn to ashes in the speaker's mouth. They lose their savour even before they are spoken, and this we do not want. (p. 6)

Years ago, this statement struck me as true, applied to my own teaching of Italian as a second language in Australia. It seemed to me that in my classrooms, despite all efforts to make the language learning activities creative and fun, sentences were reduced to ashes, stripped of all expressive meaning. At the time I was trying to implement games and dynamic activities, but they did not seem to engage students at a deeper level, as I lacked the theoretical knowledge and the practical awareness of how play could mediate learning. My intention in writing this book has been to share some insights with other L2 teachers who may find themselves surrounded by words 'turning to ashes'. Ash is a peculiar substance: residue of fire, it lacks body. Rather, it *appears* to have body but then, when firmly grasped, it smudges away. The idea of embodiment, on the other hand, conjures up a kind of learning that anchors tangible connections between language, emotions and the body.

This applies to voice and expressiveness as well. Words can be pronounced with no texture—by both the teacher and the students. Rodenburg (2015) describes such speakers as devoicers (p. 33), individuals who hold back their voices. It is not uncommon, in L2 contexts, to hear speakers devoicing entire sentences, in a perennial self-doubting tone of "Am I pronouncing this right?" Whenever this becomes a leitmotif in the speaker's intonation, the listener is likely to disengage. On the contrary, by embodying language, the listener, as well as the speaker, will become *present*. Presence, as Rodenburg (2007) intends it, is a heightened awareness state, one through which performers, teachers, athletes, and young children operate. *Presence*, for Barba (1995), is informed by "the body-in-life able to make perceptible that which is invisible: the intention" (p. 7). Recalling his experience of emigrating from Italy to Norway, he observes: "Abroad, I had lost my mother tongue and grappled with incomprehensibility […] I tried to orient myself in this labyrinth of recognizable yet unknown physicality and sounds" (p. 4). He acknowledges that these experiences, of being "plunged into the constant effort of scrutinizing behaviour which was not immediately decipherable" (p. 4), were formative to the development of his aesthetic awareness as a theatre director.

In an evocative statement, Kramsch (2008) contextualises this in second language education:

> Build on students' memories, emotions, perceptions, fantasies linked to sounds, and intonations. Ask the students: What does this word evoke for YOU? What does it remind YOU of? Bring back the emotional and the aesthetic dimension of language. (2008, p. 405, original emphasis)

Kramsch's main emphasis is on meaning as reflexive, unpredictable and mediated. She advocates the notion of symbolic competence, the ability "to play with various linguistic codes and with the various spatial and temporal resonances of these codes" (p. 400). She urges L2 educators to focus on the symbolic perspective of language learning, but she recognises that this discourse "doesn't offer a blueprint for what to do on Monday morning" (p. 405). Arguably, we cannot provide a 'blueprint for Monday morning', when dealing with an aesthetic dimension mode of knowing.

Crutchfield (2015) makes a cunning observation on the cognitive, imaginative, emotional and embodied aspects of becoming a speaker of another language:

> Knowledge of a foreign language is a special kind of knowledge. It changes the knower in profound ways—not just cognitively, but in the imaginative and emotional life as well as in the body itself: the ear, the lips and tongue, the musculature of the face, the expressiveness of the hands, the kinaesthetic sense of proximity and distance, of friendship and enmity. Learning a foreign language quite literally means becoming other. In a very real sense, once you've entered a foreign language, you can't go home again. Because the foreign language has entered you as well, and the "you" that goes home won't be the same "you" that left. (p. 110)

I have experienced this intensely in the last three years, as I have moved from Australia to Ireland. I often catch myself, as I converse in English, sensing my own voice is 'becoming other', as my mouth and jaw close around vowel sounds. As I hear myself pronouncing words like *but* and *much* with a closed [ʊ], I notice my lips tighten, the muscles in my face striving to produce a sound that may make me feel part of the Irish society, where my previously acquired Australian English doesn't fit any longer. Nothing wrong with that—the greeting *G'Day* is still present in my speech, as is *No Worries*, although I'm yet to figure out how the Irish perceive this one. Closing my lips around vowels feels forced, unnatural; yet I catch myself doing it, on purpose, perhaps to attend to the "kinaesthetic sense of proximity", as Crutchfield puts it (p. 110), embedded in my emotional identity as a speaker of English living in Ireland.

2 Towards a Phenomenology of Practice

Often in the vignettes that pepper this book I have made comments about the sound of my accent. This self-consciousness in the way I sound has accompanied me for all my life, and I suspect it is not an isolated phenomenon. Similarly, several vignettes denote an element of reflective practice, as I reflect on action about an event. This element of analysis and reflection also characterised a great part of my Ph.D. research study. Yet, as Schön (1983) argues, by over-analysing our practice, we can run the risk of becoming victims of the "centipede's paralysis" (p. 279). This condition takes its name from an anthropomorphic tale that sees a centipede as the protagonist. A fine dancer, the centipede is admired for his dancing skills by all other insects, except for the toad which, burning with jealously, approaches the centipede and asks him to explain just *how* he can dance that way. The naïve centipede, turning his conscious attention to his dancing skills, becomes stuck and cannot continue the dance. In other words, his conscious attention has inhibited the spontaneity of the movement. The poem appears in slight variations across the literature; the version titled *The Centipede's Dilemma* tells the story of a centipede who could no longer run:

> The Centipede's Dilemma
>
> A centipede was happy—quite!
> Until a toad in fun
> Said, pray, which leg comes after which?

> This raised her doubts to such a pitch,
> She fell exhausted in the ditch
> Considering how to run.

(Craster, in Connolly & Martlew, 1999)

This condition is often referred to in psychology as the centipede's effect, that is, when an automated behaviour becomes disrupted by consciously turning one's attention to it. Paradoxically, over-thinking our spontaneous gestures may impede our spontaneity. Discussing the centipede's paralysis, Schön recognises that reflecting on something may initially slow us down and result in a temporary loss of spontaneity. Arguably, in our line of work, a loss of spontaneity is a suffered loss. "Whether or not we are prepared to pay this price", Schön suggests, "depends on our ability to find a context in which we can practice at low risk" (1983, pp. 279–280).

Ideally, such a context for a teacher/artist would be provided by Initial Teacher Education programmes specialising in performative language education. However, not many such programmes are currently in place. On the one hand, this lack of belonging to a community of practice can instil a sense of isolation in teacher/artists; this may impact negatively on the motivation to continue 'practising at low risk', to echo Schön above.

On the other hand, these circumstances have pushed teacher/artists interested in performative language teaching to carve out their own niches, possibilities and contexts to practise the tricks of the trade. A rich heritage now exists of L2 practice-based performative researchers and practitioners experimenting with drama, second language learning and creative writing (Crutchfield, 2015), dance (Soulaine, 2017; Lapaire, 2016), music (Noelliste & Noelliste, 2017), circus (Mei & Cangemi, 2017), sound design (Hallsten, 2016), digital arts (Campbell, 2017a), performance art (Campbell, 2017b), playback theatre (Motos & Fields, 2015), devising (Scully, 2013, 2017) just to name a few. The resourcefulness of practice-based researchers committed to teaching through embodied approaches brings enormous potential to this inter-disciplinary field. At the same time, it is also in great need of methodological guidelines to shape the reflection-in-action that informs pedagogical choices.

For Schön, what blocked the centipede is not so much the actual complexity of his locomotion, but the lack of representational modes to make sense of it, so to express it to others: "The difficulty is not in the inherent complexity of the material brought to consciousness but in our ways of representing complexity" (1983, p. 279). In the centipede's tale above, the toad's question has a *paralysing* effect. Who is 'the toad' for us as centipedes, dancing our dance? Who asks the paralysing questions? Is it a cynical colleague? Is it a sceptical Principal? Is it a defensive participant? Is it local policy-makers? Is it the lack of Government funding for the arts? Or is the paralysing question coming from within us, our inner critic casting self-doubt? The centipede 'raises its doubts to such a pitch, that falls exhausted in the ditch'. What happens when *we* fall exhausted in the ditch? Do we stand back up? These words capture the essence of the teacher/artist attempting to integrate knowing-in-action in the ever-changing educational context, reminiscent of what Saxton (2015) calls the 'phronesis of failure'.

When failure strikes, we may let the myth of creativity as something inaccessible take over. The baggage this brings may sabotage our vision, and our appetite for practice. Creativity as a talent for the selected gifted is a long-pervasive myth, which stems back to the ancient Greeks, with creativity being related to a gift from the Muses. Building on Socrates, in *Phaedrus* Plato writes about creative madness, or divine madness, whereby a poet acts as if possessed by a God. Later, the Romantics re-packaged this myth, talking about creativity as God's gift or, as Coleridge famously described writing, "manual somnambulism, the somnial magic superinduced on, without suspending, the active powers of the mind" (in Abbs, 1989, p. 17). This was functional to create the myth of 'the artist' as a 'lone artist', a myth that Sennett (2008) also notes, which does not serve the purposes of education in the twenty-first century. By falling prey to this myth it can have a ripple effect, not only towards how we view and relate to our students, but also towards how we relate to fellow colleagues and, ultimately, to ourselves.

As Anderson and Jefferson (2016) argue, "creativity is a set of capacities or processes that can be applied to the teaching of any subject matter" (p. 158). The authors bring to the table a series of myths that still linger in the educational context, related to creativity being an elitist trait of the selected few. Teachers, in a variety of settings and contexts, may be convinced that they are, or are not, creative people, and this may directly impact on their self-efficacy and creativity in teaching. Whether we think of ourselves as particularly creative or not, we need to acknowledge that, in trying something new, it may not work perfectly the first time. To this extent, Fleming (2012) suggests it is not that helpful to ask: "What is art?" Or: "What is creativity?" but instead to ask: "What are the consequences, particularly for teaching, of seeing art, creativity, in this or that way?" (p. 3).

I recently posed this question to my Arts in Education students, pre-service teachers enrolled in a Master's degree at Trinity College Dublin. To initiate the discussion on how we see creativity and its implications for teaching, I invited the students to write on Post-it notes: 'Creativity is …' and then 'Creativity is *like*…' and complete both sets of sentences. I was struck by one of the students, who wrote: "Creativity is pairing back everything you think you know about something, and acting in that vacuum exposed" (Nick, 11 October 2017). Finding ourselves in that 'vacuum exposed' can be exciting or frightening. Not only for ourselves as teacher/artists, but also for our students, as we open up this space for them.

Answers to the second statement (Creativity is *like*…), on the other hand, gave the students metaphorical means through which to express their ideas, as platforms to discuss their views of creativity and teaching—with regard to myths and implications. As these young teachers step into the classroom for their teaching practicum, week after week, and they come back relating how they have used the strategies explored in class in their own classes, I can see the fear and the excitement in their eyes. Just what *is* this fear? Is it the fear of ridiculing ourselves as teachers, of exposing ourselves, of not knowing? This is a feeling that, to some extent, all teachers have experienced (Block, 1998).

In teacher education, intense or painful emotions related, for example, to fear of feeling inadequate as a teacher are part of the learning process. As Crutchfield (2015) argues, painful emotions in the learning process are unavoidable, and even desirable:

> To view these painful emotions – I think we can now dispense with the term "negative" – as unwanted, unnecessary, or irrelevant would be a mistake. Although their intensity and quality may differ from person to person, they are natural, perhaps even desirable, and in any case unavoidable where artistic processes are concerned – particularly where theatrical performance is a part of that process. The key to unlocking their transformative potential, however, has to do with their conscious acknowledgement, reflection and integration into what I earlier called the experiential dramaturgy of artistic process. Negative emotions must be seen as part of a dynamic whole: a coherent *phenomenology* or *trajectory of experiential moments*. (p. 112, my emphasis)

Crutchfield's point not only refers to our students, it also applies to us as teacher/artists, too; painful emotions, as a phenomenology of experiential moments, are pivotal to our own sense of growth. He argues for the conscious acknowledgment, reflection and integration of these intense emotions into artistic practice. I think back, for example, of my uncomfortable feeling captured in the poem I share in Chapter 5, when a language inspector observed my class and I had the distinct, uncomfortable feeling that I was not succeeding, as an L2 teacher, to create meaningful experiences. By virtue of making a written account of what had happened on that day, turning it into poetry, and then reflecting on those emotions years later, I chose to embrace them. Going back to Crutchfield's point, having *acknowledged* and *reflected* on those moments, and having *integrated* them into a dynamic whole, is the foundation towards a "phenomenology or trajectory of experiential moments" (p. 112). In this sense, ongoing reflexivity and knowing-in-action can guide us towards a phenomenology of practice.

3 Conclusion

In an embodied teaching perspective, it is the openness of the teacher in the reflective pauses that sets up the tone for a collaborative attitude in *obuchenie*, the Vygotskian teacher-learner interaction. As mentioned at the outset of this book, in performative language teaching a reconfiguration of hierarchy and power is related to teachers' beliefs—it requires an acknowledgement in the teachers' core values related to teaching, learning and status in the classroom. In parallel, it requires an acceptance of this shift from the students—not to be taken for granted, especially if students have been conditioned by teachers who subscribe to the 'sage on the stage' paradigm. To facilitate such a shift, it is vital to demonstrate, through listening, openness, presence, that the participants' opinions and experiences are valued. Heathcote frames this as a changing relationship between 'the teacher and the taught':

> The teacher is no longer seen as the main fount of information and the students are no longer seen as mere absorbers of knowledge. Within drama processes, teacher and students can explain what it is to be human to each other within the framework of security that teachers provide for individuals in the group, as well as the necessary protection from revelations regarding private matters. (In O'Neill, 2015, p. 56)

We ask participants to reflect. What does that *really* mean? On the surface level, to stop and go over the experience they just had. On a deeper level, we are asking them to open up, to share their opinions, values, circumstances. In this light, Heathcote above has a point.

Crucially, 'reflection' and 'revision' are not the same. While revision is based on looking over the content, reflection is about making sense of it. They serve different purposes: one may lead into the other, but reflection in process drama involves a degree of awareness of one's experience across two frames, 'play' and 'real' contexts. Meta-reflection can involve intercultural reflection on one's feelings and ideas arisen in the drama, in role or out of role; reflection on beliefs about one's or others' cultural values; about one's identity in the L1 and/or L2; reflection on voice, gender and status; reflections on one's L2 learning strategies; reflection on language register and power dynamics. This collaborative nature, which we have called, with Schön (1983), the reflective practitioner stance, is manifested in the teacher's attitude in class, mirrored in the quality of reflective pauses that arise.

In *The Art of Foreign Language Teaching*, Lutzker (2007) holds: "To realise the ideas inherent in the concept of language teaching as an art, both teachers and pupils must receive opportunities to enter into processes which encourage such developments" (p. 455). In order to feel like we are teacher/artist, we need to practise, and to feel validated *as both*. We also need to give our students the opportunity to experience such processes. In this book my aim has been to bring forth the multi-layered argument that facilitating performative language learning involves artistry. Such artistry, I have argued, relates to embodying language in action. This book represents my imperfect attempt to reflect on this claim, and I hope it will inspire others to continue exploring this exciting field. Ultimately, as Maxine Greene (1995) says, as teacher/artists, we are forever in the making.

References

Abbs, P. (1989). *A is for aesthetic: Essays on creative and aesthetic education*. New York: Falmer Press.

Anderson, M., & Jefferson, M. (2016). Teaching creativity: Unlocking educational opportunity. In P. O'Connor (Ed.), *The possibilities of creativity* (pp. 151–170). Cambridge: Cambridge Scholar.

Barba, E. (1995). *The paper canoe: A guide to theatre anthropology* (R. Fowler Trans.). London and New York: Routledge.

Block, A. (1998). 'And he pretended to be a stranger to them…' Maxine Greene and teacher as stranger. In W. Pinar (Ed.), *The passionate mind of Maxine Greene* (pp. 14–30). London: Falmer Press.

Campbell, L. (2017a). Technoparticipation: The use of digital realia in arts education. *Spark: UAL Creative Teaching and Learning Journal, 2*(3), 179–195.

Campbell, L. (2017b). Collaborators and hecklers: Performative pedagogy and interruptive processes. *Scenario: Journal for Performative Teaching, Learning and Research, 11*(2), 33–64.

Connolly, K. J., & Martlew, M. (1999). *Psychologically speaking: A book of quotations*. Leicester: British Psychological Society.

Crutchfield, J. (2015). Fear and trembling. *Scenario: Journal for Performative Teaching, Learning and Research, 9*(2), 101–114.

Fleming, M. (2012). *The arts in education. An introduction to aesthetics, theory and pedagogy*. London: Routledge.

Freiler, T. J. (2008). Learning through the body. *New Directions for Adult and Continuing Education, 2008*(119), 37–47. https://doi.org/10.1002/ace.304.

Greene, M. (1995). *Releasing the imagination: Essays on education, the arts, and social change*. San Francisco: Jossey-Bass Publishers.

Hallsten, J. (2016). *Tactics of interruption*. London: Campbell, Lee.

Immordino-Yang, M. H. (2016). *Emotions, learning, and the brain: Exploring the educational implications of affective neuroscience*. New York: Norton.

Kao, S.-M. & O'Neill, C. (1998). *Words into worlds: Learning a second language through process drama*. London: Ablex Publishing Corporation.

Kramsch, C. (2008). Ecological perspectives on foreign language education. *Language Teaching, 41*(3), 389. https://doi.org/10.1017/s0261444808005065.

Lapaire, J.-R. (2016). The Choreography of time: Metaphor, gesture and construal. In R. Gabriel & A. C. Pelosi (Eds.), *Linguagem e cognição: Emergência e produção de sentidos* (pp. 217–234). Florianopolis: Insular.

Lutzker, P. (2007). *The art of foreign language teaching: Improvisation and drama in teacher development and language learning*. Tübingen: Francke Verlag.

Maley, A., & Duff, A. (2005). *Drama techniques in language learning* (3rd ed.). Cambridge: Cambridge University Press.

Mei, J., & Cangemi, E. (2017, May 25–28). *The training of the performer in education*. Paper presented at the Scenario Forum Conference: Performative spaces in literature, language and culture education, University College Cork, Ireland.

Motos, T. T., & Fields, D. L. (2015). Playback theatre: Emboying the CLIL methodology. In N. S. Román & J. J. T. Núñez (Eds.), *Drama and CLIL: A new challange for the teaching approaches in bilingual education*. Bern: Peter Lang.

Noelliste, E., & Noelliste, J. (2017, May 25–28). *Mnemonic spaces: Music in foreign language learning*. Paper presented at the Scenario Forum Conference: Performative spaces in literature, language and culture education, University College Cork, Ireland.

O'Neill, C. (2015). *Dorothy heathcote on education and drama: Essential writings*. Abington, Oxfon: Routledge.

Perry, M., & Medina, C. (2011). Embodiment and performance in pedagogy research: Investigating the possibility of the body in curriculum experience. *Journal of Curriculum Theorizing, 27*(3), 62–75.

Rodenburg, P. (2007). *Presence: How to use positive energy for success in every situation*. London: Penguin.

Rodenburg, P. (2015). *The right to speak: Working with the voice* (2nd ed.). London: Bloomsbury.

Saxton, J. (2015). Failing better. In P. Duffy (Ed.), *A reflective practitioner's guide to (mis)adventures in drama education—Or—What was I thinking?* (pp. 253–266). Bristol: Intellect.

Schön, D. (1983). *The reflective practitioner: How professionals think in action.* London: Temple Smith.

Scully, G. (2013, July). *Let me hear your body talk: Listening to embodied knowledge for additional language acquisition.* Paper presented at the International Drama and Theatre Education Association Conference, Paris.

Scully, G. (2017, May). *From performance to the periphery and beyond: Group devised theatre for additional language acquisition.* Paper presented at the Scenario Forum Conference: Performative spaces in literature, language and culture education, University College Cork, Ireland.

Sennett, R. (2008). *The craftsman.* New Haven, CT: Yale University Press.

Soulaine, S. (2017). *An enactive approach to the training of language teachers: The example of an interdisciplinary project combining movement, dance and drama.* Paper presented at the Scenario Forum Conference: Performative spaces in literature, language and culture education, University College Cork, Ireland.

References

Abbs, P. (1989). *A is for aesthetic: Essays on creative and aesthetic education*. New York: Falmer Press.

Adžović, N. (2005). *Rom. Il popolo invisibile*. Roma: Editore Palombi.

Airey, J. (2015). From stimulated recall to disciplinary literacy: Summarising ten years of research of teaching and learning in English. In D. Slobodanka, A. Hultgren, & C. Jensen (Eds.), *English-medium instruction in European higher education: English* (pp. 157–176). Boston: De Gruyter.

Akkerman, S. F., & Meijer, P. C. (2011). A dialogical approach to conceptualizing teacher identity. *Teaching and Teacher Education, 27*(2), 308–319.

Allern, T.-H. (2001). Myth and metaxy, and the myth of 'metaxis'. In B. Rasmussen & A.-L. Østern (Eds.), *Playing Betwixt and Between: The IDEA dialogues, 2001* (pp. 77–85). Bergen: IDEA Publications.

Almond, M. (2005). *Teaching English with Drama. How to use drama and plays when teaching – for the professional language teacher*. Hove: Keyways Publishing.

Alred, G., Byram, M., & Fleming, M. (Eds.). (2003). *Intercultural experience and education*. Clevedon: Multilingual Matters.

Alsup, J. (2006). *Teacher identity discourses: Negotiating personal and professional spaces*. Mahwah, NJ: Routledge.

Anderson, M. (2015). Encountering the unexpected and extending the horizons of expectation: An autoethnographic exploration of developing through practice. In P. Duffy (Ed.), *A reflective practitioner's guide to (mis)adventures in drama education—Or—What was I thinking?* (pp. 171–182). Bristol: Intellect.

Anderson, M., & Jefferson, M. (2016). Teaching creativity: Unlocking educational opportunity. In P. O'Connor (Ed.), *The possibilities of creativity* (pp. 151–170). Cambridge: Cambridge Scholar.

Araki-Metcalfe, N. (2008). Introducing creative language learning in Japan through educational drama. *NJ: Drama Australia Journal, 31*(2), 45–57.

Aristotele. (330 BC). La poetica (G. Giannantoni, Trans.). In G. Fornero (Ed.), *Filosofi e filosofie nella storia: I Testi* (1994th ed., Vol. 1). Torino: Paravia.

Asher, J. J. (1969). The total physical response approach to second language learning. *The Modern Language Journal, 53*(1), 3–17.

Austin, J. L. (1962). How to do things with words. Oxford: Clarendon Press.

Bailey, B. (2007). Heteroglossia and boundaries. In M. Heller (Ed.), *Bilingualism: A social approach* (pp. 257–274). New York: Palgrave Macmillan.

Barba, E. (1995). *The paper canoe: A guide to theatre anthropology* (R. Fowler Trans.). Routledge: London and New York.

Barba, E. (2002). The essence of theatre. *TDR/The Drama Review, 46*(3), 12–30.

Barrett, C. (Ed.). (1966). *Wittgenstein: Lectures and conversations on aesthetics, psychology, and religious belief.* Berkeley and Los Angeles: University of California Press.

Barthes, R. (1966). *Introduction to the structural analysis of the narrative.* Birmingham: Centre for Contemporary Cultural Studies, University of Birmingham.

Barthes, R. (1977). *Image, music, text.* London: Flamingo.

Bateson, G. (1955/1976). A theory of play and fantasy. In J. Bruner, A. Jolly, & K. Sylva (Eds.), *Play: Its role in development and evolution.* Harmondsworth, Middlesex: Penguin Books.

Baumgarten, A. (1750/1970). *Aesthetica.* New York: George Olms.

Beijaard, D., Meijer, P. C., & Verloop, N. (2004). Reconsidering research on teachers' professional identity. *Teaching and Teacher Education, 20*(2), 107–128.

Bellack, A. A., Kliebard, H. M., Hyman, R. T., & Smith, F. L. (1966). *The language of the classroom.* New York: Teachers Colledge Press.

Belliveau, G., & Kim, W. (2013). Drama in L2 learning: A research synthesis. *Scenario: Journal for Performative Teaching, Learning and Research, 7*(2), 7–27.

Berdal-Masuy, F., & Renard, C. (2015). Comment évaluer l'impact des pratiques théâtrales sur les progrès en langue cible? Vers un nouveau dispositif d'évaluation de l'oral en FLE. *Lidil. Revue de linguistique et de didactique des langues* (52), 153–174.

Berghetto, R. A., & Kaufman, J. C. (2011). Teaching for creativity with disciplined improvisation. In *Structure and improvisation in creative teaching* (pp. 94–109). Cambridge: Cambridge University Press.

Berry, C. (2011). *Voice and the actor.* New York: Random House.

Berry, C., Rodenburg, P., & Linklater, K. (1997). Shakespeare, feminism, and voice: Responses to Sarah Werner. *New Theatre Quarterly, 13*(49), 48–52.

Berthoz, A. (2012). *Simplexity: Simplifying principles for a complex world* (G. Weiss, Trans.). New Haven: Yale University Press.

Blatner, A. (Ed.). (2007). *Interactive and improvisational drama: Varieties of applied theatre and performance.* Lincoln, NE: iUniverse.

Block, A. (1998). 'And he pretended to be a stranger to them…' Maxine Greene and teacher as stranger. In W. Pinar (Ed.), *The passionate mind of Maxine Greene* (pp. 14–30). London: Falmer Press.

Boal, A. (1985). *Theatre of the oppressed.* New York: Theatre Communications Group.

Boal, A. (1992). *Games for actors and non-actors.* London: Routledge.

Boal, A. (1995). *The rainbow of desire: The Boal method of theatre and therapy.* London: Routledge.

Bolton, G. (1979). *Towards a theory of drama in education.* London: Longman.

Bolton, G. (1984). *Drama as education: An argument for placing drama at the centre of the curriculum.* Essex, England: Longman.

Bolton, G. (1992). Have a heart! *Drama, 1*(1), 7–8.

Bolton, G. (2007). A history of drama education: A search for substance. In L. Bresler (Ed.), *International handbook of research in arts education* (pp. 45–66). Dordrecht, the Netherlands: Springer.

Bonomi, I. (2003). La lingua dei quotidiani. In I. Bonomi, A. Masini, & S. Morgana (Eds.), *La lingua italiana e i mass media* (pp. 127–164). Roma: Carocci.

Booth, D. (2003). Seeking definition: What is a teaching artist? *Teaching Artist Journal, 1*(1), 5–12.

Booth, D. (2015). Something's happening: Teaching artistry is having a growth spurt. *Teaching Artist Journal, 13*(3), 151–159.

Boureux, M., & Batinti, A. (2003). *La prosodia: Aspetti teorici e metodologici nell'apprendimento-insegnamento di una lingua straniera.* Paper presented at the Atti delle XIV giornate del GFS.

Bournot-Trites, M., Belliveau, G., Spiliotopoulos, V., & Séror, J. (2007). The role of drama on cultural sensitivity, motivation and literacy in a second language context. *Journal for Learning Through the Arts: A Research Journal on Arts Integration in Schools and Communities, 3*(1), 1–33.

Bowell, P. (2015). Teaching in role: Just another name is never enough. In P. Duffy (Ed.), *A reflective practitioner's guide to (mis)adventures in drama education—Or—What was I thinking?* (pp. 43–58). Bristol: Intellect.

Bowell, P., & Heap, B. (2005). Drama on the run: A prelude to mapping the practice of process drama. *Journal of Aesthetic Education, 39*(4), 59–69.

Bowell, P., & Heap, B. S. (2017). *Putting process drama into action: The dynamics of practice*. Abingdon, Oxon: Routledge.

Bowell, P., & Heap, B. S. (2001). *Planning process drama*. London: David Fulton.

Bräuer, G. (Ed.). (2002). *Body and language: Intercultural learning through drama* (Vol. 17). London: Ablex Publishing.

Brecht, B. (1964). *Brecht on theatre: The development of an aesthetic*. London: Methuen.

Brook, J., & Boal, I. A. (1995). *Resisting the virtual life: The culture and politics of information*. San Francisco, CA; Monroe, OR: City Lights; Subterranean Co. Distributor.

Brooks, P. (1984). *Reading for the plot: Design and intention in narrative* (1st ed.). New York: A.A. Knopf.

Brown, H., & Sawyer, R. D. (2016). Dialogic reflection: An exploration of its embodied, imaginative, and reflexive dynamic. In H. Brown, R. D. Sawyer, & J. Norris (Eds.), *Forms of practitioner reflexivity: Critical, conversational, and arts-based approaches*. New York: Palgrave Macmillan.

Bundy, P. (1999). *Dramatic tension: Towards an understanding of 'tension of intimacy'*. (Doctoral dissertation), Retrieved from https://www120.secure.griffith.edu.au/rch/items/dc50533c-7887-47d2-e176-f29d65389cbd/1/.

Bundy, P. (2003). Aesthetic engagement in the drama process. *Research in Drama Education: The Journal of Applied Theatre and Performance, 8*(2), 171–181.

Bundy, P. (2005). Asking the right questions: Accessing children's experience of aesthetic engagement. *Applied Theatre Researcher, 12*(6), 1–21.

Bundy, P., & Dunn, J. (2006). Pretexts and possibilities. *The Journal of the Queensland Association for Drama in Education: Drama Queensland Says, 29*(2), 19–21.

Byram, M. (1997). *Teaching and assessing intercultural communicative competence*. Clevedon: Multilingual Matters.

Byram, M. (2008). *From foreign language education to education for intercultural citizenship: Essays and reflections* (Vol. 17). Bristol: Multilingual Matters.

Byram, M. (2009). Intercultural competence in foreign languages. In D. K. Deardorff (Ed.), *The Sage handbook of intercultural competence* (pp. 321–331). Thousand Oaks: Sage.

Byram, M. (2012). Language awareness and (critical) cultural awareness—Relationships, comparisons and contrasts. *Language Awareness, 21*(1–2), 5–13. https://doi.org/10.1080/09658416.2011.639887.

Byram, M., & Zarate, G. (Eds.). (1997). *The sociocultural and intercultural dimension of language learning and teaching.* Strasbourg: Council of Europe.

Campbell, L. (2017a). Technoparticipation: The use of digital realia in arts education. *Spark: UAL Creative Teaching and Learning Journal, 2*(3), 179–195.

Campbell, L. (2017b). Collaborators and Hecklers: Performative pedagogy and interruptive processes. *Scenario: Journal for Performative Teaching, Learning and Research, 11*(2), 33–64.

Carnicke, S. M. (1998). *Stanislavsky in focus.* Amsterdam: Harwood Academic Publishers.

Cattanach, A. (1996). *Drama for people with special needs* (2nd ed.). London: A&C Black Publishers.

Clifton, J. (2006). Facilitator talk. *ELT Journal, 60*(2), 142–150. https://doi.org/10.1093/elt/cci101.

Coleman, C. (2017). Precarious repurposing: Learning languages through the Seal Wife. *NJ: Drama Australia Journal, 41*(1), 30–43.

Coleridge, S. T. (1817/1965). *Biographia literaria: Or, biographical sketches of my literary life and opinions* (Vol. 11). New York: Dent.

Connolly, K. J., & Martlew, M. (1999). *Psychologically speaking: A book of quotations.* Leicester: British Psychological Society.

Coonan, C. M. (2012). Affect and motivation in CLIL. In D. Marsh & O. Meyer (Eds.), *Quality interfaces: Examining evidence & exploring solutions in CLIL* (pp. 52–659). Eichstaett: Eichstaett Academic Press.

Cornaz, S., & Fonio, F. (2014). Présentation et premiers résultats de la conception d'un référentiel de compétences en pratiques artistiques et apprentissage des langues. *Editions du CRINI (6)*, 1–32.

Council of Europe. (2001). *Common European framework of reference for languages: Learning, teaching, assessment.* Strasburg: Cambridge University Press. Retrieved from https://rm.coe.int/1680459f97.

Council of Europe. (2018). *Common European framework of reference for languages: Learning, teaching, assessment: Companion volume with new descriptors.* Strasburg. Retrieved from https://rm.coe.int/cefr-companion-volume-with-new-descriptors-2018/1680787989.

Courtney, R. (1995). *Drama and feeling: An aesthetic theory.* Montreal: McGill-Queen's University Press.

Coyle, D. (2007). Content and language integrated learning: Towards a connected research agenda for CLIL pedagogies. *International Journal of Bilingual Education and Bilingualism, 10*(5), 543–562.

Creese, A., & Blackledge, A. (2011). Separate and flexible bilingualism in complementary schools: Multiple language practices in interrelationship. *Journal of Pragmatics, 43*(5), 1196–1208.

Crichton, J. (2008). Why an investigative stance matters in intercultural language teaching and learning. *Babel, 43*(1), 31–34.

Crutchfield, J. (2015). Fear and trembling. *Scenario: Journal for Performative Teaching, Learning and Research, 9*(2), 101–114.

Crutchfield, J. (2015a). Creative writing and performance in EFL teacher training: A preliminary case study. *Scenario: Journal for Performative Teaching, Learning and Research, 9*(1), 3–34.

Crutchfield, J. (2015b). Fear and trembling. *Scenario: Journal for Performative Teaching, Learning and Research, 9*(2), 101–114.

Crutchfield, J., & Schewe, M. (2017). Introduction: Going performative in intercultural education: International contexts, theoretical perspectives, models of practice. In J. Crutchfield & M. Schewe (Eds.), *Going performative in intercultural education: International contexts, theoretical perspectives, models of practice* (pp. xi–xxv). Bristol: Multilingual Matters.

Csikszentmihalyi, M. (2013). *Creativity: The psychology of discovery and invention*. New York: Harper Perennial.

Damasio, A. R. (1999). *The feeling of what happens: Body and emotion in the making of consciousness*. New York: Harcourt Brace.

Damasio, A. R. (2010). *Self comes to mind: Constructing the conscious brain*. New York: Pantheon.

Daniels, H. (2016). Vygotsky and dialogic pedagogy. In D. Skidmore & K. Murakami, (Eds.), *Dialogic pedagogy: The importance of dialogue teaching and learning* (pp. 34–50). Bristol: Multilingual Matters.

Davin, K. J., & Donato, R. (2013). Student collaboration and teacher-directed classroom dynamic assessment: A complementary pairing. *Foreign Language Annals, 46*(1), 5–22.

Davin, K. J., Herazo, J. D., & Sagre, A. (2016). Learning to mediate: Teacher appropriation of dynamic assessment. *Language Teaching Research, 21*(5), 632–651.

Davis, S. (2015). *Perezhivanie* and the experience of drama, metaxis and meaning making. *NJ: Drama Australia Journal, 39*(1), 63–75.

Dawson, S. W. (1970). *Drama and the dramatic*. London: Methuen & Co.

Deardorff, D. K. (Ed.). (2009). *The Sage handbook of intercultural competence*. Thousand Oaks: Sage.

Dewaele, J. (2010). *Emotions in multiple languages*. New York: Palgrave Macmillan.

Dewey, J. (1934/1980). *Art as experience.* New York: Perigee.
Dewey, J. (1925/1981). Nature, life and body-mind. In J. A. Boydston (Ed.), *John Dewey: The Later Works, 1925–1953. Volume I, 1925: Experience and Nature.* Illinois: Southern Illinois University Press.
Dewey, J. (1910/1998). *How we think.* Boston: DC Heath.
Dewey, J. (1916/2004). *Democracy and education.* New York: Dover Publications.
Donaldson, J. (2007). *The Gruffalo's child.* London: Macmillan.
Donato, R., & MacCormick, D. (1994). A sociocultural perspective on language learning strategies: The role of mediation. *The Modern Language Journal, 78*(4), 453–464. https://doi.org/10.1111/j.1540-4781.1994.tb02063.x.
Donnery, E. (2017). The intercultural journey: Drama-based practitioners in JFL in North America and JSL and EFL in Japan. In J. Crutchfield & M. Schewe (Eds.), *Going performative in intercultural education: International contexts, theoretical perspectives and models of practice* (pp. 233–240). Bristol: Multilingual Matters.
Dubois, W. E. B. (1973). *The souls of black folk.* Millwood, NY: Kraus-Thompson Organization Limited.
Duffy, P. (Ed.). (2015). *A reflective practitioner's guide to (mis)adventures in drama education—Or—What was I thinking?* Bristol: Intellect.
Duffy, P. B. (2014). *Facilitating embodied instruction: Classroom teachers' experiences with drama-based pedagogy.* (Doctoral Dissertation). Retrieved from http://scholarcommons.sc.edu/etd/2810.
Dunn, J. (2011). Analysing dramatic structures within improvised forms—The extended playwright function framework. *NJ: Drama Australia Journal, 34*(1), 21–34.
Dunn, J. (2015). Democracy over-ruled or how to deny young children's agency and voice thorugh drama. In P. Duffy (Ed.), *A reflective practitioner's guide to (mis)adventures in drama education—Or—What was I thinking?* Bristol: Intellect.
Dunn, J. (2016). Demystifying process drama: Exploring the why, what, and how. *NJ: Drama Australia Journal, 40*(2), 127–140.
Dunn, J., Bundy, P., & Stinson, M. (2015). Connection and commitment: Exploring the generation and experience of emotion in a participatory drama. *International Journal of Education & the Arts, 16*(6), n6.
Dunn, J., Bundy, P., & Woodrow, N. (2012). Combining drama pedagogy with digital technologies to support the language learning needs of newly arrived refugee children: A classroom case study. *Research in Drama Education: The Journal of Applied Theatre and Performance, 17*(4), 477–499.

Dunn, J., & Stinson, M. (2011). Not without the art!! The importance of teacher artistry when applying drama as pedagogy for additional language learning. *Research in Drama Education: The Journal of Applied Theatre and Performance, 16*(4), 617–633. https://doi.org/10.1080/13569783.2011.617110.

Dunne, É. (2016). Teaching and the event. *Journalism, Media and Cultural Studies (JOMEC) Journal, 10.* http://dx.doi.org/10.18573/j.2016.10081.

Dunne, É., & Seary, A. (Eds.). (2016). *The pedagogics of unlearning*. New York: Punctum Books.

Eagleton, T. (1976). *Marxism and literary criticism*. London: Methuen & Co.

Eisner, E. (1985). *The educational imagination: On the design and evaluation of school programs*. New York: MacMillan.

Eisner, E. W. (2002). From episteme to phronesis to artistry in the study and improvement of teaching. *Teaching and Teacher Education, 18*(4), 375–385.

Ellis, R. (1994). *The study of second language acquisition*. Oxford: Oxford University Press.

Ellis, R. (2008). *The study of second language acquisition*. Oxford: Oxford University Press.

Emunah, R. (1994). *Acting for real: Drama therapy process, technique, and performance*. New York and London: Brunner-Routledge.

Eriksson, S. (2007). Distance and awareness of fiction: Exploring the concepts. *NJ: Drama Australia Journal, 31*(1), 5–22.

Eriksson, S. (2011). Distancing. In S. Schonmann (Ed.), *Key concepts in theatre/drama education* (pp. 65–72). Rotterdam: Sense Publishers.

Ethel, R. G., & McMeniman, M. M. (2000). Unlocking the knowledge in action of an expert practitioner. *Journal of Teacher Education, 51*(2), 87–101.

Even, S. (2011). Drama grammar: Towards a performative postmethod pedagogy. *The Language Learning Journal, 39*(3), 299–312.

Even, S., & Schewe, M. (Eds.). (2016). *Performative teaching, learning, research—Performatives Lehren, Lernen, Forschen*. Berlin: Schibri Velag.

Ferholt, B. (2015). Perezhivanie in researching playworlds: Applying the concept of *perezhivanie* in the study of play. In S. Davis, B. Ferholt, H. Grainger Clemson, S. Jansson, & A. Marjanovic-Shane (Eds.), *Dramatic interactions in education: Vygotskian and sociocultural approaches to drama, education and research* (pp. 57–78). London: Bloomsbury.

Figueras, N. (2012). The impact of the CEFR. *ELT Journal, 66*(4), 477–485.

Fleming, M. (2003). Intercultural experience and drama. In G. Alred, M. Byram, & M. Fleming (Eds.), *Intercultural experience and education* (pp. 87–100). Clevedon: Multilingual Matters.

Fleming, M. (2011). *Starting drama teaching*. London: Fulton Books.
Fleming, M. (2012). *The arts in education. An introduction to aesthetics, theory and pedagogy*. London: Routledge.
Fleming, M. (2016). Exploring the concept of performative teaching and learning. In S. Even & M. Schewe (Eds.), *Performative teaching, learning, research—Performatives Lehren, Lernen, Forschen* (pp. 189–205). Berlin: Schibri Verlag.
Fonio, F., & Genicot, G. (2011). The compatibility of drama language teaching and CEFR objectives–observations on a rationale for an artistic approach to foreign language teaching at an academic level. *Scenario: Journal for Performative Teaching, Learning and Research, 2011*(2), 75–89.
Fox, H. (2007). Playback Theatre: Inciting Dialogue and Building Community through Personal Story. *TDR/The Drama Review, 51* (4), 89–105.
Freiler, T. J. (2008). Learning through the body. *New Directions for Adult and Continuing Education, 119*, 37–47. https://doi.org/10.1002/ace.304.
Gallagher, K. (2005). The aesthetics of representation: Dramatic texts and dramatic engagement. *Journal of Aesthetic Education, 39*(4), 82–94.
Gallagher, K., Freeman, B., & Wessells, A. (2010). 'It could have been so much better': The aesthetic and social work of theatre. Research in Drama Education: *The Journal of Applied Theatre and Performance, 15*(1), 5–27. https://doi.org/10.1080/13569780903480971.
García, O., & Lin, A. M. Y. (2017). Translanguaging in bilingual education. In O. García, A. M. Y. Lin, & S. May (Eds.), *Bilingual and multilingual education* (pp. 117–130). Cham: Springer.
García, O., & Wei, L. (2014). *Translanguaging: Language, bilingualism and education*. Cham: Springer.
Geertz, C. (1973). *The interpretations of cultures*. New York: Basic Books.
Gharbavi, A., & Iravani, H. (2014). Is teacher talk pernicious to students? A discourse analysis of teacher talk. *Procedia—Social and Behavioral Sciences, 98*, 552–561. https://doi.org/10.1016/j.sbspro.2014.03.451.
Goffman, E. (1959). *The presentation of self in everyday life*. New York: Double Day Anchor.
Granger, C. A. (2004). *Silence in second language learning: A psychoanalytic reading: Second language acquisition*. Clevedon, England: Multilingual Matters.
Gray, C. (1996). *Inquiry through practice: Developing appropriate research strategies*. http://www2.rgu.ac.uk/criad/cgpapers/ngnm/ngnm.htm.
Greene, M. (1988). *The dialectic of freedom*. New York: Teachers College Press.
Greene, M. (1995). *Releasing the imagination: Essays on education, the arts, and social change*. San Francisco: Jossey-Bass Publishers.

Greene, M. (2001). *Variations on a blue guitar: The Lincoln Center Institute lectures on aesthetic education.* New York: Teachers College Press.
Grosjean, F. (2008). *Studying bilinguals.* Oxford and New York: Oxford University Press.
Grosjean, F. (2010). *Bilingual: Life and reality.* Cambridge, MA: Harvard University Press.
Hall, E. T. (1959). *The silent language* (Vol. 3). New York: Doubleday.
Hallsten, J. (2016). *Tactics of interruption.* London: Campbell, Lee.
Hamachek, D. (1999). Effective teachers: What they do, how they do it, and the importance of self-knowledge. In R. P. Lipka & T. M. Brinthaupt (Eds.), *The role of self in teacher development* (pp. 189–224). Albany: State University of New York Press.
Harbon, L., & Moloney, R. (2015). Intercultural and multicultural awkward companions: The case of in schools in New South Wales, Australia. In H. Layne, V. Trémion, & F. Dervin (Eds.), *Making the most of intercultural education* (1st ed., pp. 15–34). Newcastle upon Tyne: Cambridge Scholars.
Haseman, B. (1991). Improvisation, process drama and dramatic art. *The Drama Magazine,* pp. 19–21.
Haseman, B. (2006). A manifesto for performative research. *Media International Australia Incorporating Culture and Policy, 118*(1), 98–106.
Haseman, B., & O'Toole, J. (2017). *Dramawise reimagined.* Sydney: Currency Press.
Haseman, B. C. (2007). Rupture and recognition: Identifying the performative research paradigm. In *Practice as research: Approaches to creative arts enquiry* (pp. 147–157). London: IB Tauris.
Haught, J. R., & McCafferty, S. G. (2008). Embodied language performance: Drama and the ZPD in the second language classroom. In J. P. Lantolf & M. E. Poehner (Eds.), *Sociocultural theory and the teaching of second languages.* Equinox: Oakville, CT.
Haycraft, B. (2010). Pillars of pronunciation: Approaching spoken English. *IH Journal of Education and Development, 29.* http://ihjournal.com/pillars-of-pronunciation-approaching-spoken-english-by-brita-haycraft.
Heap, B. (2015). The aesthetics of becoming: Applied theatre and the quest for cultural certitude. In G. White (Ed.), *Applied theatre: Aesthetics.* London: Bloomsbury.
Heathcote, D. (1991). The authentic teacher and the future. In L. Johnson & C. O'Neill (Eds.), *Dorothy Heathcote: Collected writings on education and drama.* London: Hutchinson Publications.
Heathcote, D., & Bolton, G. (1995). *Drama for learning: Dorothy Heathcote's mantle of the expert approach to education.* Portsmouth: Pearson Education.

Hegel, G. W. F. (1835/1975). *Aesthetics: Lectures on fine art* (Vol. 1, T. M. Knox, Trans.). Oxford: Oxford University Press.

Heider, K. G. (2009). *Ethnographic film: Revised edition.* Austin: University of Texas Press.

Heyward, M. (2002). From international to intercultural: Redefining the international school for a globalized world. *Journal of Research in International Education, 1*(1), 9–32. https://doi.org/10.1177/147524090211002.

Heyward, M. (2004). *Intercultural literacy and the international school.* (Doctoral Dissertation). Retrieved from https://eprints.utas.edu.au/423/.

Hidri, S. (2014). Developing and evaluating a dynamic assessment of listening comprehension in an EFL context. *Language Testing in Asia, 4*(1), 4.

Hodge, A. (2000). (Ed.), *Twentieth century actor training* (2nd ed.). London: Routledge.

Hornbrook, D. (1985). Drama, education, and the politics of change: Part one. *New Theatre Quarterly, 1*(4), 346–358.

Horton, M., & Freire, P. (1990). *We make the road by walking: Conversations on education and social change.* Philadelphia: Temple University Press.

Hulse, B., & Owens, A. (2017). Process drama as a tool for teaching modern languages: Supporting the development of creativity and innovation in early professional practice. *Innovation in Language Learning and Teaching*, 1–14. https://doi.org/10.1080/17501229.2017.1281928.

Immordino-Yang, M. H. (2016). *Emotions, learning, and the brain: Exploring the educational implications of affective neuroscience.* New York: Norton.

Jackson, A., & Vine, C. (2013). *Learning through theatre: The changing face of theatre in education.* London: Routledge.

Johnson, L., & O'Neill, C. (Eds.). (1991). *Collected writings on education and drama: Dorothy Heathcote.* London: Hutchinson.

Johnstone, K. (1999). *Impro for storytellers.* New York: Routledge Theatre Arts Books.

Kalogirou, K., Beauchamp, G., & Whyte, S. (2017). Vocabulary acquisition via drama: Welsh as a second language in the primary school setting. *The Language Learning Journal*, 1–12. https://doi.org/10.1080/09571736.2017.1283351.

Kant, I. (1790/1928). *Critique of judgement* (J. H. Bernard, Trans.). Oxford: Oxford University Press.

Kant, I. (1781/1990). Transcendental aesthetics (J. M. D. Meiklejohn, Trans.). *The critique of pure reason.* Raleigh, NC: Alex Catalogue.

Kao, S.-M. & O'Neill, C. (1998). *Words into worlds: Learning a second language through process drama.* London: Ablex Publishing.

Kao, S.-M. (1994). *Classroom interaction in a drama-oriented English conversation class of first-year college students in Taiwan: A teacher-researcher study*. (Doctoral Dissertation). Retrieved from https://etd.ohiolink.edu/.

Kao, S.-M. (1995). From script to impromptu: Learning a second language through process drama. In P. Taylor & C. Hoepper (Eds.), *Selected readings in drama and theatre education: The IDEA '95 papers. NADIE Research Monograph Series, 3* (pp. 88–101). Brisbane: IDEA Publications.

Kao, S.-M., Carkin, G., & Hsu, L. F. (2011). Questioning techniques for promoting language learning with students of limited L2 oral proficiency in a drama-oriented language classroom. *Research in Drama Education: The Journal of Applied Theatre and Performance, 16*(4), 489–515.

Kao, S.-M., Carkin, G., & Hsu, L. F. (2014). Questioning techniques for promoting language learning with students of limited L2 oral proficiency in a drama-oriented language classroom. In M. Stinson & J. Winston (Eds.), *Drama education and second language learning* (pp. 11–38). London: Routledge.

Kellman, S. G. (2000). *The translingual imagination*. University of Nebraska Press: Lincoln, NE.

Kempe, A., & Tissot, C. (2012). The use of drama to teach social skills in a special school setting for students with autism. *Support for Learning, 27*(3), 97–102.

Kershaw, B., & Nicholson, H. (2011). *Research methods in theatre and performance*. Edinburgh: Edinburgh University Press.

King, J., & Smith, l. (2017). Social anxiety and silence in Japan's foreign tertiary classrooms. In C. Gkonou, M. Daubney, & J.-M. Dewaele (Eds.), *New insights into social anxiety: Theory, research and educational implications* (pp. 91–109).

Kinsella, E. A. (2012). Practitioner reflection and judgement as phronesis: A continuum of reflections and considerations for phronetic judegement. In E. A. Kinsella & A. Pitman (Eds.), *Phronesis as professional knowledge: Practical wisdom in the professions* (1. Aufl. ed., Vol. 1, pp. 35–54). Rotterdam: Sense Publishers.

Kormos, J. (2017). *The second language learning processes of students with specific learning learning difficulties*. New York and London: Taylor and Francis.

Kormos, J., & Smith, A. M. (2012). *Teaching languages to students with specific learning differences*. Multilingual matters.

Kramsch, C. (1993). *Context and culture in language teaching*. Oxford: Oxford University Press.

Kramsch, C. (2008). Ecological perspectives on foreign language education. *Language Teaching, 41*(3), 389. https://doi.org/10.1017/s0261444808005065.

Kramsch, C. (2009). *The multilingual subject.* Oxford: Oxford University Press.

Krashen, S. (1985). *The input hypothesis: Issues and implications.* New York: Longman.

Kress, G. (2009). Assessment in the perspective of a social semiotic theory of multimedial teaching and learning. In C. Wyatt-Smith & J. Cummings (Ed.), *Educational assessment in the 21st century.* London: Springer.

Kristeva, J. (1980). *Desire in language: A semiotic approach to literature and art.* New York: Columbia University Press.

Laban, R. (1966). *Choreutics.* London: Macdonald and Evans.

Lantolf, J. P. (Ed.). (2000). *Sociocultural theory and second language learning.* Oxford: Oxford University Press.

Lantolf, J. P., & Thorne, S. L. (2006). *Sociocultural theory and the genesis of second language development.* New York: Oxford University Press.

Lantolf, J. P., & Poehner, M. E. (2014). *Sociocultural theory and the pedagogical imperative in L2 education: Vygotskian praxis and the research/practice divide.* Oxfordshire, England and New York, NY: Routledge.

Lantolf, J. P., Thorne, S. L., & Poehner, M. E. (2015). Sociocultural theory and second language development. Theories in second language acquisition: An introduction. In B. VanPatten & J. Williams, (Eds.), *Theories in Second Language Acquisition: An introduction* (pp. 207–226). New York and London: Routledge.

Lapaire, J.-R. (2014). À corps perdu ou le mystère de la désincarnation des langues. *E-CRINI - La revue électronique du Centre de Recherche sur les Identités Nationales et l'Interculturalité*, Editions du CRINI, (6), 1–16.

Lapaire, J.-R. (2016). The Choreography of time: Metaphor, gesture and construal. In R. Gabriel & A. C. Pelosi (Eds.), *Linguagem e cognição: Emergência e produção de sentidos* (pp. 217–234). Florianopolis: Insular.

Lapaire, J.-R. (2017, September). *Talkers as social movers.* Paper presented at the University of Padova Summer School: The role of drama in higher and adult language education – from theory to practice. Padova, Italy.

Lapaire, J.-R., & Etcheto, P. (2010). Grammaire et expression corporelle. *Langues Modernes, 2,* 1–9.

Larsen, R. J., & Prizmic, Z. (2004). Affect regulation. In R. F. Baumeister & K. D. Vohs (Eds.), *Handbook of self-regulation: Research, theory, and applications* (pp. 40–61). New York: Guilford Press.

Lee, J. (2016). Teacher entries into second turn positions: IRFs in collaborative teaching. *Journal of Pragmatics, 95,* 1–15.

Lima, M. G. (1995). From aesthetics to psychology: Notes on Vygotsky's "psychology of art". *Anthropology & Education Quarterly, 26*(4), 410–424.

Linklater, K. (2006). *Freeing the natural voice: Imagery and art in the practice of voice and language.* Hollywood, Los Angeles, CA: Drama Publishers.

Lutzker, P. (2007). *The art of foreign language teaching: Improvisation and drama in teacher development and language learning.* Tübingen: Francke Verlag.

Lutzker, P. (2016). The Recovery of experience in foreign language learning and teaching. In S. Even & M. Schewe (Eds.), *Performative teaching, learning, research – Performatives Lehren, Lernen, Forschen* (pp. 222–239). Berlin: Schibri Verlag.

MacIntyre, P. D. (2017). An overview of language anxiety research and trends in its development. In C. Gkonou, M. Daubney, & J.-M. Dewaele (Eds.), *New insights into language anxiety: Theory, research and educational implications* (pp. 11–30). Bristol: Multilingual Matters.

Mahn, H., & John-Steiner, V. (2002). The gift of confidence: A Vygotskyan view of emotions. In G. Wells & G. Claxton (Eds.), *Learning for life in the 21st century: Sociocultural perspectives on the future of education.* Malden, MA: Blackwell.

Maley, A., & Duff, A. (1982). *Drama techniques in language learning: A resource book of communication activities for language teachers* (2nd ed.). Cambridge: Cambridge University Press.

Maley, A., & Duff, A. (2005). *Drama techniques in language learning* (3rd ed.). Cambridge: Cambridge University Press.

Marcuse, H. (1978). *The aesthetic dimension: Toward a critique of Marxist aesthetics.* Boston: Beacon Press.

Marrucci, L., & Piazzoli, E (2017). *Evaluating learner engagement in arts education: Perspectives from music and drama in education.* 3rd International Conference on Higher Education Advances, HEAd '17 Universitat Politecnica de Valencia, Valencia, 2017. http://dx.doi.org/10.4995/HEAd17.2017.5516.

Marschke, R. (2004). *Creating Context, Characters and Communications: Foreign Language Teaching and Process Drama.* (Master's Thesis), Retrieved from https://eprints.qut.edu.au/16104/.

Marshall, C., & Rossman, G. B. (2006). *Designing qualitative research.* Thousands Oaks, CA: Sage.

Mazak, C. M., & Carroll, K. S. (2016). *Translanguaging in higher education: Beyond monolingual ideologies.* Bristol, UK: Multilingual Matters.

McCafferty, S. G., & Stam, G. (2008). *Gesture: Second language acquisition and classroom research.* New York: Routledge.

McGovern, K. R. (2017). Conceptualizing drama in the second language classroom. *Scenario: Journal for Performative Teaching, Learning and Research, 11*(1), 4–16.

McNeill, D. (1992). *Hand and mind: What gestures reveal about thought.* Chicago: University of Chicago Press.

Mehri, E., & Amerian, M. (2015). Group dynamic assessment (G-DA): The case for the development of control over the past tense. *International Journal of Applied Linguistics and English Literature, 4*(5), 11–20.

Mei, J., & Cangemi, E. (2017, May 25–28). *The training of the performer in education.* Paper presented at the Scenario Forum Conference: Performative spaces in literature, language and culture education, University College Cork, Ireland.

Menegale, M. (Ed.). (2016). *Drama and CLIL: A new challenge to the teaching approaches in bilingual education* (S. Nicolás Román & J. J. Torres Núñez, Eds., 2015). Bern: Peter Lang. ISBN: 978-3-0343-1629-3. 170pp.

Michael-Luna, S., & Canagarajah, A. S. (2007). Multilingual academic literacies: Pedagogical foundations for code meshing in primary and higher education. *Journal of Applied Linguistics, 4*(1), 55–77.

Morgan, N., & Saxton, J. (1987). *Teaching drama: A mind of many wonders.* Cheltenham: Stanley Thornes.

Morgan, N., & Saxton, J. (2006). *Asking better questions* (2nd ed.). Markham, ON: Pembroke Publishers.

Motos, T. (2016, April). *¿Lo tuyo es "puro" teatro? (Juego dramático versus performance)* [Is yours "pure" theatre? (Dramatic play versus performance)]. Paper presented at the 2 Congreso Internacional de Glotodidáctica Teatral en España: Fundamentos teóricos, metodología y prácticas de la Glotodidáctica teatral [2nd International Conference of Second Language Learning through Drama in Spain: Theoretical foundations, methodology and practice], Madrid.

Motos, T. T., & Fields, D. L. (2015). Playback theatre: Embodying the CLIL methodology. In N. S. Román & J. J. T. Núñez (Eds.), *Drama and CLIL: A new challenge for the teaching approaches in bilingual education.* Bern: Peter Lang.

Nanako, K. (1988). Hijikata Tatsumi: The Words of Butoh. *TRD/The Drama Review, 44*(1), 10–28.

Neelands, J. (2006). Re-imagining the reflective practitioner: Towards a philosophy of critical praxis. In J. Ackroyd (Ed.), *Research methodologies for drama education* (pp. 15–40). Sterling, VA: Trentham Books.

Neelands, J. (2010). Learning through imagined experience. In P. O'Connor (Ed.), *Crating democratic citizenship through drama education: The writings of Jonothan Neelands* (pp. 35–48). Sterling: Trentham Books.

Neelands, J. (2013). *Beginning drama 11–14* (2nd ed.). London and New York: Routledge.

Neelands, J., & Goode, T. (1995). Playing in the margins of meaning: The ritual aesthetic in community performance. *NJ: Drama Australia Journal, 19*(1), 83–97.

Neelands, J., & Goode, T. (2015). *Structuring drama work: 100 key conventions for theatre and drama* (3rd ed.). Cambridge: Cambridge University Press.

Nguyen, D. J., & Larson, J. B. (2015). Don't forget about the body: Exploring the curricular possibilities of embodied pedagogy. *Innovative Higher Education, 40*, 331–344. https://doi.org/10.1007/s10755-015-9319-6.

Nicholson, H. (1999). Aesthetic values, drama education and the politics of difference. *NJ: Drama Australia Journal, 23*(2), 82–90.

Noelliste, E., & Noelliste, J. (2017, May 25–28). *Mnemonic spaces: Music in foreign language learning*. Paper presented at the Scenario Forum Conference: Performative spaces in literature, language and culture education, University College Cork, Ireland.

Ntelioglou, B. Y. (2016). Embodied multimodality framework: Examining language and literacy practices of English language learners in drama classrooms. In M. Perry & C. L. Medina (Eds.), *Methodologies of embodiment: Inscribing bodies in qualitative research* (pp. 86–101). New York: Routledge.

Nunan, D. (1987). Communicative language teaching: Making it work. *ELT Journal, 41*(2), 136–145.

Nussbaum, M. C. (1992). Tragedy and self-sufficiency. In A. O. Rorty (Ed.), *Essays on Aristotle's poetics* (pp. 261–290). Princeton: Princeton University Press.

O'Mara, J. (1999). *Unravelling the mystery: A study of reflection-in-action in process drama teaching*. (Doctoral dissertation). Retrieved from https://experts.griffith.edu.au/publication/nb554b42fa803302bf51d8588b66d0a33.

O'Mara, J. (2006). Capturing the ephemeral: Reflection-in-action as research. *NJ: Drama Australia Journal, 30*(2), 41–50.

O'Mara, J. (2016). Thinking on your feet: A model for teaching teachers to use process drama. In *Drama and theatre with children: International perspectives* (pp. 98–112). London and New York: Routledge.

O'Neill, C. (1995). *Drama worlds: A framework for process drama*. Portsmouth: Heinemann.

O'Neill, C. (1996). Into the labyrinth: Theory and research in drama. In P. Taylor (Ed.), *Researching drama and arts education: Paradigms and possibilities* (pp. 135–146). London: RoutledgeFalmer.

O'Neill, C. (2011). *Keynote address*. Paper presented at the drama: Same difference. National Drama Conference, Swansea University (Wales).

O'Neill, C. (2015). *Dorothy Heathcote on education and drama: Essential writings*. Abington: Routledge.

O'Neill, C. (2017). Seal Wife—Random observations. *NJ: Drama Australia Journal, 41*(1), 27–29.

O'Sullivan, C. (2015a, March). *Social drama: Weaving story into the lives of children and young people with an autism spectrum disorder (keynote address)*. Paper presented at the 6th International Storyline Conference, University of Strathclyde, Scotland.

O'Sullivan, C. (2015b). The day that Shrek was almost rescued: Doing process drama with children with an Autism Spectrum Disorder. In P. Duffy (Ed.), *A reflective practitioner's guide to (mis)adventures in drama education—Or—What was I thinking?* (pp. 229–252). Bristol: Intellect.

O'Sullivan, C. (2017). *The 'Social Drama' Model for Children and Young People with Autism Spectrum Disorder: iBook version*. https://www.apple.com/itunes.

O'Toole, J. (1990). *Process, art form and meaning*. Paper presented at the 14th National Association for Drama in Education (NADIE) Conference, Sydney.

O'Toole, J. (1992). *The process of drama: Negotiating art and meaning*. London: Routledge.

O'Toole, J., & Dunn, J. (2015). *Pretending to Learn: Teaching drama in the primary and middle years*. Brisbane: Drama Web Publishing. https://pretendingtolearn.wordpress.com/.

O'Toole, J., Stinson, M., & Moore, T. (2009). *Drama and curriculum: A giant at the door*. New York: Springer.

Pavis, P. (1998). *Dictionary of the theatre: Terms, concepts and analysis*. Toronto: University of Toronto Press.

Pavis, P. (2013). *Contemporary Mise en Scène: Staging theatre today*. London and New York: Routledge.

Pavlenko, A. (2005). *Emotions and multilingualism*. Cambridge: Cambridge University Press.

Pavlenko, A. (2006). *Bilingual minds: Emotional experience, expression, and representation* (1st ed., Vol. 56). Buffalo, NY and Clevedon, England: Multilingual Matters.

Pavlenko, A. (2011). *Thinking and speaking in two languages. Bilingual education & bilingualism*. Bristol: Multilingual Matters.

Pavlenko, A. (2014). *The bilingual mind and what it tells us about language and thought*. Cambridge: Cambridge University Press.

Perry, M., & Medina, C. (2011). Embodiment and performance in pedagogy research: Investigating the possibility of the body in curriculum experience. *Journal of Curriculum Theorizing, 27*(3), 62–75.

Perry, M., & Medina, C. L. (Eds.). (2016). *Methodologies of embodiment: Inscribing bodies in qualitative research*. Oxon: Routledge.

Peter, M. (1995). *Making drama special: Developing drama practice to meet special educational needs*. London: David Fulton.

Pheasant, P. (2015). The epiphany in process drama and language learning. *p-e-r-f-o-r-m-a-n-c-e, 2*(1–2). http://p-e-r-f-o-r-m-a-n-c-e.org/?p=919.

Piazzoli, E. (2010). Process drama and intercultural language learning: An experience of contemporary Italy. *Research in Drama Education: The Journal of Applied Theatre and Performance, 15*(3), 385–402.

Piazzoli, E. (2011). Process drama: The use of affective space to reduce language anxiety in the additional language learning classroom. *Research in Drama Education: The Journal of Applied Theatre and Performance, 16*(4), 557–573.

Piazzoli, E. (2012). Engage or entertain? The nature of teacher/participant collaboration in process drama for additional language teaching. *Scenario: Journal for Performative Teaching, Learning and Research,* (2), 28-46.

Piazzoli, E. (2014a). Engagement as perception-in-action in process drama for teaching and learning Italian as a second language. *International Journal of Language Studies, 8*(2), 91–116.

Piazzoli, E. (2014b). The 'authentic teacher': Heathcote's notion of 'authenticity' in second language teaching and learning. *Drama Research Journal: International Journal of Drama in Education, 5*(1), 2–19.

Piazzoli, E. (2015). Translation in cross-language qualitative research: Pitfalls and opportunities. *Translation and Translanguaging in Multilingual Contexts, 1*(1), 80–102.

Piazzoli, E. (2016). Mapping an ethnography of change in teachers of Italian (L2) learning process drama. *Teaching Italian Language and Culture Annuals (TILCA),* 96–114. Retrieved from http://tilca.qc.cuny.edu/wp-content/uploads/2016/12/Piazzoli_Mapping-Finale.pdf

Piazzoli, E. (2017). Intercultural/Dramatic Tension and the Nature of Intercultural Engagement. In J. Crutchfield & M. Schewe (Eds.), *Going performative in intercultural education: International contexts, theoretical perspectives and models of practice* (pp. 172–197). Bristol: Multilingual Matters.

Piazzoli, E., & Kennedy, C. (2014). Drama: Threat or opportunity? Managing the 'dual affect' in process drama. *Scenario: Journal for Performative Teaching, Learning and Research, 8*(1), 52–61.

Piazzoli, E. & Kubiak, J. (2017, May). *Embodying language: A case study on students with intellectual disabilities learning Italian (FL) through Visual Arts and Drama*. Paper presented at the Scenario Forum Conference: Performative spaces in literature, language and culture education, University College Cork, Ireland.

Pink, S. (2013). *Doing visual ethnography*. London: Sage.

Piola Caselli, C. (2017, September). *Letteratura ad alta voce*. Paper presented at the University of Padova Summer School: The role of drama in higher and adult language education – from theory to practice. Padova, Italy.

Platone. (250 BC). Fedro. In G. Fornero (Ed.), *Filosofi e Filosofie nella Storia: I Testi* (Vol. 1). Torino: Paravia.

Platt, E., & Brooks, F. B. (2002). Task engagement: A turning point in foreign language development. *Language Learning, 52*(2), 365–400.

Platt, E., & Brooks, F. B. (2008). Embodiment as self-regulation in L2 task performance. In S. G. McCafferty & G. Stam (Eds.), *Gesture: Second language acquisition and classroom research* (pp. 66–87). New York: Routledge.

Poehner, M. E. (2008). *Dynamic assessment: A Vygotskian approach to understanding and promoting L2 development* (Vol. 9). New York: Springer.

Poehner, M. E., Davin, K. J., & Lantolf, J. P. (2017). Dynamic assessment. In E. Shohamy, I. Or, & S. May (Eds.), *Language Testing and Assessment, Encyclopedia of Language and Education* (pp. 243–256). Cham: Springer.

Prendergast, M., & Saxton, J. (Eds.). (2010). *Applied theatre: International case studies and challenges for practice*. Bristol: Intellect.

Prentki, T. (2013). *The applied theatre reader*. London: Routledge.

Rader, M. (1974). The imaginative mode of awareness. *The Journal of Aesthetics and Art Criticism, 33*(2), 131–137.

Ramamoorthi, P., & Nelson, A. (2011). Drama education for individuals on the autism spectrum. In S. Schonmann (Ed.), *Key concepts in theatre/drama education* (pp. 177–181). Rotterdam: Sense Publishers.

Rancière, J. (2016). Unwhat? In É. Dunne & A. Seary (Eds.), *The pedagogics of unlearning*. New York: Punctum Books.

Raquel, M. R. (2013). Towards a framework for assessing second language through drama: A Dynamic Assessment approach [Special Issue]. *Asia Pacific Journal for Arts Education, 11*(7), 159–183.

Richards, J. C., & Rodgers, T. S. (2014). *Approaches and methods in language teaching*. Cambridge: Cambridge University Press.

Richards, J. C., & Smith, D. (2010). *Dictionary of language teaching and applied linguistics*. London: Longman.

Rodari, E. (2008). *Rom, un popolo: Diritto a esistere e deriva securitaria*. Milano: Punto Rosso.

Rodenburg, P. (2007). *Presence: How to use positive energy for success in every situation*. London: Penguin.

Rodenburg, P. (2015). *The right to speak: Working with the voice* (2nd ed.). London: Bloomsbury.

Rokeach, M. (1968). *Beliefs, attitudes, and values: A theory of organization and change*. San Francisco, CA: Jossey-Bass.

Rothwell, J. (2011). *Second language learning through drama: Practical techniques and applications* (J. Winston, Ed.). London: Routledge.

Rothwell, J. (2014). Let's eat the captain? Thinking, feeling, doing: Intercultural language learning through process drama. *TESOL in Context, 24*(2), 10–12.

Rothwell, J. (2015). Laying down pale memories: Learners reflecting on language, self, and other in the middle-school drama-languages classroom. *Canadian Modern Language Review, 71*(4), 331–361.

Rothwell, J. (2017). Using process drama to engage beginner learners in intercultural language learning. In J. Crutchfield & M. Schewe (Eds.), *Going performative in intercultural education: International contexts, theoretical perspectives and models of practice* (pp. 147–171). Bristol: Multilingual Matters.

Rova, M. (2017). Embodying kinaesthetic empathy through interdisciplinary practice-based research. *The Arts in Psychotherapy*, 55, 164–173.

Rubin, L. J. (1985). *Artistry in teaching*. New York: Random House.

Ryle, G. (1949). *The concept of mind*. London: Hutchinson.

Said, E. (1978). *Orientalism*. New York: Vintage Books.

Salas, J. (1996). *Improvising real life: Personal story in playback theatre*. Kendall/Hunt Publishing Company: Dubuque, Iowa.

Sanz, E. J. (2008). Creating opportunities for expression: Interactive games in children's focus groups. In D. J. Trakas (Ed.), *Focus groups revisited: Lessons from qualitative research with children* (pp. 101–114). Berlin: LIT Verlag.

Sarason, S. B. (1999). *Teaching as performing art*. New York: Teachers College Press.

Sawyer, R. K. (2004). Creative teaching: Collaborative discussion as disciplined improvisation. *Educational Researcher, 33*(2), 12–20.

Saxton, J. (2015). Failing better. In P. Duffy (Ed.), *A reflective practitioner's guide to (mis)adventures in drama education—Or—What was I thinking?* (pp. 253–266). Bristol: Intellect.

Scarino, A., & Liddicoat, A. (2009). *Teaching and learning languages: A guide*. Melbourne: Department of Education, Employment and Workplace Relations.

Scarpa, T. (2000). *Venezia è un pesce*. Milano: Feltrinelli.

Scarpa, T. (2008). *Venice is a fish* (S. Whiteside, Trans.). Milano: Feltrinelli.

Schechner, R. (2006). *Performance studies: An introduction* (2nd ed.). New York: Routledge.

Schechner, R. (2013). *Performance studies: An introduction* (3rd ed.). London: Routledge.

Schewe, M. (2013). Taking stock and looking ahead: Drama pedagogy as a gateway to a performative teaching and learning culture. *Scenario: Journal for Performative Teaching, Learning and Research, 8*(1), 5–23.

Schewe, M. (2017, September). *The state of the art*. Key note address at the University of Padova Summer School: The role of drama in higher and adult language education – from theory to practice. Padova, Italy.

Schiller, F. (1795/1965). *On the aesthetic education of man: In a series of letters* (R. Snell, Trans.). New York: F. Ungar Pub. Co.

Schön, D. (1983). *The reflective practitioner: How professionals think in action.* London: Temple Smith.

Schön, D. (1987). *Educating the reflective practitioner: Toward a new design for teaching and learning the professions.* San Francisco, CA: Jossey-Bass.

Schonmann, S. (2011). *Key concepts in theatre/drama education.* Rotterdam: Sense Publishers.

Scully, G. (2013, July). *Let me hear your body talk: Listening to embodied knowledge for additional language acquisition*. Paper presented at the International Drama and Theatre Education Association Conference, Paris.

Scully, G. (2017, May). *From performance to the periphery and beyond: Group devised theatre for additional language acquisition*. Paper presented at the Scenario Forum Conference: Performative spaces in literature, language and culture education, University College Cork, Ireland.

Searle, J. R. (1969). *Speech acts: An essay in the philosophy of language* (Vol. 626). Cambridge: Cambridge University Press.

Seitz, H. (2016). Performative Research. In S. Even & M. Schewe (Eds.), *Performative Teaching, Learning, Research – Performatives Lehren, Lernen, Forschen* (pp. 301–321). Berlin: Schibri Verlag.

Selinker, L. (1972). Interlanguage. *International Review of Applied Linguistics in Language Teaching (IRAL), 10*(3), 209–231.

Sennett, R. (2008). *The craftsman.* New Haven, CT: Yale University Press.

Shulman, L. S. (2004). *The wisdom of practice: Essays on teachng, learning and learning to teach.* San Francisco, CA: Jossey-Bass.

Sibilio, M. (2002). *Il corpo intelligente.* Naples: Simone.

Sibilio, M. (2015). Simplex didactics: A non-linear trajectory for research in education. *Revue de Synthèse, 136*(3–4), 477–493.

Sinclair, J. M., & Coulthard, M. (1975). *Towards an analysis of discourse: The English used by teachers and pupils.* London: Oxford University Press.

Slade, P. (1955). *Child drama.* London: University of London Press.

Soulaine, S. (2017, May). *An enactive approach to the training of language teachers: The example of an interdisciplinary project combining movement, dance and drama*. Paper presented at the Scenario Forum Conference: Performative spaces in literature, language and culture education, University College Cork, Ireland.

Sparks, R. L. (2016). Myths about foreign language learning and learning disabilities. *Foreign Language Annals, 49*(2), 252–270. https://doi.org/10.1111/flan.12196.

Spolin, V. (1986). *Theater games for the classroom: A teacher's handbook*. Evanston, IL: Northwestern University Press.

St. André, J. (2011). Relay. In M. Baker & G. Saldanha (Eds.), *Routledge encyclopedia of translation studies*. London: Routledge.

St. Pierre, E. A. (2016). Afterword: Troubles with embodiment. In M. Perry & C. L. Medina (Eds.), *Methodologies of embodiment: Inscribing bodies in qualitative research* (pp. 138–148). Oxon: Routledge.

Stake, R. E. (2013). *Multiple case study analysis*. New York and London: The Guilford Press.

Stanislavski, K. (1936/1980). *An actor prepares*. London: Eyre Methuen.

Stenhouse, L. (1983). Case study in educational research and evaluation. In L. Barlett, S. Kemmis, & G. Gilliard (Eds.), *Case study: An overview*. Geelong: Deakin University Press.

Stewart, G. (1986). Reading for the plot: Design and intention in narrative. Peter Brooks. *Nineteenth-Century Literature, 41*(1), 100–108.

Stinson, M. (2009). Drama is like reversing everything: Intervention research as teacher professional development. *Research in Drama Education: The Journal of Applied Theatre and Performance, 14*(2), 225–243.

Stinson, M., & Winston, J. (2014). *Drama education and second language learning*. London: Routledge.

Stinson, M. (2008). Process drama and teaching English to speakers of other languages. In M. Jacqueline, H. John, & M. Anderson (Eds.), *Drama and English teaching: Imagination, action and engagement*. Oxford: Oxford University Press.

Stinson, M., & Freebody, K. (2006). The DOL project: An investigation into the contribution of process drama to improved results in English oral communication. *Youth Theatre Journal, 20*, 27–41.

Stolniz, J. (1960). *Aesthetics and philosophy of art criticism*. New York: Houghton Mifflin Co.

Strasberg, L. (1988). *A dream of passion: The development of the method*. New York: Penguin Books.

Styan, J. L. (1960). *The elements of drama*. Cambridge: Cambridge University Press.

Suzuki, T. (2015). *Culture is the body*. New York: Theatre Communications Group.

Svalberg, A. M.-L. (2009). Engagement with language: Interrogating a construct. *Language Awareness, 18*(3–4), 242–258.

Swain, M. (2000). The output hypothesis and beyond: Mediating acquisition through collaborative dialogue. In J. P. Lantolf (Ed.), *Sociocultural theory and second language learning*. Oxford: Oxford University Press.

Swain, M. (2006). Languaging, agency and collaboration in advanced second language proficiency. In H. Byrnes (Ed.), *Advanced language learning: The contribution of Halliday and Vygotsky* (pp. 95–108). New York: Continuum.

Swain, M. (2012). The inseparability of cognition and emotion in second language learning. *Language Teaching, 46*(2), 1–13. https://doi.org/10.1017/S0261444811000486.

Swain, M., Lapkin, S., Knouzi, I., Suzuki, W., & Brooks, L. (2009). Languaging: University students learn the grammatical concept of voice in French. *The Modern Language Journal, 93*(1), 5–29. https://doi.org/10.1111/j.1540-4781.2009.00825.x.

Syssoyeva, K. M., & Proudfit, S. (Eds.) (2016). *Women, collective creation, and devised performance: The rise of women theatre artists in the twentieth and twenty-first centuries*. New York: Springer Nature.

Taliaferro, D. M. (1998). Signifying self: Re-presentations of the double-consciousness in the work of Maxine Greene. In W. Pinar (Ed.), *The passionate mind of Maxine Greene: "I am—Not yet"* (pp. 89–121). London: Falmer Press.

Taylor, P. (1996). *Researching drama and arts education: Paradigms and possibilities*. London: RoutledgeFalmer.

Taylor, P. (1998). *Redcoats and patriots. Reflective practice in drama and social studies*. Portsmouth: Heinemann.

Taylor, P., & Warner, C. D. (2006). *Structure and spontaneity: The process drama of Cecily O'Neill*. Sterling, VA: Trentham.

Taylor, S. (2014). Globally-minded students: Defining, measuring and developing intercultural sensitivity: Part 2. *The International Schools Journal, 33*(2), 26.

Temple, B. (2002). Crossed wires: Interpreters, translators, and bilingual workers in cross-language research. *Qualitative Health Research, 12*(6), 844–854. https://doi.org/10.1177/104973230201200610.

Thompson, J. (2006). *Applied theatre*. Oxford: Peter Lang.

Thomson, P., & Hall, C. (2016). Using film to show and tell: Studying/changing pedagogical practices. In J. Moss & B. Pini (Eds.), *Visual research methods in educational research* (pp. 116–132). New York: Palgrave Macmillan.

Thorne, S. L., & Hellermann, J. (2015). Sociocultural approaches to expert-novice relationships in second language interaction. In *The handbook of classroom discourse and interaction* (pp. 281–297). Malden, MA: Wiley Blackwell.

To, L.-W. D., Chan, Y.-L. P., Lam, Y. K., & Tsang, S.-K. Y. (2011). Reflections on a primary school teacher professional development programme on learning English through process drama. *Research in Drama Education: The Journal of Applied Theatre and Performance, 16*(4), 517–539. https://doi.org/10.1080/13569783.2011.617099.

Tschurtschenthaler, H. (2013). *Drama-based foreign language learning: Encounters between self and others*. Münster: Waxmann.

Underhill, A. (1992). The role of groups in developing teacher self-awareness. *ELT Journal, 46*(1), 71–80.

Van Lier, L. (1996). *Interaction in the language curriculum: Awareness, autonomy, and authenticity*. London: Longman.

Van Lier, L. (2000). From input to affordance: Social-interactive learning from an ecological perspective. In J. P. Lantolf (Ed.), *Sociocultural theory and second language learning* (pp. 245–260). Oxford: Oxford University Press.

Van Lier, L. (2004). *The ecology and semiotics of language learning: A sociocultural perspective*. Norwell, MA: Kluwer Academic Publishers.

Van Lier, L. (2007). Action-based teaching, autonomy and identity. *Innovation in Language Learning and Teaching, 1*(1), 46–65.

Van Lier, L. (2008). Agency in the classroom. In J. P. Lantolf & M. E. Poehner (Eds.), *Sociocultural theory and the teaching of second languages*. London: Equinox.

Van Manen, M. (1997). *Researching lived experience: Human science for an action sensitive pedagogy* (2nd ed.). London and New York: Routledge.

Van Manen, M. (2008). Pedagogical sensitivity and teachers practical knowing-in-action. *Peking University Education Review, 6*(1), 1–23.

Varela, F. J., Thompson, E., & Rosch, E. (1991). *The embodied mind: Cognitive science and human experience*. Cambridge: The MIT Press, Project MUSE.

Velasco, P., & García, O. (2014). Translanguaging and the writing of bilingual learners. *Bilingual Research Journal, 37*(1), 6–23.

Vygotsky, L. (1933/1976). Play and its role in the mental development of the child. In J. Bruner, A. Jolly, & K. Sylva (Eds.), *Play: Its role in development and evolution* (pp. 537–554). Harmondsworth, Middlesex: Penguin.

Vygostky, L. (1934/1994). The problem of the environment. In R. Van Der Veer & J. Valsiner (Eds.), *The Vygotsky reader* (pp. 338–354). Oxford, UK: Blackwell.

Vygotsky, L. S. (1926/1971). *The psychology of art*. Cambridge, MA: The MIT Press.

Vygotsky, L. S. (1930/1978). *Mind in society: The development of higher psychological processes*. Cambridge, MA: Harvard University Press.
Vygotsky, L. S. (1934/1986). *Thought and language*. Cambridge, MA: MIT Press.
Vygotsky, L. S. (1930/2004). Imagination and creativity in childhood. *Journal of Russian and East European Psychology, 42*(1), 7–97.
Vygotsky, L. S., & Luria, A. (1934/1994). Tool and symbol in child development. In R. Van Der Veer & J. Valsiner (Eds.), *The Vygotsky reader* (pp. 99–105). Oxford: Blackwell.
Wagner, B. J. (1976). *Dorothy Heathcote: Drama as a learning medium*. Washington, DC: National Education Association.
Way, B. (1967). *Development through drama*. London: Longman.
Weber, E. (1907). *Ästhetik als pädagogische Grundwissenschaft*. Leipzig: Wunderlich.
Weltsek-Medina, G. J. (2007). Process drama in education. In A. Blatner & D. Wiener (Eds.), *Interactive and improvisational drama: Varieties of applied theatre and performance* (pp. 90–98). New York: iUniverse.
Wertsch, J. V. (1991). *Voices of the mind: A sociological approach to mediated action*. London: Harvester Wheatsheaf.
Winston, J. (2010). *Beauty and education*. London: Routledge.
Winston, J. (Ed.). (2012). *Second language learning through drama: Practical techniques and applications*. Padstow, Cornwall: Routledge.
Yaman Ntelioglu, B. (2011a). 'But why do I have to take this class?' The mandatory drama-ESL class and multiliteracies pedagogy. *Research in Drama Education: The Journal of Applied Theatre and Performance, 16*(4), 595–616.
Yaman Ntelioglu, B. (2011b). Drama and English language learners. In S. Shonmann (Ed.), *Key concepts in theatre/drama education*. Rotterdam: Sense Publishers.

Index

A

Abbs, P. 58, 327
Action-present 111
Active perception 63, 65
Active receptivity 58, 165
Aesthetic 53, 54, 234
    distance 143, 168, 275
    education 53, 285
    engagement 65, 85, 187, 212, 228, 233, 249, 274, 282
    experience 56, 63, 165, 249
Affect 139
Affective engagement 235
Agency 37, 164, 177, 265, 267
Alertness 263, 267
Animation 66, 67
Applied theatre 195
Apprehend/apprehension 56, 70, 80
Aristotelian elements 79
Aristotelian plot 302, 306
Aristotle 54, 79, 110
Art 5
Art form 4, 58, 65
Artistry 7
Assessment 202
Attitude 87, 88, 110
Attune 194
Attunement 43

B

Bargaining deal 250
Bateson, G. 141
Beauty 3, 283
    in education 284
'Being intercultural' 63, 268
Belief system 110, 113
Bilingual individuals 122, 123, 246, 301
Blocking 176
Bolton, G. 33, 80, 139, 142, 195
Breath 30, 200
Bundy, P. 66, 212

C

"Category three mistake" 286, 289
Centipede's effect 326
Centipede's paralysis 325
Characters 83
Character's motivation 87
Children's play 138
Chronemics 93
Classification of questions 174
Co-artists 299
Cognition/affect divide 3
Coleridge, S.T. 61, 327
Collaborative dialogue 163, 203
Collision 233
Commercial L2 classroom games 137, 194
Commitment 143
Common European Framework of Reference for Languages (CEFR) 188, 193, 202
  levels 195
  proficiency classification 190
Competence ladder model 296, 307
Comprehend/comprehension 70, 80
Confidence 156
Conflict 174
Connection 66, 67, 143, 210, 212
Conscious competence 296, 298, 307
Conscious incompetence 296, 298, 302–305, 307
Constraint 84, 101, 138, 186
Content 56
Content and Language Integrated Learning (CLIL) 145, 146
Conventions 200
Courtney, R. 98
Craft 5
Creative perception 58, 233, 282
Creative reception 63
Creativity in teaching 328
Crutchfield, J. 328
Cube 200

D

Damasio, A.R. 3, 322
Data analysis 261
Defensiveness 210
Devoicers 323
Dewey, J. 24, 109
Dialogic interaction 263
Discourse generated by process drama 266
Dissonance 85, 92, 156
Distance 86, 143, 168, 285
Double-consciousness 62, 92, 289
Drama
  in education 33, 195
  elements of 33, 65, 80, 83, 138, 201, 211, 262
  therapy 195
Drama/theatre divide 197
Dramatic focus 88, 211, 250
Dramatic irony 265
Dramatic strategies 200, 201
Dramatic tension 83, 171, 174, 186, 212, 250, 264
  in SLA 173
Dramawise model 80, 102
Dual affect 138–141, 235, 295
Dual pedagogical content knowledge 118
Dunn, J. 115, 118, 201, 296, 297, 299
Dynamic Assessment (DA) 203

E

Eddy in a stream 84
Educational neuroscience 2, 134
Educational neuroscientists 322
Eisner, E. 4, 8, 110, 312
Emancipatory detachment 124, 246
Embodied approach 9, 10, 28, 39, 40, 55, 95, 138, 194, 195, 322, 326
Embodied experience 82, 86, 116
Embodied felt-experience 27, 119, 136
Embodied knowing 25
Embodied L2 approach 33
Embodied learning 35
Embodied pedagogy 3, 25, 32, 248
Embodied drama pedagogy 154
Embodied teaching 329
Embodied time 92, 93
Embodiment 25, 322, 323
Emotional Palette 31
Emotions 2, 12, 187
   in classroom 187
   in drama 140
   emotional response 140
Engagement 277
   with the art form (creating) 235
   with the art form (perceiving) 235
   with language 165, 233, 261
Episodes 34, 299
Ethnographic filming 240
Evaluation/assessment 202
Exposure 165, 262, 265

F

Felt-experience 9, 82, 140, 141, 156, 250, 288
First-order emotions 140
Fleming, M. 200, 328
Focus 83
Foreign language anxiety 32, 192
Form 56, 229
Fourth dimension 197
Full-immersion 192, 204

G

Games 136
Gesture 28, 194, 261
Gesture studies 28, 268
Goffman, E. 98
Grasped reflection 119
Greene, M. 53, 57, 285
Groupness of the group 66, 277, 309

H

Haseman, B. 33, 250
Haught, J.R. 138
Heathcote, D. 33, 37, 79, 90, 140, 169, 170, 174, 330
Hecate 226–228, 261, 268, 274, 285
Heightened awareness 66, 67, 268, 282, 323
Hyper Cube 198

I

Identity 2, 10, 32, 113, 289, 298, 307, 322, 325
   and bilingualism 301
Imagination 34, 40, 55, 57, 58, 62
Immordino-Yang, M.H. 2, 322
Impedance 84
Impediment 84
Implicit intercultural tension 272
Improvisation 4, 306, 309
Inclination of current 84
Indirect handling 142

Initiation Response Feedback (IRF) 167, 175, 264
  exchanges 174
  pattern 167
Instrumental agenda 186
Intellectual and learning disabilities 204, 213
Intercultural aesthetic dimension 99
Intercultural aesthetic engagement 99
Intercultural competence 60
Intercultural dimension of pre-text 271
Intercultural dramatic focus 89
Intercultural dramatic mood 97
Intercultural dramatic structure 270
Intercultural dramatic tension 269, 270, 287, 288
Intercultural encounter 59, 63
Intercultural engagement 60, 233
Intercultural literacy 59
Intercultural meaning 99
Intercultural meaning-making 269, 273
Intercultural speaker 60, 63, 268
Intercultural tension
  of metaxis 92
  of mystery 91
  in pre-text 271
  of relationships 90
  of surprise 91
  of task 90
Inter-episode 300, 303, 301
Inter-episode reflection-in-action 298, 293, 307
Interlanguage 243
Interlanguage interviewing 244, 245, 247
Intra-episode 300
Intra-episode reflection-in-action 298

Ironic/irony 265, 279
Irritation 249

K

Kant, Immanuel 54
Kao, S.M. 37, 322
Kinaesthetic experiences 95
Kinaesthetic approach to focus groups 247
Kinaesthetic dimension of language learning 194
Kinaesthetic focus groups 247
Kinesics 96
Knowing-in-action 109, 111, 201, 307, 327, 329
Kramsch, C. 44, 99, 324

L

Labyrinth's metaphor 228
Language 83, 94, 137, 163, 164, 171
Language engagement 164
Large-scale forms 40, 194, 199
Limitations, of reflective practitioner methodology 248
Linklater, K. 31
Lutzker, P. 11, 330

M

Macro level 115
Macro planning 297
Make-believe 39, 175
Mantle of the Expert system 169, 199
Mask-upon-a-mask/double masking 66, 287
Master dramatists 151
Meaning 99

Mediation 135
  in drama 141
Metaphor 58, 226
Metaxis 56, 84, 85, 116, 140, 141
Micro level 115
Micro reflection-in-action 297
Mid-episode 170
Mood 83, 96, 212
Motivation 88, 211
Motos, T. 196, 200
Movement 83, 95
Myth of creativity 327

Narrative 83, 93
Narrative tension 89
Non-narrative intercultural tension 90, 97
NVIVO qualitative analysis 261, 264, 300

Object-regulation 135, 154
Oblique angle 142
Obuchenie 312, 329
O'Neill, C. 9, 30, 33–37, 43, 65, 322
Other-regulation 135, 154
O'Toole, J. 33, 84, 96

Paradoxical frame 141
Participation/non participation continuum 199, 200
Pathic knowledge 207
Pathic understanding 119
Pedagogical content knowledge 118

Pedagogical tact 110, 119, 170, 193
Pedagogy 65
People with disabilities 211
Perception-in-action 165, 233, 261
Perezhivanie 27, 85, 136, 288
Performance studies 39
Performative language
  learning 322
  pedagogy 199
  teaching 9, 28, 38, 186, 190, 194, 195, 228, 249, 329
Performative paradigm to research 229
Performative research 225, 228, 230, 231, 250
Performative(s) 40, 251
Phenomenology of practice 119, 329
Phronesis 110, 118
Phronesis of failure 122, 185, 327
Place 83
Plato 54, 327
Play 98, 136, 138, 235, 323
  as symbolic mediation 134
Play/performance continuum 199
Playfulness 35, 55, 97, 262, 265
Play theory 138
Playwright's function 299, 307–309
Plot vs. structure 307
Post-Teacher in Role (TiR) phase 170, 172, 203
Practical wisdom 110
Practice-led research 229
Praxial approach to research 206
Praxis 30, 118
Pre-Teacher in Role (TiR) phase 170, 171, 203
Pre-text 34, 37, 83, 100, 101, 270
Process/product continuum 199, 200
Process drama 9, 33, 43, 65, 80, 114
Proficiency 188

Prosodic dimension 31
Protection 142, 187
Protection mechanism 143
Proxemics 96
Purpose 87

Quadripartite response (QR) 116
Quadripartite thinking (QT) 116
Questioning 173, 174, 211

Receptive perception 58
Receptivity 165, 262, 263
Reflection 26, 32, 36, 99, 110, 119, 122, 330
Reflection-in-action 111, 114, 116–118, 125, 225, 246, 306, 310, 326
Reflective practice 110, 114, 225, 325
Reflective practitioner 112, 230, 246, 295, 330
  approach 232
  contract 112
  inquiry 311
  methodology 225
  paradigm 112
Reflexive 114, 302, 324
Reflexive attitude 298
Reflexivity 329
Reflexivity-in-practice 114
Regulation 135
Relationships 83
Resistance 210
Ritual 98
Rodenburg, P. 323
Role of emotions 2

Role plays
  as dramatic exploration 140, 141
  in drama 1340
Ryle, G. 84

savoir être 61
Scenario 40
Schechner, R. 39
Schewe, M. 9, 28, 200, 249
Schiller, F. 55
Schön, D. 110
Seal Wife 186, 187, 192, 193
Second-order emotions 140
'Self' and 'other' 59
Self-regulation 28, 135, 138, 154, 164, 261, 265
Sennett, R. 327
'Sense' of the words 286
Silence 21, 43
Simplexity 25, 53, 141, 228, 233
Situation 83
Small-scale forms 40, 194, 199, 200
Social actors 98
Sociocultural framework 261
Sociocultural theory 28, 135
Sociology of aesthetics 66
Space-time 197–199
Special needs 185
Status 87
Status hierarchy 37
Stinson, M. 115, 118, 297
Storytelling 79
Student/teacher hierarchy 37
Students with intellectual disabilities 204, 210
Sub-text 31, 96, 98
Superficial role plays 140, 141

Suspend belief 61, 233
Suspend disbelief 61, 233
Symbol 58, 83, 97, 212, 229
Symbolic competence 99, 194, 324
Symbolic forms 82
Symbolic mediation 135
Symbolic play 139

Tacit knowing 322
Teacher/artist 11, 34, 35, 82, 84, 102, 112, 117, 201, 299, 322, 326, 329, 331
Teacher in Role (TiR) 33, 37, 68, 90, 147, 148, 155, 168–171, 175, 203, 247, 250, 263, 264, 302, 305
  in L2 contexts 172
Teacher melancholia 302, 303
Teacher Talk (TT) 166, 168, 171
  speech pattern 167
Teaching as an art 4
'Tension' and 'conflict' 174
Tension of dilemma 84
Tension of relationships 84, 85
Tension of surprise 84, 85
Tension of the mystery 84, 85
Tension of the task 84
Theatre 43, 201
Theatre/drama divide 41
Theatre in Education 195
3D cube 196
Time 83
Translanguaging 123, 125, 315
  in reflective practice 125
Translating in 'cross-language research' 244

Tschurtschenthaler, H. 66, 287

Unconscious competence 297, 298, 311
Unconscious incompetence 296, 298, 301–303, 311
Underhill, A. 296, 307
Underhill's model 311
Unlearning 64, 70

Van Lier, L. 2, 164
Van Manen, M. 207
Varela, F.J. 26
Video-Stimulated Recall (VSR) 242, 247
Vigilance 166, 262, 264
Visual ethnography 241
Voice 30, 32, 323, 324
Voice studies 31
Vygotsky, L.S. 27, 55

Wide-awakeness 63
Willing suspension of disbelief 61
Winston, J. 284
Word meaning 134
Word sense 134

Zone of Proximal Development (ZPD) 136, 262–264

CPSIA information can be obtained
at www.ICGtesting.com
Printed in the USA
LVHW07*1710050718
582800LV00003B/3/P